For Reference

Not to be taken from this room

GEM HUNTER'S GUIDE

GEM HUNTER'S GUIDE

How to Find and Identify Gem Minerals

Fifth Revised Edition

RUSSELL P. MacFALL

BELL PUBLISHING COMPANY
New York

This 1989 edition is published by Bell Publishing Company,
distributed by Crown Publishers, Inc.,
225 Park Avenue South, New York, New York 10003,
by arrangement with Harper & Row, Publishers, Inc.

Printed and Bound in the United States of America

Library of Congress Cataloging-in-Publication Data

MacFall, Russell P.
  Gem hunter's guide / Russell P. MacFall.
      p.   cm.
  Reprint. Originally published: 5th rev. ed. New York :
Crowell, 1975.
  Bibliography: p.
  ISBN 0-517-68240-0
  1. Precious stones—Collectors and collecting—United States.
I. Title.
[QE392.5.U5M3   1989]
553.3'0973—dc20   89-33856
                                                         CIP

h g f e d c b a

acknowledgments

This book would not exist if countless prospectors—treasure hunters, mineralogists, and enthusiastic amateurs alike—had not gone out to every corner of North America, discovered the rich gem resources of the continent, and then shared the word of their discoveries with others. To this, the fifth edition, many persons have given generously of information and criticism, as they did in the preparation of previous editions. To their kindness and effort not only the author but all who enjoy the hobbies associated with gem hunting owe a great debt.

In particular, it is proper to acknowledge the help given by Bertram H. Johnson, of Napa, California; Norman and Betty Lemkau of Castro Valley, California; Herbert V. Corbett of Baltimore, Maryland; Professor Richard Pearl of Colorado Springs, Colorado; and Professor Jack Hanahan of Belmont, North Carolina, with locations in their respective states.

contents

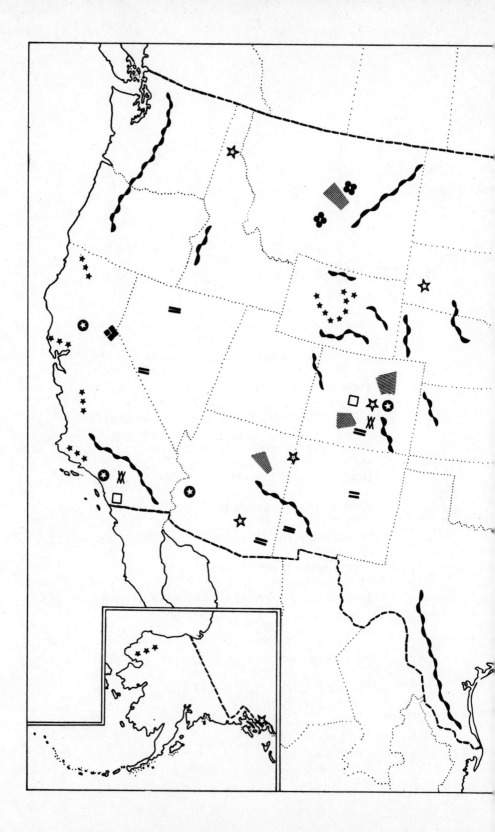

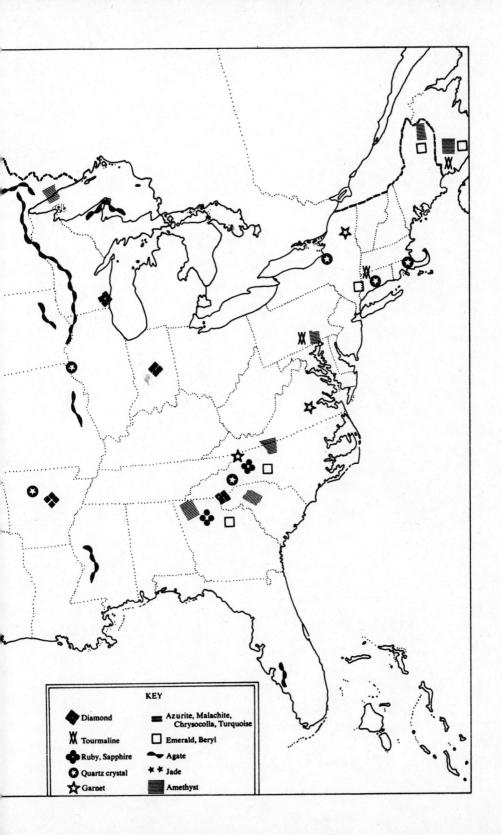

KEY

◆ Diamond

▬ Azurite, Malachite, Chrysocolla, Turquoise

Ⓜ Tourmaline

☐ Emerald, Beryl

✤ Ruby, Sapphire

〜 Agate

◉ Quartz crystal

✶ Jade

☆ Garnet

▬ Amethyst

1.
it's
fun
to hunt for
gems

Gem hunting offers many rewards—healthful and entertaining exercise for the whole family, the excitement of the search, and the thrill of discovery. No purchased stone can ever bring the pleasure that comes from opening a nodule or a pocket in rock and being the first to see a sparkling crystal fresh from nature's hoard. Furthermore, the gem hunter gains a direct, practical insight into geology and the earth sciences from his efforts. Fresh air, sunshine, and vigorous exercise are certain rewards of the prospector, whether he finds a gem or not. His quest lures him into unspoiled places off the beaten track where he would never have gone had he not been led by a purpose. As thousands of amateurs venture every year into the mountains and deserts of North America, they enjoy not only the pleasure of seeking and often of discovering but also of beholding the beauty of the wonderful land in which we live. The Appalachians, the Smokies, the Sierra Nevada, the Rockies and Black Hills, the Cascades and the Grand Canyon, the Oregon and Washington beaches, the Mojave desert of California and the Sonoran desert of Arizona, the lake beaches of the Middle West, the broad plains and the verdant hills of New England hold inestimable treasures of living things—birds and animals, trees and flowers, as well as trails and vistas to enjoy and photograph while pursuing the quest for rocks.

Wherever it may take him in this inexhaustible land, he will find that every nook and cranny offers something for him. Unlike flowers, rocks have no season. So far, there are few restrictions on collecting, fewer hunting fees or licenses, and the right kind of a collector can be fairly sure of a welcome wherever he goes. As an active outdoor hobby, its partisans believe rock and gem collecting is unmatched.

But rosy cheeks, lithe muscles, good appetites, and cheerful dispositions are not the whole story. Without destroying the beauty of the outdoors, gem and rock collectors preserve material of aesthetic and scientific value which would have eventually crumbled into dust. For nature destroys as it creates.

There are several schools of thought about man's use of the outdoors. The preservationists preach: "Take nothing but photographs; leave nothing behind but footprints." But the conservationists, in whose ranks true amateurs march, know that reasonable collecting is the only way to preserve beautiful crystals and fossils. The collector will bring out their full beauty by cleaning and trimming them; some he will cut into jewels, and some he will use to enrich museums for public enjoyment and educational institutions for teaching and research purposes. What amateurs have brought home has become a major resource of better understanding of Mother Nature's secrets.

"We in America don't realize in what close proximity we are all living to buried wealth in gems," wrote George Frederick Kunz, Tiffany's expert on the gem resources of our land. "Do you, Mr. Maine," he continued, "know that some of the finest tourmalines in the world are found not a hundred yards from your doorstep in the vicinity of Paris? . . . Have you heard, Mr. New Jersey, of your famous pearls?" citing other notable collecting areas in his rhetorical fashion. Even though Kunz wrote more than eighty years ago, yet his words still speak to like-minded gem lovers of today.

For variety of gem materials the United States is unrivaled. More than sixty kinds of gem minerals have been produced commercially from Alaska to the Mexican border and eastward to Maine and Florida. Still others are found in Canada and Mexico.

Every state, as a glance at the list of gem locations in this book testifies, offers substantial rock and gem resources. As old quarries become dumps, old mines fall into ruins and the developer's bulldozer obliterates other sites, new ones are discovered. Books and hobbyist organizations spread word of such places, and improved roads and specialized vehicles make possible access to them.

A pebble is enough to start anyone on a lifetime of profitable pleasure in the earth sciences. Many men and women, children too, who cut gems, collect crystals or fossils testify that a stone picked up during a stroll on a beach or a hike in the mountains first aroused their interest.

The earth sciences are as wide as the mineral kingdom itself, with something for everyone. How far the collector will go beyond his first acquaintance with it will be the measure of its return to him in fun, learning, and tangible possessions. Many men and women have become expert mineralogists and gemmologists and rivals in skill of the professional lapidaries. If beauty is the most alluring aspect, a cabinet of crystals will be a permanent source of pleasure and a facet of the hobby which he will be proud to show and share.

Fossils, so the saying goes, lift the veil of time. They are meaningful relics of a billion years of life on earth, rocks that once lived. Some devotees of the earth sciences find their greatest pleasure in the social satisfactions of association with like-minded people, or in the enjoyment of a hobby that has something to offer all members of the family.

Such are the reasons for the growth of interest in the earth science-related hobbies. In forty years more than 1,000 clubs with 60,000 members have sprung up as an organized body which has an estimated 300,000 to 1 million more adherents on its fringes.

Enjoyment is the real profit from any hobby, but that need not preclude tangible ones, too. In the earth sciences the chance always exists to strike it rich—a pocket of rare gem crystals, gold where no one has ever looked, or discovery of a previously undescribed fossil which will put your name in paleontological history. Every year brings news of a lucky strike—gem tourmaline by the bushel basketful in Maine and California; emerald in North Carolina, a big diamond or two in Arkansas, opal in Idaho, and so on. Old locations suddenly are brought back to life and new ones reward luck or persistent search.

The dearest, the most precious reward, however, is within the grasp of discoverer, seeker, and collector alike. It is well described by Robert Gibbings, in his *Sweet Thames Run Softly:*

> I know a man who always carries one of these stones [crystals] in his pocket, and delights to hold it in his hand. At last I have found something both exquisite and everlasting, he says. One day he has with him a cube of purple fluor-spar from Derbyshire or, perhaps, a pyramid of smoky quartz from Cumberland. The next it may be rock crystal from Madagascar. To him the sense of tenancy in life is stronger than in anyone I know. "We are passing through," he says. "Passing through. Flowers fade, timber crumbles, metal corrodes, but these stones will remain."
>
> On my own table is a section of agate, cut and polished, its concentric rings of rose, ivory and carmine enclosing a turbulent mass of amethyst. I bought it some years ago for a few shillings, and no expenditure has ever brought greater reward. Its depths are always there,

clear and refreshing, a petrified pool never to be disturbed by wind or tide.

Few people realize the beauty of even the commonest of stones; yet the insect who makes his home in a pile of gravel on the roadside lives in a palace.

For the purpose of this book, a gem material is considered to be any stone commonly used by hobbyists for jewelry or for ornaments such as bookends or tabletops. Growth of interest in these uses has broadened the range of gem materials to include more species, such as granite and satin spar, and a wider choice of quality.

But just as it is not possible to work a problem in arithmetic without knowing how to add, so knowledge of the methods for locating and identifying gems is needed if you are to prospect successfully. The basic information is neither difficult to obtain nor difficult to learn. The following chapters describe in simple language the distinguishing characteristics of gems, how to go about finding them, sources of information, and specific locations where gem materials are reliably reported to have been found.

2.
how to identify gem minerals

Most gem stones are minerals. That is, they are naturally occurring chemical elements or compounds which were formed through inorganic processes. In other words, they are not man-made, plant, or animal products; they have a definite chemical composition; and, usually, they exhibit a distinctive crystalline form. This definition distinguishes minerals from rocks, which are mixtures of minerals.

There are some exceptions, however. A few rocks, such as lapis lazuli and unakite, are made into jewelry and ornaments. Pearls, coral, pearl shell, and amber are definitely gems, although they are not minerals—pearls and coral are a product of animals and amber of ancient trees.

More than 2,000 distinct mineral species are known; only about 100 of these have been used as gems, and fewer than 30 ever appear in jewelry stores.

Aside from some exceptions, to qualify as gem material a mineral must be beautiful and rare enough to be desirable, and hard enough to stand up under wear. Gems may be beautiful because of their brilliance, as in diamonds; their color, as in emeralds; their pattern, as in moss agate; or their play of color, as in opals.

Fashion plays its part in creating a demand for certain stones. In ancient Greece, yellow stones were in high favor, while the Romans scorned yellow and preferred green gems to all others. In Renaissance times, green turquoise was greatly admired, but today bluish turquoise is the most acceptable kind. Belief that opals were unlucky long made them unfashionable, and amethyst lost some of its high status when the abundant South American supply came on the market. Promotion of diamonds as the symbol of an engagement of marriage has also helped create a steady market and a sentimental regard for that gem.

Rarity helps make stones precious, but too great rarity can be a disadvantage, because there is not a sufficient supply to make the stone known and create a demand for it. Demantoid garnet and euclase are examples of rare and comparatively unsought-after gems.

But such generalities will not help you tell a fortune in the rough from a pretty pebble. Gem hunters use a variety of methods for identifying stones, but the most useful clues are these:

1. Hardness.
2. Crystal structure—the innate shape of the mineral.
3. Cleavage—the manner in which the crystal splits.
4. Fracture—the texture of a broken crystal surface.
5. Luster—the character of the surface gloss.
6. Diaphaneity—the degree of transparency.
7. Color.
8. Pattern of surface color or light refraction.
9. Specific gravity—the density, or comparative weight, of the mineral.

These characteristics for dozens of the more important gem stones are listed in detail in Chapter 5.

Hardness

Most gem stones are as hard as or harder than silica, the very common mineral which is everywhere present in dust. A softer stone would soon become dull and scratched from abrasion by dust. Hardness is so important that it has become one of the principal means used to identify gem minerals. Like all minerals, they are rated for comparative hardness according to a table known as Mohs' scale. (See Table A.) The steps on this scale are far from equal; the diamond, for example, is rated on the scale as 10, but is actually 42.4 times as hard as talc and more than twice as hard as corundum.

TABLE A. MOHS' HARDNESS SCALE

1. Talc	6. Orthoclase feldspar
2. Gypsum	7. Quartz
3. Calcite	8. Topaz
4. Fluorite	9. Corundum
5. Apatite	10. Diamond

Sets of pencils tipped with these known minerals are used to test—by scratching—unidentified samples. But for simple field tests some rule-of-thumb methods are convenient. Minerals with a hardness of less than 2 on the Mohs' scale will mark paper. A fingernail will scratch gypsum, and a copper coin is just about as hard as calcite. A pocketknife blade will scratch apatite easily and feldspar with difficulty but not jade. Feldspar, in turn, will scratch glass. Test pencils must be used to try most of the hard gem minerals. A sharp sliver of agate, such as Montana moss agate, is also useful to test minerals near agate in hardness. In making hardness tests, it is necessary to make sure that what appears to be a scratch is not powder rubbed off the test piece. This can be done by wetting the specimen, rubbing the area, and examining it after the area dries. Tests should be made only on a smooth, unweathered surface.

Crystal Structure

Most transparent precious and semiprecious gems are crystals, which show a distinctive arrangement of their flat, smooth faces and of the angles at which the faces are placed with respect to one another. The quartz gems, for example, such as amethyst, form crystal prisms with six faces terminated by six triangular faces coming to a pointed apex. Sometimes crystals so nearly conform to the type or ideal for the mineral species that they can be identified by that characteristic alone. (See pages 10 and 11 for drawings of typical crystal forms.)

But, although crystals have been called the flowers of the mineral kingdom, they do not usually grow straight and free like blossoms in the sunshine. Instead, they are distorted by the conditions under which rocks are formed. They become twinned, or lopsided because a few faces develop at the expense of others, or complex through variation from the simple form. Yet the angles between faces remain constant, and from these angles identification of the species is often possible.

Crystallography is too detailed a science to be discussed in a book on gem hunting, although a smattering of its principles is of value. Mineralogists have assigned all crystals to six systems, according to the position of imaginary lines known as axes which intersect to form a theoretical framework or skeleton for the crystal:

The isometric system is the most regular. It includes crystals having three axes equal in length and at right angles to one another. Cubic fluorite, octahedral diamond, and trapezohedral garnet are typical examples of this system.

7

CRYSTAL SYSTEMS AND THEIR AXES

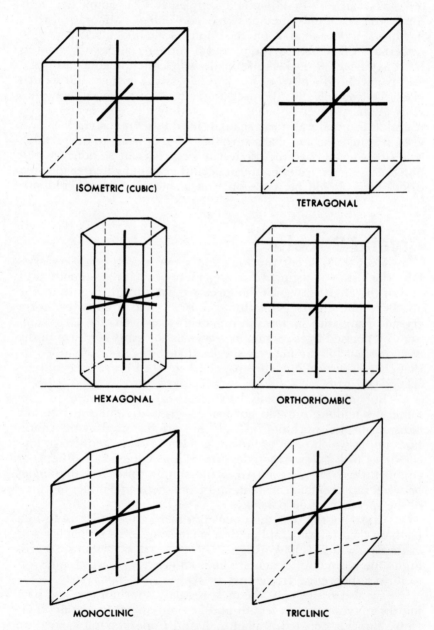

ISOMETRIC (CUBIC)

TETRAGONAL

HEXAGONAL

ORTHORHOMBIC

MONOCLINIC

TRICLINIC

Idealized drawings of a basic form for each of the six crystal systems, showing
theoretical external shape and axes of symmetry.

The tetragonal system is like the isometric system except that one axis (usually the vertical one) is longer or shorter than the other two, which are equal in length. All intersect at right angles. The crystals, such as zircon, commonly have a square cross-section.

The hexagonal system is like the tetragonal one except that there are three horizontal axes of equal length, intersecting one another at 60 degrees and intersected by a fourth vertical axis at right angles to the other three. Quartz and apatite, with their six-faced pyramid terminations, and the flat-terminated prism of beryl belong here, as well as the many variations that calcite plays on the basic form.

The orthorhombic system again has three axes placed at right angles to one another, but all three are of unequal length. Into this dominolike system fall barite and topaz, often with considerable elaboration of secondary faces.

The monoclinic and *triclinic* systems are more difficult to visualize. The former is like the orthorhombic system except that only two of the axes meet at right angles. Such crystals, including those of spodumene and orthoclase feldspar, have a droopy appearance because of the tilted axis. In the triclinic system, the axes are all of unequal length and none is at right angles with the others. Rhodonite and some of the feldspars are classified here.

In many gem materials the crystal structure is so lost in the mass that it is not evident to the eye. Minerals of this sort, such as agate and jasper, are described as cryptocrystalline. For example, an agate nodule may contain a center of easily discernible quartz crystals surrounded by chalcedony that is crystalline only to the eye of the microscope.

A few gem materials—notably opal and obsidian—are amorphous, lacking crystal structure altogether, like glass. They are a mineral jelly.

Most minerals express their individuality within their crystal system by assuming a characteristic habit, which is a variation on the basic crystal shape. Quartz, for example, is commonly twinned into a six-sided prism with a pyramidal termination but corundum, in the same system, takes a barrel-like shape; fluorite is almost always a cube, while diamond is more often an octahedron than a cube. Malachite and hematite usually take a botryoidal or reniform habit, but both may be found as needles. Tremolite and actinolite are found as needles or stout monoclinic prisms, but jade, which is the same mineral, is a mass of interwoven, felted fibers. Habit can be defined as the costume that each mineral chooses out of its crystal system's wardrobe.

TYPICAL CRYSTAL FORMS
AND HABITS

APATITE

AZURITE

BERYL

CHIASTOLITE

EMERALD

EPIDOTE

FELDSPAR
(orthoclase)

GARNET

IDOCRASE

IOLITE

KYANITE

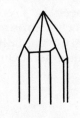

RUBY

SAPPHIRE

SPHALERITE

TOPAZ CRYSTALS

TOURMALINE CRYSTALS
(Cross-section at right)

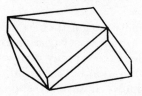

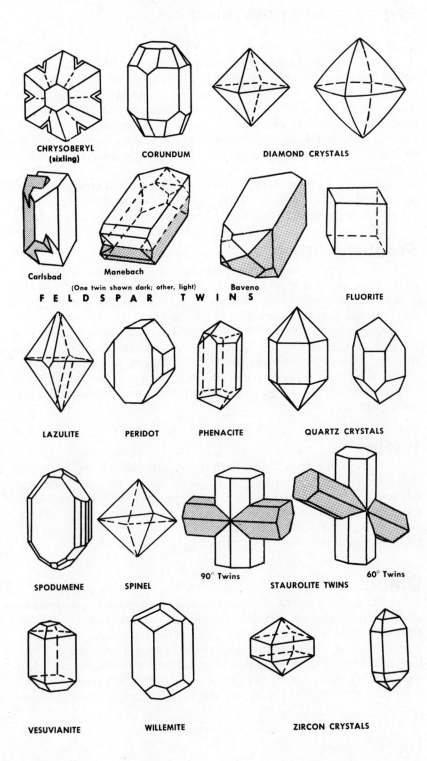

CHRYSOBERYL (sixling)

CORUNDUM

DIAMOND CRYSTALS

Carlsbad

Manebach

(One twin shown dark; other, light)

Baveno

F E L D S P A R   T W I N S

FLUORITE

LAZULITE

PERIDOT

PHENACITE

QUARTZ CRYSTALS

SPODUMENE

SPINEL

90° Twins

STAUROLITE TWINS

60° Twins

VESUVIANITE

WILLEMITE

ZIRCON CRYSTALS

Cleavage

Cleavage is a property of parting along a smooth, flat surface, which is a plane of lesser molecular cohesion in the crystal. It is like splitting wood along the grain. Cleavage cracks across the prism in the short direction of the crystal are characteristic of topaz and tourmaline, and the pearly cleavage of feldspar is unmistakable. Feldspar's cleavage surface is in sharp contrast to the fracture surface of quartz in rocks in which they are typically associated, such as granite.

Kunzite has two perfect cleavages that make cutting difficult, and easy cleavage of the diamond parallel to its octahedral faces is a property that is taken advantage of to shape the crystal for cutting.

Fracture Surface

Many gem materials fracture with a smooth, curved surface shaped like the inside of a shell. Quartz is a notable example of this conchoidal fracture. Some fracture patterns are fibrous or splintery, like the end of a broken stick, or hackly or jagged, like broken cast iron. Jade breaks with a fibrous or hackly pattern because it is formed of crystal fibers matted together into a tough mass. If a chip sparkles in the sun it is not jade. Tenacity is a quality closely allied to fracture pattern; chalcedony and jasper, because of their cryptocrystalline makeup, are tougher than their crystal counterpart, quartz.

Luster

Most gem stones have a high but nonmetallic luster. It may be vitreous or glassy, as in quartz or beryl, or the harder, glittering, adamantine luster of diamond. Other types of luster less frequently encountered among gems are described as resinous, pearly, greasy, silky, waxy, or dull. Metallic luster is brilliant, mirrorlike, such as is seen in galena or polished hematite.

Diaphaneity

Another means of discriminating among gems is provided by optical characteristics, which create much of their beauty and distinction. Most precious stones are transparent and crystalline. Some, such as the diamond and zircon, are outstanding for brilliance and fire. Brilliance depends on refractive index, the ability of a gem substance to bend light rays so that they are reflected from the back facets of a cut gem and out through the top of the stone.

Fire is the product of the gem's ability to disperse or split white light into its constituent colors, so that the stone sparkles in prismatic splendor. A material is translucent if light can pass through it but the shape of objects is not visible through it. It is opaque if it does not pass light. Agate is translucent; jasper is opaque.

Color

Color is one of the principal qualities that make a stone precious. Emerald—for example, the grass-green variety of beryl—is almost priceless, but common opaque beryl is useful only as the ore of the metal beryllium and is valued in cents per pound. The color of a fine gem should be strong and pure, neither muddy, pale, nor too dark. In transparent stones evenness of color is desirable, although some gems such as sapphire and amethyst are often so parti-colored that they test the skill of the lapidary to exploit the best areas.

Color results from optical properties of a gem material that cause it to reflect or absorb certain wavelengths of the spectrum. Ruby of the best quality passes or reflects red wavelengths most readily, then the blue wavelengths. The result is red with a bluish cast, often described as pigeon-blood red. A material that passes or reflects all wavelengths is itself colorless; one that absorbs them all is black.

Color is the most conspicuous characteristic of any mineral, so it is tempting to use color as a means of identification. For some, such as azurite or malachite, color is a primary characteristic and it becomes a reliable guide. But with most minerals, color can be misleading. A blue crystal may be diamond, aquamarine, topaz, tourmaline, kyanite, or apatite. Conversely, such a chameleon as tournaline can be found in almost every color, or even with two or more colors in a single crystal.

Pattern

Among the translucent and opaque gem stones, pattern is an important element both of value and also of identification. The pattern may be some caprice with light such as creates the unique beauty of opal or labradorite, the starry splendor of star sapphire and garnet, or the dramatic cat's-eye effect in chrysoberyl or tigereye. Or it may be the more static but inexhaustibly various patterns of agate and jasper. So typical are their patterns that these materials are described according to whether they show orbicular (eyelike), fortification (with angular, banded structure), dendritic (mossy), poppy (red spotted), tubelike, or plumelike designs.

Specific Gravity

Specific gravity, which is the ratio of the weight of a substance to the weight of an equal volume of water, is one of the most useful tools for discriminating among minerals. The apparatus is not convenient for use in the field, but experience will teach the gem hunter that comparative weight, which is a rough way to judge specific gravity, is one of the almost instinctive tests which he will apply to a puzzling specimen. Obviously malachite, an ore of the heavy metal copper, or hematite, an ore of iron, will "heft" heavy, and massive topaz is noticeably heavier than quartz, although to the eye they may appear identical.

In the laboratory, specific gravity is measured with a beam balance so arranged that the gem can first be weighed in air, then weighed again when suspended by a fine wire in a beaker of water. The weight in air divided by the difference between the two weights is the specific gravity. Specific gravity can also be determined by means of heavy liquids. Bromoform and methylene iodide are diluted to form a series of solutions of graded specific gravities in which the various gem minerals will just sink or float. A mineral that barely sinks or barely floats in a liquid has about the same specific gravity as that liquid. Some even heavier liquids are available. As gems lie in the range between opal (sp. gr. 2.1) and zircon (sp. gr. 4.7), quick and accurate determinations can be made with the heavy liquids. High cost and the poisonous nature of some of the heavy liquids are their only disadvantages.

In the laboratory, use is also made of many instruments—such as the refractometer, the dichroscope, the spectroscope, and the microscope—which not only are beyond the purse and skill of the average gem hunter, but also are useless for prospecting trips. Occasionally, he may find the Geiger counter, to determine radioactivity, and the ultraviolet lamp useful in his searches. Mainly, however, he will have to rely on simple tests and the sixth sense of experience.

Chemical Classifications

Minerals are generally classified according to their crystal structure and their chemical nature. Some are elements, such as diamond (carbon); oxides, such as corundum (aluminum oxide); carbonates, such as malachite (copper carbonate); phosphates, such as apatite; or silicates. To the large and complex silicate family belong a major part of the gem minerals.

The silicates are compounds of one or more metals—such as calcium, iron, or magnesium—with silicon and oxygen. As a family they are hard and, when pure, transparent. The common chemical tests so useful with many minerals are of little value in distinguishing one silicate from another. The visual tests that have been described, readings of specific gravity, and such optical tests as measurement of refractive index are more useful.

Among the gem minerals that are not silicates, the largest single group is the carbonates. They can be identified by the fact that they fizz in hydrochloric acid. By this means rhodochrosite (manganese carbonate) can be distinguished from rhodonite (manganese silicate). Malachite and azurite are also carbonates.

Apatite, a phosphate, can be identified by the white precipitate formed when a few drops of sulphuric acid are added to a sample previously dissolved in hydrochloric acid. Turquoise is another phosphate. Powdered turquoise moistened with hydrochloric acid and held in a flame will color the flame blue.

Fluorite (calcium fluoride) when heated in a glass tube with potassium disulphate gives off hydrofluoric acid which etches the side of the tube, leaving it gray and pitted. To differentiate smithsonite from prehnite, heat the mineral in a closed glass tube. Smithsonite (zinc carbonate) becomes coated with a film that is yellow when hot and white when cold.

Hematite is easily recognized by its weight and by the red streak it makes on a slab of unglazed porcelain. Jet, a form of coal, is easily told from plastic imitations or from glass because it is lighter and burns to an ash. Amber, which is a fossil resin, can be recognized in the same way.

Nearly all the gem minerals have been synthesized in the laboratory, either commercially or experimentally. Even diamond is now manufactured, and so is opal, since the secret of its peacock play of colors has been discovered. Under the electron microscope, precious fire opal appears formed of layer on layer of spheres of silicon dioxide arranged in symmetrical rows. When light strikes these rows, they break it up into colors determined by the precise form of the rows. In common opal, the tiny spheres lack an orderly arrangement, so they scatter the light into a milky hue.

Discoveries made in the laboratory in synthesizing gem minerals, such as corundum, spinel, chrysoberyl, emerald, and even turquoise, have resulted in other remarkable insights into their nature, but these are not major concerns of the prospector trying to find nature's gems.

3.
rock formations in which gems occur

Gold is where you find it, as the saying goes. But actually nature does not scatter her treasures blindly. Certain gems are usually associated with certain rock formations, so some acquaintance with geology makes gem hunting much easier and more fun.

Rocks are divided according to their origin into three major groups: igneous, sedimentary, and metamorphic. Gems are found in all three types.

Igneous Rocks

Igneous rocks are formed by the cooling of molten material from deep within the earth. This material reaches the surface accessible to man in two ways—either by the outpouring of the material in volcanic eruptions or by the baring of masses that had already cooled and become rock below the surface. The former are known as extrusive or volcanic rocks, the latter as intrusive or plutonic rocks.

Intrusive rocks have cooled slowly so that the crystals of their constituent minerals have had a chance to grow to a recognizable size. Extrusive rocks reach the surface rapidly, cool rapidly, and hence are fine-grained. Besides this difference in texture, igneous rocks also differ in the minerals that compose them, although each intrusive and extrusive rock has its counterpart in the other type.

Rocks are difficult to classify because the gradations of texture and mineral composition are gradual and many of the differences can only be determined by laboratory research. But a basic division is not too difficult. Coarse-grained, light-colored rock composed mainly of quartz, orthoclase feldspar, and specks of biotite mica is granite, an intrusive rock. Its extrusive equivalent is the fine-grained, light gray or pink, often-banded rhyolite.

A medium gray, coarse-grained intrusive rock is diorite, containing some quartz; plagioclase, the sodium feldspar; and the dark, iron and magnesium minerals hornblende and biotite mica. Its extrusive counterpart is andesite, of about the same color, but finer grained and often translucent in a thin chip.

Gabbro is a dark, coarse-grained, intrusive rock, rich in iron, magnesium pyroxenes, and calcium feldspar. Basalt, containing the same minerals, is the extrusive, fine-grained rock of the vast lava flows that cover the northwestern states of the United States, as well as whole regions elsewhere in the world. Basalt is the copper- and agate-bearing rock in the Michigan Upper Peninsula; underneath the whole region is the Duluth gabbro.

Some igneous rocks do not quite fit these categories. Obsidian, an extrusive rock, is a glass of much the same chemical composition as rhyolite. Pumice is obsidian in a powdery state. Much of the so-called wonderstone used for gems and bookends is a hardened and compacted pumice.

When an intrusive rock cools near the surface it may include in the hardening mass some crystals that have already formed. The result is a fairly fine-grained rock which includes large, clearly defined crystals, like croutons in soup. This is porphyry, a group of rocks that provide much excellent ornamental material for the lapidary.

Igneous rocks are important to the gem hunter for several reasons. As it cools, basalt traps gases which form pea- to football-size pockets in the hardened rock. Water carrying silica percolates into these pockets and the silica is deposited in the form of banded agate and such minerals as thomsonite and prehnite, and in the form of geodes containing crystal quartz and amethyst. Lava and pumice also engulf trees. The wood burns away as the rock cools, leaving a mold in which casts of chalcedony form. Or the tree substance may be replaced slowly by silica to form petrified wood. Lava is also the environment in which obsidian is likely to occur, and rhyolite may contain pockets of precious opal.

Granites are the home of the gem-rich areas known as pegmatites. A pegmatite is a dike of exceptionally coarse quartz and feldspar with associated minerals. The crystals are large because they were the last part of the granite mass to solidify, and this last part also often contained the less common mineral constituents that form tourmaline, beryl, topaz, smoky quartz, and such feldspars as amazonstone and labradorite.

Perhaps only one percent of the pegmatites are productive of gems. The factors that favor formation of productive pegmatites are the presence of nearby metamorphic rocks containing garnet and kyanite, a large intrusive mass of granite, and rocks that have been deformed and broken by earth movements to create cracks in which pegmatites could form.

The most productive sections of a pegmatite lie near the core of the thickest parts, where coarse quartz and feldspar are accompanied by mica. Near gemmy pockets the rock is often the type known as graphic granite because the dark quartz markings look like hieroglyphics on the feldspar mass.

Veins in massive granite may also yield quartz, phenacite, sphene, and zircon and gold and other metallic ore minerals, including rhodonite and its manganese relatives.

Sedimentary Rocks

Sedimentary rocks are silent testimony that change is the first law of nature. The everlasting hills are a poet's fantasy. Wind, water, winter's ice, and summer's sun crumble the rocks into clay, sand, and gravel. The detritus becomes consolidated into horizontal beds of shale and sandstone, while precipitation from seawater lays down beds of limestone and dolomite.

These are the most valuable rocks to industry because they are the raw materials for cement, building stone, and glass manufacture, but they are comparatively barren of gem materials. Gypsum, however, is a sedimentary rock and is the substance of such beautiful materials as satin spar and alabaster. Travertine, formed by hot springs, is another ornamental rock; so are some fossiliferous limestones. Flint and quartz geodes weather out of sedimentary rocks, and the conglomerate masses composed of rounded pebbles firmly cemented into rock are a striking example of nature's ways. If the pieces are angular, the conglomerate is called a breccia.

Some of the most costly gems are occasionally found in limestone, notably emerald and sapphire, and other beryls and corundums.

Metamorphic Rocks

A metamorphic rock is one that has undergone change from its original form through the effects of heat, pressure, mineralizing solutions and vapors, or contact with other rocks. Metamorphism may change a rock's chemical composition, its physical appearance, and its crystal structure.

Shale, a stratified sedimentary rock, becomes hard, dense slate, in which the clay has been recrystallized. Heat from a large intrusion of igneous rock will turn a dolomitic limestone into marble. An igneous gabbro rich in olivine when attacked chemically by hot waters from an intrusion is changed to serpentine, and through swelling and fracturing it becomes the ornamental rock striped with dolomite that is known as verd antique.

Most metamorphic rocks are layered, like sedimentary rocks, but the layers are light and dark instead of being uniform as they are in sedimentary beds. They are hard like the igneous rocks and usually crystalline. The commonest is schist, easily recognized by its banding, its tendency to split, and the large mica flakes in its composition. Schist results from the effects of great pressure and heat on sandstones, impure limestone, basalt, and other dark rocks. Granite under the same influences becomes gneiss, a hard, markedly banded rock.

Areas of contact metamorphism, where igneous dikes, for example, intrude the country rock, are potential sources of many gem materials, such as chiastolite, the corundum gems, garnet, jade, kyanite, lapis lazuli, and vesuvianite. In such places heat and mineralizing solutions have full play to create valuable crystals.

Weathering, a process to which all rocks are exposed, also creates and concentrates gem minerals. The action of air, water, and dissolved carbon dioxide changes the chemical character of minerals, especially ore minerals lying close to the surface. Malachite and azurite, for example, are formed from copper sulphides by the action of carbon dioxide dissolved in ground water. Erosion removes broken pieces of rock, which are sorted by size and specific gravity by moving water. Gem minerals are usually heavier and more durable than the other rocks, and they become concentrated, like gold, in streams and on gravel bars. From such formations come the sapphires in the Missouri River near Helena, Montana, and the star garnets of Idaho.

Distribution in America

Rocks of all these types are found in the United States, which offers a great diversity of collecting areas. Geologically, the United States comprises three major divisions: the mountains of the East, the mountains of the West, and the broad plains these mountains enclose. In the East, an ancient mountain system of folded and metamorphosed sediments and igneous rocks, the Appalachians, sweeps down from the province of Quebec to Alabama, affording a challenge to the collector, especially in Maine, New Hampshire, Connecticut, New Jersey, Virginia, and North Carolina.

In the West, the Rockies, the Sierra Nevada, and the Coast ranges dominate a vast geological complex which includes the lava plains of the Northwest, the arid Great Basin, and the rugged and highly mineralized Southwest. Crystalline rocks of many kinds are exposed in the smaller mountains, canyons, and deserts that diversify the landscape.

The more level plains between the mountains are less dramatic, but they are by no means lacking in variety. At the foot of the Rockies, the High Plains roll east to meet the Mississippi Valley. To the north lie the granite rocks of Canada and the lavas of the Lake Superior region, and to the south the Mississippi delta and vast coastal plain. In the Black Hills and the Ozarks, crystalline mountains break the broad sweep of the prairie.

Debris eroded from the Rockies covers the High Plains, and glacial sand, silt, and pebbles cloak the glaciated areas of the Mississippi Valley. It is idle to look for such gem minerals as agates in these regions except where water has brought them to the surface or concentrated them by stream action.

Geology is the fundamental clue to gem locations. Since hard-rock mining is too expensive for amateurs, the hobbyist will do most of his collecting where the forces of nature or the efforts of man have exposed minerals. He will pick over stream beds, gravel pits, mine dumps, road cuts, and quarries. Some gems—agate, petrified wood, crystals—may also be dug from easily worked soil, disintegrated rock, and beds of volcanic ash.

Specific directions to promising sites are listed by states in chapter 11. But neither the directory of locations nor the discussion of geology and prospecting techniques in this volume is exhaustive. Their sole purpose is to give the gem hunter some basic information, to tell him what the American gem materials are and where they have been found. Description of a location in the directory should not be regarded as a guarantee that gem-grade materials will be found there. It merely means that such materials are reliably reported to have been found there and that it is a promising place in which to search. Some locations long abandoned as mining sites have been included because of renewed interest in them. Likewise, the growing interest in working with ornamental stones has prompted listing of a number of collecting sites for these materials.

4.
how
to hunt
for
gems

Careful planning is essential if a gem hunting trip is to be successful. First, decide where you are going. Second, become familiar with the appearance of what you hope to collect. Third, acquaint yourself with how and where to look for it.

Don't plan too ambitious a program. The attempt to crowd in visits to too many locations, to do in a day what you will discover requires a week, is certain to cause disappointment and frustration. Each year brings more collectors into the field; many of the easily reached locations are closed or depleted; driving on poor roads and time-consuming preparations to reach an obscure location may be required, and a lot of pick-and-shovel work must be done to get down to worthwhile material.

The days of casual collecting are over; only methodical field-work and the will to dig deeper than in past years will spell success.

Assistance

Museum displays and shops dealing in gems and minerals are the places to look at the kind of rough material you hope to find on your trip. From owners of such shops or from a fellow collector or a hobby magazine, the name of a person who lives near the place you plan to visit can often be obtained. Write or call him and ask his help. It may prove invaluable in such ways as obtaining information about whether and when certain collecting locations are open. New Jersey's Limecrest quarry, for instance, is open to collectors only one day a year; the Foote quarry in North Carolina one day a month.

Information of the same kind can frequently be obtained from a Chamber of Commerce, the geology department of a nearby college, the state geologist, or a local mineral club.

21

In addition to such advance preparations, it is often possible to find a guide, perhaps a fellow collector, in a town near your destination. A high school science teacher, a college graduate student, a filling station operator, a druggist, or a postman—all these are natural sources of information and guidance. A specimen of what you will be looking for will often elicit more information than many words of description. Landmarks have a way of changing; place names are unreliable; roads are relocated in this restless country. A local source of information can clear up such confusions.

Fee areas have grown in number and popularity recently. These are places where the owner builds access roads, removes overburden from the gem deposit, and otherwise offers incentives to the visitor in return for money. In this way money has opened up many areas that would otherwise have been closed and has made collecting easier and more profitable both for the collector and the owner. Often the latter also supplies some collecting equipment, such as screens, buckets, and a flume with running water, as at the ruby mines near Franklin, North Carolina, and the sapphire areas in Montana.

For a few dollars at the gate and perhaps a reasonable charge for material taken away by the collector, fee areas offer the chance to find diamonds in Arkansas, emeralds in North Carolina, opals in Idaho and Nevada, jade in California and Wyoming, and agate on many Oregon and Washington ranches. Such operations have a way of closing without notice, so that it is prudent to make sure whether ones included in a trip are open. The Priday ranch thunder egg beds, for example, long a noted source of agate, are closed, although the owners still sell material from the ranch and have announced plans to reopen.

Some mineral and gem clubs have leased or purchased sites so that they could control and protect reasonable collecting. Usually these are open to visitors if permission is obtained.

In a few states, rock-hound parks for camping and collecting have been established. One of these is near Deming, New Mexico (described in this book's Locality Guide), and another is thirty-five miles southeast of Des Moines, Iowa, near Knoxville.

It is reasonable to take the weather and the seasons into account when planning a trip. Much of Utah, southern California, and Arizona is uncomfortably hot in the summer, although the dry heat is less unpleasant than the moist heat of other regions. Montana and Vermont and the Sierra Nevada offer more to skiers in winter than to rock hounds. But most of the United States is comfortable the year round, especially the richly endowed West Coast states. In hot weather, gem hunting is most pleasant in the early morning, the coolest time of day, and the afternoon is a splendid time to look over the morning's gatherings and to loaf in the shade.

High altitude makes some persons lethargic and depressed. But much of this feeling can be removed by gradually exposing the person to heights, a process known as acclimation.

Maps

Maps are essential. Road maps, such as those provided by filling stations and state tourist bureaus, are invaluable.

Frequently, however, more detailed maps are needed, such as the topographic maps published by the United States Geological Survey. Each map shows a quadrangular area designated by the name of a town or prominent natural feature. Maps for areas east of the Mississippi River may be ordered from the Distribution Branch, Geological Survey, 1200 S. Eads Street, Arlington, Va. 22202. Those for areas west of the Mississippi River may be ordered from the Distribution Center, Geological Survey, Federal Center, Denver, Colorado 80225. Index charts, provided free by the Survey, also list dealers in some cities who stock maps.

Maps of national forests may be obtained from the United States Forest Service, Washington, D.C. 20415.

The Geological Survey's topographic maps record natural features of the earth's surface by means of contour lines. They also include place names, symbols, and man-made features, such as roads and towns, as well as boundaries of civil divisions and parallels of latitude and meridians of longitude. Symbols and conventional representations of roads, marshes, and so on are explained on the reverse sides of the maps.

Understanding contour lines is the key to productive use of topographic maps. Contour lines show the relief and configuration of land surfaces. Each line connects points of the same elevation above or below sea level. The elevations delineated by the contour lines are spaced at some convenient fixed distance, such as 100 feet apart. Thus contour lines are like steps with risers of uniform height and treads varying in width according to the pitch of the slope. On a steep slope the treads or contours will be close together; on a gentle slope they will be far apart. With practice it becomes easy to visualize the peaks, valleys, and other natural features of a mapped surface.

Topographic maps are of primary value to the gem hunter intent on finding a described location. Geologic maps, which add further information about rock formations, help guide the hunter to rocks associated with the gems he is seeking.

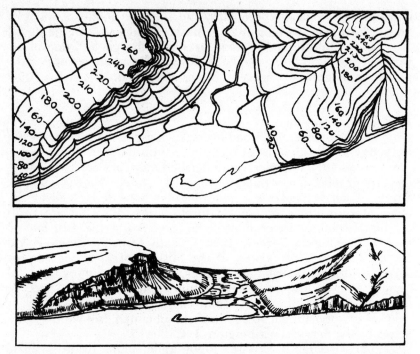

A river valley between a cliff and a hill and draining into a lake is shown in the drawing. Above it is the same scene as it would be pictured on a topographic map. Note how close the lines are where the cliff rises sheer and how they are spaced on the gently rising hill. (Drawing by U.S. Geological Survey)

On geologic maps, colors and symbols identify sedimentary and other types of rocks, as well as faults, direction of pitch and strike, and deformations. Interpretation of such maps requires more practice and more knowledge of geology than other maps. But the rock hunter who can use geologic maps can direct his search to the rock masses in which the gems he is seeking are likely to occur. Herkimer "diamonds," for example, are found only in exposures of the Little Falls dolomite; these would be defined on a geologic map of certain quadrangles in upper New York State. Likewise, petrified bone and wood are associated in the Southwest with such formations as the Morrison and Chinle sandstones.

Traveling

The rock-hunting vehicle, whether jeep, camper, trailer, or family car, should be put in first-class condition before it is taken on a trip. Gem minerals must be collected today in places far from major highways. Most modern cars are not designed for rutted roads or dim trails across the desert. A four-wheel-drive vehicle is ideal for venturing where only a mountain goat or antelope would feel at home, and some old-model cars with a bit of daylight under them are serviceable.

Two spare tires give a feeling of comfort when the collector is forty miles from nowhere; so does a roll of chicken wire for traction in desert sand. A towrope, spare fan belt, and a bumper jack belong in the trunk in a place where they can be easily reached. If the excursion leads far from a source of supplies, it is well to have a change of crankcase oil, a five-gallon metal safety can filled with gasoline, and an equal amount of radiator water in a spout-type can.

A few cans of food and fruit juice and a supply of drinking water may make an emergency less grim or make possible a sudden change in plans.

Not only should the car be in good shape; so should the driver. A few thousand miles of driving coupled with strenuous hiking, climbing for gem materials, and carrying heavy loads of rocks is taxing for an outdoorsman, much more so for an office worker. Doctors advise: Don't overdo, don't drive too fast or too far, don't drive when sleepy or tired.

Instead of abusing your vehicle on mountain roads or in desert sands, it is often sensible and economical to rent a car and even engage a driver-guide for the rough going. In some regions where strangers may not be welcome, such as in or near an Indian reservation, this is imperative.

Travel-wise collectors take the extra trouble to pack the car for a trip, then unpack it and unroll everything to make sure they have not forgotten something essential. They then repack it in such a way that each item will be readily accessible when it is needed. They advise: Don't overload the car, and don't place packages where they will interfere with the driver's vision or where the packages will be hurled forward in the event of a panic stop.

Gasoline mileage can be increased five percent by installing a fresh air filter, clean or new spark plugs, and having the distributor and carburetor properly adjusted. Tires will wear longer if they are properly balanced and the wheels are aligned. A jumper cable is invaluable in that not-uncommon event of a run-down battery.

Prospecting Equipment

The choice of clothing and prospecting equipment depends on the type of area where gems will be sought, but there are some items that are always needed. One is a prospector's pick with a square hammerhead on one end, and a pick point on the other. These can be bought at any large hardware store. With it should go a cold chisel with a one-inch blade: a flat-bladed chisel for splitting rock, and one chisel with a square point. Often a large pickax, a sledgehammer, large and small crowbars, and a shovel and trenching tool are needed. A screen should be included if gravel is to be worked over, either dry or in a stream or lake. A metal detector, although popular with prospectors working over ore dumps, is rarely useful in gem hunting.

To make sure that good specimens are not ruined on the way home, the car should carry some cardboard boxes, burlap and paper bags, egg cartons, wrapping paper, and labels. Bruised or broken crystals cause gem specimens to lose most of their value, so that it pays to pack them well.

For collecting in the field, a carpenter's apron with big pockets is often used. So is a knapsack or a shoulder bag. If the trip calls for going into caves or mines, candles, a flashlight, or a miner's headlamp should be included.

Clothing should cover the whole body, even in hot weather. Clothing protects the skin against sunburn, insect bites, and abrasion by rocks and cactus. Women will find jeans or slacks more comfortable than skirts. Stout shoes are essential for both men and women. The most comfortable and the safest for climbing on rocks are shoes with six-inch uppers and broad toes like the army last, of medium-weight leather. They should be broken in at home before undertaking the trip. Such shoes are more comfortable if two pairs of socks—thin inside and heavy outside—are worn.

High boots are too hot and too exhausting except where snakes or marshy ground make them indispensable. Armor, however, is not the best protection against snakes; being careful where you put your hands and feet is.

Work gloves save hands from blisters, cuts, and broken fingernails when climbing on rocks, wielding a pick, or handling specimens. A hat is the best protection against sunstroke and a boiling-red forehead, and sunglasses are helpful at high altitudes. Suntan lotion and insect repellent belong in the personal kit, along with a pocketknife, a magnifying glass, and a few raisins, nuts, and a candy bar for that midafternoon craving. Someone in the party should have a first-aid kit.

Federal regulations and common sense dictate the wearing of a hard hat, safety glasses or goggles, and safety-toe shoes in an operating quarry or mine. They are prudent precautions against disaster in any situation where there is danger of rock falling from a cliff, of flying rock chips from hammer blows, or of a crushed foot.

Conduct in the Field

One thing that must not be forgotten and left at home on a trip is common courtesy and good manners. Scores of areas still rich in gem materials have been closed forever to collectors because someone was careless, insolent, hoggish, or a litterbug. For your own good, the good of the property owner, and the good of those who will wish to collect after you, it is well to remember:

1. Always obtain permission to enter private property, even unfenced range, a deserted cabin, or a mine dump. Be ready to sign a waiver absolving the owner of responsibility for any accident you may suffer. Have a clear understanding with the owner where you may go, what you are seeking, and how you plan to find and get it. Strictly observe this understanding by staying within its limits.
2. Know and heed the laws governing collecting on public lands.
3. Be careful with fire. Wet down campfires when leaving, bury the embers, and crush out cigarette butts. Be careful not to start grass fires.
4. Clean up your campsite. Either bury all debris, cans, and garbage, or take it away with you.
5. Don't contaminate wells or creeks.
6. Fill in holes that you dig. Stock may be injured by falling into pits. Be careful not to alarm range cattle. They may stampede and be injured.
7. Leave gates as you find them, open or closed.
8. Don't trespass on growing crops or drive across grasslands, especially if the ground is soft. Stay on roads in farming country.
9. Do not meddle with tools or machinery.
10. Report any vandalism you find. This is for your own protection.
11. Leave firearms and blasting materials at home unless you know how to use them, have a reason for using them, and have permission from authorities and property owners to use them.

Mineral collecting clubs, especially in the far West, have organized field trips to pick up litter along highways, in national forest campgrounds and parks, and at popular collecting areas.

Under the program known as HELP (Help Eliminate Litter Please) they have passed out litter bags to motorists, and by lectures and distributing kits to teachers have carried into the schoolroom their message of restoring the beauty of the outdoors.

Litter is a major problem. One state, Mississippi, has found that the cost of clearing its state highways of litter costs taxpayers 300,000 dollars annually, and it is not a heavily populated state, either.

Courtesy also includes moderation; the gem hunter should take only what he needs, leaving some for the next fellow. So-called truck collectors, who haul away everything in sight, have given everyone else a bad name. Grade your specimen on the spot by chipping away a small corner of it. If you don't want it, leave it for someone else who may prize it. Nodules and geodes should not be broken in the field. Take them home intact and saw or break them where the fragments will not litter the landscape.

The field manners of some collectors have been so outrageous that many once-productive locations have been closed. "The flower agate locations south of La Junta have been fouled up by rockhounds who left gates open and cut fences to the point where the ranchers are liable to welcome you with a gun," writes a Colorado collector. "As far as Texas is concerned," says a Texan, "the legislature, prodded by ranchers and leasers of state land, has passed a trespassing law that has virtually killed the ambition of any rockhound. . . . The law makes it illegal to even enter another's property without having written permission . . . to camp, cook a meal, or rest."

And from a New Hampshire state bulletin: "A number of mines are posted and permission to collect must be obtained. . . . With mineral collecting one of the fastest growing hobbies, care and courtesy are a 'must' if New Hampshire mineral collecting grounds are to remain available to the amateur."

A group that broke into an abandoned mine was rescued by company police and warned, then went back in and had to be brought out again. These and other instances of vandalism caused closing of most properties in the copper mining region of Upper Michigan. For a century this has been a Mecca for collectors. Only after strenuous efforts by mineral clubs was the closing modified to allow groups in under proper supervision.

Vandals in off-road vehicles using high-speed drills, jackhammers, and bulldozers have destroyed or removed many of the ancient carvings and rock paintings in the Mojave desert of California. Federal officials estimate that nearly a quarter of these archeological treasures, five thousand years old and among the finest in the world, have already disappeared. They fear all will be gone within fifteen years.

Vandalism, excessive collecting, and damage done to the delicate balance of life in desert regions by off-road vehicles have brought about federal regulations in California that have closed some areas altogether, restricted travel of all kinds in others, controlled use of off-road vehicles, and set up a permit and fee system. Similar regulations are in force or in preparation on federal lands in Oregon, Utah, and elsewhere. They are harbingers of the shape of things to come for all collecting.

State and federal legislation requiring reclamation of lands strip-mined for coal also impinge on amateur collecting because they require filling in of excavations and limit access to strip-mine spoil piles.

Regulations on the amount of petrified wood that may be taken by one person have been in force for several years. The limit is 25 pounds a day plus one piece per person, and 250 pounds a year. Two noted areas in national forests—the Emerald Creek garnet area in Idaho and the Moat Mountain smoky quartz area in New Hampshire—are now federally administered and controlled under a fee system. Even more comprehensive action shrinking the boundaries of easily accessible collecting appears in proposals for roadless areas in 22 million acres of federal lands.

Collecting, of course, has always been forbidden in national parks, national monuments and historical sites, in lands, lakes, and reservoirs administered by the U.S. Army Engineers, in areas under the wild and scenic rivers program and in some Bureau of Land Management tracts, some national forests, state parks, and ocean beaches, such as in Oregon.

The major effect of federal regulation is felt in the western states and Alaska, where most federally owned land lies. In the Midwest, the East and the South, most land is either privately owned or belongs to the state.

States have put few restrictions on collecting for personal use on state-owned lands, aside from the exceptions mentioned above, but vertebrate fossils and Indian artifacts are protected under the federal antiquities law. They are off bounds to amateurs, who are asked, however, to report discovery of such materials to a museum, university, or federal agency.

The law of trespass is the one that primarily concerns the amateur collector. It forbids, on penalty of fine or imprisonment, entry on privately owned property without permission of its owner. Accidental trespass may be excused by the owner but it is not legally defensible. In Colorado recently a property owner cut across the land of another person to reach his own, was arrested and fined one hundred dollars. Land does not have to be posted against trespassers or even fenced in some states.

Mine and quarry owners are often reluctant to give permission for collectors to enter because in most states they would be liable for injury to the collector. The owner's liability insurance company for this reason forbids him to open the property to anyone not in the place on business. Sometimes the owner will allow an overlooked trespass to avoid taking any responsibility, or he may ask for a signed waiver of responsibility. Some states have passed laws absolving an owner of liability for the death or injury of a person allowed to come on the property.

Hazards

Prospecting, like any other outdoor activity, is not without physical hazards. Rocks can fall from a shattered quarry wall, a frost-weakened cliff, or an overhanging mass. A fellow collector working above you on a rocky slope may start a slide or dislodge a boulder. Never collect above another person or under one.

Open mine shafts are obvious dangers; so are water-filled quarries. One of the major sources of accidents occurs when a collector digging in gravel or soft earth causes it to cave in on him. He may be crushed or suffocated.

In almost any collecting area, children and pets must be kept close at hand and constantly supervised. Better yet, leave them at camp or at home. Kids are reputed to say the darndest things; they do them, too, and often with tragic results. Several children at play dug around a concrete cap sealing a shaft of a copper mine in Michigan. A small child with them slipped into the hole they had dug and fell a mile beneath the surface to her death.

Safety in prospecting, like safety anywhere, is based on common sense and moderation. The first step after reaching a collecting site is to look it over for any obvious hazards.

The greatest risk is getting lost. Even here common sense comes into play. Leave word where you will be going and when you expect to return so that a search can be started when you become seriously overdue. Unless you are thoroughly familiar with the country, it is a sound rule to stay within sight of your vehicle. An automobile is a first-rate survival kit. It provides shelter, fuel, and safety, and it is much easier for a search party to find than a wandering, delirious man or woman. Radiator water not contaminated with antifreeze is potable in an emergency and enough for a family of four for several days. Headlights and horn can be used to draw the attention of a rescue team, and engine oil burned in a hubcap sends up a smoke signal visible for miles. The steel car body is proof against cold and animals.

An Arizona sheriff who has searched for hundreds of lost persons advises: Don't send your partner for help; don't start walking unless you are dead sure you can make it to help; and don't get panicky; someone will find you.

If the supply runs dry, there is a way recommended to get water from desert soil. Dig a hole 30 inches deep, place an empty can or pan in the bottom, spread over the hole a sheet of thin plastic, and make a dimple in the center of the sheet so that water evaporating from the soil will condense on the underside of the sheet and drip down into the can. The method is said to yield a pint a day. The yield can be tripled if cactus or other desert vegetation is broken up and placed in the hole.

Some outdoor hazards are in the nature of things; but going into old mines is not one of them. The best advice from experts is to stay out. Poison gases, rotten timbers, hidden shafts, roof rocks ready to fall at the least vibration, snakes and wild animals can make an old mine a deathtrap.

Dynamite is often abandoned around ghost towns and old mine sites and quarries. It has become touchy with age and may explode at the least jolt. With dynamite there may be old blasting caps. These look like long .22 rifle cartridges of copper or aluminum. They are very sensitive and can blow off the hand that picks one up.

Ranchers on the western range often set cyanide guns to kill coyotes. The deadly chemical is buried with an explosive charge and an exposed piece of cloth saturated in something to attract the animal. The area around such traps is supposed to be marked with signs, but sign or no sign, pulling on the bit of cloth will spray the chemical on a man and could kill a child if it reaches the child's face.

Rocks in some desert areas harbor a fungus that can cause serious illness. The careless collector who licks a rock to make its pattern visible could contract the disease. A number have. Even breathing the dust stirred up by collecting activity may spread the infection. In any kind of collecting it is advisable to wash up thoroughly before eating, as many rocks carry poisonous minerals.

Old hands offer these suggestions for driving in the desert: Use second gear in soft sand. If you get stuck, do not dig sand away from the wheels—this only softens it and makes the wheels sink deeper. Instead try these remedies:

1. Tamp the sand down hard in front of the wheels.
2. Lay chicken wire under the wheels.

3. Place burlap bags, filled half full of sand and tied, under the wheels.
4. Let air out of the tires until they are about half deflated. You can reinflate them later with a carbon-dioxide gas "bomb" or spark-plug pump or a regular tire pump (available from auto accessory stores).

Campers in desert regions are advised to avoid dry stream beds and canyons where they may be trapped in their tent or vehicle by a flash flood.

In only a few places in the United States are wild animals a danger. Poison oak and ivy are prevalent, however, and learning to identify them is elementary education for the outdoors. Prompt use of soap and water after exposure will be adequate for most persons.

Rattlers are the most commonly encountered poisonous reptile. The best way to avoid being bitten by a rattlesnake is to stay away from it. Usually it will avoid human beings unless it is accidentally cornered and strikes to protect itself. Snakes take shelter from midday heat under bushes and logs and sun themselves in cool weather in open spots. They are more active by night than in the day.

For safety's sake, keep hands and feet out of holes, crevices, and other places where a snake cannot be clearly seen. Wear stout shoes, thick wool hose, loose trousers, and gloves. Look closely at the ground, move slowly, and make some noise to avoid unwelcome encounters. In known snake country, it is well to turn over rocks with a stick or a long scoop made for that purpose.

Besides rattlesnakes, coral snakes, copperheads, and water moccasins are regarded as venomous. The Gila monster is generally too lethargic to be dangerous, and the black widow spider is usually thought to be less fearsome than its reputation.

Modern first aid for snakebite calls for rushing the victim to a hospital or doctor. Meanwhile the victim should be kept quiet to avoid accelerating the circulation of venom through the body. A tourniquet or constricting bandage should be placed between the bite and the heart. On an arm or leg, the usual scene of a bite, place it two or three inches above the bite. It should restrict but not stop the circulation, and it should be loosened once or twice an hour.

The bite should be cleansed with sponges saturated in alcohol, an incision made to connect the fang marks and a quarter inch beyond, but without severing muscles or nerves. The wound then can be squeezed gently with the fingers. Ice wrapped in clean cloth and applied to the wound is helpful. If the victim cannot be taken to a doctor, administer antivenin. The snakebite kit should include the antivenin, a disposable scalpel in sterile foil, two surgical prep sponges sealed with alcohol in foil, and a flat elastic tourniquet.

One way to invite trouble in some areas is to sleep on the ground—an open invitation to a snake or scorpion to crawl into a snug warm place. Scorpions, which are small, straw-colored and highly venomous, hide in clothing and shoes. Shaking out such articles before donning them is standard practice wherever scorpions can be expected.

Ticks are more of a nuisance than a real danger, now that the Rocky Mountain spotted fever virus, which ticks carry, can be treated with antitoxin and antibiotics. Ticks hang out in warm weather on underbrush, waiting to hitch a ride on the first passerby. It follows that the best way to avoid ticks is to stay out of brushy spots, at least from June until after August, when the tick menace fades away.

Once it has found a host, the tick burrows under the skin to feast on blood. Unless it is well under the skin, a tick can often be removed with tweezers or induced to withdraw by touching it with the heated point of a pin or nail or by application of a drop of turpentine. If these fail, the best remedy is to have a physician cut out the tick.

Collecting Techniques

Psychologists say that knowledge makes us conscious of things we would otherwise ignore. This means that if we are out riding we may not be conscious we have passed a lot of trees, but if we are interested in trees we will notice them and identify the several varieties along the way. A corollary to this is the observation that we see what we are looking for. We may go looking for agates and while finding them pass over other stones on the beach.

Finding gem material takes some science, some skill, some perspiration, and some luck. The first axiom is to look wherever rock is exposed, such as a road or railroad cut, a quarry, mine dump, excavation, gravel pit, beach, river bar, or plowed field. Sometimes it is rewarding to examine streams and washes for fragments of gem materials and then trace them back to their source, much as a gold seeker pans the streams back toward the mother lode.

The second axiom is to look for the rocks and other conditions associated with the gem material. Oregon thunder eggs, for example, are in volcanic rocks; tourmaline, beryl, and kunzite occur near the quartz segregations in the feldspar mass of pegmatite dikes. Garnets and corundum settle with other heavy materials to the bottom in river gravels. The expert agate hunters of Minnesota say that big ones are found only where the stones are large, usually in gullies and on the gravelly uplands, not in the streams. In desert regions, agates and other silica minerals often can be distinguished from the other rocks by a white coating caused by weathering under arid conditions. Where much of the surface material has already been picked up, watch for a corner of rock sticking inconspicuously from the ground. It may be a winner that has been overlooked. When looking for agates in gravel, notice whether quartz and jasper pebbles appear in the gravel. If not, it is unlikely that agates will be found there.

When searching a gravel bar for agate and jasper, walk slowly with the sun at your back and keep your eyes on the gravel a yard or so ahead. Agate and jasper pebbles, being hard and compact, emerge from the hurly-burly of stream and wave action with a better polish than other stones. They shine, especially when wet, and catch the practiced eye at once. Both agate and jasper are forms of chalcedony, but agate is translucent, jasper is opaque.

The best collecting time on open ground and beaches is in the spring or after storms, when fresh material is exposed. On the other hand, a storm may wash away the beach pebbles or cover them with sand.

Much good gem material comes from mine dumps. There are tricks to lightening the labor of working at such sites and to working them effectively. The best specimens are usually in the oldest part of the dump, which is buried under newer debris. Dig in from the side to reach the old part and to avoid working over the top material. Dig where there is tree or shrub growth, as that will be an older, undisturbed part. Break up boulders; they may contain unscrutinized material. When you find a good piece, note the level in the dump and the associated rocks, and look elsewhere for the same combination. And it is often profitable to rework a spot where someone else has hit pay dirt.

Sometimes it is more rewarding to wander away from the described area to look for an overlooked or undiscovered exposure of gem-bearing rock or a mine dump.

Material that is not fragile can be shipped home by truck in hundred-pound lots in burlap or heavy paper potato bags. It should be labeled "Country Rock" and sent C.O.D. Specimens from several localities can be segregated and labeled in separate bags within the shipping bag.

Perhaps once in a lifetime an industrious prospector will discover a bonanza of gem or ore minerals. He can make it his own by filing a mining claim, which calls for putting up a location notice, staking the four corners of the claimed area, and filing in the county land agent's office. In addition he has to show that the claim contains minerals of reasonable commercial value.

The claim can be kept alive by doing 100 dollars' worth of work a year on developing it. Notice must be made annually that this has been done. The claimant may remove minerals but he may not build a house on the ground. He can patent or make the claim permanent by application to the federal Bureau of Land Management. Details are set out in "Staking a Claim on Federal Lands," obtainable from the Superintendent of Documents, U.S. Printing Office, Washington, D.C. 20402, and in "Mining Claims: Questions and Answers," obtainable from the Bureau of Land Management, Interior Building, Washington, D.C.

Not all mineral treasures come from the earth. As the astronauts have demonstrated, rocks from outer space are of great interest and scientific significance. Two types of rocks from the sky— meteorites and tektites—are within the reach of anyone who searches the great open spaces of our land.

Meteorites, which are believed to be fragments of a crumbled planet, are found in several forms. The commonest and the most difficult to identify are stony meteorites, which have a blackish crust when fresh and are gray or white inside with a texture like concrete. In the mass will be some small blobs or granules of metal. Stony meteorites look so much like other rocks that they can easily be overlooked. They disintegrate more rapidly than the other types.

Stony-iron meteorites, the second type, are like the stony ones except that they are filled like a fruitcake with pieces of metal. Neither type should be broken in an effort to identify it as a meteorite. The approved method is to grind off a corner to see whether the metal blobs are present. Both types are fairly smooth on the surface and fairly heavy.

To the third type belong the nickel-iron meteorites, very heavy and black on the surface, which is usually marked with curious, thumbprintlike indentations. Inside these meteorites is a silvery mass of iron-nickel alloy. Meteorites may range in size from marbles to masses weighing many tons. They are usually irregular in shape, often like a cone but almost never spherical or flat.

Deserts, prairies, and dry, unforested lands are the easiest places to find meteorites. Like other rocks, they work toward the surface through freezing and thawing of the ground. Where one has been found is a sensible place to search for others because meteorites often fall in a number of pieces. Most universities and large museums are willing to examine a suspected meteorite. So will the Center of Meteorite Studies at Arizona State University, Tempe, Arizona.

Tektites are still objects of mystery, but they are almost certainly visitors, too, from outer space. Tektites fall as showers of thousands of small, rounded, black or dark green blobs of glass. In size and color a typical one resembles the obsidian pieces known as Apache Tears, except that the tektite's surface is wrinkled and warty. Tektites are found on the ground in several southern and southeastern states, but notably in Texas. The Texas specimens are called bediasites from Bedias, a town in Grimes county.

Gold is a subject by itself, but because the gem hunter will be brought near locations where gold is found, brief mention should be given to this companion form of prospecting. Gem minerals are often hunted in streams, where their weight segregates them with gold. Hard-rock mining for gold is beyond the capabilities of most amateurs, but panning for gold is a diversion that can be profitable.

A frying pan or cake pan will serve but a regular gold pan is better. It should be broken in so that the surface is slightly roughened. Gold panning is easier to do than to describe. Gold is heavy; it settles into crevices in the rock underlying a stream or into the bottom stratum of gravel. So dig down to bedrock, scrape out the cracks, and scoop up the gravel below the upstream point of a bar. Fill the pan half full with the gravel, sit close to the stream, fill the pan with water, break up any lumps, and jiggle the pan as you turn it slowly. Pick out and discard the big pebbles, then lower the pan beneath the surface of the stream and twist and tip the pan so that the top layer of gravel spills slowly over the side. Continue doing this until less than a cupful of fine material remains. Look now in the pan for any nuggets, pick them out, twist the pan clockwise, then rapidly the other way so that the material in the pan swirls across the pan. Look for the glint of gold. Continue this until only black sand and gold remain. Pick out the gold flakes with tweezers. Or you can dry the concentrate, lift out the black sand with a magnet, and separate the gold.

In the East, Georgia, North and South Carolina, and Virginia have been the major gold producers, mostly from placer mining. Colorado, Idaho, Montana, Nevada, Utah, and South Dakota have had their bonanza years, both from placers and hard-rock mining. Arizona and New Mexico and the West Coast states of California, Oregon, and Washington also had their golden days, and so did Alaska.

To summarize, when you hunt gem material, know what you're looking for. Know how to recognize it when you find it. Give yourself plenty of time. Go prepared for the kind of work you'll have to do. Respect the rights of the man who owns the land you're hunting on, even Uncle Sam, and of those other gem hunters who will follow you.

Remembering these points, and putting them into practice, you'll find gem hunting a fascinating and exciting hobby.

5.
characteristics of important gem stone materials

TABLE B

Name and Specific Gravity	Hard-ness	Composition	Color or Pattern
Agate 2.6	7	Cryptocrystalline chalcedony	Varicolored in bands or patterns
Alabaster 2.3	2	Hydrous calcium sulphate	Variegated patterns
Amazonstone 2.5 to 2.6	6	Microcline feldspar	Leek green often dappled with white
Amber 1.0 to 1.1	2+	Fossil tree resin	Yellow, reddish, brown
Amethyst 2.6 (ăm'-ê-thĭst)	7	Variety of crystal quartz	Purple or lavender
Apatite 3.2 (ăp'-à-tite)	5	Calcium fluophosphate	Yellow, green, blue, pink, purple
Aquamarine 2.6 to 2.7 (ăk-wȧ-mȧ-rēn')	8	Crystal variety of beryl	Sky blue to blue green

The descriptions in these tables are of gems and ornamental materials found in the United States that are generally considered to be worth collecting and cutting.

Diaphaneity and Luster	Fracture and Cleavage	Other Characteristics	Associated Rocks
Translucent; vitreous luster	Conchoidal	Patterns include iris, eyes, bands, fortification, moss, dot, flower and plume; also sagenitic	Nodules and veins in volcanic and sedimentary rocks; also in gravel
Opaque; grainy		Form of gypsum; satin spar is another variety	Sedimentary rocks
Opaque; pearly luster	Perfect cleavage	Well-developed crystals, often banded by twinning	Pegmatite
Transparent to translucent; subvitreous luster	Conchoidal	As lumps and masses	Marl and clay
Transparent; vitreous luster	Conchoidal	Color often in zones	Lining nodules; massive in veins
Transparent to opaque; vitreous luster	Conchoidal	Yellow crystals often called asparagus stone	Pegmatite, metamorphic rocks, and ore veins
Transparent; vitreous luster	Conchoidal; basal cleavage	Crystals are hexagonal, often very large	Pegmatite and granite druses

TABLE B (*Continued*)

Name and Specific Gravity	Hard-ness	Composition	Color or Pattern
Aragonite 2.9–3.0 (e-rag'-e-nīt)	3.5	Calcium carbonate	Colorless, yellow
Augite 3.3 (aw'-jīt)	5–6	Calcium aluminum silicate, a pyroxene	Black
Axinite 3.2 (ăk'-sĭ-nīt)	7	Complex calcium aluminum borosilicate	Clove brown
Aventurine 2.6 (ă-ven'-tchu-rīn)	7	Quartz colored by mica flakes or an iron mineral	Green, brown, yellow, red, spangled with mica
Azurite 3.8 (ăzh'-ū-rite)	3+	Hydrous copper carbonate	Deep blue
Benitoite 3.6 (bĕ-nē'-tō-ite)	6+	Barium titanium silicate	Sapphire blue crystals
Beryl 2.6 to 2.9 (bear'-ĭl)	8	Beryllium aluminum silicate	Varieties: aquamarine is bluish; emerald, grass green; goshenite, colorless; heliodor, yellow; morganite, pink; also asteriated
Bloodstone 2.6	7	A jasper	Dark green with red spots

Diaphaneity and Luster	Fracture and Cleavage	Other Characteristics	Associated Rocks
Vitreous; transparent to opaque	Perfect cleavage	Fizzes with acid	Substance of pearls, and of cave formations
Opaque, glassy	Hackly	A major rock former	Found with lavas such as basalt
Transparent to opaque		Wedge-shaped crystals	Granite
Translucent to opaque; pearly luster	Semi-conchoidal	Massive	Pegmatite
Translucent to opaque; vitreous luster	Conchoidal	Crystals or botryoidal masses; often with malachite	Copper ores
Transparent; vitreous luster	Conchoidal	Wedge-shaped crystals in natrolite	California, only locality
Transparent to translucent; vitreous luster	Conchoidal; basal cleavage	Crystals are prisms	Pegmatite and schist; limestone
Opaque	Conchoidal to hackly fracture	Also called St. Stephen's stone and heliotrope	Igneous rocks and in gravel

TABLE B (*Continued*)

Name and Specific Gravity	Hard-ness	Composition	Color or Pattern
Calcite 2.7 (kăl'-site)	3	Crystalline calcium carbonate	Colorless, pale brown, yellow, red
Carnelian 2.6 (kär-neal'-yăn)	7	Variety of chalcedony	Red-brown, often from heat treatment
Chalcedony 2.6 (kăl-said'-ō-nĭ)	7	Cryptocrystalline variety of quartz	White, varicolored, and often patterned
Chiastolite 3.2 (kĭ-as'-tō-lite)	7	Aluminum silicate	Gray; cross-shaped black inclusions in cross section
Chlorastrolite 3.1–3.5 (klōr-as'-trō-lite)	6	Silicate of calcium and aluminum, mostly pumpellyite	Dark green eyes ringed in white or pale green; chatoyant
Chrysoberyl 3.7 (krĭs'-ō-bear-ĭl)	8½	Beryllium aluminum oxide	Yellow, green; alexandrite is green-red; cat's-eye is chatoyant
Chrysocolla 2.5 (krĭs-ō-kŏl'-a)	7	Quartz colored by copper silicate	Greenish blue to sky blue

Diaphaneity and Luster	Fracture and Cleavage	Other Characteristics	Associated Rocks
Transparent to opaque	Two perfect cleavages	Onyx is massive, striped variety. Marble and travertine other forms. Fizzes with acid	Sedimentary rocks
Translucent; vitreous luster	Conchoidal	Sard is brown. Sardonyx is sard or carnelian, striped with white or black	As nodules, usually in desert areas
Translucent; waxy to vitreous luster	Conchoidal	Agate, carnelian, sard, jasper are some varieties	Seams or lining of cavities in sedimentary and volcanic rocks
Opaque; waxy luster	Uneven fracture	Cigar-shaped prisms; a variety of andalusite	Schists; metamorphic rocks
Opaque	Fibrous fracture, brittle	Amygdaloids or beach pebbles. Often called greenstones	From basalt and gravel of Lake Superior district
Transparent; vitreous luster	Conchoidal	As crystals	Schists and pegmatite
Translucent to opaque; vitreous luster	Conchoidal	Massive, enamellike surface	Copper deposits

TABLE B (Continued)

Name and Specific Gravity	Hard-ness	Composition	Color or Pattern
Chrysoprase 2.6 (krĭs'-ō-praise)	7	Chalcedony colored by nickel oxide	Apple green
Citrine 2.6 (sĭt'-rĭn)	7	Crystalline quartz	Yellow to red-brown
Coral 2.6	3+	Organic aragonite	Red is precious coral; pink known as angel's flesh; also black and white
Cordierite 2.6 (kôr'-di-e-rite)	7+	Hydrous magnesium (iron) aluminum silicate	Light to smoky blue
Corundum 3.9 to 4.0 (kō-rŭn'-dŭm)	9	Aluminum oxide	Ruby red, sapphire blue; many other colors, also asteriated and cat's-eye
Datolite 2.9 to 3.0 (dăt-ō-lite)	5+	Calcium borosilicate	White, copper red, yellow, green
Diamond 3.5	10	Carbon	Colorless, blue, yellow, pink, brown, black

Diaphaneity and Luster	Fracture and Cleavage	Other Characteristics	Associated Rocks
Translucent to opaque; vitreous to waxy luster	Conchoidal	Massive	In veins with nickel deposits
Transparent	Conchoidal	Often from amethyst by heat treatment	From cavities in igneous and sedimentary rocks
Translucent; dull luster	Hackly fracture	Branching	From salt water coral formations
Transparent; vitreous luster	Conchoidal	Also called iolite or dichroite; crystals are white or pale blue in one direction, dark in the other	Gravel and metamorphic rocks
Transparent to translucent; subadamantine luster	Conchoidal	Platelike or blunt, barrel-shaped six-sided crystals	Metamorphic and igneous rocks
Massive is opaque; crystals transparent	Subconchoidal	Massive form looks like porcelain; crystals, very bright	Massive form in Michigan copper mines; crystals in trap rock cavities
Transparent adamantine luster	Octahedral cleavage	Cubic or octahedral crystals with rounded edges	Peridotite and gravel

TABLE B (*Continued*)

Name and Specific Gravity	Hard-ness	Composition	Color or Pattern
Dumortierite 2.8 (dū-môr'-tĭ-ēr-ite)	7	Complex aluminum borosilicate impregnating quartz	Blue, violet, pink
Emerald 2.6 to 2.9	8	Variety of beryl	Grass green
Enstatite 3.1 to 3.5 (ĕn'-stȧ-tite)	5+	Magnesium iron silicate; a pyroxene	Bronzite, the green variety, shows iridescent bronzy colors. Also often asteriated
Feldspar 2.5 to 2.8	6	Silicates of aluminum with potassium, barium, sodium, or calcium	Moonstone is shimmering white; amazonstone, green; labradorite, yellow or gray with play of colors; sunstone is red spangled
Flint 2.6	7	Earthy variety of chalcedony	Various pale colors, black

Diaphaneity and Luster	Fracture and Cleavage	Other Characteristics	Associated Rocks
Translucent to opaque; subvitreous luster	Fibrous fracture	Usually massive	In schists and gneiss
Transparent; vitreous luster	Conchoidal fracture; basal cleavage	Crystals are hexagonal	Limestone, in Colombia; schists and pegmatite
Transparent to opaque; vitreous luster	Hackly fracture	Usually massive. Hypersthene is iron-rich and closely related	Igneous rocks
Transparent to opaque; vitreous to pearly luster	Perfect cleavage	Orthoclase and microcline are potassium feldspars; albite is the sodium feldspar; anorthite is the calcium feldspar. Oligoclase and labradorite lie between albite and anorthite. These four are the plagioclase feldspars. They are usually striated on cleavages	Principal constituent (with quartz) of igneous rocks
Opaque	Conchoidal	Rarely of gem quality. Chert is much like flint, usually duller in hue	Nodules in limestone, and chalk

TABLE B (*Continued*)

Name and Specific Gravity	Hard-ness	Composition	Color or Pattern
Fluorite 3.0 to 3.2 (floo'-ō-rite)	4	Calcium fluoride	Green, blue, purple, red, brown, colorless
Garnet 3.4 to 4.3	6+ to 7½	Silicates of aluminum, with magnesium, manganese or iron, or of calcium with iron, aluminum or chromium	Pyrope is wine to blood red; almandine, violet red; spessartite is orange to brownish red; grossularite, green, reddish brown, or yellow; andradite, green, or black; rhodolite is red-purple, a mixture of pyrope and almandine
Hematite 4.9 to 5.2 (hĕm'-à-tite)	5+ to 6+	Iron oxide	Black or steel gray
Jade (nephrite) 2.9 to 3.0 (nĕf'-rīt)	6+	Silicate of calcium, magnesium and iron; an amphibole	White, green, brown, and black
Jade (jadeite) 3.3 to 3.4 (jād'-ite)	7−	Sodium aluminum silicate; a pyroxene	Green, gray white, less commonly blue, red, lavender
Jasper 2.6 to 2.9	7	Impure chalcedony	Varicolored; usually patterned. Prase is dark green; plasma light green

Diaphaneity and Luster	Fracture and Cleavage	Other Characteristics	Associated Rocks
Transparent; vitreous luster	Perfect cleavage	Cubic, less commonly octahedral, crystals	Usually in limestone
Transparent to opaque; vitreous to resinous luster	Conchoidal to uneven fracture	Pyrope almost never crystals; almandine is the "carbuncle," often asteriated; grossularite is known as essonite or cinnamon stone; when green, as Transvaal jade; crystals often dodecahedral	Pyrope in volcanic rocks; others in metamorphic rocks, and in gravel. Spessartite in pegmatite
Metallic luster	Hackly fracture; streak red	Massive, some from Minnesota is chatoyant	Iron deposits
Translucent to opaque; subvitreous luster	Splintery fracture	Compact and massive; very tough	With diorite and serpentine in metamorphic rocks
Translucent to opaque; subvitreous luster	Granular fracture	Compact and tough; best green is the "imperial" jade	In metamorphic rocks
Opaque; vitreous to dull luster	Conchoidal	Massive, with eye, moss, dot, or stripe patterns	Veins, nodules in igneous rocks

IMPORTANT GEM STONE MATERIALS

TABLE B (Continued)

Name and Specific Gravity	Hard-ness	Composition	Color or Pattern
Jet 1.1 to 1.4	2+	Carbon, a form of coal	Black
Kyanite 3.5 to 3.7 (kī'-à-nite)	4+ to 6+	Aluminum silicate	Spotty blue or green
Labradorite 2.7 (lăb'-rà-dôr-ite)	6	Plagioclase feldspar	Gray with blue, green and golden play of color. Transparent yellow variety has no play of color
Lapis lazuli 2.5 to 2.9 (lă'-pis lăz'-ū-lī)	5+	Mixture of lazurite with calcite, pyrite, etc.	Deep blue
Lepidolite 2.8 (lĕ-pĭd'-ō-lite)	7	Quartz containing a lithia mica	Lilac to rose red
Malachite 3.8 to 4.0 (măl'-à-kite)	3+	Hydrous copper carbonate	Light to dark green; often banded or orbicular
Marble 2.7	3−	Calcium carbonate	Usually light but many patterns and colors
Mariposite 2.8 (marĭ-pōs'-īte)	varies	Muscovite mica colored by chromium	Green mottling in quartz and schists
Moonstone 2.6	6	Orthoclase and albite feldspar in layers	Colorless with blue or milky "moon"

Diaphaneity and Luster	Fracture and Cleavage	Other Characteristics	Associated Rocks
Opaque; resinous luster	Conchoidal	Feels warmer than glass or plastic	Coal deposits
Transparent to translucent	Perfect cleavage	Bladed crystals harder in one direction than in other	Metamorphic rocks
Transparent to opaque	Perfect cleavage	Massive	Igneous rocks
Opaque; vitreous luster	Uneven fracture	Massive; the best is nearly free of white and contains specks of pyrite	Metamorphic limestone
Pearly luster; opaque	Uneven fracture	Massive	Pegmatite
Opaque; silky luster	Conchoidal to uneven fracture	Massive; often botryoidal, and mixed with azurite	Copper deposits
Opaque	Grainy fracture	Massive. Onyx, travertine are forms. Also often fossiliferous	Metamorphic rocks
Opaque	Irregular	Grass green flakes in rock	Metamorphic and igneous rocks
Transparent to translucent	Perfect cleavage	Best has strong schiller	Pegmatite

TABLE B (*Continued*)

Name and Specific Gravity	Hard-ness	Composition	Color or Pattern
Obsidian 2.3 to 2.4 (ŏb-sĭd′-ĭ-ăn)	5+	Volcanic glass	Black, green, brownish red, or gray
Onyx 2.6 (ŏn′-ĭks)	7	Variety of chalcedony	Varicolored in layers or bands; often dyed
Opal 1.9 to 2.3	6+	Hydrous silicon dioxide	Precious opal has colorless, gray or black body with varicolored fire
Pearl, and Pearl Shell 2.6 to 2.7	2+	Aragonite and organic matter	White, pink, blue, green, or black
Peridot 3.3 (pĕr′-ĭ-dŏt)	7	Magnesium iron silicate	Oily bottle green. Also known as olivine and chrysolite
Peristerite 2.6 (pĕ-rĭs′-tĕ-rīte)	6+	Albite feldspar	White or pale pink with blue flash
Perthite 2.5	6	Mixture of albite and other feldspars	Flesh red
Petrified wood (bone or coral) 2.6	7−	Variety of chalcedony or opal	Varicolored, often showing wood grain
Phenacite 2.9 (fĕn′-à-site)	7+	Beryllium silicate	Colorless or pale yellow or red

Diaphaneity and Luster	Fracture and Cleavage	Other Characteristics	Associated Rocks
Transparent to translucent; vitreous luster	Conchoidal	Massive; lacks crystal structure	Volcanic rocks
Translucent; vitreous luster	Conchoidal	Cryptocrystalline. Banded calcite is also known as onyx	Igneous rocks
Transparent to opaque; vitreous luster	Conchoidal	Amorphous, in veins, often as fossils. Cherry opal is red, usually without fire	In sandstone, lavas, or hot spring deposits
Translucent; pearly luster	Shell has splintery fracture	Abalone and pearl shell cut for jewelry	From pearl oyster. Also abalone, conch and freshwater mussels
Transparent; vitreous luster	Conchoidal	Crystals usually water-worn	Volcanic and metamorphic rocks
Opaque, pearly luster	Perfect cleavage		Igneous rocks
Opaque, pearly luster	Perfect cleavage	Has a golden labradoritelike flash	Igneous rocks
Opaque	Conchoidal to splintery	Often limbs or trunk masses	In volcanic ash or lava; coral in sedimentary rocks
Transparent; vitreous luster	Conchoidal	Crystals look like quartz	Pegmatite or metamorphic rocks

TABLE B (*Continued*)

Name and Specific Gravity	Hardness	Composition	Color or Pattern
Porphyry (por'-for-y)	varies	An igneous rock	Crystals of another mineral in rock mass
Prehnite 2.8 to 3.0 (pray'ñite)	6	Hydrous calcium aluminum silicate	Oily pale green or yellow
Pyrolusite 4.4 to 5.0 (pie-rōw-lú-sīte)	6+	Manganese dioxide	Black
Quartz 2.6	7	Silicon dioxide	Rock crystal is colorless; amethyst, purple; citrine, yellow; smoky quartz, brown; chrysocolla, blue; chrysoprase, green; rose quartz, pink
Rhodochrosite 3.4 to 3.7 (rō-dō-krō'-site)	4	Manganese carbonate	Pink to red
Rhodonite 3.5 to 3.7 (rō'-dō-nite)	6	Manganese silicate	Red, rose or pink, often veined in black
Rose quartz 2.6	7	Variety of quartz	Rosy pink, often asteriated
Ruby 3.9 to 4.0	9	Variety of corundum	Pink to red; often asteriated
Rhyolite (rye'-ō-līte)	7	Quartz and feldspar	Light color with swirls of red and brown

Diaphaneity and Luster	Fracture and Cleavage	Other Characteristics	Associated Rocks
Opaque	Irregular fracture	Variety of colors and crystal inclusions. Llanite is a form	Igneous rocks
Translucent; vitreous luster	Uneven fracture	Botryoidal masses	With zeolites in dark volcanic rocks
Metallic luster	Brittle	Psilomelane, a barium manganese oxide, is closely related	Manganese and iron deposits
Transparent; vitreous luster	Conchoidal	Crystals are 6-sided with pointed terminations	In cavities of many kinds of rocks
Translucent to opaque	Uneven, granular fracture	Usually massive	With manganese and base metal deposits
Transparent to opaque; resinous luster	Uneven fracture	Crystals or compact masses	Manganese ores
Translucent; vitreous luster	Conchoidal	Massive; deep color rare	Pegmatite
Transparent; subadamantine luster	Conchoidal	Crystals are plates or keg-shaped	Schists; limestone or igneous rocks
Opaque	Hackly	Massive, a fine-grained granite in composition	In lava flows

IMPORTANT GEM STONE MATERIALS

TABLE B (*Continued*)

Name and Specific Gravity	Hard-ness	Composition	Color or Pattern
Sagenitic quartz 2.6 (săj-é-nĭt-ĭk)	7	Quartz containing needles of rutile, tourmaline, actinolite, or hornblende	Colorless or smoky; often called rutilated quartz; Venus or Thetis hair stone
Sapphire 3.9 to 4.0	9	Variety of corundum	Colorless, blue, yellow, green, violet; also asteriated
Scapolite (wernerite) 2.6 to 2.7 (skăp'-ō-lite)	6	Complex silicate	Colorless, yellow, pink, and gray
Serpentine 2.5 to 2.6 (sûr'-pĕn-teen)	2½ to 4	Hydrous magnesium silicate	Green, white, yellow, often mottled or striped
Sillimanite 3.5	6+	Aluminum silicate	Blue, white, yellow
Smithsonite 4.3	5	Zinc carbonate	Blue, green, yellow, pink
Smoky quartz 2.6	7	Variety of quartz	Yellow, brown to black
Sodalite 2.2	6	Sodium aluminum silicate	Colorless to deep blue with white veins or orange cancrinite
Soapstone 2.7 to 2.8	1 to 2.5	Magnesium silicate	White or gray, with a greasy feeling

Diaphaneity and Luster	Fracture and Cleavage	Other Characteristics	Associated Rocks
Transparent; vitreous luster	Conchoidal	Crystals shot through with green, golden, red, or black needles	In cavities in many types of rocks
Transparent; subadamantine luster	Conchoidal	Crystals often particolored	Schists, limestone or igneous rocks
Transparent to opaque; vitreous to resinous luster	Conchoidal to hackly fracture	Sometimes cat's-eye	Pegmatite or metamorphic rocks
Translucent to opaque; greasy luster	Splintery fracture	Massive; variety names such as williamsite, ricolite, bowenite, verd antique	In magnesian rocks
Opaque; silky luster	Uneven to hackly fracture; tough	Fibrous, often chatoyant	As stream pebbles
Translucent; resinous luster	Uneven fracture	Compact masses, often botryoidal	Zinc deposits
Transparent; vitreous luster	Conchoidal	Sometimes known as cairngorm	Pegmatite, igneous rocks
Translucent to opaque; subvitreous luster	Uneven fracture	Massive	Igneous rocks
Opaque; pearly luster	Granular	Massive, for carving; also known as talc, steatite	Serpentines and metamorphic rocks

TABLE B (*Continued*)

Name and Specific Gravity	Hard-ness	Composition	Color or Pattern
Sphalerite 3.9 (sfal'-ĕ-rīte)	3½	Zinc sulphide	Yellow, red, or black
Sphene 3.5 (sfēēn)	5+	Titanium calcium silicate	Yellow, brown, green, black
Spodumene 3.2 (spŏd'-ū-meen)	7−	Lithium aluminum silicate	Yellow; kunzite pink; hiddenite, green
Staurolite 3.6 to 3.8 (stôw'-rō-lite)	7+	Iron aluminum silicate	Reddish brown
Sunstone 2.6	6	Oligoclase feldspar	Reddish, spangled with inclusions
Syenite (sigh-ĕ-nīte)	varies	A granite lacking visible quartz	Usually light
Thomsonite 2.3 to 2.4	5+	Hydrous sodium calcium aluminum silicate	Orbicular patterns in red, green, black
Topaz 3.5	8	Aluminum fluosilicate	Colorless, wine-yellow, golden, blue, or red

Diaphaneity and Luster	Fracture and Cleavage	Other Characteristics	Associated Rocks
Adamantine, rarely transparent	Perfect cleavage	Major ore of zinc	With zinc deposits
Resinous to subadamantine luster	Brittle	Also known as titanite	Gneiss and granite
Transparent; vitreous luster	Perfect cleavage	Some massive spodumene is cat's-eye	Pegmatite
Opaque; dull luster, rarely transparent	Distinct cleavage	Crystals twinned in cross form known as fairy stones	Schists
Opaque	Perfect cleavage	Massive; imitated with glass "goldstone"	Igneous rocks
Opaque	Uneven fracture	Nepheline syenite is found with gem minerals	Igneous rocks
Opaque; luster, porcelaneous	Splintery fracture; brittle	Lintonite is a clear, olive green form	Basalt in Lake Superior district; elsewhere, as crystals with zeolites
Transparent; vitreous luster	Perfect basal cleavage	Prisms with many-faced terminations	Pegmatite and rhyolite

TABLE B (*Continued*)

Name and Specific Gravity	Hard- ness	Composition	Color or Pattern
Tourmaline 3.0 to 3.2 (tōor'-mȧ-lĭn)	7+	Complex sodium, aluminum borosilicate	Rubellite is red; indicolite blue; achroite colorless; usual color of gem material is deep green
Turquoise 2.6 to 2.8	6−	Hydrous copper aluminum phosphate	Sky blue to green
Unakite 2.9 to 3.2 (ū'-na-kite)	6+	Mixture of quartz, feldspar, and epidote in granite	Mottled pink and green in quartz
Variscite 2.5 (văr'ĭs-cite)	5	Hydrous aluminum phosphate	Dark to pale green
Vesuvianite 3.4 (vĕ-su'-vĭ-ăn-īte)	6+	Complex calcium aluminum silicate	Yellow, green, brown, or blue
Zircon 4.0 to 4.7	7+	Zirconium silicate	Colorless; red-brown, orange, blue, green
Zoisite 3.3 (zois'-ite)	6	Hydrous calcium aluminum silicate	Thulite is pink. Tanzanite is blue heat-treated zoisite

Diaphaneity and Luster	Fracture and Cleavage	Other Characteristics	Associated Rocks
Transparent; vitreous luster	Subconchoidal to uneven cleavage across prism	Crystals long, with rounded, triangular cross-section, often parti-colored, along length or breadth of crystal, as a pink center with green edges	Pegmatite and metamorphic rocks
Opaque; waxy luster	Conchoidal	Nodules in claystone or veins in rock	Usually in desert regions
Opaque	Hackly fracture	Massive	Mostly in eastern U.S.
Opaque; subvitreous luster	Conchoidal	Nodules and masses often patterned with other phosphates	Shales and slates, mostly in Utah
Transparent to opaque; vitreous to greasy luster	Splintery fracture	Massive form known as California jade; blue known as cyprine	Metamorphic rocks
Transparent; adamantine luster	Conchoidal	Crystals; blue and colorless by heat treatment	Granites and gravel
Transparent to opaque; vitreous to greasy luster	Uneven fracture; one perfect cleavage	Crystals to massive	Metamorphic rocks

IMPORTANT GEM STONE MATERIALS

The history of man's interest in gems can be traced through the names he has given to them. Some of these, such as quartz, zircon, beryl, corundum, and tourmaline are of doubtful or unknown origin. But the ending *ite* comes down from Greek classical times, in such a mineral as hematite, which derives its stem from the word for blood. Agate gets its name from the Achates river in Sicily, and amethyst from the Greek words meaning "not drunken" because of the belief that it could prevent intoxication. Jade has a similar origin in allusion to its supposed efficacy for kidney disease.

The name for amazonstone is derived from the place where it was first found; aragonite from Aragon, Spain; vesuvianite from Mt. Vesuvius; labradorite from Labrador, and turquoise from Turkey, the first market for the gem. Likewise, benitoite comes from San Benito county, California. Many gem materials are named for people—alexandrite for Czar Alexander II, uvarovite garnet for Count Uvarov of Russia, prehnite for Dutch Colonel von Prehn. smithsonite from the donor of the Smithsonian Institution, thomsonite for a Canadian mineralogist, kunzite for George F. Kunz, and morganite for J. P. Morgan.

Chrysocolla's use in metallurgy is alluded to in its name, which in Greek means "gold glue," and pyrolusite's name derives from words meaning "fire" and "wash" because it decolors melted glass. Rhodonite and rhodochrosite both carry the Greek word for "rose" in their names, as does the garnet variety called rhodolite. The name of grossular garnet derives from the Latin for gooseberry; that of sagenite goes back to the Latin for "net," alluding to its inclusions of the mineral, rutile; lapis lazuli is Latin for "blue stone," and that of fluorite is derived from the Latin *fluere*—to flow. Aquamarine gets its name from the Latin word for "seawater," alluding to its color.

Chiastolite and staurolite, both names of gems, are related words in Greek, one meaning "marked with an X" and one meaning "marked with a cross."

6.
black light
for
your
minerals

Drab rocks can be awakened to glow with incomparable colors by a magic lamp that thousands of hobbyists are using today. The lamp radiates invisible ultraviolet light and the phenomenon this light produces is known as fluorescence.

To understand fluorescence, you need to understand something about light. Light rays visible to the human eye are only part of a great electromagnetic spectrum (see page 65), a vast pattern of radiant energy vibrations ranging from very short cosmic rays to long, alternating current rays. Visible light consists of the colors seen in the rainbow. Ultraviolet light lies just outside this visible light band and is commonly called black light.

To identify wavelengths in the various bands of light, the Angstrom unit is used. The ultraviolet band is divided into three parts—far ultraviolet from 2,000 to 2,800 *au* (Angstrom units), middle ultraviolet from 2,800 to 3,200 *au,* and near ultraviolet from 3,200 to 4,000 *au.* Above this band is visible violet. The lense of the human eye recognizes only wavelengths between 4,000 *au* and 8,000 *au,* which is why true black light is invisible.

Far ultraviolet radiation is exceedingly active. In addition to causing many materials to fluoresce, it will kill airborne bacteria. In its mineralogical and scientific applications it is known as shortwave UV. Middle UV radiation produces vitamin D by its effect on the skin as well as burning skin badly with overexposure. Near UV is the wavelength group used to produce theatrical and advertising effects as well as fluorescence in some substances not affected or only slightly affected by the shorter wavelengths. It is commonly called long UV.

What happens when ultraviolet radiation penetrates a mineral and makes it fluoresce is not entirely clear even though many practical applications have been made of the phenomenon. According to the most generally accepted theory, the radiation's energy disarranges the electronic structure of the atoms. As the atoms re-arrange themselves they return the energy imparted by the ultraviolet light, but in the form of visible light.

Another theory maintains that the vibrations of the electrons in the ultraviolet radiation produce a resonance seen as light when they strike an electronic structure in a mineral that they are attuned to. This is like the phenomenon in music where a note produces harmonics.

More important for the amateur interested in his fluorescent minerals, however, is the fact that fluorescence does happen with some minerals and not with others. He soon recognizes that the color of a mineral in ultraviolet light has no relation to its color in ordinary light. He will also find that in some specimens the fluorescing effect lingers on after the source of ultraviolet light has been removed. Such minerals are described as phosphorescent.

Many minerals need to contain a trace of some other compound, commonly a metallic salt, before they will fluoresce. This foreign compound is called an activator and the host material the base. For instance, the activator may be a manganese salt and the base zinc orthosilicate, as in the mineral willemite. Freedom of the base from other substances, the heat at which base and activator were fused together, and harmony between the crystal structure of the two materials are some conditions that determine how fluorescent a substance is. This is true, also, of artificial minerals and compounds prepared for fluorescent lamp coatings. The activator must be present in just the right amount. Calcite from Franklin, New Jersey, fluoresces a fiery red from specimens containing 3 to 9 percent manganese. If less than that amount is present, the calcite will not fluoresce. As the amount of manganese in excess of 9 percent increases, the fluorescence of the specimen decreases until at 17 percent it is extinguished. Some other elements, notably iron compounds, are fluorescent poisons; they depress or destroy the ability of a specimen to react. A few minerals seem to have an inborn reactivity; scheelite and hydrozincite are among them and so are certain uranium minerals. Most metallic minerals do not respond.

In general, though, only certain specimens from certain localities where conditions are favorable can be counted on to be fluorescent. Furthermore, mineral substances can be choosy about the wavelength of the light to which they are expected to respond. One may make its best display under shortwave UV, another only under long-wave UV. A few respond in different ways to the two light sources, such as the calcite from Miles, Texas, which

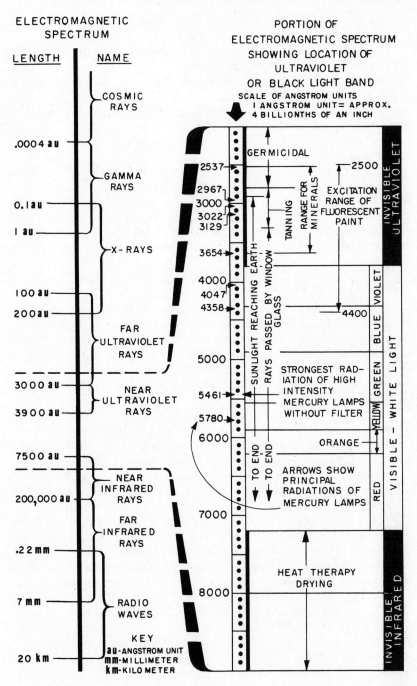

ELECTROMAGNETIC
SPECTRUM

LENGTH   NAME

COSMIC RAYS

.0004 au

GAMMA RAYS

0.1 au

1 au

X-RAYS

100 au

200 au

FAR ULTRAVIOLET RAYS

3000 au

NEAR ULTRAVIOLET RAYS

3900 au

7500 au

NEAR INFRARED RAYS

200,000 au

FAR INFRARED RAYS

.22 mm

7 mm

RADIO WAVES

20 km

KEY
au - ANGSTROM UNIT
mm - MILLIMETER
km - KILOMETER

PORTION OF
ELECTROMAGNETIC SPECTRUM
SHOWING LOCATION OF
ULTRAVIOLET
OR BLACK LIGHT BAND
SCALE OF ANGSTROM UNITS
1 ANGSTROM UNIT = APPROX.
4 BILLIONTHS OF AN INCH

GERMICIDAL

2537   2500

2967   EXCITATION
3000   TANNING   RANGE OF
3022   FLUORESCENT
3129   PAINT

3654

4000
4047
4358   4400   VIOLET

5000

STRONGEST RAD-
IATION OF HIGH
5461   INTENSITY
       MERCURY LAMPS
5780   WITHOUT FILTER

6000   ORANGE

ARROWS SHOW
PRINCIPAL
RADIATIONS OF
7000   MERCURY LAMPS

HEAT THERAPY
DRYING

8000

RANGE FOR MINERALS

SUNLIGHT REACHING EARTH

RAYS PASSED BY WINDOW GLASS

TO END   TO END

INVISIBLE ULTRAVIOLET

BLUE   GREEN   YELLOW   RED

VISIBLE — WHITE LIGHT

INVISIBLE INFRARED

fluoresces pink at 3,650 *au* and a blue fluorescence and phosphorescence at 2,537 *au*.

Calcite is the most versatile performer under the ultraviolet lamp. Seven distinct colors are on record from as many as twenty-five different localities, as well as the ones, like that from Texas, which give a double play. Franklin, New Jersey, calcite with its fiery red glow is perhaps the most spectacular, but nearby Weehawken, New Jersey, calcite from the Palisades, and that from Newry, Maine, and Cornwall, Pennsylvania, are not far behind it among Eastern sources.

Calcite from Terlingua, Texas, may be blue, pink, or even green in its response. Sage Creek, South Dakota, appropriately provides a green one.

Heat will bring out a latent fluorescence in some calcites, such as those from Bernardsville and North Plainfield, New Jersey. In one huge region, the Gaspé peninsula of Quebec, nearly all the calcite exposures are fluorescent.

The most popular and versatile apparatus to generate ultraviolet light is a hand-held lamp not much larger than a hairbrush. Inside the black plastic housing is a small tube of high-silica glass or fused quartz. It is filled with argon gas and contains a small amount of mercury. At each end is an electrode. When current is turned on, it ionizes the argon and the discharge across the tube vaporizes the mercury. The mercury then radiates light especially strong in the ultraviolet bands. A filter of special glass screens out most of the visible light.

By controlling pressure within the tube and by using different types of tube material, the wavelength of the radiation can be adapted to varying uses. With low pressure the principal radiation is at 2,537 *au*—shortwave; medium pressure gives the longer wavelengths for "black light bulbs," and high pressure is used in lamps producing visible light. Lamps are made to produce both short- and long-wave *au*.

These compact lamps, supplied with a portable power source, are popular for hunting fluorescent minerals at night, when the response is most evident and when the eye is most sensitive to color. With such a lamp, a strongly fluorescent specimen can be seen as far as twenty feet away.

Less expensive generators of ultraviolet light, such as the 2½-watt argon bulb and the 250-watt Purple X bulb, have been used, but the response to their light is weak.

Many of the lamps used for mineral displays provide long-wave UV radiations in the region of 3,200 to 4,000 *au*, with peak intensity at 3,650 *au*. Fluorescent paints, dyes, and fabrics sensitive to this long-wave radiation are used by theatrical and display designers; many minerals will also respond well to long-wave. But the most spectacular minerals, such as the Franklin calcites, react best to shortwave mercury vapor and quartz lamps radiating light at the 2,537 *au* band.

Some minerals will appear to be fluorescing when they are really only reflecting the visible light from the ultraviolet source, usually purple in color. If a sheet of glass inserted between the radiation source and the mineral fails to cut out the apparent response, the mineral is not fluorescent.

The most famous source of fluorescent minerals is Franklin, New Jersey. From its zinc mines came calcite which fluoresces a fiery red, willemite (zinc orthosilicate) which displays a brilliant green, and esperite (formerly called calcium larsenite) a calcium-lead-zinc-silicate, which has a yellow fluorescence. A similar calcite comes from Langban, Sweden. Collecting at Franklin is now confined to the Buckwheat and Trotter dumps. Wyoming contributes the Sweetwater moss agates, Specimen Hill chalcedony, and Eden Valley petrified wood, which owe their reactivity to traces of uranium minerals. Clay Center, Ohio, fluorite owes its response to oily hydrocarbon inclusions. A few diamonds fluoresce blue, and some of the rarer ones fluoresce green, orange, yellow, or red. Table C lists fluorescent minerals, their color response, and localities where they have been obtained.

Fluorescence is widely employed in many commercial forms such as detecting counterfeit money or postage stamps, exposing alterations in oil paintings and forged documents, and revealing flaws in castings which have been soaked in an oil carrying a fluorecent dye. In fact, fluorescence follows mankind from the cradle, when the baby may be stamped with fluorescent ink in the hospital for identification, to the grave, when a fluorescent embalming fluid may be used.

The hobbyist is not restricted to minerals. He can experiment with fluorescent woods, such as sumac, black locust, and Oregon graperoot; petroleum jelly (blue-green), several kinds of plastics, cheap glassware (yellow-green), false teeth (yellow-white), quinine in acid solution (bright blue), fresh eggs (scarlet), or stale eggs (purple), a number of dyes, waxes, and leathers. UV light makes real teeth and fingernails fluoresce white and shows up freckles. Gardenias or other cut flowers, placed with their stems in water containing the dye fluorescein, will take up the dye in their petals, which will then fluoresce a brilliant green. Rhodamine and eosin dyes can also be used.

Fluorescing minerals can be photographed in color. Exposure

varies so greatly that most photographers use a trial-and-error test sequence to arrive at the proper aperture and time. Photographs taken for one magazine article were made at *f*. 22 on Ektachrome color film Type A with a Wrattan 2A filter, and the exposure time varied from twelve minutes for a brilliant piece of hydrozincite to twenty times that long for a chalcedony geode.

TABLE C. FLUORESCENT MINERALS: Their color and wavelength of response, and where they are found

---

Adamite: Mapimi, Durango, Mexico—green (shortwave)

Agate: Sweetwater Valley, Wyo.—yellow-green—all wavelengths; Goldfield, Nev.—yellow-green; Prescott, Ariz.—cream; San Diego, Calif.—yellow-green

Alunite: Marysville, Utah—light blue (longwave)

Amber: Baltic Sea—greenish yellow; Maryland—green (longwave); Texas—yellow; Washington—yellow

Amethyst: North Carolina—deep blue

Andalusite: Oreville, S.D.—pinkish (longwave)

Andersonite: Hillside Mine, Ariz.

Anglesite: Phoenixville, Pa.—yellow (longwave); Black Hills—yellow

Apatite: Brinton's Quarry, Delaware Co., Pa.—orange; Hull, Que. —yellow; Ontario—dark green

Apophyllite: Paterson, N.J.—yellow

Aragonite: Bisbee, Ariz.; Crestmore, Calif.—yellow; Death Valley, Calif.—light green; La Junta, Colo.—cream-white; Livingston, N.M.—red; Platte Mound, Wis.; Chuckawalla Mts., Calif.— white; Vernonia, Ore.—cream; Franklin, N.J.—cream

Autunite: Chesterfield, Mass.; Rumford, Me.; Alexander Co., N.C.; Grafton, N.H.; Branchville, Conn.; Black Hills; Daybreak mine, Spokane, Wash.—all yellow-green (all wavelengths)

Axinite: Franklin, N.J.—red

Barite: Franklin, N.J.—cream or blue; Palos Verdes, Calif.—yellow (also phosphorescent); Elk Creek, S.D.—brown

Barylite: Franklin, N.J., blue (shortwave)

Benitoite: San Benito Co., Calif.—blue (all wavelengths)

Beryl: Elba, N.Y.—bluish white; Gillette Quarry, Haddam Neck, Conn. (morganite)—orange

Bone: Mastodon tusk, Kansas—yellow

Brucite: Wood's Chrome mine, Texas; Pa.—blue-white

Bustamite: Franklin, N.J.—orange

Calcite: Franklin, N.J.—red—2,925 to 3,128 *au;* Bagdad, Ariz.— deep blue; Deming, N.M.—blue (shortwave), orange (long-

wave); Casa Grande, Ariz.—blue; Bisbee and Nogales, Ariz.—
red; Granby, Mo.—light green; Keller, Wash.—pink; Picher,
Okla.—deep green; Terlingua, Tex.—pink at 3,650 au, blue
by shortwave; Texas calcite containing petroleum—yellow to
orange; Barrego Valley, Calif.—rose; Brewster, Tex.—blue;
Hollywood Hills, Calif.—red; Miles, Tex.; Paicines, Calif.—
white; Randsburg, Calif.—orange; Eagle Ford, Tex.—cream
and purple; Lovington, N.M.—green; Deming, N.M.—
yellow, green; Hope, Ind.—phosphorescent; Charcas, San
Luis Potosi, Mexico; Rosiclare, Ill.—cream

Calomel (mercury chloride): Terlingua, Tex.—orange to pink
(long-wave)

Cerussite: Good Springs, Nev.—blue (shortwave); Salt Lake City—
orange (long-wave)

Chalcedony: Aguila, Ariz.; Barstow, Calif.; Wasco County, Ore.—
yellow-green (all wavelengths)

Chlorapatite: California—orange

Clinohedrite: Franklin, N.J.—orange by shortwave, pink by long-
wave

Colemanite: Death Valley, Calif.—white

Coquina (shell): Florida—white

Coral: Petoskey stone, Little Traverse Bay, Mich.—mustard yellow;
Tampa Bay, Fla., cream

Corundum: Franklin, N.J.—red (long-wave); Franklin, N.C., area

Crocoite: Tasmania and Ural Mts., Russia—brown

Cuproscheelite: Milford, Ore.; Plumas County, Calif.—yellow
(shortwave)

Curtisite: Scaggs Springs, Calif.—yellow-green

Diamond: Arkansas, South Africa, Brazil—most commonly blue, but
other colors are known

Diaspore: Chester, Mass.—pale yellow

Diopside: Franklin, N.J.—blue

Dolomite: Palos Verdes, Calif.—yellow; Bloomington, Ind.—
gray-green

Dumortierite: San Diego County, Calif.—gray

Epsomite: Death Valley, Calif.—pale blue

Esperite: Franklin, N.J.—yellow (shortwave)

Eucryptite: Center Strafford, N.H.—red, pink

Feldspar: Amelia, Va.—amazonite, gray-green; Franklin, N.J.—
anorthite, blue; Gillette Quarry, Haddam Neck, Conn.—albite, orange; Broken Hill, Australia—amazonite

Fluorite: Castle Dome, Ariz.—blue—3,650 $au;$ Clay Center, O.—
cream; Keller, Wash.—blue; Duncan, Ariz.—green; Durham,
England—blue; Cave-in-Rock, Ill.—white and purple; Frank-

TABLE C. FLUORESCENT MINERALS: Their color and wavelength of response, and where they are found (*Continued*)

lin, N.J.—chlorophane—green; Westmoreland, N.H.—violet; Trumbull, Conn.—phosphorescent, green

Fluorapatite: Center Strafford, N.H.—orange

Forsterite: Monterey, Calif.—blue-white

Gay-lussite: Washington—pink

Glauberite: Borax Lake, Calif.—blue

Gypsum: Grand Rapids, Mich.—green (long-wave)

Hackmanite: Bancroft, Ont.—orange, yellow, or pink (long-wave) (Shortwave radiation changes color of rock temporarily from gray to purple, which fades in daylight.)

Halite (salt): Amboy, Calif.—red; Kansas—green

Hanksite: Searle Lake, Calif.—pale blue, green (phosphorescent).

Hardystonite: Franklin, N.J.—violet (shortwave)

Hemimorphite: Good Springs, Nev.—green; Adelanto, Calif.— green (both shortwave); Superior, Ariz.—cream

Hexagonite: Edwards, N.Y.—red

Hiddenite (spodumene): North Carolina—weak red or lilac

Howlite: Lang, Calif.—orange (long-wave)

Hydrozincite: Good Springs, Nev.; Utah; Keeler, Calif.—blue by shortwave, yellow by long-wave; Dragoon, Ariz.—blue; Franklin, N.J.—blue-white

Inyoite: Death Valley, Calif.—white

Kunzite (spodumene): Pala, Calif.—reddish yellow

Kyanite: Tyrol—greenish white

Leadhillite: Arizona—yellow (shortwave)

Lepidolite: Keystone, S.D.—pale green

Manganapatite: Portland, Conn.; Center Strafford, N.H.; St. Mary's Lake, B.C.; Valyermo, Calif.—bright orange; Franklin, N.J. —orange

Margarosanite: Franklin, N.J.—violet

Meyerhofferite: Death Valley, Calif.—yellowish

Mooreite: Sterling Hill, N.J.—red (shortwave)

Norbergite: Franklin, N.J.—pale yellow

Opal: Bagdad, Ariz.; Barstow, Calif.; Beaver, Utah; Bishop, Calif.; Connell, Wash.; Fulton, Nev.; Lind, Wash.; Salmon, Idaho; Stone Mountain, Ga.; Coso Hot Springs, Calif.; 29 Palms, Calif.—all green; San Luis Potosí, Mex.—hyalite opal—green (all waves); Alpine, Tex.; Big Fork, Mont.; Lovington, N.M.; Virgin Valley, Nev.—common opal—green; Eden Valley, Wyo.; Goldfield, Nev.; Huntsville, Tex.—opalized wood— green; Spruce Pine, N.C. (hyalite opal)—brilliant white

Ozokerite: Utah, Brazil—yellow-brown

Pectolite: Paterson, N.J.—yellow; Franklin, N.J.—yellow

Powellite: Beaver, Utah; Bishop, Calif.; Lordsburg, N.M.; Randsburg, Calif.—yellow; Nogales, Ariz.—white; Franklin, N.J., yellow

Priceite: Death Valley, Calif.—yellow

Quartz: Red Desert, Wyo.—blue-white

Ruby: Siam—weak red; Burma and North Carolina—strong red; Ceylon—yellow (see Synthetics)

Sapphire: Ceylon—yellow or orange; Montana—blue or lavender

Scheelite: Inyo, Kern, and San Bernardino Counties, Calif.; Mill City, Nev.; Lucin, Utah—blue (shortwave)

Schroeckingerite (dakeite): Wamsutter, Wyo.—yellow green (all waves)

Selenite: Hay Springs, Neb.—pale yellow; Lovington, N.M.—yellow

Septaria: Utah—orange

Sodalite: Hastings Co., Ont.—white; Moultonboro, N.H.—orange red

Sphalerite: Iturbidie district, Mexico; Tsumeb, Southwest Africa—orange; Trona, Searles Lake, Calif.—blue; Arizona—orange; Franklin, N.J.—pale orange, pink, or blue (shortwave)

Sussexite: Franklin, N.J.—pink to red

Svabite: Franklin, N.J.—orange

Synthetics: Ruby—strong red at 3,000 *au;* sapphire—orange to red, strongest in white variety; spinel—red

Tarbuttite: Rhodesia—orange

Thaumasite: Paterson, N.J.—white (shortwave)

Thenardite: Newport Bay, Calif.—pale yellow

Thomsonite: Franklin, N.J.—pale blue (long-wave)

Torbernite (and metatorbernite): yellow-green (all waves)

Tourmaline (red variety): Pala, Calif.; Newry, Me.—lavender (long-wave)

Tremolite: Jefferson Co., N.Y.—orange-pink; St. Lawrence Co., N.Y.—red; Franklin, N.J.—green

Uranophane: Grafton, N.H.—green

Variscite: Fairfield, Utah—pale green

Wavellite: Mt. Holly, Pa.—blue

Wernerite (scapolite): Eganville, Ont.—yellow; Sparta Junction, N.J.—yellow

Willemite: Casa Grande, Ariz., Franklin, N.J.—green

Witherite: Cave-in-Rock, Ill.—white

Wollastonite: New Jersey—orange spots; Riverside, Calif.—golden

Wurtzite: Utah—golden

Zircon: Placer Co., Calif.; Henderson Co., N.C.; Oregon; Idaho; Montana; Wyoming; Ontario in placer sands—orange

Many natural petroleum derivatives—pitch, bitumen, asphalt, as well as oil—fluoresce; so do some coals.

7.
judging
quality
and
value

Not many hobbyists get rich from their field trips, or even cover expenses. Few expect to. But this does not prevent them from having a lively interest in the cash value of gem minerals. Partly it's plain curiosity, but only partly, for gem hunters trade with other amateurs, and occasionally sell their surplus to dealers. Some skill at judging quality is essential if rough materials are to be finished for display or made into jewelry.

Experience alone will develop the ability to evaluate gems in the rough. You have to practice, first estimating quality and then checking your judgment by cutting the rough into gem stones. You soon learn to watch for defects peculiar to certain types of stone and to judge specimens in the light of their fitness for lapidary purposes.

Values of Quartz Minerals

Nine-tenths of the stones that the amateur works with belong to the quartz family, of which agate is the most versatile and popular member. Agate sells in the rough for one to four dollars a pound, although especially beautiful pieces, such as Oregon flower agate, sell far above that level.

Lake Superior and Montana moss agates are unsurpassed, but they are prone to cracks and flaws which mar their fine patterns. Mexican and Oregon agate nodules have not suffered buffeting of streams and the action of frost, but many are hollow and others show dull coloring or patterns. Only sawing can determine their worth, so agate nodules are a gamble—but a fascinating one. As in any patterned material, there is much waste in agate when it is cut. All these elements must be considered in your evaluation.

Much more costly are chrysoprase, chrysocolla, and cabochon-quality amethyst, smoky quartz, and citrine. They bring from forty cents to one dollar an ounce. High grade Australian chrysoprase retails at two to four dollars an ounce. Good color is the most important quality, but the rough should be translucent and free from major blemishes and cracks. Judging color in the large piece of rough can be deceptive. Rose quartz, especially, may have vigorous color in the chunk but retain only a ghost of its beauty when cut.

Other valuable materials are bloodstone that is well marked with small, bright red spots, and carnelian of a rich, red-brown hue. Good material which is sound and fracture-free may bring as much as six dollars a pound.

Most jaspers are the poor relations of the quartz family, although a few stand out for unique pattern or color. They sell in the rough for less than one dollar a pound. They and their relatives, the petrified woods, frequently have so porous a texture that they are valueless for cutting. A homespun test can be used to check for porosity. Just wet a sawed or chipped surface. Any porous spots quickly become dull as the moisture soaks in. Solid material remains shiny.

Pale, dull-patterned, or very dark gem materials rarely possess value unless some unusual quality, such as the black and white contrast of snowflake obsidian, redeems their drabness. Obsidian varies greatly in texture; some has a pitchy texture which refuses to take a satisfactory finish. Too much pattern is as bad as too little; some Texas plume, for example is more like a pile of feathers than a gorgeous array of red or black plumes.

Rutilated quartz, aventurine, and rose quartz of average quality retail for about four dollars a pound. Especially desirable pieces, such as rose quartz of deep color and translucence that fit it for faceting, may be much higher. Coarse rutile inclusions in quartz may create cavities which retain polishing compounds and disfigure the finished stone.

Feldspar

The feldspar family has one weakness—easy cleavage. Deposits that have been blasted or exposed to weathering are likely to be shattered. Often a handsome, large specimen will yield only a few sound pieces. Amazonite, labradorite, and sunstone, the major gem varieties, retail for as much as six dollars a pound. Moonstone is obtainable only in small pieces and will bring much higher prices.

Jade

Nephrite jade of top quality should have a rich, translucent green color and should be fairly free from black inclusions. Most American nephrite is too dark, too gray and pale, or peppered with too many inclusions to be attractive. Top-quality Wyoming jade is expensive, but some satisfactory material has been coming from the Fraser River in Canada, from Alaska, and occasionally from California. It may be had for as little as five dollars a pound or three dollars a square inch.

Much Alaskan jade has a pronounced grain which causes it to chip in grinding, and some will not take a good polish. Only the test of the grinding wheels will evaluate it properly. Monterey jade from California is often disfigured by schistose spots. Black jade from Wyoming, however, is free from almost all defects and is easy to cut and polish.

Garnets are almost always small and brittle, often with cracks and disfiguring inclusions. Almandine and pyrope—the red gem varieties—may be too dark. Those that do not show rich, bright color when examined under—not against—a shaded light are too dense to make a gem.

The most attractive rhodonite is deep pink veined with black. It sells for three to seven dollars a pound. Unakite and sodalite of good color and pattern are in the same range.

Banded or orbicular malachite, now mostly obtained from Africa, is among the more expensive materials. It sells for fifteen to fifty dollars a pound, and is so heavy that a pound does not bulk large. South American lapis lazuli brings half as much, but top-grade American and Afghanistan lapis—deep blue, solid, and spangled with pyrite—sells for six to twelve dollars an ounce. Top-grade turquoise, too, is costly at ten dollars and more an ounce, while Persian turquoise retails at two dollars a carat. Much porous and off-color turquoise is waxed, oiled, or treated with plastic to "improve" it. Such sophisticated material is suitable for cutting into finished gems and ornaments if it is honestly priced.

Opal is the aristocrat of the cabochons, and it is priced as high as several hundred dollars an ounce, although Australia continues to produce a lot of surprisingly good stones for from ten to fifty an ounce. Most Australian white opal is seam material which shows its best fire on the side; a thick piece that can be sawed parallel to the side will yield the flashiest stones and is worth more. Pieces cut so that the top or bottom of the seam material is used for the top of the finished stone show less intense fire. This is not true of Mexican or American opal, which is of the nodular variety.

Virgin Valley opal, for all its rare black beauty, has a bad reputation for crazing after it is cut.

The comparative value of cutting rough and a square inch of slab can be calculated as follows: A pound of rough should yield about 30 square inches of slabs. It costs five cents a square inch to saw such material as agate, and the loss of weight in sawing is about one-fourth, so the formula is 1¼ times the cost per pound plus $1.50 per pound equals the cost per square inch when divided by 30.

To compare whether slabs or rough is the better buy, measure the sawing width of the rough in inches, multiply by 4 to get number of slabs, estimate the gross number of square inches, and take half this number as the net yield, then compare the cost of a square inch of the rough with the quoted price for already slabbed material.

Stones for Faceting

Material of faceting quality, suitable for cutting into jewelry stones, is much more expensive than cabochon rough. Close evaluation of the yield in finished gems becomes essential. Flaws that would be ignored in cabochon rough become glaring in a faceted stone and make the rough undesirable at any price (except for a gem such as emerald, which is rarely found free of defects). You can detect inclusions, cracks, and incipient cleavages by studying the stone under the edge of a lampshade, holding the piece so that it is illuminated but does not reflect light into your eyes. Defects will show up as the stone is slowly turned.

Relative freedom from flaws is only one of the criteria for judging value in a facet-quality piece of rough. Color is equally important, often more so, as in emerald. Pale amethyst or citrine, for example, may be worth ten cents a gram, even though flawless, while material of rich, deep color and transparency would bring three dollars a gram.

Other factors enter into values, of course. One is scarcity; a ruby or emerald of any size is rare and hence precious. Likewise, a cat's-eye chrysoberyl or a star sapphire or even a bicolor tourmaline will far exceed in cost an unfigured stone of equal quality. Fashion also plays its part. Right now colored stones are in great demand. This demand, coupled with the nationalistic feeling that prompts producing nations to retain their precious rough and cut it themselves, as well as political situations that have closed off the supply from several regions, has driven up the price of good colored gem rough. Diamonds, too, have risen, representing as they do an assured value in times of inflation and social unrest.

For economy, the shape of the rough piece should be close to that desired in the cut gem. Long, thin, irregularly shaped pieces are extravagant purchases when judged by what can be made from them. It is more economical to buy several small pieces of rough to cut several small stones, as for a bracelet, than to buy and saw up one large piece.

Color zones, characteristic of sapphire and amethyst, are a serious defect unless the rough can be manipulated to place a spot of color at the bottom of the gem, where it will suffuse the stone.

A sense of values depends in part on recognition of the comparative size of the units in which faceting rough is quoted. There are 28.35 grams to the avoirdupois ounce, and 5 carats to the metric gram. The table below will give essential comparisons that can be extended easily into the higher values:

TABLE D

CARAT VALUE	GRAM VALUE	OUNCE VALUE
1 cent	5 cents	$1.42
2 cents	10 cents	$2.83
3 cents	15 cents	$4.25
4 cents	20 cents	$5.67
5 cents	25 cents	$7.09
10 cents	50 cents	$14.17

Artificial Coloring

Much has been done in recent years to alter the color of gem materials by heat treatment and atomic bombardment. Aquamarine is customarily heated to drive off any tint of yellow and improve its blueness. Some amethyst made green by the same treatment came on the market a few years ago, and most citrine is derived from amethyst and smoky quartz by careful heating. Carnelian's color deepens when the rough is baked, and both the blue and white zircons of commerce are the result of careful heating of brown stones from southeast Asia.

Atomic bombardment of yellow diamonds changes them to green, brown, or even light blue, while kunzite's lilac becomes an impermanent blue-green and some colorless topaz comes out of the atomic pile a rich yellow. Atomic treatment is also said to intensify the color of many sapphires.

As no gem hunter can hope to visit all the collecting areas in person, he can diversify his materials by exchanging with other collectors or by buying from dealers. Names of the latter can be obtained from the American Gem and Mineral Suppliers Association, P.O. Box 274, Costa Mesa, California, or from the advertisements in magazines listed on page 323.

Mineral conventions, such as those held annually by the American Federation of Mineralogical and Geological Societies and by its six regional federations and those held by individual clubs, offer almost unlimited opportunity to meet other collectors from all parts of North America, to patronize dealers who have display booths at the conventions, and to learn about new gem materials, new products, and new methods.

Swapping by mail or at what are called swap shows is one inviting way for the gem hunter to diversify and enrich his collection by exchanging material he has collected for material from a fellow collector. A swap in that way can be as productive as several field trips as well as less expensive and time-consuming. It is often the only available way to get gem material from a privately owned area to which he does not have access.

Swapping is a way to meet and share experiences as well as specimens with other lapidary and mineral enthusiasts. A diligent swapper can within a few years build up a roster of friends from Maine to Mexico.

Like all arts, swapping has its techniques. Horse traders learned that centuries ago. Experienced swappers advise the beginner to keep his best specimen for his own collection, then grade the rest. Take to the swap the very good and the good—the material he would expect another collector to admire—and discard or give away the culls. Label each specimen with locality and mineral type, trim and clean it, and show it in its own clean padded box or tucked with others in tissue-paper nests in a cardboard flat.

In the swap tent or area, place the material on a table, then walk around and look over what is offered by others. If you see something you want, ask its owner to walk over to your table and find something he would like to have in exchange.

A sense of values is useful here, but interest in getting what you can use is even more important. Experts reason that the first consideration is to turn your own surplus into material you do not have or can use, although monetary value is not to be forgotten altogether.

Be generous with youngsters but not to the extent that you let them wheedle you out of your best specimens. Likewise, beware the pitiful old gentleman who may arouse your sympathy but who is likely to have some good swapping material of his own if he has to disclose it.

At a big national show, attended by many persons from far places, bring local material because the visitors will be looking for gems from celebrated areas near the show site. At small club shows, bring more exotic material because many there will have only local stones.

There are more than a thousand organized mineral and gem collecting clubs in the United States and a growing number in Canada. Most of these hold their own shows annually with swapping as a feature, and many states hold a swap for all the clubs in the area. Finally, it is a sound principle to swap with rock hounds and to buy from dealers. That keeps both sources open for the future.

Trading by mail has long been a favored means of making friends and augmenting a collection. Etiquette requires that the person initiating the trade offer material by letter. If he receives an encouraging reply, he sends what he has and tells what he would like to have in exchange. Only good to excellent material should be involved in such long-distance exchanges, and scrupulous attention should be given to packing, mail regulations, especially in foreign trading, and detailed labeling.

8.
collectors
and
collections

Precious stones have been actors in some of the most lurid scenes of history. The Koh-i-noor diamond, before it came to rest in the British crown, passed from hand to hand as the prize of 650 years of violence. It was taken from the Mogul emperor in Delhi, India, in 1793 by the founder of Afghanistan. His grandsons fought over it until the victor fled to Lahore. There the rajah extorted it from him as the price of hospitality. In 1849 the British East India company seized it and gave it to Queen Victoria.

Another ornament of the British crown, the Black Prince's ruby, sealed the death of the king of Granada, who was killed for it by the king of Castile. He gave it to the Black Prince, son of Edward III of England. A later king, Henry V, wore it on his helmet on the famous day at Agincourt when England broke the power of feudal France. It helped deflect a nearly fatal sword blow at Henry's head. The stone, a spinel, has been polished but left in its natural shape.

Jewels have been the last resource of fugitives from war and revolution for ages. Napoleon pledged the Pitt diamond, now in the Louvre in Paris, to raise money for his wars. After World War I, the Russian Communists sold many of the Imperial treasures to strengthen the financial position of their country.

The Great Collections

It was not until the nineteenth century that gems began to be collected for their scientific interest rather than their beauty and cash value. As mineralogical science developed, wealthy Europeans created a vogue for assembling cabinets of minerals.

King Christian VIII of Denmark, for example, formed a fine collection in the mid-nineteenth century, which is now in the Royal

Museum in Copenhagen. Philadelphia was the first center of collecting in the United States. One of the first gem and mineral collections there was formed by J. R. Cox of the University of Pennsylvania and was later owned by Professor Joseph Leidy of the University, founder of paleontology in America.

A wealthy machine-tool manufacturer in Philadelphia, Clarence S. Bement, created the outstanding cabinet of his time by purchasing collections abroad and in the United States. J. Pierpont Morgan bought the 12,000 Bement specimens and gave them to the American Museum of Natural History in New York.

Philadelphia was also the home of the notable Vaux family. William S. Vaux gave his collection of 13,000 specimens to the Philadelphia Academy of Natural Sciences; his son George bequeathed his 10,000 specimens to Bryn Mawr college; and his grandson, George, Jr., augmented the gifts of his father at Bryn Mawr.

Of equal stature among these princely collectors was Colonel Washington A. Roebling, builder of the Brooklyn Bridge, who brightened years of invalidism in Trenton, New Jersey, by assembling the great collection of 16,000 specimens which he gave to the National Museum of the Smithsonian Institution in Washington, D.C.

Buying with a lavish purse, under expert advice, in a time when major European collections were being dispersed and when the demands of industry were opening mines all over the world, these men brought together treasures that are the foundations of the displays of uncut and cut gems in the American Museum of Natural History and the National Museum.

The National Museum dates the formation of its gem collections to 1884, when it was authorized to buy material for an exhibit at New Orleans. Ten years later the valuable and well-chosen gems assembled by Isaac Lea, Philadelphia publisher and naturalist, were given to the museum by his daughter; her husband supplemented these with his own collection. Since then, Colonel Roebling and many other donors have added rich gifts.

Notable among these is the collection of 7,000 specimens from the zinc mines at Franklin, N.J. This was formed by Frederick A. Canfield, of Dover, N.J. and expanded by his son, who gave the collection to the National Museum.

The collections of the National Museum have grown impressively in the last few years. In addition to the Hope blue diamond of 44½ carats, a jewel with a historic past, the museum has the 127-carat Portuguese diamond and the Eugenie blue of 31 carats, as well as several superb necklaces from the Napoleonic era.

In rubies it now has the superb Rosser Reeves star ruby of

139 carats, a bracelet with 31 rubies, and in sapphires the 330-carat Star of Asia as well as the 316-carat Star of Artaban, and another sapphire of 423 carats. Such gems are beyond the dimensions of jewelry.

So are a 911-carat giant Brazilian aquamarine, and another beryl from California, a 113-carat morganite, an emerald crystal of 858 carats and an almost unparalleled cut one of 38 carats as well as two emerald necklaces of royal proportions.

Other stars in the National Museum's crown are two colossal topazes—a yellow one of 7,725 carats, and a greenish one of 12,000 carats; the largest known alexandrite of 66 carats, two big chrysoberyl catseyes, one of 40 carats; the largest known peridot of 310 carats, as well as the largest cut benitoite, the 7,000 carat rock crystal (quartz) faceted egg; a quartz sphere 12⅞ inches in diameter, and the famous Roebling black opal from Nevada.

These are only the highlights of the collection, which also includes a display of rarely cut minerals.

Another treasury of rare gems in the United States is at the American Museum of Natural History in New York. It owes much of its outstanding American material to George Frederick Kunz, who was vice president of Tiffany & Co., the famous New York jewelers. He encouraged his company to form a collection of American gems for exhibition in Paris in 1889. J. Pierpont Morgan bought that collection for the museum. Eleven years later Dr. Kunz again exhibited in Paris—and took a grand prize for the Tiffany collection of precious stones from world-wide sources. And once more Morgan bought the prize-winning collection for the museum. He also donated the Bement minerals, which included many famous gem specimens. Morgan Memorial Hall was set up in the museum to house the gifts of its benefactor. After that time substantial gifts and endowments were added by William Boyce Thompson, copper and sulfur-mining magnate.

Among notable American specimens in the museum are American fresh-water pearls, diamonds from Wisconsin and Alabama, some of the finest known tourmalines from Maine and southern California, and, appropriately, many examples of two gems named for the men most closely associated with the collection, the lilac spodumene, kunzite, and the pink beryl, morganite. Morgan Hall contains such unique displays as a magnificent cabinet of sapphires given by Morgan's son, J. P. Morgan: the 100-carat DeLong star ruby; the 536-carat Star of India, largest known blue star sapphire; a carved morganite crystal 6 inches high; a 600-pound gem-quality topaz crystal; a fine 71-carat red spinel; a 9.29-carat hiddenite; and the largest cut blue zircon, of 208 carats.

Smaller Museums

Three university museums in the East also offer the hobbyist first-rate collections for study. The Mineralogical Museum at Harvard University in Cambridge, Massachusetts, is the show window of a great research department with well-housed and well-displayed collections. It was started in 1892 with the acquisition of the Hamlin tourmaline collection from Maine. The Peabody Museum of Natural History of Yale University at New Haven, Connecticut, also is a center of research; and the collection at Wesleyan University, Middletown, Connecticut, is smaller but of high quality.

The Hall of Gems in the Field Museum of Natural History in Chicago is without a peer in the Middle West. It grew out of a collection that Kunz brought to the World's Columbian exposition in 1893. This was expanded by Oliver Farrington as curator and by later aquisitions. Among its outstanding gems is the Sun God opal which was once in the Hope collection, and giant Russian aquamarines, Brazilian amethysts and tourmalines, a gem sapphire carved as a woman's head, and an engraved diamond. An aquamarine from Stoneham, Maine, is regarded as the finest ever found in the United States. Russian sculptures in rock crystal and rhodonite make up a unique display, and the case of topazes is certainly the finest of its kind in the United States.

In a nearby room is the Hall of Jade with examples from the collection formed in China by Berthold Laufer tracing the use of jade over five thousand years.

Cranbrook Institute of Science, in Bloomfield Hills, a suburb of Detroit, also has a good collection in quarters well designed for viewing.

Two smaller museums of high quality are the Lizzadro Museum of Lapidary Arts in Wilder Park in Elmhurst, a suburb of Chicago, where a center has been created for hobbyists; and the Walker Art Center in Minneapolis, which houses T. B. Walker's collection of two hundred pieces of jade, principally from the seventeenth, eighteenth, and nineteenth centuries.

The best displays on the West Coast are the Warner collection of the California Institute of Technology at Pasadena, and the California Division of Mines Collection in the Ferry Building in San Francisco. Both are exceptionally strong in the gem minerals of that state.

Canada's most diversified gem collection is in the Royal Ontario Museum of Geology and Mineralogy in Toronto.

Amateur Collectors

Present-day interest in gem collecting goes back to the first amateur club formed in New York in 1886, and the Mineralogical Society of Pennsylvania formed about the same time. A magazine, the *Mineral Collector,* served the interests of these pioneer clubs, but the real growth of the hobby may be dated from the first appearance of *Rocks and Minerals* magazine in 1926. Five years later a club group was formed in Joliet, Illinois, and in the same year the Mineralogical Society of Southern California was organized in Pasadena. Today there are more than one thousand mineral and gem clubs.

Such clubs grow out of the needs of the beginner who comes home from a vacation trip with a bag full of stones. What can he do with them? Most likely he will buy some machinery, or get acquainted with someone who already has the equipment, and cut his stones to bring out their full beauty. Amateurs have invented machinery for cutting gems and have provided a market for companies that manufacture it. Many have developed skill equal to that of professional lapidaries.

Gem cutting is divided into two major branches: faceting and the fashioning of cabochons. Ordinarily only transparent material free from disfiguring flaws is faceted. Such material is more costly than the equally colorful nontransparent materials—the agates and jaspers—that are used for cabochons. Faceting, consequently, is generally regarded as the advanced step in amateur gem cutting.

Cabochons

Cabochons are fashioned in four major operations. The large piece of rough material is clamped in a vise, and a circular saw blade containing diamond grit embedded in its edge revolves against the stone, sawing it into slabs usually ¼ to ³/₁₆ inch thick. Chosen areas are marked on a slab with a template and an aluminum pencil. These blanks are cut out by holding the slab against a smaller diamond saw.

If blanks are large enough, they are grasped in the fingers and ground to the marked shape on a wet abrasive wheel. The base is made to conform to the pencil line, and the top is ground to a dome or some other chosen shape. If the blank is too small to hold, it is mounted on the end of a stick with sealing wax. This is known as a dop stick. The shaped stone is now given a smooth surface by successive sandings with abrasive cloth of finer and finer grades, up to 600 grit. This is usually done on a wheel covered with the cloth or on a wet belt sander.

When the surface is satiny and free of defects after sanding, it is ready to polish. This is done on a rotating wheel covered with leather, or made of wood or hard felt, using a slurry of a polishing agent, such as tin oxide or fine aluminum oxide. The stone is pressed against the damp wheel, and within seconds, if it has been carefully prepared, it takes on a mirror finish which reveals all the innate beauty of the gem.

Ornamental objects, such as bookends or lamp bases, are formed by sawing to shape, sanding, and polishing in the same way. To polish large flat surfaces, special equipment—a power buff made of carpeting, a rotating flat plate, or vibrating plates—has been developed. It has become fashionable to make tabletops of gem materials, with the pieces laid close together in mortar and polished like a single slab or imbedded in plastic. Transparencies consisting of unpolished slabs cemented between glass plates and viewed against a lamp form another means of displaying the color and pattern of gem materials.

Tumbling has become one of the most popular ways of fashioning gems because it eliminates most of the handwork of forming and polishing and because it exploits a lot of material formerly too shattered or flawed for cutting. The rough pieces, usually all about the same size and hardness, are placed in a rotating or vibrating container with water and abrasive. As the container turns slowly, the stones slide on one another, grinding away rough edges. When the rough grinding is completed, the process is repeated with finer abrasive, and then finally with polishing agents. The product consists of irregularly shaped, highly polished stones. If they have been well chosen in the beginning and preshaped to fit small, bell-shaped mounting caps, they can be made into attractive costume jewelry.

Faceting

Until the amateurs took up faceting about forty years ago, this delicate work was done with tools as primitive as those used in the Middle Ages. High skill alone enabled the professional faceter to do wonders. His only equipment was a horizontally revolving lap wheel and a dop stick jammed into a hole in a block of wood to give the proper angle for the facet. But amateurs compensated for their lack of this skill by devising machinery that would give even more precise results.

The stone to be faceted is roughed into shape on a grinding wheel. Then it is cemented to a metal dop stick which fits into a fixed metal post. The angle at which the stone touches the horizontal grinding wheels can be set with a protractor. It is possible to place the facets exactly where they belong to bring out maximum fire and brilliance in the gem.

Increasing use of diamond as a grinding and polishing agent has been made possible in recent years by the availability of synthetic diamond. Small tabletop units fashion the cabochon with revolving discs coated with diamond grit embedded in plastic or metal. For faceting similar discs rotating horizontally enable the amateur to create precise angles on his gem. The use of diamond in this way allows more rapid and more closely controlled cutting with more compact machinery.

Displays

Most cut gems find their proper place in jewelry, and many amateurs have become skillful at making mountings. But since there is a limit to the amount of jewelry that a family or its friends can wear, many collectors exhibit unmounted stones in a number of ways. In regions of abundant gem resources, such as the Far West, collectors take pride in comprehensive displays of cabochons. Many faceters enjoy the challenge of cutting uncommon gem materials, which, either because of rarity, softness, or fragility, are not suitable for use in jewelry. Others cut or collect special types, such as star stones, opals, jade, or tourmaline.

Collections are displayed in many ways. A case of shallow drawers such as an antique spool cabinet suits a small collection. For a larger one, a case with shallow drawers designed for architectural drawings is satisfactory. In such cabinets, typical rough material, the sawed slab, and the finished gem can be laid out together to tell the entire story of the gem.

Smaller lots of gems can be displayed safely and yet be handled in Riker mounts, which are shallow black cardboard boxes with glass lids. They are filled with cotton and held together with pins.

Individual stones can be housed in small plastic boxes of the size used for micromount minerals. The top of the box forms a magnifying lens that brings out the beauty of what is inside.

The best opportunity to display handiwork as a gem cutter is at club shows, the bigger shows put on by their regional federations and the annual national one. Displays may be entered in two cate-

COLLECTORS AND COLLECTIONS

gories—competitive and noncompetitive. The former are judged under strict rules.

Official cases for such shows are limited for competition to 12 square feet in area, either shallow, glass-topped cases or a boxlike case with glass front containing risers to display the contents. Lighting should be hidden, and for gems should be incandescent rather than fluorescent to preserve color values.

Cases are usually lined with an off-white material free of exposed edges or folds to make the background as unobtrusive as possible. As a veteran exhibitor said: "You are showing gems, not background."

Each stone should be labeled, and for display this requires certain information and a limit on the number of items displayed. Educational exhibits are free of many of these restrictions, and so are noncompetitive ones.

Only perfect gems of high quality, free of fingerprints and other disfiguring marks, are suitable for public display under the high standards set by modern shows.

9.
diamonds
in the
united states

The vast forces of nature that produced diamonds as a by-product of the molding of continents and oceans did not spare North America. Diamonds have been found in the United States all the way from North Carolina to California and from Georgia to Wisconsin. Some are found in the rock in which they were created by volcanic fires. Others have washed out of the rock formations of the East and West Coast mountains, while the diamonds of the Midwest region of the United States were carried there by great glaciers that crunched down from Canada.

The Great Lakes region is the most extensive diamond field in the United States and it undoubtedly contains a thousand stones for every one that has been recognized. Millennia ago this area was planed smooth by a succession of glaciers that advanced and retreated; the southern limit of this glaciated region is marked roughly by the Ohio and the Missouri rivers. As the glaciers retreated they left behind great moraines or dumps of boulders, gravel, and clay which the ice had carried along. Diamonds are found in the moraines at the outer limits of the glacial advance in an area 600 miles long and 200 miles wide, which trends in a northwest-southeast direction from above Milwaukee, Wisconsin, to Cincinnati, Ohio.

Study of the glacial pathways indicates that the Wisconsin diamonds, at least, were brought down by the thick ice sheet from a source near the summit east of James Bay and south of Hudson Bay in Labrador. The diamonds found in glacial drift in Indiana and Ohio may have been transported by another glacial lobe descending almost due south from Canada. But both theories of the origin of Midwest diamonds remain unsupported until a diamond-bearing rock formation is discovered in Canada. Organized searches have so far failed to discover one.

Some fifty diamonds have been found in the Great Lakes region, and undoubtedly only the difficulty of recognizing them in this thinly scattered field has kept others from being discovered. An uncut diamond has none of the luster and the transparency of the cut jewel. It is usually a frosted, greasy looking, rounded crystal, shaped like a fat double pyramid with the bases together. Because diamonds are so much harder than any other stone, they can wander far without becoming worn. The distinctness of their rounded crystal faces helps to distinguish them from quartz, a softer mineral.

The largest Midwest diamonds have been found near Milwaukee. Others have been found in central Indiana, near Cincinnati, and at Dowagiac, Michigan. Few have been reported in recent years, perhaps because of the decline in placer mining for gold in this region, and also because income tax laws penalize such disclosures. Table E lists authenticated finds in this Midwestern region.

Dots show where diamonds have been discovered in Midwestern states. Broken line marks southern advance of glaciers.

TABLE E. DIAMOND FINDS IN MIDWESTERN STATES (FOR FINDS IN INDIANA, SEE TABLE F)

Place	Date	Weight	Description
Eagle, Waukesha County, Wis. (while digging well on Thomas Devereaux farm)	1876	$15^{12}/_{32}$ cts.	Slightly distorted crystal with yellowish cast
Plum Creek, Rock Elm Twp., Pierce County, Wis.	1880s	13 stones largest $^3/_4$ ct.	From stream bed, with platinum and gold in mining operations. Stones tinged yellow and green
Saukville, Ozaukee County, Wis. (on Conrad Schaefer farm)	1881	$6^{13}/_{32}$ cts.	Distorted white crystal
Kohlsville, Washington County, Wis.	1886	$21^4/_{16}$ cts.	$^1/_2$ white $^1/_2$ cream colored. Known as the Theresa diamond
Oregon, Dane County (found by boy in clay bank on Devine farm)	1893	$3^{14}/_{16}$ cts.	Distorted and pitted white stone
Dowagiac, Cass County, Mich.	1894	$10^{14}/_{16}$ cts.	In gravel pit at Cook Lake. Cut into four ring stones
Milford, Clermont County, Ohio	1897	6 cts.	A white stone of fine quality
Burlington, Racine County, Wis.	1903	$2^1/_{16}$ cts.	A white twin crystal

The Eagle diamond had a curious history. Its finder, not knowing it was a diamond, sold it for one dollar to a Milwaukee jeweler, who learned later that he had bought a diamond and sold it to Tiffany & Co., only to be sued by the original finder. The courts decided that the jeweler had acted in good faith.

DIAMONDS IN THE UNITED STATES

Wisconsin diamonds have a characteristic dodecahedral shape. Some sixteen are reliably known to have been found in the state. African rough diamonds are usually octahedral in form.

The largest number of Midwestern diamonds has been taken from glacial drift in Brown and Morgan counties in Indiana, south and southwest of Indianapolis, probably because gold panning has been carried on for years in the creeks there. These creeks wash down and concentrate the heavy material, including diamonds, in the glacial debris and leave it deposited in crevices in the bedrock over which they flow. The diamonds here are associated with sapphire, garnet, black sand, and, occasionally, native copper and chlorastrolite carried down from the Lake Superior region. Recorded finds of Indiana diamonds number more than twenty (see Table F).

In the Appalachian region, diamonds have been reported from Virginia, West Virginia, North Carolina, Georgia, Alabama, Kentucky, and Tennessee. These mountains are so ancient, so eroded, and have undergone such extensive geological changes that one can only guess at the origin of the Appalachian diamonds.

Dots show where diamonds have been discovered in Southern states.

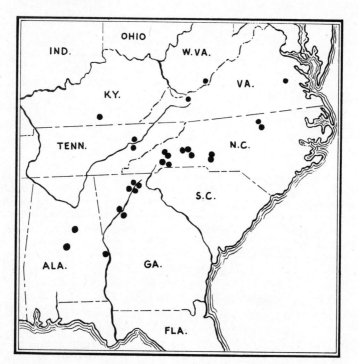

TABLE F. INDIANA DIAMOND LOCATIONS

Place	Date	Weight	Description
Goss Creek (tributary of Little Indian Creek), Morgan County	About 1863	3 cts.	Good quality with a greenish cast
Lick Creek, Brown County	1882		Yellowish white of good quality
Lick Creek, Brown County	About 1882	$^1/_8$, $^3/_{16}$, $^5/_{32}$ ct.	Pink, yellow, and brownish, respectively
Gold Creek, Morgan County		$^{11}/_{16}$ ct.	A blue stone
Brey, Morgan County (on Dr. Clark Cook farm)	1903	2 tiny stones $^1/_8$ ct. or less	Pinkish
Branch of Gold Creek, Morgan County	1900	$4^7/_8$ cts.	Greenish yellow, with a small flaw
Lick Creek, Brown County	1898	$1^{21}/_{32}$ cts.	Clear
Salt Creek, Brown County		3.06 cts.	
Morgan County		3.64 cts.	
Brown County (owned by state)		1.05 cts.	
Gold Creek, Morgan County (all found by Dr. Kelso of Mooresville)	1904	$1^1/_4$ cts. .625 ct. $^3/_4$ ct.	
Morgan County	1908	1.00 ct.	
Peru, Miami County (found in field by farmer)	1949	3.93 cts.	

In addition, a veteran gold panner of Brown County, James Merriman, is said to have found eight small stones in Salt Creek. Two cut stones, one of .87 ct. from Brown County and one of 2.5 cts. from Gold Creek, Morgan County, are also known.

Most of the stones were found in the course of gold mining. Consequently two active mining states, North Carolina and Georgia, have supplied most of them. Records are incomplete, but Table G lists well authenticated finds.

TABLE G. NORTH CAROLINA AND GEORGIA DIAMOND LOCATIONS

Place	Date	Weight	Description
		North Carolina	
Brindletown Creek, Burke County	1843	2 stones	
Twitty gold placer, Rutherford County	1845	1$\frac{1}{3}$ cts.	Clear, flawless, and faintly yellow
Placer on Levinthorpe property, Rutherford County		.84 ct.	
Placer, Cottage Home, Lincoln County	1852	$\frac{1}{2}$ ct.	Greenish, clear
Todd's Branch, Mecklenburg County	1852	2 stones one of 1 ct.	Fine crystal
Portis Mine, Franklin County	1853	2 stones	One of fine water
Muddy Creek headwaters, McDowell County		2 or 3 small stones	
McDowell County	1877	2$\frac{3}{8}$ cts.	White, flawed
Dysortville, McDowell County	1886	4$\frac{1}{3}$ cts.	Greenish, twin crystal
King's Mountain, Cleveland County	1893	$\frac{3}{4}$ ct.	Canary yellow
		Georgia	
Branch of Muddy Creek, Williams' Ferry, Hall County	1843		
Horshaw Mine, Nacoochee Valley, White County	1866	Less than $\frac{1}{8}$ ct.	Opaque
White County		1 ct.	Fine quality

Place	Date	Weight	Description
Daniel Light farm, $^3/_4$ mi. NE of Morrow, Clayton County	1887	$4^1/_4$ cts.	Slightly yellow
11 mi. NE of Macon, Twiggs County		Several	
Stockeneter branch at the Glades, 13 mi. NE of Gainesville		Several	
Near Atlanta	1889		Defective and poor color

In addition, diamonds have been reported from placers in Lumpkin, Dawson, and perhaps in Habersham, Banks, Forsyth, Gwinnett, Cherokee, Bartow, Haralson, Carroll, Paulding, and Cobb counties in Georgia.

A 4.27 carat diamond was found about 1900 in Shelby county, Alabama, 30 miles south of Birmingham, and one of $2^2/_5$ carats was found in 1905 on the Isbell property of Prescott Siding in St. Clair county, 20 miles northeast of Birmingham. One found in 1901 in Lee county, Alabama, not far from Columbus, Georgia, weighs $4^3/_5$ carats. All Alabama stones are of good quality and have a greenish cast.

The two most famous American diamonds are the Punch Jones, of 34.46 carats, found by William P. ("Punch") Jones in a vacant lot at Peterstown, West Virginia, in 1928, and the Dewey, of 23¾ carats, dug up by Benjamin Moore, a laborer leveling a hill on Dr. Samuel Taylor's estate at Manchester, Virginia, now within the city limits of Richmond, in 1854. The former, which was uncovered by a pitched horseshoe during a game, was not identified as a diamond until 1943. It is of good color and apparently is free of imperfections. The surface was covered with tiny circular marks, believed to have been caused by blows from other stones when they were all tossed together in a stream. The Dewey diamond is transparent, has a slightly greenish cast and one large flaw. It was cut to a stone of 11.69 carats. It is presumed that the Punch Jones diamond was carried down by Rich Creek; the Dewey, by the James River. In 1913 a diamond was cut in New York that was reported to have been found by Frank Brewster in a cornfield at Pounding Mill, Tazewell county, Virginia.

Rivaling these two is the 27.21 carat diamond which Mrs. Pellie Howard of Searcy, Arkansas, about 50 miles northeast of Little Rock, sent to Tiffany & Co. in 1946 for identification. She said she found it while chopping cotton. The stone, which is of good quality and faintly yellow in color, was bought by Tiffany. In 1970 an 18.2 carat diamond was found in a yard at Princeton, Louisiana. (Princeton is near Shreveport.) It was cut into three stones. Since then six more diamonds with a total weight of 4 carats have been recovered from the Gifford Hill gravel pit in Sibley, Louisiana, which is only 20 miles from Princeton.

A 3 carat stone, bought by a Knoxville, Tennessee, jeweler in 1889, and one of 1.69 carats bought by the same jeweler in 1900, are the only ones reliably reported from Tennessee. The former is supposed to have been found in the Clinch River in Roane county, the other on the bank of Flat Creek in Luttrell, Union county. A light yellow stone, weighing .78 carat, was reported found in 1888 on the Henry Burris farm, near Cabin Fork Creek in Adair county, Kentucky. It is also likely that diamonds have been found in South Carolina.

The West Coast, one of the most intensively mined areas in the United States, has yielded a great many diamonds. In California, diamonds were found soon after placer mining began with the gold rush. One was reported in 1849, a crystal the size of a small pea and of a straw-yellow color, and since then about 500 have been found, mostly from the counties north and east of Sacramento. Most of these have been small and off-color and of a pale yellow tinge, but several have been more than 2 carats in size and of good quality, and one was of 7¼ carats. California diamonds have been found only in placer gravels and black sands and concentrates. It is presumed that they came from the igneous rocks from which the serpentines of the Sierra Nevada were derived. Discovery of a serpentine "pipe" resembling the vertical pipes penetrating the horizontally bedded rocks of diamond-bearing districts in South Africa led to sinking of a shaft near Oroville, but no diamonds were found. Table H, based on one made by Joseph Murdoch of the University of California at Los Angeles, for the California Division of Mines, summarizes California finds.

TABLE H. CALIFORNIA DIAMOND LOCATIONS

Place	Date	Number	County	Largest Size
Jackass Gulch, near Volcano		60–70	Amador	1.57 cts.
Rancheria, near Volcano	1883	1	Amador	1 ct.
Loafer Hill, near Oleta		1	Amador	

Place	Date	Number	County	Largest Size
Indian Gulch, near Fiddletown	1855–67	5	Amador	
Plymouth	1934	1	Amador	2.57 cts.
Cherokee Flat	1853–1918	300	Butte	2.25 cts.
Oroville		10	Butte	
Yankee Hill, near Oroville	1861	1	Butte	1 1/2 cts. (cut)
Thompson's Flat, near Oroville	1915–16	11	Butte	6 cts.
Smith River			Del Norte	Microscopic stones
Foresthill	Before 1867	40–50	Placer	1.5 cts.
Smith's Flat	1859–1912	47	El Dorado	1.88 cts.
Unrecorded	Before 1873	12	El Dorado	
White Rock Canyon, Cedar Ravine, near Placerville		3–4	El Dorado	1.25 cts.
Webber Hill		3	El Dorado	
Lower Trinity River			Humboldt	
French Corral		2	Nevada	7.25 cts.
Gopher Hill and Upper Spanish Creek		2	Plumas	
Sawpit Flat			Plumas	
Nelson Point		1	Plumas	
Near Junction of Trinity and Klamath rivers		1	Trinity	2 cts.
Alpine Creek	1895	1	Tulare	Many minute stones

DIAMONDS IN THE UNITED STATES

Operations at the Rock Flat gold placer 5 miles east of New Meadows, Adams County, Idaho, have yielded three small stones, grayish in color, the largest ⅛ carat. Several years ago the finding of a 19½ carat diamond at this mine was reported, but the authenticity of the report is doubtful. Microscopic fragments are also found in Owyhee county and in the sands of the Snake River. Placer miners in southwest Oregon have found perhaps one hundred small stones, mostly flawed and yellowish, including a 3 carat stone from Josephine county and a 2½ carat stone from Malheur county, and a few tiny ones have been reported from Oregon and Washington beach sands. A 4 carat stone was found in Skamania county, Washington, in 1932. A scattering of other reported discoveries included a 2¼ carat stone from Montgomery county, Texas, another found in 1911 in Foard county, Texas, and a tiny diamond from near Syracuse, New York. More doubtful are ones reported from Santa Fe, New Mexico; Yankton, South Dakota; the Santa Maria River, Arizona; Cleveland, Ohio; and San Juan county, Colorado.

Montana has reported at least five diamond discoveries, including one found in 1883 at Nelson Hill, Deer Lodge county; a .22 carat stone found the next year in the same place; and three small stones sent to New York by A. F. White of Butte.

The nation's most spectacular diamond occurrence, however, is in the hills of southwestern Arkansas. Two and one-half miles southeast of Murfreesboro (which is southwest of Little Rock and Hot Springs) on a 72-acre tract lie the only deposits of diamond-bearing rock in the western hemisphere. These are almost precisely like the geological formations in South Africa that during the past 100 years have sent a flood of diamonds to world markets.

Geologists believe that more than 200 million years ago a rock known as peridotite was squeezed under great pressure and heat from deep within the earth, like toothpaste from a tube, creating the vertical pipes from which the Arkansas and South African diamonds come. This rock, a bluish green material containing fragments of shale and sandstone engulfed as it reached the surface, weathers to a yellowish, slick mass.

John W. Huddleston, an unlearned but shrewd farmer who suspected that there was copper in the yellow and blue ground near Murfreesboro, traded a mule as down payment on it. According to one account, he was plowing to plant his turnip greens in August, 1906, when he turned up first one, then a second shiny stone. Suspecting that they were diamonds, he took the stones to Murfreesboro; from there they were sent to New York and their nature authenticated. The two stones, of 1.35 and 2.75 carats, are still preserved in the Pike county bank in Murfreesboro.

Huddelston's good fortune was soon known, and a group of business men bought his farm for $36,000. The subsequent history of the attempts to operate the tract as a diamond mine is one of 40 years of bickering, bald-faced thefts and breach of trust, mismanagement, law suits and shots in the night, arson and intimidation.

In 1950, 32 acres of the diamondiferous area, known as The Crater of Diamonds, were opened to the public to collect for a fee. The attraction became so popular that in 1972 the state of Arkansas bought 867 acres, including the 78-acre area in which the four diamond-bearing pipes are located. In addition to the 750,000 dollars it paid for the property, the state has spent 1,000,000 dollars to develop the property as a state park.

A fee of 2 dollars a day is charged to hunt diamonds in the park, and any lucky finds will be appraised without cost, according to the Department of Parks and Tourism.

Altogether, it is estimated that one hundred thousand diamonds have been recovered from the Arkansas mine, including the thousands "high graded" by miners and neighbors. The largest, known as the Uncle Sam, weighed 40.23 carats when it was found in 1924. It was cut to a rosy-tinted gem of 12.35 carats.

In 1956 Mrs. Arthur L. Parker, of Dallas, made the most spectacular discovery since the Crater of Diamonds was opened to the public. This stone, called the Star of Arkansas, was 1½ inches long, ⅝ inch thick and ¼ inch wide. It weighed 15.31 carats in the rough and was cut to a marquise weighing 8.28 carats. Another Texan, Mrs. Don Macrae of Irving, found a 3.11 carat diamond in 1957 near the spot where Mrs. Parker had been lucky.

The biggest gems reported since that time are one of 13.5 carats found by Mr. and Mrs. Jim Beggs of Carlisle, Arkansas, in 1966, and a 10.4 carat yellow stone in 1963. Neils Bach of Ludington, Michigan, turned up a 6.43 carat stone in 1960, and seven more of more than 3 carats have been reported, including one of 3.91 carats found in 1973 by Barbara Stanoil, of Osage, Oklahoma. Some steady customers of the Crater of Diamonds have reported finding from thirty to eighty diamonds each over the last twenty years.

The Arkansas stones have included a number of superb canary and pink diamonds. The white ones are noted for their exceptional freedom from color, like the so-called river stones of Africa. Arkansas diamonds have an unusually high luster in their natural state, resembling the Brazilian gems, and show complex crystallization, which makes the crystals very rounded. They are said to be harder than the African stones. The white stones make up 40 percent of the total, the yellow and canary 22 percent, the brown 37 percent, and bort 1 percent. About 10 percent of the white stones are gem quality.

Rough diamonds are valued by the same criteria as cut stones—color, flawlessness, and weight. The finest color is a total absence of color, or at least of any yellowish tinge. A diamond of the first water (the professional phrase) is as clear, colorless, and sparkling as a drop of spring water. Such quality is the rarest attribute of a diamond. Next most desirable quality is comparative flawlessness, which means the absence of imperfections visible to a trained eye through a 10-power magnifying glass. Weight, of course, is important in valuation, because small diamonds are much more common than large ones. Consequently, the value of a 10 carat stone is much greater than the total value of ten 1-carat stones.

The quality of rough diamonds is estimated by experts who chip a tiny window so that they can see behind the dull, rough skin into the stone. They decide in the same way how the stone shall be cut to eliminate flaws and give the greatest marketable weight in finished gems.

10.
pearls
in the
united states

Among the varied U.S. gem sources are its streams and rivers which have produced rare and valuable pearls that rival the best from the Orient. Some worth thousands of dollars have been found in the Middle West in the last one hundred years; they can still be found today. Quantities of these gems have been dug from the graves of the ancient Indian mound builders, and in 1542 De Soto found the natives of the southeastern states rich in them.

But modern exploitation of American pearl resources dates back only to 1857, when a New Jersey carpenter found a 93-grain pink pearl in Notch Brook, near Paterson, New Jersey. He sold it to Tiffany & Co., which dubbed it the Tiffany Queen and sold it to the Empress Eugenie of France.

News of this good fortune started a "pearl rush" to the rivers of the East; the rush quickly spread West. Pearls of remarkable luster and in a great variety of colors were found in southwestern Wisconsin and in the Illinois River by about 1900, and silvery pearls in the Wabash River. The search for pearls was rapidly taken up in Tennessee and Arkansas. The first important pearl found in Arkansas was a 27-grain gem found in the White River in 1888, and good pearl fishing grounds were developed at Bald Knob, Cypress Bayou, and in the Black, St. Francis, and Cache rivers.

By 1908, midwestern streams were producing nearly 500,000 dollars in pearls annually, mostly from tributaries of the Mississippi. Soon, however, intensive fishing depleted the shallower streams, and industrial wastes and sewage destroyed many shellfish. And when Japanese cultured pearls depressed the market for genuine pearls, pearl fishermen turned to gathering shells for the button factories, principally in Muscatine, Iowa. They began to fish in the Mississippi and in its deeper tributaries, and the search for

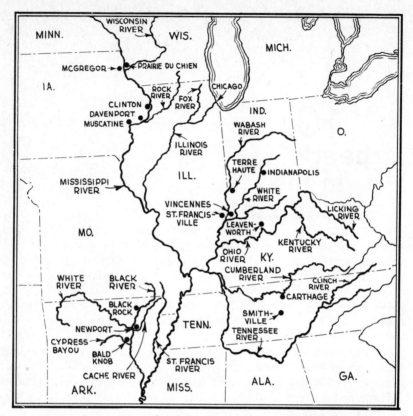

Dots show where freshwater pearls have been found.

pearls became incidental to the shell industry. Today the Tennessee River and its tributaries are major sources of freshwater shell and pearls; some still come from Arkansas, and Oklahoma has developed a thriving shell-fishing industry in the Verdigris river.

The Wabash river has also become important in production of mussel shell, with several thousand licensed fishermen, and a major market for shell in Terre Haute, Indiana. The buyer there, Cohen & Son, has developed a method of flushing loose the mussels from the river bottom with submerged water jets that force the shells onto a conveyor belt.

The largest pearl found in the Mississippi river area is one of 210 grains—nearly an inch in diameter—from near Genoa, Iowa. In 1953 Albert Langsford received 400 dollars for one found at Lansing, Iowa, and 225 dollars for one found at Harper's Ferry, both near the Mississippi river. As late as 1966 a black pearl reported as large as an old-fashioned shoe button was taken from the Cedar river in Iowa and was sold for 1,200 dollars.

The Wabash river yielded a 300-dollar pearl in 1961, after having been the source of one sold for 400 dollars in 1953 and one almost as valuable in the same year.

From a less appropriate source came 2,000 dollars in pearls recovered by a farmhand cleaning the pens of pigs fed on mussels at Marley, Illinois. Pearls before swine!

Of the nearly one hundred varieties of American mussels, about twenty-five have the pearly shell lining characteristic of pearl mollusks. In the Middle West the most plentiful of these is the niggerhead, almost round and black and rough on the outside, which forms large beds. A good-sized niggerhead is 4 inches across. The best pearl mussel is the three-ridge, named for a characteristic of the shell. Sand shells, found singly in mud banks and on beaches, are 5 to 6 inches long when mature, and very narrow. The buckhorn is long, narrow, and has a rough brown exterior. The butterfly, a mussel whose shell is marked with dotted stripes, produces excellent pearls. Some other varieties are the pimpleback, monkey face, pigtoe, washboard, mucket, maple leaf, grandmaw or pocketbook, eggshell or glass back, warty back, and creeper.

Most pearl and shell fishermen are farmers, woodsmen, or trappers who make a part-time occupation of pearling from June to October. In Arkansas, about fifteen hundred families take part each year.

Since plastics have destroyed the pearl button business, most pearls are purchased by roving buyers representing New York jewelers. One described the average pearl-fishing family as living in abject poverty in a one- or two-room cabin, sleeping on a filthy mattress and using boxes for table and chairs. This buyer said he made his rounds of the states in the Mississippi valley, cultivating the trust of the natives and listening for news of a pearl discovery. Most pearl fishermen, he said, were close-mouthed about their work and dealt in secrecy with buyers.

The buyer reported that the mussels were cooked until they opened in an oil barrel cut in half lengthwise and welded together into a long trough. The trough was supported on blocks, filled with water, and the clams were put into the trough in gunnysacks and steamed. Then the opened clams were searched for pearls and slugs in the mantle or a bulge near the hinge of the shell. The shells were cleaned and sold to a buyer.

The method most commonly used for taking mussels from the river bottom is called crowfooting. This is done with a 12- to 20-

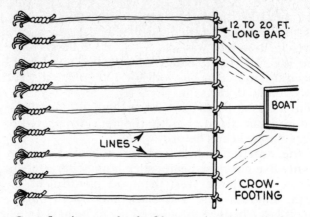

Crowfooting method of harvesting mussels from river bottom.

foot-long iron bar, to which are attached lines ending in crowfeet made of heavy twisted wire bent back into four prongs like a bird's foot. This rig is dragged behind a boat as it floats downstream. (See drawing.) The mussels, which lie half open against the current as they feed, close on the prongs, and the rig is pulled periodically into the boat. With such an outfit, 200 to 800 pounds of shell can be harvested in a day.

A "hogger," who wades in the shallow water at night hunting the mussels with a flashlight, can bag 25 to 100 pounds. A net is often used to scoop up the shell from soft, muddy bottoms, or they can be taken with a long rake in swift water, or with shell tongs (two rakes hinged and used like tongs) in deep water. Diving with a helmet and an inflated suit is the most costly method, and is resorted to only in very deep water.

The best pearls come from shells taken from swift-running streams with clean, sandy bottoms. Fishermen always expect to find a good pearl in an old, deformed shell but often are disappointed. Some idea of the good hunting grounds can be gleaned from the pearl-buying centers of past years. These include Prairie du Chien, Wisconsin; McGregor, Clinton, Davenport, and Muscatine, Iowa; Newport, Black Rock, and Bald Knob, Arkansas; Clinton, Carthage, and Smithville, Tennessee; St. Francisville, Illinois; and Vincennes and Terre Haute, Indiana.

As the Midwestern pearl-shell catch has diminished in recent years, such conservation methods as licensing of fishermen, minimum limits on the size of shells that may be taken, and "resting" of streams have been put into force. Indiana, for example, has a closed season on shelling from November 1 until April 15.

Pearl hunting in other parts of the United States is not systematically pursued any more, except in California, where the abalone gives interesting green and blue pearls, and in Florida, where beautiful deep pink pearls are found in the conch shell.

Abalone blister pearls are sought on the Pacific Ocean side of Baja California, Mexico. In the southern part of the long peninsula, around Punta San Francisquito on the Gulf side, the western wing shell and a heavier shell known as *Pinctada mazatlania* are gathered for their pearls, which are often pink or black. La Paz is the center of this pearl trade. The local pearls are also imitated by cutting spheres from the shell.

A Salisbury, Maryland, jeweler, Hans Schilling, has made a collection of more than six hundred pearls from cherrystone clams found off the Delaware and Maryland coasts. The best are button-shaped and they range in color from milky white through cream and orange to mauve and purple and, rarely, black. Some are as large as a half-inch across. The pearls, which lack the fine iridescence of gem pearls, are a by-product of commercial shell fishing, and most of them are found by shuckers preparing the clams for restaurant use.

A valuable pearl has a regular shape, a definite color or tint, an even, clear skin without blemishes, and the real pearl luster. The most valuable are usually spherical or egg-, pear-, drop-, or button-shaped. Freshwater mussels are noted for the variety of odd-shaped pearls they form, such as the long, dogtoothed hinge pearls, and others resembling a wing or a petal. Irregular pearls of an attractive shape are known as baroques, unattractive ones as slugs, and tiny ones as seed pearls.

Pearls usually are the color of the lining of the shell of the mussel or oyster in which they form, and, especially in freshwater varieties, exhibit an astonishing spectrum which includes rose, cream, white, black, gray, bronze, and shades of lavender, blue, yellow, mauve, orange, brown, and green. The first four mentioned are the most desirable.

Unlike most other gems, the pearl is of organic origin. Around a foreign particle—a sand grain or a tiny parasite—the mussel secretes layer after layer of a substance which is about 6 percent conchiolin (an organic material like tooth enamel), 2 percent water, and the rest calcium carbonate (the same substance as limestone or marble). The thin, semitransparent layers, arranged and crinkled like the leaves of a well-formed cabbage, break up the light that falls on them, reflecting back the peculiar iridescence or orient which is the pearl's unique glory. Gems with the thinnest, most symmetrically arranged layers have the finest luster. By careful peeling, layers can be removed from a pearl until a blemish is eliminated or a layer of good luster exposed.

Weights of pearls are expressed in pearl grains, of which there are 4 to the metric carat, so that the grain is 50 milligrams. Because large pearls are rare, pearl values increase rapidly with size. The usual method is to grade the pearl according to shape, color, luster, and perfection, then assign a unit value, which is the value it would have if it weighed 1 grain. This unit or base value is multiplied by the square of the number of grains the pearl weighs to give its value. For example, if the base value were 1 dollar, a 2-grain pearl would be worth 4 dollars, a 5-grain pearl 25 dollars.

High prices and the steady demand for fine pearls have inspired efforts to cultivate them. The Chinese practiced this art in the fourteenth century, when they learned that small beads or lead images of Buddha inserted into the body of the mussel would become coated with pearly nacre within a few months. In the last fifty years, experiments in pearl culture have been carried on in the Gulf of California and at Cedar Rapids, Iowa.

Pearl culture was brought to its present state in Japan, where a high degree of skill, infinite patience, and low labor costs are favorable circumstances. By the method usually credited to the late Kokichi Mikimoto, a piece of the mantle of a living pearl oyster is removed and used as a bag to hold a bead made of Mississippi valley freshwater pearl shell. This bead measures from 80 to 90 percent of the linear diameter of the cultured pearl. The bag is inserted into the tissue of a three-month-old pearl oyster. The oysters are kept in the ocean in baskets, inspected annually, and cleaned to speed their growth. They are allowed to grow for three to eight years. But only about 5 percent yield perfect pearls big enough for an expensive necklace, the rest being baroques or defective.

More recently, the Japanese experimented with growing pearls in fresh water in Lake Biwa, northeast of Kyoto. Not only are these freshwater pearls, but they do not have a nucleus. They are started by inserting bits of mantle from another oyster into the pearl oyster. The oysters are hung in wire baskets and the pearls removed when they are less than two years old. The pearls become oval if they are allowed to grow older and larger, and even the young ones are not perfectly round.

A fine necklace of cultured pearls may cost as much as 25,000 dollars, or as little as 50 dollars. Only an expert can tell cultured pearls from natural pearls, and the expert will usually rely on X-ray photographs and the endoscope, a tiny probe with a mirror on the end which is inserted into the hole drilled into a pearl for stringing.

It can "see" the mother-of-pearl core of the cultured gem. Both natural and cultured pearls are worlds above the imitations, which are made of glass beads lacquered with a preparation of fish scales called pearl essence, or of hollow glass balls filled with the essence and wax.

11.
directory and maps
of gem hunting
locations

It is the purpose of this book to discuss gem materials available (chiefly in the United States), to offer suggestions about the best means of prospecting for them, and to tell the amateur where to look for them. It is not its purpose to enable the collector to gather commercial quantities of gem rough. It is always possible to strike a rich new location, of course, but generally speaking a gem hunting trip should be looked on as recreation. It should not be expected to return a financial profit.

This directory of locations has been made up from state and federal reports, from other published materials, from personal communications from collectors, from museum lists, and from other reliable sources. New gem locations are discovered every season; old ones become exhausted. Constant revision of such a list as this is therefore necessary. The current Rand McNally Road Atlas has been taken as the standard reference, and with few exceptions the following locations appear in it.

It is not always possible, however, to pinpoint locations, especially in the West, where the absence of man-made landmarks prevails over vast areas. Other areas have been only vaguely described or even kept secret by their discoverers to prevent commercial collectors from stripping them. A number of dormant eastern locations have been included only because mining may again be resumed at them, making possible the discovery of gems as a by-product, or because interest in them has been renewed.

Many areas have been closed, either by state or federal authorities, or by private owners who have other uses for their land or who have been annoyed by thoughtless collectors. Storm, fire, urban expansion, and road changes may occasionally make localities inaccessible. For these reasons, it is wise to inquire about locations before undertaking a long trip to them. Neither the availability of locations described in this book nor the quality of the material can be guaranteed.

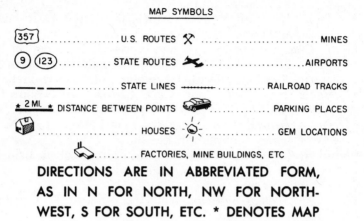

MAP SYMBOLS

357 ...............U.S. ROUTES ✗ ....MINES

9 123 ....STATE ROUTES ✈ ....AIRPORTS

— — — ....STATE LINES ++++++ ....RAILROAD TRACKS

★ 2 MI. ★ DISTANCE BETWEEN POINTS 🚗 ....PARKING PLACES

🏠 ....HOUSES ☀ ....GEM LOCATIONS

⚒ ....FACTORIES, MINE BUILDINGS, ETC

DIRECTIONS ARE IN ABBREVIATED FORM, AS IN N FOR NORTH, NW FOR NORTH-WEST, S FOR SOUTH, ETC. * DENOTES MAP

United States

Alabama

A coastal plain formed of sedimentary rocks, sand, and gravel makes up the lower half of the state. The northern half rests on sedimentary beds, rich in coal and iron, while a small wedge-shaped area of about six counties in east central Alabama offers an area of metamorphic rocks to the gem hunter.

- *Athens, Limestone County* QUARTZ NODULES: NW 18½ miles on Hwy 99 to Good Springs, then S on Hwy 26, go a mile to Dobbins Branch and collect in field downstream.
- *Blountsville, Blount County* AGATE NODULES: W 2 miles on Hwy 27 on way to Holly Pond.
- *Brookwood, Tuscaloosa County* SAGENITIC AGATE: Hwy 116 W for 4 miles, then take road N to strip mines to collect in pits. Also look for petrified wood.
- *Cedar Bluff, Cherokee County* QUARTZ: Take Hwy 9 for 3½ miles, then left ½ mile to search in fields.
- *Dadeville, Tallapoosa County* SOAPSTONE: E 12 miles at Garfield Heard farm at Dudleyville.
- *Delta, Clay County* QUARTZ, KYANITE, BERYL: NW 2½ miles at Smith Mica mine and at old Delta mine.

- *Erin, Clay County* APATITE, BERYL: To S along Gold Mine creek and to E of creek.
- *Hissop, Coosa County* BERYL: Take Crewsville road NE for a mile, then left ¾ mile to fork, take left fork to end of road at Thomas Prospect.
- *Hollis Crossroads, Cleburne County* BERYL: E 1½ miles on Hwy 431, left on SACP road 4199 for ½ mile, then left on dirt road ½ mile. Collect in pegmatite in left-hand ditch.
- *Jackson, Clarke County* SEAM AGATE: In road cuts NW on Hwy 1, 5½ and 14½ miles NW of junction with U.S. 43.
- *Leesburg, Cherokee County* AMETHYST: On Lowe farm to N. See Mrs. James Hampton in Leesburg.
- *Lineville, Clay County* TURQUOISE: In railroad cut at Erin NW on Hwy 49; and also S of Pleasant Grove church on the Hobbs farm.
- *Our Town, Tallapoosa County* EPIDOTE, QUARTZ: To E in fields and along Wind Creek.
- *Paint Rock, Jackson County* AGATE, JASPER: N on Hwy 65 to collect to N in tributaries of Paint Rock River and on Jacobs Mountain.
- *Phil Campbell, Franklin County* CARNELIAN: In gravel pits 2 miles N of town on Hwy 43.
- *Pinetucky, Randolph County* APATITE, RHODOLITE GARNET: At Jones Mica mine W of road to Milner, and with beryl to SW and NE in pegmatite mines.
- *Pyriton, Clay County* BERYL, FELDSPAR: Take road E to church, then N to first graded road and E to Lake Simon sign to turn N on logging road.
- *Quenelda, Clay County* RHODONITE: NW 2 miles on Watts farm.
- *Rockford, Coosa County* BERYL: S 5 miles on Hwy 231 to Pentonville, then W on Hwy 14 for ½ mile to fork, take right fork 1½ miles to mine at Williams Prospect.
- *Sylacauga, Talladega County* MARBLE: 1 mile W on Hwy 8, then S to quarry.
- *Talladega, Talladega County* AZURITE, MALACHITE: Go 11 miles SE near Coleta, turn left on Hwy 7, then S to where Hatchett creek crosses road. Collect ¼ mile farther S on E side of road.
- *Tuscaloosa, Tuscaloosa County* QUARTZ, PETRIFIED WOOD: NE on Hwy 116 to Girls' 4-H club camp sign, then ¼ mile more and N to Brookwood location to collect in strip mine area.
- *Wetkumpka, Elmore County* GARNET: At dam to N.
- *Winterboro, Talladega County* SOAPSTONE: In quarries.

Alaska

The largest of the states resembles the Western United States in topography. A chain of mountains borders the Pacific, including active volcanoes, separated by a basin from another mountain chain which includes Mt. McKinley, highest in North America. These mountains are formed of sedimentary rocks intruded by igneous rocks. Northeast of these ranges lies an arctic plain like the great plains of the West. South of the main plateau of Alaska lies a panhandle with many islands, and the Aleutian chain stretches west almost to Asia. The geology of Alaska is complex and is made more difficult for the gem prospector by frozen ground, vast distances, and lack of transportation.

- *Alcan Highway* SMOKY QUARTZ: Around poles on right hand side of road at Milepost 1225½.

   AGATE, BLOODSTONE: Upstream in Caribou creek at Milepost 118.

- *Anchorage* JASPER: Along Matahuska River at Milepost 72 on Glenn Highway.

   AGATE: At Fire Island, reached by cannery barge.

   AGATE NODULES: At Luster's Claim in Talkeetna mountains.

   AGATE, JASPER: In Kenai River to S.

   PETRIFIED WOOD, AGATE: In Anchor River.

- *Admiralty Island* AGATE NODULES: On beaches from Gambier Bay to Wilson Cove and near Point Gardner.

- *Fairbanks* AGATE, OBSIDIAN: To E in 40-mile area.

   FOSSIL IVORY: In gold dredge gravels.

- *Healy* AMETHYST: With agate and quartz.

- *Juneau* GRAY SAPPHIRE, STAR RUBY: In Copper River gravels.

- *Kenai* (On Cook Inlet) AGATES: At Salamatoff beach.

- *Kobuk River* DARK GREEN AND GRAY JADE: Boulders in Dahl Creek about 150 miles inland from Kotzebue Sound. At headwaters of creek at 5,000 ft. level.

   GRAY JADE: At Shungnak River, 14 miles W of Dahl Creek.

   GREEN JADE: Fairly free of black spots. At Jade Mountain, 30 miles NW of Dahl Creek, and in Jade Creek.

- *Kotzebue Sound* FOSSIL IVORY: In scarp on S side of sound.

- *Lake Iliamna* AGATE, BLOODSTONE: On beaches, best in spring.

- *Platinum* FOSSIL IVORY: Near Cape Newenham on Bering Sea.

- *Popof Island* CHALCEDONY PEBBLES: On beaches near Sand Point.

- *Port Heiden* AGATES: On beaches all the way to Port Moller.

- *Port Houghton* GARNET: To S with TOURMALINE.
- *Point Barrow* AMBER: In beach deposits.
- *Prince of Wales Island* EPIDOTE: Near Summit Lake on Green Monster Mountain.
- *Sand Point, Shumagin Islands* PETRIFIED WOOD: On NW side of Unga Island, reached by boat or plane.
- *Takeen, Marble Island, off Prince of Wales Island* MARBLE.
- *Tok Highway* NODULES: In stream at Mentasta Lodge.
- *Sitka* RHODONITE: At head of Silver Bay on Baranof Island.
- *Wrangell* AGATE NODULES: At Agony Beach, reached by plane.
    ALMANDINE GARNET (mostly specimen grade): Near mouth of Stikine River.

Arizona

The Colorado plateau, with its sandstone formations containing fossil wood and bone, extends over the northern third of Arizona. It is set off sharply from the rest of the state by an escarpment, the Mogollon Rim. South of the Rim lies a semidesert region of plains broken by low mountains, from which chalcedony minerals erode. The east central and southern areas are a major copper mining district.

- *Ajo, Pima County* CHALCEDONY ROSES: Hwy 85 N for 20 miles, then right on road 7½ miles to far end of Black Mesa.
    CHALCEDONY: S of road.
    SHATTUCKITE: In veins at New Cornelia Mine.

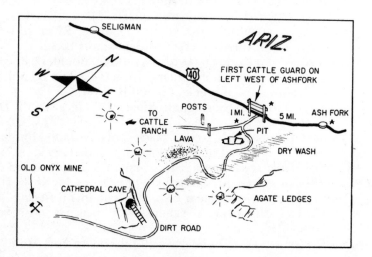

• *Alpine, Apache County* MOSS AGATE: Go NW on U.S. 260 27 miles to sawmills, then E into Escudilla Mountains, and collect on N side.

　PLUME AGATE: Take national forest road NE to state line.

• *Ash Fork, Yavapai County* * AGATE: Int. 40 W for 5 miles, then left on dirt road at first cattle guard on left side of road for mile, then take left fork across a wash (which contains agate), and agate will be found along roadside where road passes under ledges from which agate is weathering. Continue to Cathedral Cave. About 500 ft. from cave entrance are ledges containing white agate spotted with colors. (Beyond cave about ¾ mile is abandoned onyx mine.)

• *Bisbee, Cochise County* SHATTUCKITE: At Shattuck Mine.

• *Boulder City (Nevada)* BLACK AGATE, BROWN JASPER: In Mohave County 3 miles SE of Hoover Dam and W ¼ mile to hill.

• *Bouse, Yuma County* SEAM AGATE: In black volcanic butte, 1 mile E of Bouse.

• *Bowie, Cochise County* FIRE AGATE: Take road N past railroad tracks, then take right fork and keep right as you go NE 21 miles toward the Peloncillo Mountain collecting area.

• *Casa Grande, Pinal County* AGATE, JASPER: South past Chuischu 12 miles. E to Wild Horse pass.

• *Cibola, Yuma County* CHALCEDONY, PETRIFIED WOOD: In river gravels 7 miles N of town.

● *Clifton, Greenlee County* * RED JASPER, VEIN AGATE, BRECCIA
AGATE: Take road NE from Clifton, following San Francisco River. Cross on steel bridge, turn left and go 2 miles to Limestone Canyon on right.

PURPLE AGATE: Three miles farther up Limestone Canyon, Mulligan Peak area to right can be reached on foot; N of peak.

NODULES: W of peak. Similar material is also found beyond on side of Granite Mountain.

FIRE AGATE, JASPER: At Crystal Mountain, trail to right around peak.

JASPER, BLUE AND BLACK AGATE: In nodules and boulders. Above Bobcat Canyon, cross river at Colorado Gulch and take road on right at cattle guard to Ash Spring Canyon. Found 2 miles from cattle guard.

NE of Ash Spring Canyon agate lies in foothills of Sunset Peak.

Nearer Clifton, west of the river, jasper and agate occur in Rocky Gulch and Weaver and Potter Canyons.

BLUE AGATE, CARNELIAN: N from Clifton on U.S. 666; found in first canyon to left a mile S of the Apache National Forest.

FIRE AGATE: Farther N road to left marked Upper Eagle, if followed to bottom, will lead to deposit.

OBSIDIAN NODULES (APACHE TEARS): Three miles farther N, road to right goes to Fritz ranch 16 miles.

CARNELIAN, CHALCEDONY: Continue N on U.S. 666. The 6K6 ranch sign points to this area 2 miles away.

OPALIZED WOOD: Exposed by road cuts. Farther N at Engineer Springs, 3 miles beyond Rose Peak lookout, old road to left for ½ mile.

AGATE GEODES: SE of Clifton on Hwy 75 and 4 miles up cemetery road in Wards Canyon.

S on Hwy 75, Mule Creek road leads E to Davis Ranch road, which is first road to right past tank in canyon, to dig for agate nodules.

OBSIDIAN NODULES: Continue on to state line on Mule Creek road; nodules lie scattered on hillsides.

FIRE AGATE, CARNELIAN: About 15 miles S of Clifton on Hwy 75 in the Apache Creek area E of highway. (Note: Many of these Clifton areas lie on rough roads and are on private property. Permission should be obtained to collect.)

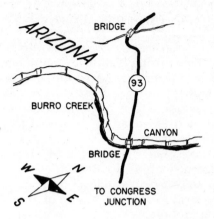

- *Colorado City, Coconino County* PETRIFIED WOOD: S to Pipe Springs National Monument to collect on the Arizona strip.
- *Congress, Yavapai County* * PINK AGATE: Under bridge of Burro Creek which lies 47 miles NW on Hwy 93.

   BLUE AGATE, JASPER: In canyon above bridge. In lava outcrop along highway E of bridge.

   PASTEL ROCK: NW of Burro Creek bridge is sign to Bogle ranch. Go 12 miles E to collect.

   PURPLE AGATE: A few miles NE of crossing of Signal Road at Burro Creek is a deposit of purple agate in white tufa.

   OBSIDIAN NODULES, OBSIDIAN, BANDED AGATE: N of bridge 5½ miles and beyond another bridge a lava and a limestone ridge meet, forming a collecting area.

   QUARTZ CRYSTALS: Found on Gypsy ranch, reached by taking Hwy 93 N to ranch sign and turning N 2 miles to diggings along road.
- *Courtland, Cochise County* TURQUOISE: At Turquoise Ridge ¾ mile NW.
- *Dragoon, Cochise County* CHALCEDONY, CHRYSOCOLLA: At Arizona Mines, 3 miles N.
- *Duncan, Greenlee County* FIRE AGATE, CHALCEDONY ROSES: SE 26 miles on Hwy 70, then take road W for 20 miles to Brister Willow Springs ranch. Follow dirt road at last cattle guard before ranch and go 3 miles to collect.
- *Florence Junction, Pinal County* CARNELIAN, CHALCEDONY ROSES: Take blacktop road W of town, go N and W for 5 miles, then N on faint road past corral.

- *Fort Defiance, Apache County* PYROPE GARNET, PERIDOT. (See Buell Park under New Mexico.)
- *Fredonia, Coconino County* PETRIFIED WOOD, AGATE: To SW in area of Pipe Spring National Monument.
- *Ganado, Apache County* PETRIFIED WOOD: At Nazlini Canyon, N of Ganado.
- *Gila Bend, Maricopa County* OBSIDIAN: Go 10½ miles S on Hwy 85, then left 36 miles on jeep road to Javelina camp to NW at base of mesa.

    GEODES IN WASH: NE at base of mesa. (Get permission from Lynn Cool in Gila Bend.)

    GEODE, AGATE: Go 24 miles S on Hwy 85, then 7 miles E on jeep road to area on W side of Hat Mountain to N in Sauceda Mountains.

    AGATE, BANDED: Go 14 miles W on U.S. 80, N on dirt road 5 miles, then NW 4 miles around red butte, where material is loose on ground.
- *Gleeson, Cochise County* TURQUOISE: E to graded road N to Courtland, then 2 miles N to dim road W around ridge.
- *Globe, Gila County* CHALCEDONY, MOSS AGATE, PINK JASPER: Go SE on Hwy 70 7 miles and take road to Coolidge Dam. Take winding road in front of dam to bridge and gravel pits for agate.

    Search in hills along big bend in river and below for agate and jasper.

    YELLOW AND BROWN ANDRADITE GARNET: Take dirt road S 10 miles E of dam to Stanley Butte, then go 1½ miles S to shack for garnets in vugs in gneiss.

    SERPENTINE, GOLDEN AND GREEN: On mine dumps at Apache town 35 miles NE on Hwy 77. Go W to the Chrysotile mine, then N to turnoff to the Phillips and other mines in the Salt River canyon.

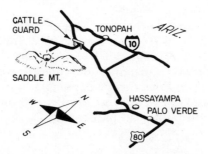

PERIDOT: In basalt and stream gravels S on Hwy 70.
E on dirt road to Peridot and Tolkai (on San Carlos Indian Reservation; ask permission).

VARIEGATED JASPER: W to Hwy 88, then 21 miles to Young Road, then N 15 miles to windmill, E to dry wash.

•*Hassayampa, Maricopa County* * WHITE CHALCEDONY: Take Int. 10 to Tonopah exit, then go 3 miles S and W 5 miles to turnoff at a cattle guard onto a dirt road, then S and W 1⁴/₅ miles to a faint road S across flats to base of Saddle Mountain. White and pink chalcedony mixed with brown is found in rhyolite, and quartz crystals, and chalcedony roses.

FIRE AGATE: Is found in a cliff high on E side of the saddle between peaks of mountain, and some in the fan below peak.

CHALCEDONY GEODES: S 8 miles on Gillespie Dam Road, then 21 miles W to Fourth of July Peak. Search in debris on S side of pass.

•*Holbrook, Navajo County* PETRIFIED WOOD: In draws and banks all around Petrified Forest National Park (no collecting in park).
Two fee places to collect are at Dobell diggings, 19 miles from Holbrook on Hwy 180 E, and at Greer's Milky ranch. It is SE 7 miles on Hwy 180 past the National Park entrance to sign indicating ranch road.

• *House Rock, Coconino County* PETRIFIED WOOD: Along Hwy 89 to E to Marble Canyon.

• *Hyatts Camp, Maricopa County* LAZULITE: N 1¼ miles on Phoenix-Cavecreek Road.

• *Jerome, Yavapai County* PINK AGATE: N 9 miles on Perkinsville Road, deposit in place to left of road.

• *Kingman, Mohave County* TURQUOISE: In porphyry cutting schists, 15 miles NW at Ithaca Peak in Cerbat Mountains.

AMETHYST: NE of Boulder Spring, near McConnico 4 miles SW on U.S. 66.

• *Lees Ferry, Coconino County* PETRIFIED WOOD: In Paria and Colorado Rivers.

• *Mayer, Yavapai County* BROWN AND VARIEGATED ONYX: NE of town across Big Bug Creek and to E on Hwy 69.

• *Mesa, Maricopa County* CHALCEDONY ROSES: Go 25 miles on Bush Hwy, then right on Stewart Mountain Lake Road 4 miles and turn left toward lake.

AMETHYST: On Bush Hwy 3 miles farther to Cottonwood Ranch Road and right to end of road, then hike to Four Peaks where amethyst is found.

- *Miami, Mineral County* TURQUOISE: From miners at Castle Dome mine and at Sleeping Beauty mine.
- *Mineral Park, Mineral County* TURQUOISE: SW at Cerebras ranch.
- *Moenkopi, Coconino County* PETRIFIED WOOD: 9 miles NW at Willow Springs.
- *Morristown, Maricopa County* * JASPER, AGATE, QUARTZ CRYSTAL: Go 25 miles NE to Castle Hot Springs (where there is an excellent hotel); in area just above hotel, in creek to S, and in draws off main canyon in which stream flows.

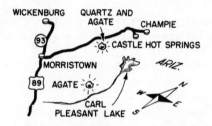

From Castle Hot Springs, Champie Ranch is reached by road N. Here, agate nodules may be collected for a fee. (Area is in rugged Bradshaw Mountains.)

New River, Maricopa County RED JASPER: S in Skunk Creek. BLACK AND RED JASPER: In New River.

- *Oatman, Mohave County* * AGATE AND NODULES: Take Kingman road NE for 5²/₅ miles to curve in Meadow Creek Canyon; some on slopes above canyon, but best material, including chalcedony roses, agate and sard, is just below Hwy at curve and to N of Hwy on buttes and ravines.

FIRE AGATE: Can be collected at Sitgreaves Pass at Ed's Camp (fee).

16 miles to NW at bend in Colorado River near Bullhead City, agate is found as float over a wide area.

- *Parker, Yuma County* CHALCEDONY: Loose on ground along Santa Fe right-of-way E of town.
- *Paulden, Yavapai County* DENDRITIC AGATE: W 3 miles along road.
- *Payson, Gila County* QUARTZ CRYSTALS: Kohl's Ranch road, take left fork for 24 miles to Diamond Point for crystals in sandstone, loose in washes.

VEIN AGATE: Road W past new part of town and left to fork of North Peak and Cypress thicket roads for agate in the area between the roads.

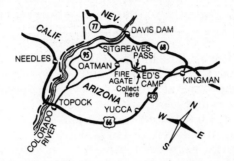

•*Perkinsville, Yavapai County* PINK AGATE: S 5 miles on road to Jerome, collect in low hill that road cuts through.

•*Phoenix, Maricopa County* AGATE, ONYX: N 1 mile to Cavecreek road and 5 miles E to old house and Maricopa agate bed.

RED JASPER: Take Int. 17 N to Carefree road, go E 12 miles to Black Mountain ranch sign to collect opposite sign on S side of road.

AGATE: NW 35 miles NW to Agua Fria river, collect in hills across river to W of New River station.

•*Prescott, Yavapai County* RED JASPER: N on Alt. 89 to collect just N of Granite Dells.

•*Quartzsite, Yuma County* MOSS, PLUME JASPER: E 17 miles on Hwy 60 in area S of road.

QUARTZ CRYSTALS: S 9 miles on Hwy 95, then E 5½ miles to fork, and N ¼ mile to celebrated Crystal Hill area. Crystals, many containing chlorite inclusions, are dug from beds N and S of hill and in hills E of Crystal Hill, and loose on flats.

CHALCEDONY ROSES: From Crystal Hill take pipeline service road 12 miles around deep gully where pipeline is exposed, walk ½ mile S to collect.

Also 27 miles S on Hwy 95 and dig in alluvial fan E of road.

FIRE AGATE: Go 19 miles S on Hwy 95 to Kofa mine sign, then E 6 miles to road S 5 miles and then W 2 miles.

GRAY AND PINK OPAL: Go 22 miles S on Hwy 95 to Cibola Road, then W 4½ miles and S a short distance to Opalite Hill.

LAZULITE: Take old highway W for 2 miles, then dirt road S to a bend to right into trees. Find poor road left under phone wires; go to last low hill, turn left over saddle, and collect in trenches in basin. There is pyrophyllite here, too.

- *Safford, Graham County* GREEN MOSS AGATE, RED AGATE, OB-
SIDIAN NODULES: Take Hwy 70 to Hwy 666, continue on
Hwy 666 7 miles to faint road NW to chalcedony field
and fire agate field NE of it (fee).

  FIRE AGATE: Return to Hwy 666, go 3 miles and turn N
through gate at Milepost 141½ over cattle guard for 1⅔
miles N and E of parking place.

  WHITE CHALCEDONY ROSES, RED AGATE: Are found in
draws in hills NW of Hwy 666.

  NODULES, PALM ROOT, MOSS AGATE, RED AGATE: Continue
on Hwy 666 toward Thumb Butte; collect where road
passes hill.

  OBSIDIAN NODULES: Scattered over hills.

  AGATE, PETRIFIED WOOD, BONE: Take U.S. 70 3½ miles
past U.S. 666 intersection and S to 111 ranch. Collect on
hillsides a mile S.

- *St. Johns, Apache County* MOSS AGATE: In gravels to S.

  AGATE, JASPER: 11 miles S on Hwy 260 at right of highway in blue sandstone.

  AGATE: N 5 miles on Hwy 666; collect on both sides of
road in weathered hills.

- *Salome, Yuma County* MOSS AGATE, CARNELIAN: To S in Eagle
Tail Mountains.

  CHRYSOCOLLA: SE 10½ miles at Socorro mine.

- *Show Low, Navajo County* RED JASPER: Along Mogollon Rim
road 47 miles W.

- *Superior, Pinal County* CHALCEDONY ROSES: Go W on Hwy
60 to Florence Junction, then 2 miles on old highway
to bridge, turn onto dirt road and follow under power
line to hills.

  OBSIDIAN NODULES: Roads W of Superior and S of Hwy
60 cut through perlite beds containing Apache tears.
There are fee places to collect, such as Mike Guzeman's.

- *Topock, Mohave County* AGATE, BLACK JASPER: Go 5 miles N on
road to Oatman, pebbles loose on ground.

- *Tucson, Pima County* BANDED AND MOSS AGATE: Take Int 10 N
to Cortaro, left across gas pipeline to Wade Road, then
right to desert roads to Little Peak area, and hike to Safford Peak.

  RHYOLITE (WONDERSTONE): Near Tumamoc Hill and Sen-
tinel Hill 2 miles SW.

- *Wickenburg, Maricopa County* CHALCEDONY ROSES, OBSIDIAN
NODULES: Take Hwy 60 W to Aguila, then N on dirt road
toward E end of Harcuvar Mountains to gem field.

QUARTZ CRYSTALS, AMETHYST: Take Constellation Road NE 6 miles to cattle guard, then left ½ mile to amethyst in hills. Return to cattle guard, go S ½ mile to collect quartz crystals.

Continue on Constellation Road 4 more miles to top of ridge for quartz crystals.

QUARTZ: Take Hwy 60 22½ miles to sign for Date Creek ranch, then road to ranch house 3½ miles. Drive 2 miles to tracks right to Campfire Circle, park and go in any direction to collect.

JASPER: NW on Hwy 93 to Santa Maria river area.

AGATE: NW 7 miles on Hwy 93 to intersection with Hwy 71, then 4 miles NW on Hwy 71 to Alamo road. Take it 8 miles to fork, take right fork to a T, take dirt road right 7 miles to Anderson mine. Collect near mine office.

•*Woodruff, Navajo County* PETRIFIED WOOD: As chips and limb sections in area.

•*Young, Gila County* SERPENTINE (verd antique): 10 miles SE between Cherry and Canyon Creeks.

•*Yuma, Yuma County* * AGATE: F on Hwy 80 to Ligurta, then 4 miles further, go NW on dirt road and then N and E along the Muggins Mountains for 3 miles. Drive N into the foothills toward the highest peak 3¾ miles to edge of agate field, which extends a mile to the N.

PALM ROOT SPECIMENS, JASPER, AGATE: The collecting area NE of Yuma lies in a military reservation; permission to collect should be obtained from the Yuma Test Station. The road to Martinez Lake in the Colorado river turns W from Hwy 95 at a windmill and a branch road leads to the Test Station. In the large area from a mile S of the Yuma Test Station to 10 miles N and from Hwy 95 to the Colorado river, palm root, jasper, and agate can be collected lying loose on the ground.

119

Arkansas

Southern and eastern Arkansas are sandy river delta and coastal plain, while the northern and western areas are rugged plateaus shared with Missouri and Oklahoma. Most of the plateaus are formed of hard sedimentary rocks, but a small area including Hot Springs and Pike counties is underlaid by crystalline rocks. This is the quartz crystal and diamond producing region.

- *Hot Springs, Garland County* QUARTZ: The area N and W of Hot Springs is famous for its crystal quartz groups found in the Ouachita Mountains, notably at Jessieville, 10 miles N on Hwy 7 at the Coleman Crystal mine (fee); at Mt. Ida, 30 miles W on Hwy 270; at the Ocus Stanley mines 10 miles SE of Mt. Ida; at High Point and Fisher Mountain (fee); and at Lewis Crystal mine (fee), Crystal Springs, 20 miles W on Hwy 270, at Crystal Mountain. Other locations are at Glenwood and Mountain Valley.
- *Malvern, Hot Springs County* NOVACULITE: On dumps along Rock Island railroad tracks near Butterfield station and in talus near Remmel Dam. Also on E side of Hot Springs mountain on bypass around Hot Springs.
  SODALITE: In old Diamond Joe syenite quarry on S side of Magnet Cove.
- *Mountain Pine, Garland County* VARISCITE: At Dug Hill, near Cedar Glades.
- *Murfreesboro, Pike County* DIAMOND: In peridotite. (See chapter on diamonds for details.) Now a state park.
- *Yellville, Marion County* SMITHSONITE: Take Hwy 14 S, turn E to Rush, collect in old mine dumps. There is agate on the mountain and in Clabber Creek. See Fred Durst at Rush as guide.

California

California's heart is a great central valley fringed with high mountains. Along the ocean rises the broken Coast range, and on the east towers the Sierra Nevada. These meet in northern California in a welter of glacier-cut valleys dominated by majestic Mt. Shasta and linked to Oregon's Cascade Mountains. In the south the Coast range and the Sierra Nevada swing together below Bakersfield to enclose the valley at that end. Below this point California's arid lands belong to the Great Basin and, like Nevada, are cut by short ranges. The Sierras tower in sheer cliffs above the narrow strip at their base, formed by the sinking of this part of the Great Basin. Within a few miles are the highest point in the continental United States, Mt. Whitney, and the lowest, Death Valley.

In the north, volcanic activity is still evident, and the abundant lavas yield obsidian to the gem hunter, while elsewhere metamorphism has created jade and serpentine. In the south, agate materials are plentiful in the arid deserts and eroded mountains, and in the coarse granites of the mountains north of San Diego are treasures of tourmaline, topaz, and beryl.

- *Acton, Los Angeles County* AGATE NODULES: W on Escondido Canyon road at Sir'Kegian gem beds, with amethyst and bloodstone.
- *Adin, Modoc County* RYOLITE (WONDERSTONE): 12 miles S on Hwy 139, then left 4 miles.
- *Alturas, Modoc County* OBSIDIAN NODULES: N 15 miles and one mile E of Davis Creek in gravel pits.
- *Amargosa, Inyo County* AGATE: S almost 8 miles on Hwy 127 to Deadman Pass Road. Collect float agate along road.

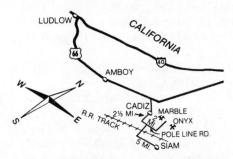

- *Amboy, San Bernardino County* * ONYX, MARBLE: E to Chambless on Hwy 66, S to phone line for 2⅓ miles and E for 2 miles, to collect in quarry to N.
- *Applegate, Placer County* SILICIFIED ASBESTOS: At Best Bet Mine. (Fee; see Mr. Moore at Iowa Hill.)
- *Arroyo Grande, San Luis Obispo County* TRAVERTINE: Take road N to Routzahn County Park, then E along creek almost 10 miles; then hike on S side of creek to veins of travertine in hills.
- *Auburn, Nevada County* AGATE: At Pilot Hill.
- *Avenal, Kings County* PETRIFIED WOOD: Near airport.
- *Bagby, Mariposa County* JADE: N-NE 2½ miles between David Gulch and Flyaway Gulch.
- *Bagdad, San Bernardino County* OBSIDIAN: Go ½ mile E on Hwy 66, take road N across railroad tracks and take left fork to power line, then go left ⅔ mile, right under power line and take rough road to collect in hills to N and W. AGATE: Farther along on same road.

121

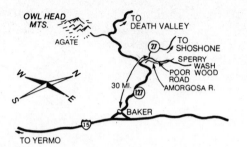

- *Baker, San Bernardino County* * RED AND YELLOW AGATE, PET-RIFIED WOOD: Take Hwy 127 N to Milepost 174, turn E 10½ miles, passing Sperry Station ruins and through canyon into open space at Sperry Wash. (Location closed to collecting at present by U.S. Bureau of Land Management.)

  SAGENITIC AGATE, JASPER: Take Hwy 127 N to Salt Spring, go left on Furnace Creek Road 13 miles, and left 13 miles and N 3 miles into Owlhead Mountains collecting area.

  OPALITE, JASPER: Go 22 miles W on Int. 15, then S to Afton Canyon.

- *Bakersfield, Kern County* ROSE QUARTZ, AGATE: NE on Hwy 178, then W to Greenhorn Mountain Park, get permission at park office and collect 1 mile E at Little Acorn mine, and a half mile farther at Huckaby mine. Then go N and E 15½ miles to rose quartz location.

- *Bankhead Springs, San Diego County* RHODONITE: On Hwy 80 go E for 2½ miles to dirt road, and take it N to end.

- *Barstow, San Bernardino County* SAGENITIC AGATE, JASPER: E on Int. 15 to Calico road NW. Take it 1 mile, then NE on Mule Canyon road 1 mile or more to onyx diggings N of road (fee), then on 2 miles and N in Tin Can Alley road more than a mile for moss agate and sagenitic agate. Return to first fork E and go a mile to jasper and agate diggings. Return to Mule Canyon road and go E a mile to dig for palm wood.

  Return to Calico road and go N 1½ miles, then N on Doran drive to the loop drive in Odessa Canyon. At its north extremity a trail goes into Green Hill for sagenitic agate.

  TRAVERTINE: From Central Barstow exit take road to end, then left to Fort Irwin sign and follow signs 15 miles N to power line to dig for travertine.

122

CHALCEDONY NODULES: From Tiefort village in the Fort Irwin reservation Goldstone road goes W 2½ miles. Collect there.

JASPER: Take Fort Irwin road 5 miles N, then Superior Valley road 2 miles N to faint road ¼ mile E. Collect in wash and on hillsides.

JASPER, AGATE: E 2½ miles on Int. 15, then S on dirt road ⅓ mile.

PETRIFIED WOOD: E on Int 15 35 miles, turn off at Afton exit, go back a mile on N side of freeway, then N nearly 5½ miles to collect on hills and in washes.

• *Berkeley, Alameda County* IRIS AGATE NODULES: Take MacArthur Freeway to Warren Freeway, turn off at Walnut Creek, go through Caldecott Tunnel to Fish Ranch road. Park by microwave station, climb wall and go down slope to collect.

• *Bigpine, Inyo County* QUARTZ CRYSTALS: Go E through Westgard Pass, and continue 12 miles through Deep Spring Valley to cattle guard, turn left along fence and collect in rocky hills.

TURQUOISE: To E in Last Chance range almost on Nevada line. (See Roy Cummings, Big Pine.)

• *Bishop, Inyo County* OBSIDIAN: At Montgomery Pass; take Hwy 6 for 2 miles past Nevada line, then left through wash and take trail to diggings.

Return to Hwy 6 and turn right to collect at Queen Mountain.

PETRIFIED WOOD: Continue on Hwy 6 through Montgomery Pass to intersection with Hwy 10, turn right and collect in hills S of Hwy 6.

QUARTZ: In washes to W near Mt. Tom in Buttermilk area. Also N on Hwy 6 to Laws, then E into Silver Canyon in White Mountains.

• *Blythe, Riverside County* PYROLUSITE, PSILOMELANE: Take Lovelin Blvd. 21 miles NW to Inca Siding, cross tracks, turn left ¼ mile and then right for 9 miles to Arlington Mine.

AGATE: In gravel S of Hwy 60 about 8 miles W of Blythe.

• *Bodie, Mono County* LAZULITE: Mile W of Green Lake in Green Creek Canyon.

• *Bridgeport, Mono County* QUARTZ: Go N on Hwy 22, take Sweetwater road halfway to Wellington, turn right into canyon and just before reaching ranch turn left ¾ mile to collect.

• *Camarillo, Ventura County* SAGENITIC AGATE: E 3 miles on Hwy 101, turn N to county park and hike mile up private road to diggings.

• *Carlsbad, San Diego County* AGATE, JASPER PEBBLES: On beaches S to Cardiff-on-the-Sea.

• *Cedarville, Modoc County* AGATE, OPALIZED WOOD: One mile S and 4 miles W in Deep Creek area.

AGATE, PETRIFIED WOOD: W 4 miles on Hwy 299, then S to Cedar Creek. Also S 35 miles on Hwy 81 to Duck lake, then 2 miles through pass to dirt road W to Tuledad canyon. Go 2 miles more to turnoff N to steep hill and dig in ravine for agate. Petrified wood is 5 miles farther on the same road.

• *Chilcoot, Plumas County* SMOKY AND SCEPTER QUARTZ: Take Hwy 70 to U.S. 395, N on U.S. 395 7 miles and E 1½ miles to Crystal Peak (fee).

ORCHID STAR QUARTZ: Take road N for 5 miles, turn right and go NE for 8 miles; turn right and go ⅓ mile, then left less than a half mile and turn right. Park and walk uphill to left to collect.

• *Clio, Plumas County* FIRE OPAL: In ironstone 3½ miles N at Laura quartz mine.

IDOCRASE (CALIFORNITE): E 7 miles.

• *Coalinga, Fresno County* * JASPER, PETRIFIED WOOD: S on Merced road to Lost Hills road to Jacolitos Canyon and continue W up canyon; look in creek bed. Chert and fossil coral are also found there.

JADEITE: Take Hwy 198 W to Hwy 25, then NW to Bitterwater and on E to Hernandez. Follow Clear Creek

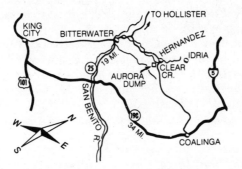

road 3 miles to jade mine sign. The dark green jadeite, streaked with light green and white, is found as boulders in the creek and lenses in the walls of the canyon. It is also found as far south as Santa Rita peak.

SERPENTINE: On the Aurora Dump is cutting quality serpentine. (Get permission at the Idria store.)

•*Cobb, Lake County* MASSIVE QUARTZ: Hunt in road cuts on Hwy 291 and at Manke ranch, NW of Cobb.

•*Coulterville, Mariposa County* MARIPOSITE: Take Hwy 132 W for less than a mile, collect on N side of road.

NEPHRITE JADE: At Jade King mine 2 miles S (fee) and at nearby Ming, Green Dragon and Four Jacks claims.

•*Covelo, Mendocino County* NEPHRITE JADE, JADEITE: NE 15 miles on top of Leech Lake Mountain.

Also in N fork of Eel River, where road N to Mina crosses river, at Dos Rios to SW and at Dryden ranch 6 miles E reached by Mendocino Pass road (fee).

•*Davis Creek, Modoc County* OBSIDIAN: N on Hwy 395 4 miles, then take right fork 4½ miles and E 3 miles across creek to Rainbow mine (fee). Or continue N instead of turning off, go 2 miles and collect in hills. Obsidian is also found E on the Lake City road 5 miles to second creek crossing, then hike parallel with and E of road ¼ mile to collect at base of hills. Beyond here toward Lake City 2½ miles is golden sheen obsidian in creek.

•*Desert Center, Riverside County* AGATE NODULES, SEAM AGATE: E 22 miles on Int. 10, then S on Army Road 6 miles to right fork, continue 9 miles to fork, and left to Chuckawalla Spring. Collect geodes in hills below camping place and in Augustine Pass area to W, and seam agate SE at Graham Pass.

Take Int. 10 E for 21 miles, cross Bridge 23, turn S past

125

gravel pits for 2½ miles. Collect float agate on desert and along W side of road.

- *Earp, San Bernardino County* JASPER, AGATE: Take Wall Canyon road N for 1 mile, collect on E side of road.
  Take boat S on Colorado River to collect agate and jasper pebbles on beaches and in cliffs along river, especially where Vida Wash empties into it.
- *El Centro, Imperial County* PETRIFIED WOOD, JASPER, AGATE: On Int. 8, 48 miles E, take dirt road N to old army camp to collect NE and S of camp.
- *Escondido, San Diego County* TOURMALINE, BERYL: At Mack mine. Take Hwy 6 N 16½ miles through Valley Center and Rincon reservation to red house, then right to mine.
- *Etna, Siskiyou County* MARBLE: Take Sawyers Bar road for 3 miles into mountains.
- *Eureka, Humboldt County* NEPHRITE JADE, JADEITE PEBBLES: On beaches from Patrick Point State Park, 28 miles N on U.S. 101, to Dry Lagoon, 8½ miles farther N. Also 40 miles E in Trinity River.
- *Exeter, Tulare County* ROSE QUARTZ: At Gasenberger ranch 8 miles SE.
- *Fairfield, Solano County* BANDED ALABASTER: E for 5 miles, at Tolenas quarry (fee).
- *Fallbrook, San Diego County* QUARTZ CRYSTALS: Go 2 miles NE of De Luz school, to dig in granite ledge 700 feet S of Murrieta-Fallbrook road.
- *Fresno, Fresno County* AGATE, JASPER: In Panoche Pass; take Hwy 180 W to road through Panoche hills.
- *Furnace Creek, Inyo County* TRAVERTINE: Take Hwy 190 N for 13¾ miles to abandoned quarry W of road; 1 mile E of Death Valley Monument boundary. Also collect in ravine near road ½ mile farther N. No collecting in monument.
- *Georgetown, El Dorado County* WHITE GROSSULARITE GARNET, PREHNITE, VESUVIANITE (CALIFORNITE): 2½ miles SE in serpentine along Traverse Creek.
  VESUVIANITE: 4 miles S at Stifle claim on Meadow Brook road off Hwy 193 (fee).
- *Glamis, Imperial County* NODULES, PETRIFIED WOOD: Take Hwy 78 NE 12 miles, then S 4½ miles on road to Ogilby, and ⅓ mile E for palm wood. Continue S 6½ miles and go E under power line 8 miles to Indian Pass for petrified wood and dumortierite. Return to Ogilby road and go 4 miles S to Gold Rock Ranch for petrified palm wood, and

5 miles farther S is road E to Bluebird mine for palm wood, kyanite, and dumortierite.

N of the intersection of the Ogilby road and Hwy 78 lies the Midway Well area. Take Hwy 78 N for 6½ miles and collect in the area of Buzzard Peak about a mile E of the road.

•*Goffs, San Bernardino County* GREEN OPAL, PETRIFIED WOOD: Take Lanfair Lane, a dirt road, 11 miles NW to Hackberry wash.

•*Goleta, Santa Barbara County* PETRIFIED WOOD, JASPER: NW on Hwy 154, then take road E on S side of Lake Cachuma, collect in hills SE of lake.

•*Grass Valley, Nevada County* PETRIFIED WOOD: E on Hwy 174 to U-Bet sign, then N 5½ miles to old house where road swings left, then go 1 mile more and N to park. Dig in area N and W of parking area.

•*Halloran Spring, San Bernardino County* TURQUOISE: In area about 10 miles N and W of Halloran Spring in dumps of old claims in the Turquoise Mountains, including Toltec.

•*Happy Camp, Siskiyou County* RHODONITE: Go 9 miles N to Mt. Thompson, collect on E side between Indian and Thompson creeks (fee).

VESUVIANITE: Take road N and then left across bridge where S fork of creek joins Indian Creek; continue mile across second bridge to ranch house, where road ends. (Get permission; hike up creek a mile.)

NEPHRITE JADE: To N at Chan jade claim on S fork of Indian Creek.

Also with serpentine 5 miles E on Hwy 96, then N past dump.

•*Hemet, Riverside County* SMOKY, ROSE QUARTZ: At Juan Diego flat; take Hwy 74 E 4 miles, then S 17 miles and turn left.

SMOKY QUARTZ, PINK BERYL: At the Williamson mine just S of Juan Diego flat at Coahuila Mountain.

•*Hinkley, San Bernardino County* * CHALCEDONY NODULES, GREEN OPAL: At Opal Mountain and Black Canyon. Go 6½ miles N and take right fork 4 miles to a left fork, continue on left fork 6½ miles into canyon, dig for nodules on Black Mountain to S; continue to summit, collect cherry opal at Opal Mountain to NE; continue left and then right for almost three miles to small white hill in Black Canyon and dig green dendritic opal.

JASPER, NODULES: N 9 miles on Hinkley road, then W a mile and N 2 miles and then 3 miles W, stay left of road 4¾ miles into valley.

•*Hornbrook, Siskiyou County* MOSS AND DENDRITIC AGATE: E 11 miles on road along Klamath River at Jenney Creek.
AGATE, PETRIFIED WOOD: N of river as far as Copco and into Oregon.

•*Independence, Inyo County* QUARTZ CRYSTALS: Take Hwy 395 N for 5⅓ miles, then new road N for 3 miles to Colosseum Road. Take that E for 1 mile, then keep generally E under power line and across old railroad for 5 miles. Go SE past national-forest sign 1½ miles, to dig at Crystal Ridge.
OPALITE: E on Mazouka Canyon road to collect at old mine on left side of canyon.

•*Indio, Riverside County* * JADE, VESUVIANITE, AGATE: Int. 10 E for 26 miles, take turnoff into Joshua Tree National Monument NE for 26 miles, then E 8½ miles to Storm Jade mine.

•*Inyokern, Kern County* OPALITE, RAINBOW JASPER: S on road, and as it curves toward U.S. 395, cut off S 5 miles on power line road, take road W 2 miles to collect.

•*Johannesburg, Kern County* * AGATE, BLOODSTONE: Take road N toward Westend, but take right fork skirting S end of Searles Lake 19 miles to Wingate Pass for vein agate. This road goes through a naval ordnance testing station, and special permission will be required to use it. To S is Brown Mountain, and 4 miles SE is bloodstone.
BLACK MOSS AGATE: At Sheep Spring; go N on U.S. 395 for 21½ miles, turn S where road crosses railroad tracks for 8 miles and E to Sheep Spring to collect in hills E of spring.

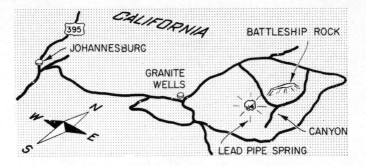

BLUE CHALCEDONY AND NODULES: Go E from Johannesburg on a fair road to Granite Well, then NE nearly 12 miles to road turning S that is beyond a narrow ridge visible to the S known as Battleship Rock. Curve around rock to a canyon and take a branch road into it. Leave car and find specimens in volcanic ash.

FIRE OPAL, NODULES: Farther up and higher.

SAGENITE AGATE: In nodules, lies farther up the canyon.

FIRE OPAL, BLUE AGATE NODULES: Back at canyon mouth, take road on W a short distance and turn S again to Lead Pipe Spring, where gems can be dug from red rhyolite, particularly to the SE.

JASPER, AGATE: Back near the road.

AGATE, OPAL: Back to road, next turn S goes to diggings. The road curves N shortly farther W and goes back to road to Granite Wells. (Note: Area is Naval Ordnance Testing Station. For permission to collect, write Commandant, N.O.T.S., China Lake, California 93555.)

PLUME AGATE: Take Steam Wells road E 7 miles to Brown's ranch, then 4⅔ miles N on dirt track to dry lake, keep left here less than 1 mile to collecting area.

•*Kane Spring, Imperial County* PETRIFIED WOOD: In clay hills 15 miles W.

•*Kramer, San Bernardino County* * PETRIFIED WOOD, PALM WOOD: From Kramer Junction, go 17 miles W on Hwy 58, then N past some new houses and through gap in reddish hills, keeping left at fork to large dry lake which contains best petrified wood, including palm wood.

BLOODSTONE, AGATE, PETRIFIED WOOD: Go on and keep left toward Castle Butte, where bloodstone, agate, and petrified wood can be dug on east slope and in area just

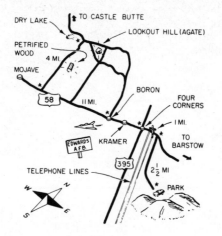

NE of butte. Right fork before reaching dry lake leads to small dry lake and hills containing wood.

AGATE: E 1½ miles from the intersection of Hwys 395 and 58 near Kramer lie the Kramer Hills, reached by following a road that parallels telephone lines about 3 miles S of Hwy 58, turning off to the SE into the hills to park. Collect agate around parking area and to W of phone lines.

BORON WOOD: 11 miles W of Boron a road N leads to a dry lake where the noted Boron wood is dug from the soil. Some is also found on dry lake areas E of the road.

AGATE, NODULES: To the SE of this region lies Lookout Hill, high spot in the area, where agate and nodules are found.

• *LaGrange, Stanislaus County* RHODONITE: At Sturtevant ranch, 14 miles NE on Coulterville Road (fee).

• *Lake City, Modoc County* AGATE, PETRIFIED WOOD: In stream gravels from Fort Bidwell to Cedarville.

• *Lakeport, Lake County* JASPER: S on Hwy 29 to fork above Kelseyville, then take Big Valley road SW and hunt around reservoir.

OBSIDIAN: Along Bottle Rock road, 2½ miles E of Kelseyville off Hwy 29, and farther E near Soda Bay and Red Hill roads, as well as in Cold Creek.

QUARTZ (Lake County diamonds): From Hwy 29, go E to Lower Lake and take roads W and S toward Siegler Springs for 5 miles to collecting area between Perini Hill and Hoborg's Airport.

- *Lakeside, San Diego County* GARNET, EPIDOTE: Take Wiliat Canyon road NE 11 miles to Wright Canyon, go E for 1⅔ miles, then left to dig at old mine.
- *Lang, Los Angeles County* HOWLITE: At U.S. Borax and Chemical company mine.
- *Laporte, Plumas County* QUARTZ CRYSTALS: NE 22 miles at Nelson Point.
- *Lemoncove, Tulare County* ROSE QUARTZ: N 5 miles on ridge W of Dry Creek.

  RHODONITE: N 3 miles on N side of ravine which is ⅓ mile NE of Kaweah river and mile E of Ward ranch.
- *Lindsay, Tulare County* CHRYSOPRASE, GREEN OPAL: SE one mile in pits on N end of Venice Hill.

  VESUVIANITE: On ridge S of Lewis creek.
- *Little Lake, Inyo County* OBSIDIAN: Go N for 2½ miles on Hwy 395 to cinder road, E into naval test station, and then 3 miles E into hills. (Open weekends; get pass at China Lake office.)
- *Littlerock, Los Angeles County* AGATE: In Agate Valley, 2 miles W of Little Rock Dam and 3 miles S near quarry.
- *Livermore, Alameda County* CITRINE QUARTZ: At Newman mine to SE near Cedar Mountain.
- *Lodoga, Colusa County* JASPER; JADE: In gravels of Stonyford creek.
- *Lompoc, Santa Barbara County* PETRIFIED WHALEBONE: At Jalama Beach, 18 miles S, with travertine.
- *Lone Pine, Inyo County* AMAZONITE: From N edge of city, turn right on road past railroad station, cross Owens River and go almost to second railroad tracks, turn S ½ mile to Kern Knob, a granite mass, and collect from seams in canyons between it and the Inyo Mountains.

  OBSIDIAN: Take U.S. 395 S 12 miles, go E 1 mile and then 2 miles S and E to road parallel to U.S. 395 to collect nodules.
- *Los Angeles, Los Angeles County* HOWLITE: Take Golden State Freeway NW to Palmdale cutoff (Hwy 14), go on old Sierra Hwy NE to Solemint Junction. Continue NE 6 miles to Davenport Road, then E for 1½ miles and N to dumps of Sterling Mine in Tick Canyon.

  AGATE: In beach gravels at El Segundo, Hermosa, and Redondo beaches.
- *Los Banos, Merced County* PLUME AGATE: S 11½ miles to Mercy Springs exit, follow power line uphill W of freeway to intersection with main power line on top of hill.

- *Los Olivos, Santa Barbara County* SAGENITIC AGATE, JASPER: Take Figueroa Mountain road 8 miles past end of pavement, then trail down hill to collect along creek.
- *Lower Lake, Lake County* CHRYSOPRASE: E 21 miles to Knoxville and S 3½ miles at Lone Pine chromite mine.
  QUARTZ ONYX: N 2 miles of Knoxville at Manhattan mine (fee).
- *Lucerne, Lake County* GREEN TRAVERTINE: At Hitchcock ranch (fee).
- *Lucerne Valley, San Bernardino County* SERPENTINE (VERD ANTIQUE): N on Barstow Road 12 miles and W 5⅓ miles to faint road, then S 3 miles into Sidewinder Mountains.
  RHYOLITE: Go 5 miles E on Old Woman Springs Road to Camp Rock Road, then 14 miles N and NE, turning NW into East Ord mountain area near old gold mine.
- *Lucia, Monterey County* NEPHRITE JADE, RHODONITE: Farthest N location is at Limekiln Creek Beach, where jade pebbles are found with rhodonite (fee).
  NEPHRITE JADE: To S on Hwy 1 at Plaskett Creek and just S of it at Jade Cove, and next cove S is another spot. Look for a new botryoidal jade and a reddish jade.
  Farther S is Willow Creek Beach and Salmon Creek even farther S. Some jade is in place and some has been recovered by skin diving. (This is on a military reservation and blasting and camping are prohibited.)

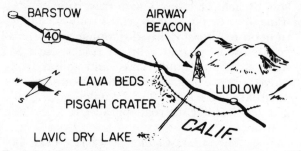

- *Ludlow, San Bernardino County* * Int. 40 exits are at Newberry, Hector, and Ludlow. Use them to reach old Hwy 66.
  JASPER: Take Crucero Road N 7½ miles, take a jeep road SW for 12 miles into Cady Mountains. Collect in basin between Flat Top Peak and Mt. Afton, and on Mt. Afton and canyon to N.
  JASPER, AGATE: Take any road N of Int. 40 between Ludlow and the airplane beacon to W and collect in hills and canyons of Cady Mountains 2 or 3 miles N of hwy.

CARNELIAN: Go 9 miles W on Int. 40 to old hwy, go S for $^2/_5$ mile, hike in and collect on hill and slopes ½ mile W.

CHALCEDONY ROSES: Go 11 miles E on Hwy 66, take road N 3 miles and collect them along road, or go 4 more miles into hills and collect them there.

PINK CHALCEDONY: SE 12 miles to Siberia along railroad and 3½ miles W to gulch near Ash Hill.

OBSIDIAN: S of Int. 40, for ½ to 1½ miles E.

JASPER, CHALCEDONY: S of Int. 40 and between Milepost 114 and airway beacon 44-18.* Good jasper is also found at Milepost 121.

WIND-POLISHED CHALCEDONY, AGATE PEBBLES: N of Pisgah Crater, embedded in lava-formed bay. Farther W collect just W of where lava flow crosses road.

JASPER, AGATE: Farther E, at Milepost 114, turn from the road S across the railroad at Lavic Station, and on down to Lavic jasper field. (Area S of railroad is under claim.) About 3 miles farther S, the road leads to a dry lake and a military-reservation sign. Turn E here 8 miles on poor road into mountains for agate.

CHALCEDONY ROSES: E on Hwy 66 for 9¼ mile, take old road S for 1⅓ mile, then mine road W to Ash Hill, also look for carnelian and chalcedony with red spots.

• *Mammoth, Mono County* RHODOCHROSITE: Take road to Agnew Meadows camp, then Shadow Lake trail 1 mile to River trail. Go left ½ mile to ridge on left and collect in talus of the ridge.

• *Manix, San Bernardino County* YELLOW JASPER, SEAM AGATE: Take road N almost 9 miles into Spanish canyon, collect there and to right in side canyon.

AGATE, PETRIFIED PALM WOOD: Go E on old Hwy 91, collect on both sides of hwy in dry lake bed.

JASPER, PETRIFIED PALM WOOD: Take Int. 15 W for 11 miles and then road N for 6 miles to Alvord Mountains.

• *Mendota, Madera County* NODULES, PETRIFIED WOOD: Hwy 11 SW for 20 miles to ranch house, then S 3 miles into Panoche Hills. Collect E of road, and then go 3⅓ miles farther for petrified wood.

• *Mesa Grande, San Diego County* BICOLORED TOURMALINE, MORGANITE, AQUAMARINE: World famous locality for pegmatite gem minerals. On Gem Hill, 2¾ miles NW of Mesa Grande, are the Himalaya and San Diego mines.

PINK AND DARK GREEN TOURMALINE, MORGANITE AQUAMARINE, CITRINE QUARTZ: NW of Gem Hill 1½ miles at the

Esmeralda mine. (This mine and those on Gem Hill are privately owned.)

• *Middletown, Lake County* QUARTZ (Lake County Diamonds): To N on road to Lower Lake and SE to area N of Pope Valley.

• *Mojave, Kern County* * PETRIFIED WOOD, AGATE, JASPER: Last Chance Canyon is a favorite collecting place. To reach it take Hwy 14 N through Red Rock Canyon for 21 miles to Cantil store, then 13½ miles N to ruins of Hart's Place. Turn E, pass Holly mine at 5 miles, go mile farther to fork, take right fork to a T, go left into Last Chance Canyon to collect in side canyons and red hills to W. Go back to T, turn S there to camp ground and through it right to a canyon often called the Hidden Forest to dig agate and jasper. There is also some collecting in Red Rock Canyon.

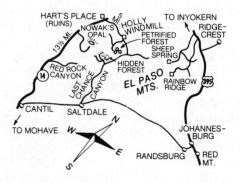

AGATE, JASPER, PETRIFIED PALM WOOD: E on Hwy 58 to Clay Mine Road, N almost to end of pavement (about 3 miles), then W for ¼ mile, and collect along ridge and S of ridge.

OPAL: At Leo Nowak diggings, at sign 7⅔ mi N of Randsburg road turnoff (fee).

PETRIFIED PALM WOOD: E 8 miles on Hwy 58, then S 1½ miles across railroad tracks and 1½ miles to area near butte to collect on flats and ridge.

• *Mokelumne Hill, Calaveras County* QUARTZ CRYSTALS: Take Glencoe Road, turn off on road to ghost town of Jesus Maria, then to bridge and 9½ miles through Jesus Maria, park at turn, take trail to right, down slope and to left into gulch.

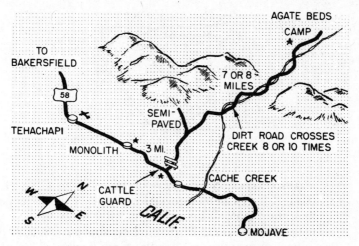

- *Monolith, Kern County* * MOSS AND PLUME AGATE: At Horse Canyon. Go 3 miles E on Hwy 58 to Cache Creek Road and turn N about 9 miles, keeping right. Heavy digging, and there is fee and limit on amount taken.
- *Morgan Hill, Santa Clara County* ORBICULAR JASPER: At Paradise Valley. (fee)

  MOSS AGATE, JASPER: Go NW on Hwy 101 to Cochran Road, then E to parking area near Anderson Lake at dam, and hunt along lake.
- *Moss Beach, San Mateo County* PETRIFIED WHALEBONE: On beach just N of parking area. Beach is 11 miles S of San Francisco.
- *Needles, San Bernardino County* * AGATE, CHALCEDONY ROSES, OPALITE: Hwy 95 S to Lake Havasu road, then 1½ miles farther to Turtle Mountain road. Take it 10½ miles W to Essex road NW, then take Essex road 2 miles and turn S on faint road for 2 miles to collect sagentic agate, and opalite at hill. Return to Essex road, take it NW 2 miles to butte ¼ mile N of road for chalcedony roses and fire agate. S from Essex road near this butte is road that goes ½ mile to place to collect so-called bacon agate.

  AGATE NODULES, JASPER: S on Hwy 95 23 miles to dirt road W.

  CHALCEDONY ROSES, CARNELIAN: Along the above road. Continue 11 miles, then S for chalcedony roses and agate to E and S in washes, and S and W to Mohawk Springs.

135

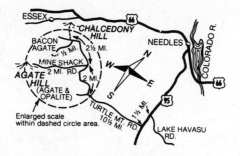

AGATE, JASPER: S on Hwy 95 16 miles to Lake Havasu road E into Chemehuevi Mountains. Take it to power-line, then S along line to dig in hills below wash.

BLUE-GREEN AGATE: In rhyolite on above road. (Get directions and permission, Needles Gem Society, 308 D St.)

JASPER, CHALCEDONY ROSES: Go 39 miles S on Hwy 95, then E at milepost 270 for 2 miles to jasper field SE of knoll. Hike half mile NE across basin into canyon for chalcedony roses.

• *Nevada City, Nevada County* OPALIZED WOOD: Hwy 20 E for 5 miles, then 3 miles N to Scott Flat Lake. Collect along shore.

• *Newberry, San Bernardino County* AGATE NODULES: Use Int. 40 exit, go 2 miles S on Newberry road, keeping right to end of road. Walk ½ mile W into canyon and collect in blue-white ash in walls.

• *Newport Beach, Orange County* PETRIFIED WOOD, PETRIFIED BONE: Turn W on Cherry Street to sea cliffs, take trail to beach near Arch Rock; collect on beach and in ravines.

• *Nipomo, San Luis Obispo County* SAGENITIC AGATE: In bean fields, or at Freddi's ranch (fee).

• *Nuevo, Riverside County* GARNET, STAR QUARTZ: Go 2 miles N and take road E a mile and then S to Mountain View ranch. Also at Southern Pacific silica quarry nearby.

• *Ocotilla, Imperial County* PETRIFIED WOOD: NW on Hwy S2 for 8½ miles to collect in hills nearly on San Diego–Imperial County line.

• *Pala, San Diego County* TOURMALINE, KUNZITE, BERYL: Famous for tourmaline are the Pala Chief mine on Pala Chief Mountain; the Tourmaline King and Tourmaline Queen mines on Tourmaline Queen Mountain. These mines and two on Hiriart Hill, 2 miles NE of Pala, the Senpe and the Vanderburg, are noted for morganite beryl. The Pala Chief, and the Katerina, Vanderburg, and San Pedro on Hiriart Hill are mines noted for kunzite. (Mines are privately owned and closed to collecting).

• *Palmdale, Los Angeles County* AGATE NODULES: Go 5 miles S on Hwy 14, then SE to Little Rock Dam, and take jeep trail 5 miles to Agate Valley.

• *Palo Verde, Imperial County* JASPER, CARNELIAN, FIRE AGATE: S 7 miles on Hwy 78, then W at pole rack ⅔ mile to Palo Verde Pass (fee).

AGATE, PETRIFIED WOOD: 6 miles W of town in old Colorado River terraces.

• *Palos Verdes, Los Angeles County* PETRIFIED WHALEBONE, AGATE: From Fountain square follow Pasco de Mar to bluff, then walk to beach to collect there.

• *Paradise, Butte County* QUARTZ: In pockets in quartz veins in Sawmill Peak. Some of crystals contain inclusions.

• *Petaluma, Sonoma County* NEPHRITE JADE: As lenses and veins in serpentine, SW 5 miles and on E side of Massa Hill on Vonsen ranch.

JASPER, PETRIFIED WOOD: 5 miles N of adobe mission.

• *Pinehurst, Fresno County* QUARTZ: Take Hwy 180 into King's Canyon National Park to Camp Joaquin sign, turn right to campsite at Chimney Rock.

• *Placerville, Eldorado County* NEPHRITE JADE: Take Hwy 49 N for less than a mile, then take road right to S fork of American River. Cross bridge, turn right on dirt road along river for 2 miles, and collect in rock along river and in river.

QUARTZ: After crossing bridge, take Rock Creek road 9½ miles to Mosquito Creek road to Pino Grande.

ROSE QUARTZ: E 18 miles in road cut along Hwy 50.

• *Porterville, Tulare County* NEPHRITE JADE: NE 2 miles at commercial workings of Januko Brothers.

CHRYSOPRASE, SERPENTINE: E of Plano and 1½ miles S, also 8 miles E and ½ mile S of Deer Creek.

• *Pulga, Butte County* IDOCRASE, MASSIVE GROSSULARITE GARNET: In spoil piles from gold dredging in Feather River E of town, and in outcrops ½ mile from river in hills above town to W.

• *Quincy, Plumas County* ROSE QUARTZ, RHODONITE: Take Meadow Valley road W, then N ¾ mile into hills to collect.

- *Ramona, San Diego County* * DARK GREEN TOURMALINE, AQUA-MARINE, MORGANITE: Another of the celebrated pegmatite gem-producing districts. At the ABC mine, 3½ miles NE of Ramona.

  DARK GREEN TOURMALINE, TOPAZ, SPESSARTITE GARNET: At the Little Three mine, 3¾ miles NE of Ramona in the Hatfield Creek valley.

  SPESSARTITE GARNET: In the Spaulding and Hercules mines.

  EPIDOTE, GROSSULARITE GARNET: At McFall Mine, 7½ miles SE.

- *Randsburg, Kern County* JASPER: At Rainbow Ridge. Take U.S. 395 3 miles past intersection with Ridgecrest Road, turn S on road along power line slightly more than 5 miles and W into El Paso Mountains to collect. (Get permission: Charles Bishop, Box 354, Red Mountain, Calif 93558.)

  RHODONITE: At Main Street turn S for 7½ miles to Sunshine Mine Road. Turn here, go for 1 mile to end of pavement, continue straight on dirt road for 1 mile. In next ½ mile take two left turns, then turn right to mine dumps. Collect in vein and dumps.

  FLOWER AGATE: Take Trona Road 1½ miles N, then go 6 miles E on Steam Well Road and N for 5½ miles from Brown's ranch, to collect in hills.

- *Rincon, San Diego County* TOURMALINE, AQUAMARINE, MORGANITE: At the Victor mine, 2 miles SE.

  MORGANITE, AQUAMARINE: At the Clark and Mack mines.

- *Rosamund, Kern County* JASPER, PETRIFIED WOOD: Take Willow Springs road W for 3 miles, Mojave-Tropico road N for 4½ miles, and then go W ½ mile to collect in Rosamund Hills to S and E. Area is known as Gem Hill.

- *Sage, Riverside County* TOURMALINE, LEPIDOLITE: N 2½ miles on Hwy 79 and then E on dirt road to Anita mine.

- *St. Helena, Napa County* ONYX: At Erdahl ranch (fee).

- *San Diego, San Diego County* * DUMORTIERITE: Go E on Int. 8 to Alpine, take Taven Road ½ mile to Arnold Way and go 2½ miles S to Dehesa Road and short distance SW to road S into quarry.

- *San Francisco, San Francisco County* CHALCEDONY PEBBLES, PETRIFIED WHALEBONE: At beaches at Bodega Bay, Bolinas Bay, Tomales Bay, Drakes Bay, and Duxbury Point, all in Marin County and at Coyote Point Beach, 11½ miles S.

- *San Jose, Santa Clara County* DENDRITIC AGATE: Take Coleman Road to end at Guadalupe Mine.

- *San Miguel, San Luis Obispo County* BRECCIATED JASPER: Take Parkfield Road 17 miles, turn N for 9 miles and then go 2 miles E into Stone Canyon. (Get permission from Mrs. Hope Bagby, Hidden Valley Rancho, San Miguel.)
- *Santa Barbara, Santa Barbara County* PETRIFIED WHALEBONE: At Gaviota Beach, 32 miles W on Hwy 101; also Refugio Beach, 20 miles W.
- *Santa Cruz, Santa Cruz County* AGATE, PETRIFIED BONE: N 30 miles on Hwy 1 at Steele Beach.
- *Santa Monica, Los Angeles County* SHELL CONGLOMERATE: Go NW for 30 miles N to Coquina Beach for shells in dark matrix.
- *Siam Crossing, Riverside County* AGATE NODULES: Take old Hwy 66 6½ miles NE to Danby, then S on road across railroad tracks, and SW 7 miles along tracks in hills to E.
- *Sky Valley, Riverside County* TRAVERTINE: S on VeeBee road from Dillon road, then W ⅓ mile to deposit on slopes.
- *Susanville, Lassen County* AGATE, BLACK AND WHITE PETRIFIED WOOD: W 8 miles on Hwy 36, then S toward Stephens ranch.
  Also N on Hwy 139 11 miles, then W to collect along road.
- *Tecopa, Inyo County* PRECIOUS OPAL: Go 3½ miles W to Hwy 127, 2½ miles N on it to ruins of stage station. Collect in gray-green area in hills to W.
- *Tehachapi, Kern County* MARBLE: Take Curry Street S to Highline road, then S to Antelope Canyon Ranch to collect in quarry.

139

• *Tennant, Siskiyou County* OBSIDIAN: NE 4 miles from Medicine Lake at Glass Mountain.

• *Tollhouse, Fresno County* VESUVIANITE (CALIFORNITE), GROSSULARITE GARNET: On E side of Watts Valley, 1½ miles S of Hawkins School.

• *Trinidad, Humboldt County* BRECCIATED JASPER: On beach 1 mile N and S and in boulders on cliffs and at Patrick Point.

• *Trona, San Bernardino County* ONYX: N on Panamint Valley Road to summit, then 3 miles to sharp left turnoff, 2 miles to road to left and through rough country to house and around to right to Onyx Hill for Death Valley onyx (fee).

• *Ukiah, Lake County* ONYX: N on Hwy 20 for 6 miles, then left to Potter Valley and Lake Pillsbury to collect at NW side. (See Enrique Mahnke at Cobb.)

• *Upland, San Bernardino County* LAPIS LAZULI: 12 miles N in N fork of Cascade Canyon.

• *Valley Ford, Sonoma County* JASPER, AGATE: Take Hwy 1 to Bodega, then 8 miles N to Shell Beach for pebbles.

• *Valley Springs, Calaveras County* MOSS AGATE, PETRIFIED WOOD: At Marie Costa ranch 2 miles N on Paloma road (fee).
AGATE, OPAL: E on Hwy 26 to Hwy 12, then S to Hogan reservoir road to Hooten ranch to collect in hidden valley (fee).
BLUE DENDRITIC OPAL: Take Hwy 12 E then N a block and 2 miles to turnoff S to Snyder ranch (fee).

• *Ventucopa, Santa Barbara County* ALABASTER: S 3 miles on Hwy 33, then E through gate for a block to take steep trail up canyon. Collect in ridges on top.

• *Victorville, San Bernardino County* VERD ANTIQUE: N on Int. 15 to Bell Mountain exit, go NE 3 miles on exit road to dirt road, take it NE 7 miles, then E to quarry on mountain.

• *Vidal Junction, San Bernardino County* CHALCEDONY: Take U.S. 95 N for 10 miles, at Milepost 270 marker turn E 12 miles, passing wash to collect in Whipple mountains and farther E in gravels of Parker Dam area of Colorado River.

• *Visalia, Tulare County* SERPENTINE: E 8 miles at S end of Venice Hill, with chrysoprase.

• *Warner Springs, San Diego County* MORGANITE: At Pearson mine, 13 miles NW on Hwy 79 to Oakgrove and E to mine.

MORGANITE, TOPAZ: At Aguanga Mountain, 10 miles NW on Hwy 79 and W to Mountain Lily mine.

TOPAZ, BLUE-GREEN TOURMALINE: At Ware mine near summit of Aguanga Mountain.

- *Weed, Siskiyou County* AGATE: To N in Willow creek.
- *Westmoreland, Imperial County* OBSIDIAN: To N at Obsidian Butte.
- *Westwood, Lassen County* AGATE, PETRIFIED WOOD: E on Hwy 36 to Willard Creek road S for ½ mile, collect along creek.
- *Wiley Well Area, Imperial County* * CHALCEDONY ROSES, FIRE AGATE: Take Int. 10 E from Desert Center (Riverside County) 31 miles and turn S after crossing bridge. Cross Niland Road at 8 miles and go 3 miles more to left-hand road leading into Coon Hollow in the Mule Mountains. Specimens along road.

Road E out of Coon Hollow goes mile to fire agate and chalcedony diggings.

Other road NE out of Hollow goes less than mile into Mule Mountains and then hike about a block to bed of white nodules.

OBSIDIAN NODULES: About 13½ miles W of Wiley Well on the road along the power line, turn off N 1½ miles into sandy flat to hills between Big and Little Chuckawalla Mountains for nodules on stony slopes.

BANDED AGATE, SEAM AGATE, BLACK CHALCEDONY, FLOAT AGATE, PLUME AGATE, CHALCEDONY ROSES: In Palo Verde Mountains. Back on Wiley Well Road, go on S and then E to Twin Buttes Road which leads up a ridge and at 1½ miles it forks. Right fork leads to Twin Buttes nodule beds, a great variety of colors and materials. Left fork

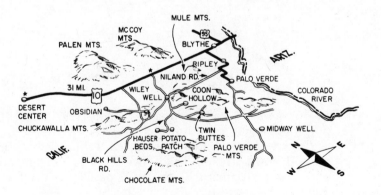

leads into a mountain basin where float agate, including some plume, is found. Rough road goes on toward buttes to a field of chalcedony roses.

Palo Verde mountains are E of Twin Buttes. Collect seam agate there.

SEAM AGATE, GEODES, AMETHYST: Back on Wiley Well Road N almost to Coon Hollow Road but turn W on Black Hills Road. At 5⅔ miles it splits into three branches. The southernmost branch goes almost 2 miles S, then forks left between two hills where seam agate is found, and into the Potato Patch, a deposit of crystal-lined geodes, and some amethyst, now deep with the debris of digging. Branch veers to W and at 3½ miles reaches old Hauser bed and new bed a half mile farther up canyon for agate-filled geodes lying 3 to 5 ft. below surface.

CARNELIAN, RED VARIEGATED JASPER: On faint fork left nearly a mile farther on.

AGATE, CARNELIAN, JASPER: Next branch N off Black Hills Road leads 3½ miles through flats where these occur as float, and to trail up wash a half mile to blue nodule (Long Beach) bed.

Northernmost branch of Black Hills Road * goes 3 miles to fork, then left to end of passable road. Hike up wash to geode bed in side of hill.

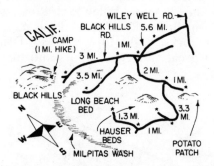

- *Willits, Mendocino County* * JADEITE, ACTINOLITE: Take Hwy 306 E to Hearst to hunt in Eel river.
- *Willow Creek,* * *Humboldt County* JADE: In Trinity River; both up and down stream. Take Hwy 96 N to Orleans area, and look in Klamath River. Road parallels river for 30 miles.

- *Winterhaven, Imperial County* AGATE NODULES, CHALCEDONY ROSES: Take Imperial Dam Road 2½ miles past Laguna Dam, turn off on road across canal and toward Ferguson Lake, but keep to left on this road, cross ridge into a basin, dig on W side for nodules and on S edge for chalcedony roses. Distance from canal to basin is 10 miles.
- *Wrightwood, San Bernardino County* RHODONITE: Go mile to Heath Canyon, collect up 1,000 feet.
- *Yermo, San Bernardino County* PETRIFIED WOOD, JASPER: E on Int. 15 to Minneola exit, cross freeway and take access road N, then E a half mile to road NE. Follow it a mile under pole line and continue N a mile to roads E into hills, the Green Ash Hills in the Calico mountains.
  Turn W into Mule Canyon for palm wood on the N side, and go about 2 miles to road N into Tin Can Alley a mile

143

to collect in canyon to E for moss agate and farther N for sagenitic agate. Continuing on the Mule Canyon road will reach the Calico road SE to Int. 15. Just before junction with Calico road there is a deposit of onyx to N in hills at the Calico Silver Onyx mine (fee).

•*Yreka, Siskiyou County* * BLOODSTONE, JASPER: 18 miles NE.

Colorado

Colorado is a state of startling physical contrasts: The eastern third is part of the High Plains like Kansas and Nebraska; the mid-state area is formed of massive mountain chains enclosing fertile basins; the western slope meets Utah in a welter of mesas and plateaus that comprise the wildest part of the state. Sedimentary rocks have been raised or pushed aside by the great igneous intrusions that formed the spectacular Front Range and created Colorado's mineral wealth.

- *Artesia, Moffat County* AGATE: 25 miles E on U.S. 40, then N on road between Big and Little Wolf creeks and hike mile to hill.
- *Baxterville, Rio Grande County* BLUE AND GRAY AGATE NODULES: Go SW on Hwy 160 7¾ miles beyond Wolf Creek Pass and collect in loose rock below road, but be careful; it's dangerous.
- *Bedrock, Montrose County* PETRIFIED WOOD, PETRIFIED BONE: One mile S on south bank of Dolores River.
- *Buena Vista, Chaffee County* ROSE QUARTZ: Take Hwy 24 to Trout Creek pass, collect at Clora May mine at top of hill.
- *Burlington, Kit Carson County* MOSS OPAL: In S fork of Republican River 20 miles N.
- *Canon City, Fremont County* AGATE: At Curio (Specimen) Hill, 7 miles S; loose in soil or in limestone ledge near top of ridge.

  BERYL: In Mica Lode, Meyers and School section mines at Eightmile Park.

  SATIN SPAR, PETRIFIED BONE, QUARTZ GEODES: 8 miles N on Shelf Road up Fourmile Creek to mouth of Felch Creek. Collect just W of Fourmile Creek.
- *Colorado Springs, El Paso County* AMAZONSTONE, SMOKY QUARTZ, WHITE TOPAZ: In pegmatites at Crystal Park, at foot of Cameron Cone, 2 miles S of Manitou Springs (use toll road on E slope of Pikes Peak). Crystals found for mile

NW and SW of park, especially in Bear Creek Canyon and at Specimen Rock in canyon.

- *Creede, Mineral County* AMETHYST: N past courthouse, left on road to North Creede, at 1½ miles pass Commodore mine, take left fork to old buildings, park, return to plank bridge and climb path into dumps. Green sphalerite and wire silver are found with the amethystine quartz. The upper dump is the most productive but is unsafe.

  CHALCEDONY, OPAL NODULES: Drive to W end of Rio Grande Reservoir to Trail Creek, hike S through rough country to Ute Creek. Collect along creek.

- *Del Norte, Rio Grande County* PLUME AGATE: Take Hwy 112 N for ½ mile, then left 4 miles to fork, go on to second fork and stay left to Del Norte Agate Beds sign near bridge (fee).

- *Elbert, Elbert County* PETRIFIED WOOD: In headwaters of Bijou and Kiowa Creeks, in gravels of rivers to SE, along Hwys 157 and 217, in Union Pacific railroad cut and as far S as Peyton and Calhan. Some from Peyton and Kiowa areas contains carnotite.

  One specific location is N for 7½ miles from U.S. 24 to collect in a wash near a farmhouse.

- *Elizabeth, Elbert County* PETRIFIED WOOD: At Kit Carson Monument.

- *Elk Springs, Moffat County* AGATE: In gravels at SE edge of town and along Hwy 14 off U.S. 40 for a few miles.

  JASPER, AGATE: Take U.S. 40 8 miles W to Hwy 16 and N 19 miles to road junction.

  SPOTTED AGATE: Take dirt road from junction 6 miles to cabin.

  PETRIFIED BONE: Continue W on U.S. 40 4½ miles from intersection with Hwy 16 and take trail N ½ mile, search on ridges.

  AGATE, JASPER, PETRIFIED BONE: N of U.S. 40 in gravels and outcrops within two miles of highway all the way to Blue Mountain.

- *Florissant, Teller County* * AMAZONSTONE, SMOKY QUARTZ: Take Hwy 67 N to a Y fork. Take left fork 2 miles to pits and other diggings in pegmatite outcrops in the woods. From these diggings, once known as the American Gem Mines, have come spectacular gem specimens. Much of the area is under private claims. Farther along Pine creek are amazonstone diggings.

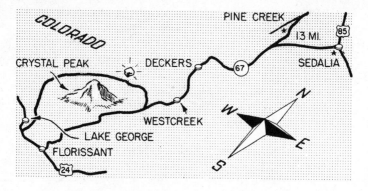

WHITE TOPAZ, PHENACITE: Found in pegmatite near Crystal Peak, especially ½ mile NW of peak.

•*Fort Collins, Larimer County* AMETHYST: On Hwy 287 22 miles NW and W on Hwy 200 to Red Feather Lakes. Deposit is about 5 miles W on mountain at claim.

SATIN SPAR, ALABASTER: Take U.S. 287 17 miles N to quarry in Owl Canyon.

•*Fruita, Mesa County* OPALIZED WOOD: Go S on Hwy 340, cross railroad tracks and bridge, take gravel road right for 1¾ miles, stay straight at fork, and right at next fork, a half mile farther take left fork and Opal Hill is on right. Collect there.

PETRIFIED BONE: W 4 miles and S of Int. 70 at Dinosaur Ridge.

•*Glade Park, Mesa County* AGATE, OPALIZED WOOD: Take road S toward top of mesa for 8½ miles, take left fork and keep right for 3 miles; collect along road and at house ½ mile farther along road.

•*Golden, Jefferson County* AQUAMARINE, SMOKY QUARTZ: W 15 miles at Centennial Cone on Termantozzi ranch. Collect in pegmatite on N side of cone. Don't enter without permission.

•*Granby, Grand County* BLOODSTONE: On ridges in Middle Park near junction of Willow Creek and Colorado River.

•*Guffey, Park County* BLUE AGATE: At 31 Mile Mountain 8 miles W.

•*Gunnison, Gunnison County* LAPIS LAZULI, GROSSULARITE GARNET: At Italian Mountain. Take Hwy 135 19 miles N to mouth of Cement Creek. Follow creek on bad road 12 miles. Mountain is mile NE of end of road. Collect on W side of north mountain near top and just above ledges of slaty black limestone. Difficult to find without guide.

BLUE CHALCEDONY: In rhyolite in Gunnison River above Black Canyon.

AGATE: E on U.S. 50 to mile E of Sargents; take dirt road left and hunt in streams.

‣*Hartsel, Park County* MOSS AGATE, PETRIFIED WOOD: Along Hwy 9 SE 1½ miles; also along U.S. 24 just W.

‣*Idaho Springs, Clear Creek County* RHODOCHROSITE: At Moose Mine. Take Virginia Canyon road to Russel Gulch Road and to Willis Gulch. Mine is ½ mile below head of gulch.

ROSE QUARTZ: In pegmatite at Santa Fe Mountain prospect; 3 miles SE on ridge NE of mountain, and reached by road up Sawmill Gulch from U.S. 6.

•*Jefferson, Park County* TOPAZ, SMOKY QUARTZ: Take graded road SE into Tarryall River valley for 30 miles to Spruce Grove campground, then take trail along ridge ½ mile SE to collect in pegmatite.

•*Kalouse, Weld County* AGATE: Along Two Mile River.

•*La Junta, Otero County* FLOWER AGATE, PETRIFIED BONE: In washes and streams to S.

•*Leadville, Lake County* TURQUOISE: At Turquoise Chief mine, 7 miles NW just below crest of ridge between Turquoise Lake and basin to N. (Private claim.)

•*Manassa, Conejos County* TURQUOISE: At King mine (private claim). Take Hwy 142 E for 6⅔ miles; S ⅓ mile to mine dumps at bottom of hill.

•*Mt. Antero, Chaffee County* * AQUAMARINE, PHENACITE, QUARTZ: Take Hwy 162 from Nathrop up Baldwin Gulch to saddle, climb from there, or by U.S. 285 S for 3½ miles from Nathrop and taking trails up Browns Creek. It is about 6 miles and 6,000 feet up to the collecting area in pegmatite within 500 feet of top in Mt. Antero and White Mountain, and collectors are exposed to sudden storms.

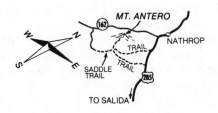

BERYL, SMOKY QUARTZ: At the California mine, 2 miles SW of Mount Antero, at 12,500 ft. and reached by either trail. Mine is on S slope of divide between Browns Creek and Baldwin Gulch, on what is known as Carbonate Mountain.

•*Nathrop, Chaffee County* SPESSARTITE GARNET, WINE-COLORED TOPAZ, OBSIDIAN NODULES: Just to N on U.S. 285 at Ruby and Sugarloaf Mountains E of river, and Dorothy Hill W of river. Stones are very small.

•*Naturita, Montrose County* PETRIFIED BONE: Take oil road W 4 miles, then S 6 miles on road toward Paradox to fork in road. Take this fork NW past Bitter Creek mine to collect dinosaur bone.

•*Ouray, Ouray County* RHODOCHROSITE: At Silver Bear mine, to S near Bear Creek Falls.

•*Parker, Douglas County* PETRIFIED PALM WOOD: One mile S.

•*Peyton, Elbert County* PETRIFIED WOOD: N on county road from gas station for 7½ miles, stop at first farmhouse on right and get permission to hunt in wash W of house. Continue N on road then W along gravel road for a total distance of 10 miles from Peyton, park near windmills and collect S in dry wash and pastures.

•*Rico, Dolores County* RHODOCHROSITE: At Newman Hill and Enterprise mines.

•*Saguache, Saguache County* AGATE GEODES: Take Hwy 114 W for 21 miles, then S 8½ miles and dig W of road.

•*Salida, Chaffee County* PETRIFIED WOOD, JASPER: In hills to SW on S side of U.S. 50, from Poncha Springs to Sargents.
SAPPHIRE, GROSSULARITE GARNET, SAGENITIC QUARTZ: In schists at Calumet iron mine, in E wall of Railroad gulch. Take Hwy 291 N from Salida, right on Hwy 180 to Hwy 190, then left on Hwy 31 to gulch.

•*Sargents, Gunnison County* AGATE: 1 mile E on U.S. 50, then N on dirt road, collect in small streams that road crosses. At 7-mile point collect slag in ruins of Cosden smelter.

•*Sedalia, Douglas County* TOPAZ, SMOKY QUARTZ: In pegmatite pockets at Devils Head, just S of peak at top of ridge below highway. Take Hwy 67 SW to Rampart Range Road and S, a total of 21½ miles.
Also across from Virgin's Bath picnic grounds.
AMAZONSTONE, SMOKY QUARTZ: Take Hwy 67 SW 13 miles to Pine Creek store, then down Pine Creek road 2 miles to dump above stream.

•*Silverton, San Juan County* RHODONITE: On dump on N side of Sunnyside Mill at Eureka, 9 miles NE of Silverton on Hwy 110.

At Gold Prince mine, Terry Tunnel of Sunnyside mine, and Golden Fleece mine and American Tunnel at Treasure Mountain. Buy from miners.

•*Villa Grove, Saguache County* TURQUOISE: At Hall mine (private claim). Take U.S. 285 NW 2⅔ miles, then side road 2⅔ miles W to edge of Cochetopa National Forest, and then 2 miles to cabins that are ½ mile below mine.

CHALCEDONY, RHODOCHROSITE: N on Hwy 285 to road W to Bonanza, where road turns N walk across Kerber creek and collect in canyon. Return to road, pass ranch, and collect rhodochrosite N of Hayden's Peak.

Connecticut

A central lowland valley divides eastern Connecticut from the western part of the state. This valley is cut by ridges of trap rock, while the eastern and western uplands are broken by mountain ranges and valleys, affording exposures of crystalline rocks containing gem materials. The trap rocks of the Connecticut valley yield agate and jasper, and amethyst and prehnite in cavities.

•*Branchville, Fairfield County* * GOLDEN BERYL, ROSE AND SMOKY QUARTZ, SPODUMENE: The quarry, a short distance NE of Branchville, has long been noted for these gem minerals. Work on the dumps is required to uncover fresh material, however.

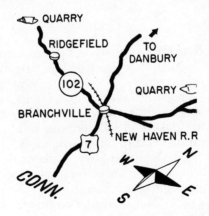

West of Branchville, a short distance out of Ridgefield, is a pegmatite that has been worked, containing some beryl, as well as quartz crystals and rose quartz. It is reached by following Conn. 102 W 1½ miles from the stoplight in Ridgefield, then turning N, crossing a bridge, and taking dirt road to left just beyond bridge. Drive to end, park and hit trail ¼ mile to area of pit and dumps. Area's future is uncertain; it may be closed.

• *Canton, Hartford County* AMETHYST: Take Hwy 44 E for ¼ mile, then East Hill road N to a road left and hike to area in and near stream where quartz veins are exposed.

• *East Hampton, Middlesex County* * GOLDEN AND BROWN BERYL, ROSE QUARTZ: In Slocum Quarry. Take Hwy 196 SW to Daniel Road, then to paved road N. Continue 2 miles to fork, take left fork past farmhouse (fee).

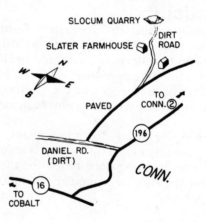

• *East Haven, New Haven County* AMETHYST, SMOKY QUARTZ: Collect at Cinque quarry back of Weeping Willow restaurant on Laurel Street.

• *Glastonbury, Hartford County* AQUAMARINE, SMOKY QUARTZ: Take Isenglass Hill road E from Hwy 17 to Thompson Hill road. Take Old Glastonbury road ½ mile N to old truck entrance left to Simpson quarry.
N of Isenglass road on Hwy 17 about 4 miles is a road E to the dumps of the Howe quarry, a good place for beryl and other pegmatite minerals.
E on Isenglass Hill road to Thompson Hill road. Take it S to Cotton Hill road E, stop at power lines and hike N

uphill to the Case quarries for good beryl and pegmatite minerals.

- •*Guilford, New Haven County* IOLITE: In gneiss at Hungry Horse Hill.

- •*Haddam, Middlesex County* * TOURMALINE, BERYL, GARNET, AMAZONSTONE: The noted Gillette quarry is reached by taking Hwy 9 to Hwy 82 exit, across river to E Haddam, then N on Hwys 149 and 151 to Haddam Neck. A road from Haddam Neck leads to the quarry near the Connecticut river. Collect in the dumps (fee).

  Nearby just off Hwy 151 is another mine notable for lepidolite. From a farmhouse as Hwy 151 veers E a dim road leads a half mile to the dump.

  BERYL (GOSHENITE), SMOKY QUARTZ, TOURMALINE: Take Jail Hill road to small bridge, take left fork and go ½ mile to Turkey Hill mine sign (fee).

- •*Meriden, New Haven County* AMETHYST, PREHNITE: Take Hwy 71 to road cut in Hwy 6, also quartz in reservoirs around Hubbard Park.

- •*Middletown, Middlesex County* * BERYL, RUBELLITE TOURMALINE: At White Rocks Quarry.

- •*Milford, New Haven County* SERPENTINE (VERD ANTIQUE): Take U.S. 1 from turnpike exit 39 for 2⅓ miles NE past Hwy 152, park near thrift shop and walk W to dig.

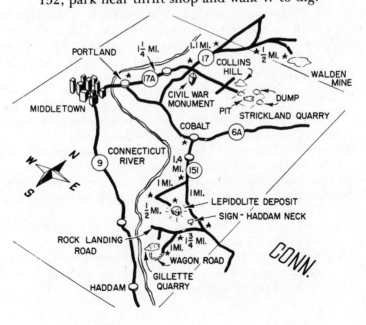

- *Monroe, Fairfield County* ROSE QUARTZ: NE of East Village beyond old canal in feldspar quarry.
- *Morris, Litchfield County* SMOKY QUARTZ: Take path from Hwy 109 to S end of Morris reservoir, collect in quarry to W.
- *New Milford, Litchfield County* BLUE AND GOLDEN BERYL, SMOKY QUARTZ: NW 5 miles at Upper Merryll in George Roebling (Merryll) Mine.

   KYANITE: Take Hwy 67 E to Judd's Bridge, collect one mile N.
- *Old Saybrook, New London County* AGATE, MOONSTONE: Collect on beach on W side of point toward Long Island Sound.
- *Portland, Middlesex County* * BERYL, TOURMALINE, SPODUMENE, GARNET, APATITE, SMOKY QUARTZ, CITRINE: The Strickland Quarry, NE of Portland, has produced these, some in varied colors. Take Conn. 17A out of Portland to a brown Civil War monument. Turn right here and keep right until the road ends in a T. Keep straight ahead up a rough road on Collins Hill to the quarry. The pit, before it was flooded, was a choice collecting spot and the dumps have yielded many specimens to collectors.

   AQUAMARINE: SE of the Strickland quarry and W of a clearing for power lines are the Hale Walker quarries, reached by taking Collins Hill road S and a road E to the cleared strip and then N.

   TOURMALINE, BERYL: At Walden farm. Take Hwy 17 to Hwy 26, then go N 3 miles to Cotton Hill road (fee).
- *Ridgefield, Fairfield County* QUARTZ: N on Hwy 35 to Farmingville road, then E to new road, take it N and path past ball park NW to collect in exposed rock.
- *Roxbury, Litchfield County* KYANITE: From Hwy 67 and 199 junction, go N on Hwy 199 3⅔ miles, turn left and left again at a small park, then 1⅔ miles to park entrance. Park and take path left to collecting area.
- *Roxbury Falls, Litchfield County* GARNET, STAUROLITE: SE ⁴/₅ mile from Hwy 199, turn off E on road to Green farm, garnet in dump, staurolite deposit beyond farmhouse (fee).
- *Southford, New Haven County* BERYL, ROSE QUARTZ: 1¾ miles SW in quarry.
- *Unionville, Hartford County* FELDSPAR, MOONSTONE, CORDIERITE: 1½ miles NE in road cut S of Biglow Pond.
- *Wallingford, New Haven County* AMETHYST: Exit 15 from Wilbur Cross parkway, then E to Hwy 68 and N to New Haven Traprock quarry.

- *West Redding, Fairfield County* GARNET, CLINOZOISITE: In quarry 2,000 feet from railroad station and near Simpaug turnpike.
- *West Stafford, Tolland County* QUARTZ: Hwy 190 E across brook and past firehouse to path N to Diamond Ledges.
- *Woodbury, Litchfield County* BERYL, AGATE, ROSE QUARTZ: In Flanders Quarry.

Florida

Florida is a peninsula not far above sea level but containing a diversity of natural features, ranging from the hilly area in the northwest to the coastal plain on the east, and marked by many lakes and the huge Everglades Swamp to the south. Underlain by limestone, it lacks the formations that would yield a variety of mineral or gem specimens.

- *Lake City, Columbia County* AGATE: N on Hwy 41 to White Springs; at north gate of Foster Memorial turn right, go 1¾ mile on sand road to second wooden bridge and just beyond it to cross roads. Turn right and collect in creek bed.
- *Lakeland, Polk County* CHALCEDONY, FOSSIL CORAL: On Lake Parker Beach for chalcedony and fossil coral.
  On canal near Kathleen, 7 miles NW.
- *Miami, Dade County* AGATIZED CORAL: Turn E at auditorium, cross bridge and collect in debris piles at port of Miami.
- *New Port Richey, Pasco County* AGATIZED CORAL: To S at Bailey's Bluff.
  Coral may be expected along a vast area of the coast wherever dredging brings up material from the ocean.
- *Perry, Taylor County* AGATIZED CORAL: Go 20 miles W on U.S. 98 and ¼ mile past the Oconfina River, turn ½ mile S on Hwy 14 and go E to parking place. Dig there and in river area.
- *Tampa, Hillsborough County* AGATIZED CORAL: In Hillsborough Bay off Ballast Point.

Georgia

With representative rocks of almost every geologic period exposed on the surface, it is not surprising that Georgia exhibits a variety of rocks and minerals. The southern half of the state is part of the coastal plain underlain by sedimentary rocks. North of this is the Piedmont Plateau and, in the extreme northeast, a highlands, both formed of crystalline rocks containing minerals of interest. The extreme northwest corner consists of ancient folded and eroded sedimentary rocks.

- *Albany, Dougherty County* RED JASPER: In Flint River.
- *Apalachee, Morgan County* AQUAMARINE: To W on Adair plantation.
- *Athens, Clarke County* GREEN BERYL: In field along Alps Road across from new airport.
- *Ball Ground, Cherokee County* RUTILATED QUARTZ, BERYL: NE 2½ miles at Cochran mine near old tenant house.
  STAUROLITE: Take Fairview Church road W to collect along Sharp Mountain creek. Also on Oscar Robertson and James Spear farms (fee).
  ALMANDINE GARNET: In prospects along Hwy 5 toward Canton.
- *Blairsville, Union County* RUBY: On S side of Track Rock Gap.
  KYANITE: S of Hwy 76 W, especially ½ mile E of Akin Mountain and 5 miles NW in Teece Creek valley a mile below highway.
- *Blue Ridge, Fannin County* STAUROLITE: Take Hwy 2 W one mile, then blacktop road left to gravel road on left, follow to second house on left and turn left to Hackney farm (fee).
- *Bremen, Haralson County* QUARTZ CRYSTALS: W 1½ miles.
- *Buford, Gwinnett County* AGATE, MOONSTONE: On Addison Lowe farm.
- *Clarkesville, Habersham County* AGATE: W 2 miles.
  RUBY WITH MARGARITE: At Alec Mountain in Piedmont Orchards, 6 miles NW by road up Beaver Dam creek.
  KYANITE: On grounds of North Georgia Vocational school, ½ mile E of grounds in gravel of small stream and in bank of Soque River, in schist belt through farms NE, and near Turnerville, and Stonepile Church.
- *Clayton, Rabun County* AMETHYST: On dump of the North Georgia Company Mine 4 miles N.
  Also at Ledbetter Mine dump, N on Hwy 23 to Rabun Gap and one mile E to S side of Black Creek.

Also at W. T. Smith Mine at junction of road E from Clayton with Hwy 28.

Also at Wilson farm 4 miles SE.

Also N on Hwy 23 on mine dumps near dam at Mountain City.

Also, take U.S. 76 W, turn N, follow Tallulah River into Towns County, then left on Upper Charlie Creek to diggings.

KYANITE: At lower end of Burton Lake near dam.

BERYL, QUARTZ CRYSTALS: E 8 miles, at Mark Beck farm via Warwoman and Dick's Creek roads.

CORUNDUM: E to Pine Mountain, then 1½ miles NE to Laurel Creek Mine.

ROSE QUARTZ: E to road N to crossing of Walnut Fork, in dumps of Kell Mica Mine.

- *Clyattville, Lowndes County* * AGATIZED CORAL: Leave Int. 75 at Valdosta exit, turn W on Hwy 31 5 miles to Clyattville, take Main street W 1½ miles, then S on Bland's Dairy road 4 miles to the Withlacoochee river. Collecting is only possible at low-water stages.

- *Columbus, Muscogee County* PETRIFIED WOOD: Near Bull and Randall Creeks.
- *Commerce, Banks County* BERYL: Along Hwy 59, 5 miles E of Jackson-Banks County line.
- *Cumming, Forsyth County* AMETHYST: E 6 miles at the I. H. Gilbert farm.
- *Dallas, Paulding County* ALMANDINE GARNET: On surface near Little Bob Copper Mine 6 miles SE.
- *Elberton, Elbert County* SMOKY QUARTZ: NE 10 miles in Chapman mine on N side of Cold Water Creek.

  AMETHYST: Take Hwy 17 5 miles NW to Deweyrose, then go 2 miles N to W. B. Perkins place.

- *Fayetteville, Fayette County* AMETHYST, RUTILATED QUARTZ: on Homer Kellin farm.
- *Greenville, Meriwether County* GARNET, TOURMALINE: Take Hwy 109 to the first millpond, then first road left of millpond to fourth house on left, the Ernest Strozier farm (fee).
- *Griffin, Spalding County* BLUE BERYL, SMOKY QUARTZ AND ROSE QUARTZ: Take Hwy 92 NW to Vaughn, and go 2 miles NE to T. J. Allen property; collect crystals in pegmatite and loose in soil.
- *Hartwell, Hart County* BERYL: Take U.S. 29 E to access road to Hartwell dam and collect in quarry to right.
- *Hiawassee, Towns County* PINK CORUNDUM: Often with smaragdite, 2 miles SW at Hog Creek Mine.
  Also at Bell Creek Mine 4 miles N at head of Chatuge Lake and in beach deposits and outcrops along Chatuge Lake, especially near Elf.
- *Hillsboro, Jasper County* BLUE QUARTZ: From Baptist church just N on Hwy 11 to dirt road 3 miles to Barron Fullerton farm. Hunt near farmhouse.
- *Hiram, Paulding County* SERPENTINE (VERD ANTIQUE), APATITE: Go W at Dunn store, follow pavement to end, take graded road ¼ mile to fork, take right fork, turn on dirt road to Verd Antique quarry, which is a mile SW of town.
- *Kingston, Bartow County* RED AND BROWN AGATE: To S along Etowah River.
- *La Grange, Troup County* BERYL, ROSE QUARTZ: Take Hwy 219 S to Cleveland Crossroads to Big Beryl (Hogg or Foley) mine (fee).
- *Lithonia, DeKalb County* EPIDOTE, THULITE: In Rock Chapel quarry and on N side of Arabia Mountain.
- *Macon, Bibb County* AGATE: At Holton Quarry, 7½ miles NW. BERYL: N of Calloway airport at road junction.
- *Madison, Morgan County* AMETHYST: Take U.S. 278 E to Buckhead and go 2 miles E to Ray farm.
- *Marble Springs, Chattooga County* MARBLE: In local quarries.
- *Maysville, Banks County* QUARTZ CRYSTALS: In Commerce area along railroad (see Alton Hayes in Maysville).
- *Milledgeville, Baldwin County* JASPER: At State Farm.
- *Mineral Bluff, Fannin County* STAUROLITE: Take road a mile NW on Windy Ridge, collect at Richards and Arp properties and on ridge along dirt road at end of paved road.
- *Monroe, Walton County* AQUAMARINE: On surface at Malcolm farm; take Hwy 83 SE to Blasingame, then 6½ miles on dirt road.

- *Nacoochee, White County* GREEN APATITE: In cut on N side of Hwy 17 3 miles E.
- *Monticello, Jasper County* BERYL: In pegmatite 9 miles S on J. R. Parker property.
- *Nicholson, Jackson County* BERYL: In pegmatite on W side of U.S. 441 at dirt side road just N of the town.
- *Norcross, Gwinnett County* MOONSTONE: Hwy 141 N to crossing of Chattahoochee; in pegmatite on Green farm.
- *Powder Springs, Cobb County* CORUNDUM: S 2 miles on Turner property.
- *Roswell, Fulton County* CORUNDUM: E 3½ miles.
- *Rutledge, Morgan County* CORUNDUM: Take dirt road from Hwy 12 for 2 miles SW of the Georgia railroad to collect on Bill Oxford farm.
- *Sparta, Hancock County* CHERT: Along Sinclair reservoir to W, a colorful jasper.
- *Summerville, Chattooga County* AGATE: W on Hwy 48 to fish hatchery, turn right, then right again at Baptist church sign and again at church, go ¼ mile, collect along road. Also 3 miles S on U.S. 27 over top of first ridge to collect on east slopes.
- *Sylvania, Screven County* FOSSIL AGATE: Take Hwy 301 N almost to Savannah River, turn left for 8 miles to a sharp turn, take dirt road there ½ mile, collect along road.
- *Tate, Pickens County* GOLDEN BERYL, AQUAMARINE: In pegmatite SE of Rock Creek on Ralph Cook farm near Refuge Church.
  MARBLE: in quarries.
- *Thomaston, Upson County* CORUNDUM: NE 7 miles at the Kelly place.
  MOONSTONE, APATITE: SE 7¼ miles and a mile NW of Waymansville on a branch of Tobler Creek, collect at the Mitchell Creek Mica mine. Also at Blount and Joe Persons mines.
  AGATE: NE 6 miles at Wilmot's Ravine.
  STAUROLITE, GEMMY KYANITE: SW 3½ miles on Dolly Cherry property. Take U.S. 19 S 2 miles to Shepherd school, go 1¾ miles on dirt road, turn right and go mile.
- *Toccoa, Stephens County* QUARTZ CRYSTALS: S 9 miles.
- *Warm Springs, Meriwether County* AGATE: One mile S on Southern Railroad.
  ROSE QUARTZ, BERYL: 15 miles W at Pine Mountain valley.
- *Washington, Wilkes County* GREEN SPINEL: Take highway to Lincolnton and county line, take a right fork, then a left fork

to Magruder Mica mine on hill to right.

- *Yatesville, Upson County* BERYL: ¼ mile E at Herron Mine and 3 miles N at Adams mine.
- *Young Harris, Towns County* CORUNDUM: On S side of Track Rock Gap reached by road S from U.S. 76 2½ miles W of Young Harris.

Hawaii

The state of Hawaii is a group of islands in the Pacific Ocean. The major islands are volcanic domes formed of basaltic lava cut by erosion into ridges and valleys, and marked in places by coral reefs. The islands show craters and other marks of former volcanic activity, and on the largest island, Hawaii, are two of the world's largest active volcanoes, Mauna Loa and Kilauea. Gem minerals are relatively few under such conditions.

- *Halemaumau, on Kilauea, Hawaii* OBSIDIAN: Droplets known as Pele's Tears.
- *Kailua, on north shore of Oahu* QUARTZ CRYSTALS: In basalt ridges, in ravines from Mount Olokanu, in washes of Keolu hills and in H & D quarry, with jasper, also jasper in Lanikai golf course washes and in Wahiawa Valley.
- *Kaneohe, on north shore of Oahu* JASPER: On ridges in Koolau range.
- *Lahaina, on south shore of Maui* BLACK CORAL: In deep water offshore.
- *Manele Bay, on SE shore of Lanai* FELDSPAR SUNSTONE: In cinder cone.
- *Olomana Peak, Oahu* BANDED AGATE: In gullies, and also in crater of West Molokai volcano.
- *Puna district, on island of Hawaii* OLIVINE: In lava flow; also in green beach sands of Oahu and South Point, Hawaii.
- *Pohakea Pass, in Waianai Range,* CLEAR YELLOW LABRADORITE.

Idaho

Its diversity of geographical features, ranging from the rugged mountains of the northeast and central parts of the state to the arid wastes of the south and the basalt plateaus of the north, makes Idaho a state rich in mineral and gem resources. The Salmon and Clearwater river regions are one of the last frontiers of collecting in the United States—a wilderness of canyons and forests.

- *Arco, Butte County* QUARTZ, AMETHYST GEODES: In Antelope Creek and Road Creek areas and Upper Lost River valley, and quartz crystals in veins in Wildhorse Canyon on E side of Hyndman Peak.

  AGATE: In lava to E and S of Hwy 93A.
- *Ashton, Fremont County* AGATE: In volcanic rocks to N and then E of U.S. 191 in Island Park Caldera.
- *Avery, Shoshone County* KYANITE, STAUROLITE: To S on divide between headwaters of the St. Joe and Clearwater rivers.
- *Avon, Latah County* GREEN BERYL: In mica mines between Deary and Princeton, especially the Levi Anderson and Muscovite mines.
- *Bliss, Gooding County* BROWN OPALIZED OAKWOOD: In volcanic ash along Clover Creek. Wood has flashes of fire opal.
- *Boise, Boise County* AQUAMARINE: To E along Middle Fork of Boise river as far as Atlanta in scattered beryl mines and prospects.
- *Bruneau, Owyhee County* PETRIFIED WOOD: W 2 miles to Hwy 51, then S 9 miles and E to collect in conglomerate formations in and around low hills.

  PURPLE AGATE: SE 8 miles to Indian Hot Springs, then S past ranch 8½ miles to collect at Indian Bathtub.
- *Burgdorf, Idaho County* CORUNDUM, QUARTZ: In placer mining dumps at mouth of Grouse Creek S of road to Warner. Also beyond Secesh Creek at Ruby Meadows in placer mining dumps.
- *Camas, Jefferson County* TOPAZ, FIRE OPAL: In rhyolite near source of E branch of tributary to S fork of Camas Creek.
- *Carey, Blaine County* MOSS AGATE: W on Muldoon Summit.
- *Cascade, Valley County* SMOKY QUARTZ: Dig in pegmatites on mountain just to N, also with agate to S and E of U.S. 55 and in placer tailings along Big Creek.
- *Challis, Custer County* * AGATE, PETRIFIED WOOD: Hwy 93 S to Hwy 93A, then 8 miles S on Hwy 93 to bridge; stay on

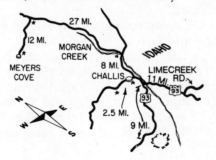

Hwy 93 another 1½ miles to Malm Gulch, hike or take jeep trail 2½ miles E to petrified forest on ridge, or collect along the way.

AGATE, BLACK WOOD: S on Hwy 93 through gorge, collect on hills and in valleys to right, and 2 miles on road to left collect black wood.

AGATE: Hwy 93 to Hwy 93A, take Hwy 93A 11 miles SE, then Lime Creek road E for 2 miles, hunt in hills.

SEAM AGATE IN VOLCANIC ASH: N of Challis about 8 miles is turnoff at Morgan Creek almost due N for 27 miles, then sharply left toward Meyers Cove. Look along road to cove.

• *Cuprum, Adams County* ANDRADITE GARNET: In limestone in contact zone where copper is mined in the Seven Devils district. Epidote is found with the garnet.

• *Deary, Latah County* GARNET: E on Hwy 8 to Helmer, hunt in Boulder Creek.

• *De Lamar, Owyhee County* PETRIFIED WOOD: To NW in Cow and Soda Creeks.

• *Emmett, Gem County* FIRE OPAL: At Black Canyon Dam. Go toward Horseshoe Bend to small pond E of road; take trail to canyon and go mile to diggings on left side.

JASPER: To S in both forks of Willow Creek E of road to Hwy 44.

• *Fernwood, Benewah County* STAR GARNET: This famous locality is now open by obtaining a federal permit to collect. The areas are reached from Fernwood by going SE on Hwy 3 along the St. Maries River. The turnoff W to Emerald Creek is 4½ miles S on Hwy 3. Take the dirt road and follow the E fork of the creek. One collecting area is along a tributary 8 miles in from the highway, the other is farther along on the E fork. Shorty's Diggin's, a concession area, is open (fee).

Purdue Creek crosses Hwy 3 a short distance N of Bovill. Take a dirt road E 1¼ mile, then hike in 3 miles along the left fork.

• *Hailey, Blaine County* JASPER, PETRIFIED WOOD: SW 5 miles to Bellevue and E to Little Wood River.

• *Homedale, Owyhee County* * (also see Adrian, Ore.) AGATE: Take Hwy 95 S 3 miles, turn right to Graveyard Point Monument, collect to W of monument near foot bridge, then continue to road bridge and S to collect S of bridge and W of road. Go on 2 miles to collect W and a mile farther to collect S of road. Latter areas can also be reached

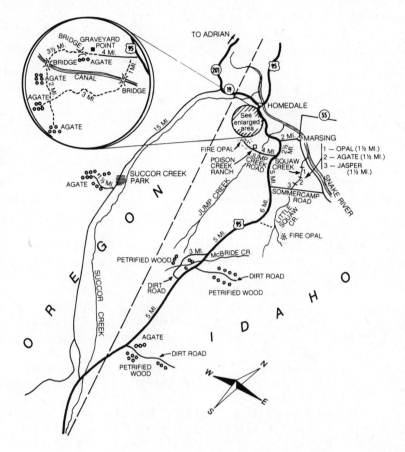

from Hwy 95 by going S a mile across canal bridge, then taking trail 3 miles W.

Succor Creek agate is reached by taking Hwy 19 in Oregon from its intersection with Hwy 201 and along the stream 15 miles, then past the state park a mile and W up the mountainside 1½ miles for agate nodules. A mile beyond is another location, and common opal is found in rhyolite back of park.

•*Idaho City, Boise County* QUARTZ, GARNET: In placer tailings and mine dumps, especially at the Gold Hill mine.

FIRE OPAL: At More's Creek.

•*Kooskia, Idaho County* PETRIFIED WOOD: Go N on Hwy 13, then NE to collect.

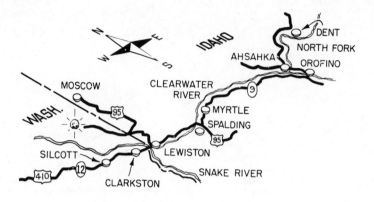

- *Lewiston, Nez Perce County* * FIRE OPAL: Just N of Lewiston a dirt road turns W from Hwy 95. Take it for 10 miles, then hike up ridge a half mile, turn right and follow along cliffs to diggings.

  A mile or so farther along the dirt road and across the Snake River is a big gravel pit at Silcott. Opposite it on N side of river and 900 ft. up, caves are reached by a trail. Diggings are in caves.

  BLUE AGATE: Take first gravel road left after starting up Lewiston Hill; go 9 miles to place just below pit in Snake River.

  FIBROUS SILLIMANITE, AGATE: Found E and N from Lewiston in the Clearwater River and in its N fork for 50 miles. The best hunting is between the Cheerylane and Myrtle bridges and at Big Eddy above Spalding. The sillimanite is blue, yellow, green, or white pebbles.
- *Lost River, Custer County* AGATE, JASPER: On the North Fork of Lost River.
- *Mackay, Custer County* GEODES, JASPER SPOTTED WITH CHRYSOCOLLA: Found in Alder Creek mines and on ridges.
- *Marsing, Owyhee County* * PETRIFIED WOOD, AGATE, FIRE OPAL: Go W to junction of Hwy 95 and Hwy 55, then take Hwy 95 S for 2½ miles to Jump Creek road. Follow it W to Poison Creek ranch, about 4 miles, and continue on a mile to dig fire opal.

  From the Jump Creek intersection on Hwy 95 go 5 miles S and E to reach collecting area along Squaw Creek. Jasper, agate and opal are found along the creek to the NE. Farther S 6 miles along Hwy 95 is an access road NE

to a fire opal area just downstream from where Little
Squaw Creek enters Squaw Creek.

Five miles farther S on Hwy 95 is McBride creek. To W
are dirt roads and trails to several petrified wood locations. Five miles beyond McBride Creek and E of Hwy 95
near the Oregon line is the Coal Mine Basin E of the
highway. Here petrified wood and agate are found.

- *May, Lehmi County* FIRE OPAL: On W side of Pahsemeroi valley
  in ledge of porphyry paralleling Panther Creek and
  about 6 miles from its source.
- *Montpelier, Bear Lake County* JASPER: Colored red by hematite
  and green by malachite at Humming Bird Mine dump in
  Paris Canyon.
- *Moore, Butte County* BLACK AGATE: Follow Antelope Creek can-
  yon road 13½ miles W, then drive or walk trail left to Big
  Piney Mountain.
- *New Meadows, Adams County* RUBY, GARNET: Take Hwy 55 7
  miles E, dirt road left, and pan or screen sands of stream
  at Rock Flat for small stones.
  RHODONITE: A few miles S in foothills.
- *Pierce, Clearwater County* ALMANDINE (STAR) GARNET: In
  streams near Headquarters 12 miles N on Hwy 11.
  SAPPHIRE, EPIDOTE: In placer tailings along Rhodes and
  Orofino creeks.
- *Riggins, Idaho County* GARNET: For several miles to N in Little
  Salmon River.
- *Rocky Bar, Elmore County* SMOKY QUARTZ, TOPAZ: N 10½ miles
  toward Steel Mountain, then S to trail W into Dismal
  Swamp. Also in placer tailings in area.
- *St. Anthony, Fremont County* YELLOW FELDSPAR (ANDESINE)
  CRYSTALS: At Crystal Butte, 18 miles N, where they have
  weathered out of lava.
- *Silver City, Owyhee County* AGATE, QUARTZ, CASSITERITE: In
  mine dumps in Long Gulch ¾ mile S.
- *Spencer, Clark County* FIRE OPAL: In Spencer Opal mine (fee).
  Write Mark Stetler, Box 113, Spencer, Ida. 83446. The
  Wilson & Jepperson mining company has another fee
  opal dig over the hill from the Stetler dig.
- *Wallace, Shoshone County* KYANITE, GARNET: Go S to Goat
  Mountain, collect on S side of mountain.
- *Weiser, Washington County* AGATE NODULES: W on Hwy 70 5
  miles through Eaton, N on Old's Ferry Road a mile to
  crossroads, W 2 miles, then right up hill 5½ miles into
  saddle. Nodules are loose in decomposed rock.

Also on road left from Eaton to end of road for nodules and cinnabar-colored jasper in Hog Creek area.

BLACK AND WHITE OPALIZED WOOD: Take Hwy 95 N 13 miles to Mann's Creek guard station sign, turn W on dirt road 8½ miles to Mann's Creek and Fourth of July Creek Canyon. Dig in right bank.

RED AGATE: U.S. 95 N 6 miles to rest area, hike 2½ miles into Sage Creek ravine, collect there.

• *White Bird, Idaho County* AGATE: S and E of U.S. 95 6 miles.

• *Yellow Pine, Valley County* WHITE OPAL (MYRICKITE): Stained red by cinnabar in mercury mine dumps.

Illinois

Most of the state consists of prairie underlain by sedimentary rocks yielding coal, oil, and glass sand and deeply buried by glacial sand and gravel. The Ozark plateau and coastal plain of the southwestern part of the state, and the unglaciated "driftless" area in the northwest corner contain fluorite, lead, and zinc mines.

• *Grand Chain, Pulaski County* BROWN JASPER: In rail cut mile to NE.

• *Hamilton, Hancock County* * BROWN JASPER: Old gravel pit.
GEODES: In Railroad creek, East Fork of Crystal Glen Creek and other creeks to S crossed by Hwy 96.

• *Nauvoo, Hancock County* * GEODES: in creek a mile N of Nauvoo State Park.

• *Niota, Hancock County* * GEODES: On W side of creek at second bridge 2 miles S and in streams crossed by Hwy 96 S to Nauvoo and Hamilton. Many of the geodes are oil-filled.

• *Rosiclare, Hardin County* FLUORITE: From mines N of Cave In Rock and to W toward Golconda.

• *Warsaw, Hancock County* WATERWORN AGATE PEBBLES: In gravel pits.

GEODES: Found in area 100 miles long and 60 miles wide from eastern Iowa almost to St. Louis, especially in area N to Niota and Ft. Madison, Ia., and W to Keokuk and Kahoka, Mo. Best are in small streams. One area near Warsaw is called Geode Glen.

Indiana

Like Illinois, Indiana rests on the sedimentary rocks laid down by ancient seas, which are rich in fossils but poor in gem minerals. Where the glacial drift that covers most of the state lies on bedrock, streams sort out gold and some gem minerals such as diamond. Although most of the state is flat, resistant ridges and glacial moraines in the southern half create scenic variety.

• *Heltonville, Lawrence County* GEODES: In Salt Creek and to W toward Guthrie.

• *Martinsville, Morgan County* BROWN CHATOYANT SAPPHIRE: In gravels of Highland Creek 7 miles NW

• *Medora, Jackson County* GEODES: 5 miles W and S in creek near Jackson-Lawrence County line. Also in fields at Tunnelton.

• *Morgantown, Morgan County* SAPPHIRE, GARNET: In Gold Creek and other small streams through glacial drift and running on bedrock.

• *Salem, Washington County* GEODES: At Jim Day farm on E edge of Salem on Hwy 56. Also 10 miles N on Hwy 135 to Minnie Holstine farm. Also N on Hwy 135 to river, turn W and hunt in bottom lands.

• *Scottsburg, Scott County* PETRIFIED WOOD: In shale beds throughout county.

• *Trevlac, Brown County* QUARTZ GEODES: In Bear Creek. Streams east of Bloomington, Monroe County, and in Brown County and as far S as Washington County contain quartz-filled geodes.

Also in Bummets creek off Hwy 46.

• *Vallonia, Jackson County* GEODES: S on Hwy 135 to Delaney Creek road, go W to right fork, take it to steel bridge and Nazarene church and on to end of pavement, then follow gravel road to bridge over creek. Collect in creek.

Iowa

Iowa is a moderately rolling prairie tableland of glacial materials resting on sedimentary rocks except in the northeast corner, which was not touched by the glaciers. Here cliffs and hills make a more rugged topography, and in the extreme west, where mound-like bluffs rise from the Missouri River's flood plain. Geodes eroding from sedimentary rocks and quartz gem materials from the glacial drift can be expected in such circumstances.

• *Bellevue, Jackson County* * CARNELIAN, BANDED AGATE, PETRIFIED WOOD: Lake Superior agates from Mississippi River gravels: Take U.S. 52-67 N from Bellevue ¼ mile to gravel pit, which is privately owned and is operated most of the year. Search big piles of washed gravel for specimens. Inch to 2-inch agate is large. Occasional big ones go into oversize gravel discard pile near loading dock.

Similar gravel operations can be found up and down the Mississippi River, especially at Muscatine, Burlington, at Davenport, in Block Co. gravel operation at 4th St. and River Dr., near Clinton, and upstream in Wisconsin.

• *Chapin, Franklin County* GEODES: N to Sheffield along U.S. 65.
• *Donnellson, Lee County* GEODES: in gravel pit to S.
• *Des Moines, Polk County* PETRIFIED WOOD: In strip coal mines.
• *Dubuque, Dubuque County* * AGATE: There are two gravel operations at Dubuque: Molo Sand and Gravel Co. N of U.S. 20 bridge at E. 3d St.; the other just across the river in East Dubuque, Ill. Waterworn Lake Superior agates may be hunted in the stock piles (with permission).

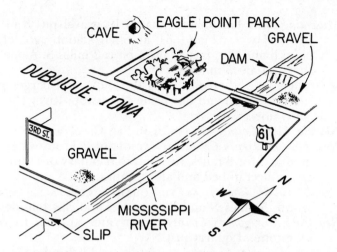

SATIN SPAR: On the bluffs above the city, just W of Y.M.C.A. camp in Eagle Point Park.

• *Farmington, Van Buren County* GEODES: In riverbanks.
• *Granger, Dallas County* GEODES: SW 3½ miles in gravel pit.
• *Iowa City, Johnson County* SILICIFIED CORAL: In stream and quarry at Coralville.
• *Keokuk, Lee County* GEODES: S on 5th Street W of Union Carbide plant, in upper shale. (Also see Warsaw, Ill.)
• *Keota, Washington County* * AGATE: Cold water agate at Kaser Construction Co. quarry; also at Ollie 10 miles S on Hwy 77, then W 4⅔ miles on Hwy 78 past church, N ½ mile and W 1 mile, and then N ⅓ mile to quarry.
• *Keswick, Keokuk County* AGATE: Nodules in quarry.
• *LaPorte City, Black Hawk County* AGATE: In gravel pit.
• *Mount Pleasant, Henry County* AGATE: In gravels of Big Creek and Skunk River and in pits.

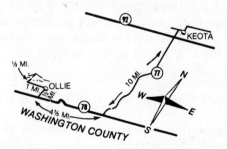

- *Muscatine, Muscatine County* AGATE: In gravel pits S of town. Leave Hwys 92 and 61 at Shell station, go left past church and S to pits. Hahn's pit is 2 miles S. Acme and a third pit are 5 miles S.

  There are other pits along the shore and barges pumping gravels up and down the Mississippi River from Missouri northward.
- *Nevada, Story County* AGATE: In Indian Creek gravels to E.
- *New London, Henry County* AGATE GEODES: From water tower go due S for 8 miles, turn left to tributary of Shunk creek and collect in bed and along banks.
- *Orient, Adair County* AGATE, QUARTZ CRYSTALS, PETRIFIED WOOD: 5 miles N and E in washes and clay hillsides.
- *Red Oak, Montgomery County* CHERT (RICE AGATE): In vein in limestone of quarry just NW.
- *Sheffield, Franklin County* GEODES: In field behind quarry.
- *Shell Rock, Butler County* AGATE: Lake Superior type just N at gravel pit.
- *Steamboat Rock, Hardin County* QUARTZ GEODES: Along Iowa River
- *Vinton, Benton County* AGATE: Cold-water type. Hwy 101 N across river, take first turn right and go 4½ miles along Cedar River, then left ½ mile to gate. Get permission and walk to collecting area (fee).
- *Waterloo, Black Hawk County* GEODES: At Burton Avenue quarry and Mitchell Avenue gravel pit near Cedar River.

Kansas

Extensive sedimentary beds underlie Kansas. They contain coal, salt, and world-famous fossils. The surface is formed of sand and gravel derived from erosion of the Rockies and carried eastward by water. These deposits create the gently eastward sloping High Plains, a region where agates and other quartz materials may be expected. East of the Colorado High Plains are the Smoky Hills in the north and the Great Bend Prairie. East of them is a strip known as the Flint Hills, north to south across the state, and in the northeastern corner of Kansas is a glaciated region. The prairie surface is diversified by broad plains, isolated hills, and moderate valleys.

- *Ashland, Clark County* MOSS OPAL: To N in hills along Bluff creek.
- *Bonner Springs, Wyandotte County* QUARTZ CRYSTALS: In geodes in Lone Star Quarry.

- *Buffalo, Wilson County* AGATE: Along Verdigris River.
- *Concordia, Cloud County* PETRIFIED WOOD, AGATE: To N in glacial gravels of Old River bed.
- *El Dorado, Butler County* GEODES: In large road cut near the Butler-Greenwood County line.
- *Elkader, Logan County* AGATE: W in river terraces.
- *Ellsworth, Ellsworth County* AGATE, JASPER, PETRIFIED BONE AND WOOD: In gravels N of Kanopolis Lake.
- *Kiowa, Barber County* AGATE, JASPER: Along Medicine Lodge river to Aetna.
- *Medicine Lodge, Barber County* PETRIFIED WOOD: 10 miles S.
- *Quinter, Sheridan County* MOSS OPAL: In limestone at Saline river and S fork of the Solomon River and in outcrops on U.S. 24 from Hoxie to Hill City.
- *Ransom, Ness County* AGATE, PETRIFIED WOOD: To NE in Seybert sand pit near Smoky Hill River bridge at Hwy 283.
- *Sharon Springs, Wallace County* AGATE, PETRIFIED WOOD: in sand pit to N.
- *Topeka, Shawnee County* AGATE: Agates of the Lake Superior type in glacial moraines near city.
- *Wallace, Wallace County* OPAL: Cacholong opal with green fire 5 miles S near S branch of the Smoky Hill river; dendritic opal in Ladder Creek to S.
- *Yates Center, Woodson County* QUARTZ CRYSTALS: In granite 8 miles S.
  AMETHYST: In quartzite 4 miles W and 10 miles S.

Kentucky

Rugged eastern Kentucky belongs to the Allegheny plateau, a region of sharp ridges and deep valleys which includes extensive coalfields. The rest of the state is divided into the Mississippian plateaus and coalfields to the south and southwest and the blue-grass region of rolling hills to the north, all sloping gently to the Mississippi river. Like the Plains states, Kentucky is underlain by sedimentary rocks but is unglaciated and hence more varied in character.

- *Columbia, Adair County* GEODES: In Shamrock stone quarry.
- *Glasgow, Barren County* GEODES: In stream to E.
- *Marion, Crittendon County* FLUORITE: In mines to W with quartz crystals. Many of the mines are not operating.
- *Sandy Hook, Elliott County* PYROPE GARNET: At Isonville 6 miles SE.

- *Stanford, Lincoln County* GEODES: S 6 miles on Hwy 78 near Hall's Gap on the banks of the Green River.
- *Wickliffe, Ballard County* JASPER: In gravel pit.

Louisiana

Much of Louisiana has been built by the Mississippi River from mud and sand carried down from the north. On the west side of the river lie areas of low hills and plains becoming marshes to the south. There are agate-bearing gravel deposits in these hills, 20 to 45 miles W of the river, and petrified wood near Alexandria. No gem materials occur south of an east-west line through Baton Rouge. The east side of the river is low flood plain.

- *Alexandria, Rapides Parish* AGATE: In gravel pits and stream bars to N, such as in the Ouachita River valley near Monroe and near Pollock and Farmerville, with some petrified wood.
- *Amite, Tangipahoa Parish* AGATE: On banks of Amite river and to E in rivers and gravel pits of the Tangipahoa, Bogue Chitto, and Pearl rivers.
- *Gulfport, Harrison Parish* PETRIFIED WOOD, JASPER: In creek beds to the NW.
- *Leesville, Vernon Parish* PETRIFIED WOOD: E as far as the Red river, as far W as the Sabine river, and N as far as Shreveport.
- *Monroe, Ouachita Parish* BANDED AGATE, PETRIFIED WOOD, SILICIFIED CORAL: Scattered over wide area to south and east. To south, some of the prominent locations are Pollock, Grant Parish; Woodworth, Rapides Parish; Turkey Creek, Evangeline Parish; and, farther east, St. Francisville and Jackson, in Feliciana Parish; and Watson in nearby Livingston Parish.

  In the extreme east these materials are found near Bogalusa and Franklinton in Washington Parish; and in Tangipahoa Parish along the Tangipahoa River from Kentwood south to Independence. Most of the gem materials are found in stream gravels.

Maine

Southern Maine is a rolling upland broken by hills and isolated mountains and valleys; the northern part is hilly and often swampy. Glacial action caused many lakes to form behind debris damming the normal drainage, and stripped the rocks of soil, laying bare the crystalline rocks that are the source of Maine's splendid tourmalines and other gems. Oxford County, particularly the area just northwest of Auburn, is world-famous for the many mines and quarries that have poured out mineral wealth for more than a century.

- *Albany, Oxford County* BERYL, ROSE QUARTZ, SMOKY QUARTZ: At Scribner ledge and Wardwell quarry.

  BERYL: Nearby on Lovejoy Mountain at Stearns and Guy Johnson quarries.

- *Andover, Oxford County* * TOURMALINE, ROSE QUARTZ: Hwy 5 S for 7 miles to Abbot farm, drive ¾ mile NW and park; trail SW goes to Nevel and Dunton pits and farther S to Bell pit. W from parking area ¼ mile is Scotty pit and ¾ mile farther another pit, all on Halls Ridge of Plumbago Mountain. A spectacular find of tourmaline was made in the Dunton-Nevel quarry in 1973, and later the area was closed to amateur collecting.

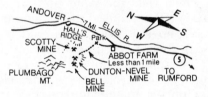

- *Blue Hill, Hancock County* RHODONITE: 1¾ miles SW on Hwy 176 at Blue Hill manganese mine.

- *Bethel, Oxford County* BERYL, ROSE AND SMOKY QUARTZ: At the Bumpus quarry 6½ miles SE on Hwy 5. Dumps are along E side of highway.

- *Brunswick, Cumberland County* BERYL: At LaChance Mine 4 miles S.

- *Buckfield, Oxford County* BERYL: At Fletcher Mine 2 miles SW on Hodgson Hill and 2½ miles SW at Robinson Dudley Mine.

  BERYL, APATITE, ROSE QUARTZ, TOURMALINE: At Paul Bennett Quarry 3 miles W on back road to Mount Mica (fee).

  BERYL: At Irish Mine 3 miles SE.

- *Byron, Oxford County* RED JASPER: In Swift River.

- *Canton, Oxford County* AMETHYST: In brook at Ragged Jack Mountain.

- *Deer Isle, Hancock County* LAVENDER GRANITE: On Moose and Crotch Islands.

- *Denmark, Oxford County* AMETHYST, SMOKY QUARTZ: In Warren Quarry on W side of Pleasant Mountain.
- *Dixfield, Oxford County* BERYL, GARNET: On south slope of Hedgehog Hill.
- *Fryeburg, Oxford County* GARNET, SMOKY QUARTZ: To S on E side of Stark Mountain at Eagle Granite Quarry.
- *Greenwood, Oxford County* * BERYL, ROSE, SMOKY AND STAR QUARTZ: Stanley Perham, of Trap Corner, was a leader in making Maine gem sources available to collectors. One of his mines, the Heikkinen mine, is reached from Greenwood by going S 500 feet, then to the Rawleigh Hayes house on Hayes Hill, and walking ¾ mile on the mine road.

  Another is the Harvard quarry, reached by driving S for 2½ miles to a crossroad below Mud Pond. Turn left 1,000 feet to a rise above Nestor Tamminen's house and walk ½ mile to mine on SW brow of Noyes Mountain. Tourmaline, beryl, and purple apatite are found here.

  Nearby are the Tamminen mine and the Waisanen quarry, which yield the same gem minerals as the Harvard quarry. (Directions at the Tamminen house.)

  PINK BERYL, ROSE QUARTZ: Take road W to Patch Mountain school, then N to end of road and hike to Emmons quarry. The mine is on the east face of Uncle Tom mountain. W of this quarry is the Tiger Bill quarry, noted for purple apatite, aquamarine, and golden beryl.

  QUARTZ: S 1½ miles to gravel road between Hicks and

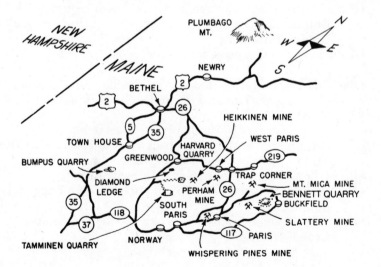

172

Mud Pond. Hike up Noyes Mountain, which lies to left of the road from Greenwood and collect at Diamond Ledge. (Permission at Rawleigh Hayes house.)

- *Hebron, Oxford County* GREEN BERYL, TOURMALINE: N 2½ miles at quarries at Number 4 hill—the Mills, Foster Haverinen, and Mt. Marie mines.

  PINK TOURMALINE, APATITE: N 2 miles to Mt. Rubellite quarry on steep ridge just north of a church.

  GOLDEN AND BLUE BERYL, ROSE QUARTZ: 1½ miles N at Hibbs Mine.

- *Lisbon Falls, Sagadahoc County* BERYL, GREEN FELDSPAR, QUARTZ: E on Hwy 125 past Hwy 201 to Stoddard's Pond, then N on road past marsh to Coomb's mine.

- *Litchfield, Kennebec County* SODALITE: At Spear's Corner.

- *Machiasport, Washington County* JASPER PEBBLES: At Jasper Beach.

- *Minot, Androscoggin County* TOURMALINE, PURPLE APATITE: Hwy 121 E to Haskell's Corners, then left 2 miles to Hatch road to right to quarries on side of Mt. Apatite. There are several other quarries along Hatch road. Nearby are the Pulsifer & Wade quarries, notable for apatite and lepidolite; the Maine Feldspar mine, with pink beryl; the Littlefield quarry, which yields smoky quartz, and the Phillips mine, for amethyst and smoky quartz.

- *Mount Desert, Hancock County* AMETHYST, SMOKY QUARTZ: At Hall's Quarry.

- *Newfield, York County* VESUVIANITE: In boulders in the game preserve.

- *North Lovell, Oxford County* BLUE BERYL: 3 miles N at Chapman Hill.

- *Norway, Oxford County* TOURMALINE: At B.B No. 7 Mine at Nobles Corner 8 miles NW.

  TOURMALINE, ROSE QUARTZ: N 2 miles at Tubb's Ledge.

- *Paris, Oxford County* * TOURMALINE, BERYL, SMOKY QUARTZ: Mount Mica's open pits and dumps lie 1⅓ miles E and are reached by a mine road to left up a hill. Herderite and amazonite are also found here. (Get permission from Mrs. Howard Irish in Buckfield; fee.)

  SMOKY QUARTZ, AQUAMARINE: In Slattery mine. Take right turn from Paris and go a half mile to mine road. Walk 1,000 feet to dumps. (Get permission at Perham store.)

  ROSE QUARTZ, CHRYSOBERYL: At Hooper's Ledge on S side of Paris Hill.

- *Pembroke, Washington County* RHYOLITE, JASPER: At Gleason Cove.

- *Perry, Washington County* AGATE: At Loring Cove to N off U.S. 1.
- *Phippsburg, Sagadahoc County* BERYL: At Thomas mine at Parker's Head.
- *Poland, Androscoggin County* GREEN TOURMALINE: In Berry quarry.
- *Roxbury, Oxford County* JASPER: At bend in Swift River around Thomas Intervale.
- *Rumford, Oxford County* TOURMALINE, LEPIDOLITE: N on Hwy 120 10 miles to Roxbury Notch, turn left on dirt road 2 miles to mine road to left, to Black Mountain quarries.
- *Sanford, York County* BROWN VESUVIANITE: In pit and on dump. Go 1½ miles E on School Street at Goodhall farm.
- *South Paris, Oxford County* * ROSE, CITRINE, SMOKY QUARTZ: At Whispering Pines mine 6 miles S on Hwy 26 and at mine by road E.

  CITRINE QUARTZ: At Blueberry Mountain.
- *Stoneham, Oxford County* TOPAZ, PURPLE APATITE: At Lord Hill. Take Hwy 5 N to Kezar Lake, then W through Narrows and N 1⅔ miles, take left fork and go 2 miles to mine in ledge near top of hill. At Melrose quarry on Pleasant Mountain E of Lord Hill, aquamarine is found.
- *Stow, Oxford County* AMETHYST, APATITE: Hwy 113 N for 5 miles, then E on dirt road and take trail N up valley ½ mile to CTA trail. Take it E when it heads up mountain. Dig in new area over top and down on E side. Jeep trail leads to Eastman Ledge, and a trail leads beyond it over top of hill. (Get permission: Harry Eastman in Fryeburg.)
- *Topsham, Sagadahoc County* GARNET, TOURMALINE, SMOKY QUARTZ, BLUE BERYL: At quarries. Take Hwy 24 for 3 miles N; turn on left fork at Topsham Quarry Company sign; cross Cathance River and go mile to top of hill. Turn left on dirt road to Fisher (the best), Consolidated, Staples, and Willes quarries.
- *Westford, Middlesex County* CHIASTOLITE: In soil and stream at Small's Falls, Madrid twp., Franklin County.
- *West Minot, Androscoggin County* GARNET: At Pitts & Tenny mine N 1 mile on Hwy 119 to quarry on W. (Get permission at Perham store at Trap Corner.)
- *West Paris, Oxford County* * SMOKY QUARTZ, APATITE: The Perham mine is reached by taking High Street to a sign reading "Perham Mine," thence a half mile up the mine road. In the open pits in feldspar are found smoky

quartz crystals, sometimes with pale amethyst tints. (Get permission from Bell Mineral Company of West Paris.)
• *Winslow, Kennebec County* BLUE BERYL: In Winslow Mine.

Maryland

The easternmost part of Maryland along the line of Baltimore and Washington is coastal plain, backed up by the Piedmont plateau of crystalline rocks containing a diversity of mineral wealth, and giving way in the west to mountains and valleys of the Appalachian system, made up of sedimentary and metamorphic rocks of lesser mineral interest.

• *Baltimore, Baltimore County* SERPENTINE: In Bare Hills Serpentine quarry ½ mile N at Falls and Pimlico roads. Quarry E of Falls road is owned by the city. (Get permission from Baltimore Department of Parks.)
• *Beltsville, Prince Georges County* PETRIFIED WOOD: In stream beds to N.
• *Cape Sable, Anne Arundel County* AMBER: In sedimentary deposits on the Magothy River.
• *Cockeysville, Baltimore County* MARBLE, QUARTZ, TOURMALINE, DIOPSIDE: At H. T. Campbell quarry. Take Padonia exit off Int. 83 N of Int. 695. Collecting permitted only on Saturday mornings with advance permission.
• *Elk Mills, Cecil County* BERYL, GARNET: From U.S. 40 go N on Hwy 280 to Cherry Hill, then E on Hwy 277 to quarry on E bank of Elk Creek. Get permission.
• *Granite, Baltimore County* QUARTZ: Loose in soil on Nash farm.
• *Hancock, Washington County* QUARTZ: S on Hwy 522 to Pennsylvania Sand corporation pit.
• *Jarrettsville, Harford County* SERPENTINE: At Reed chrome mine.
At Wilkins chrome mine 1½ miles SE along road to Cooperstown. Both mines are on private lands and collecting is discouraged.
• *Ocean City, Worcester County* QUARTZ: Crystals like Cape May "diamonds" in beach sands at Point Lookout.
• *Point of Rocks, Frederick County* BRECCIA: In abandoned quarry near Potomac river.
• *Reistertown, Baltimore County* SERPENTINE, CHALCEDONY, JASPER: Off Hwy 140 2 miles S, turn right on Nicodemus road at quarry. Get permission.

• *Rock Springs, Cecil County* SERPENTINE (WILLIAMSITE), CHAL-
CEDONY: The area at the Maryland-Pennsylvania line
offers some of the world's finest serpentine to the collector. One location for this translucent green material is
the Line Pits (Lowe chrome mine) dumps north of Con-
owingo dam on the Susquehanna River. Hwy 222 leads N
to the Pleasant Grove road to the left, then a short trail
through the woods leads to the dumps. Information can
be obtained from Mrs. Glenn Holdsworth, 3730 Chestnut St., Baltimore, Md. 21211 (fee).
East of the Line Pits are scores of prospect pits and mines
in the chrome serpentine deposits, including the Wood
Chrome mine just N of the state line in a meander of Oc-
toraro creek, the Jenkins or Rock Springs mine, and the
Cedar Hill quarries in Pennsylvania.

• *Rockville, Montgomery County* DIOPSIDE, GROSSULAR GARNET:
NW on Hwy 28 for 3½ miles to Travilah road, then left 1
mile to Piney Meeting House road, take it left to Hunting
Hill quarry to collect a rock formed of massive diopside
and grossular garnet known as rodingite.

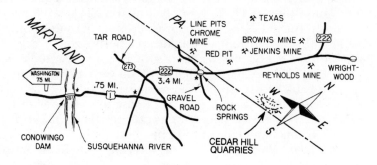

• *Simpsonville, Howard County* AMETHYST, QUARTZ CRYSTALS: In
Maryland mica mine on Arrington farm.

• *Springfield, Montgomery County* JASPER: Take first road on left
from school marked "Vaughn Summit" to concrete
bridge. Collect under it in stream.

• *Union Bridge, Carroll County* QUARTZ CRYSTALS: SW 3 miles in
Mountain View lead mine ¼ mile W of Beaver Dam
Church on Beaver Dam road.

• *Westminster, Carroll County* QUARTZ CRYSTALS: N of New
Windsor Road ¼ mile at Hyde limestone quarry.

Massachusetts

Massachusetts, like Connecticut, is divided into two geographical provinces by the Connecticut River. East of the river, the land falls with few elevations toward the ocean, although the underlying rocks are contorted metamorphic schists; to the west lies an Appalachian Mountain region. Most gem-producing areas lie in the Connecticut River valley or just east of it, except the Essex County area in the extreme northeast part of the state.

- *Amherst, Hampshire County* AMETHYST, PREHNITE: In Lane Traprock quarries on Hwy 116, with datolite.
- *Bolton, Worcester County* SCAPOLITE: 2¼ miles E in dumps of Bolton Lime quarry (fee).
- *Cape Cod, Barnstable County* JASPER: Pebbles on beach with epidote between Sandwich and the Plymouth County boundary.
- *Chester, Hampden County* JASPER: In W branch of Westfield river.
- *Chesterfield, Hampshire County* RHODONITE, KYANITE: N of meetinghouse 1 mile on old Searle farm.
- *Cohasset, Norfolk County* JASPER: With epidote as pebbles on shore of Massachusetts Bay.
- *Conway, Franklin County* JASPER: In Deerfield River, and in breccia in SE part of town.
- *Deerfield, Franklin County* AGATE: In Deerfield River and a mile E of Deerfield Academy.
- *Fitchburg, Worcester County* GOLDEN BERYL: In pegmatite in W side of Rollstone Hills.
- *Gay Head, Dukes County* AMBER: On shore eroding from greensand deposits.
- *Gloucester, Essex County* SMOKY QUARTZ, AMAZONSTONE: In Pomroy quarry.
- *Greenfield, Franklin County* AMETHYST, CHALCEDONY: In Cheapside quarry, S of village, with datolite and prehnite.
- *Marshfield, Plymouth County* JASPER PEBBLES: At beach.
- *Middleboro, Plymouth County* AGATE, CHALCEDONY: In vein running N from Rochester to Middleboro and SW to Fairhaven.
- *Nantucket, Nantucket County* AMBER: On sea beaches eroded from deposits of greensand.
- *Newburyport, Essex County* SERPENTINE: On turnpike 2 miles to Newbury, then first road left for 2 miles. Park, walk to Devil's Den, and look in mine dumps.

- *Pelham, Hampshire County* SERPENTINE, APATITE: At asbestos mine. 4 miles SW.
- *Pittsfield, Essex County* GREEN QUARTZ: In SE part of town.
- *Plainfield, Hampshire County* RHODONITE: In Betts manganese mine and another mine 1 mile W.
- *Rockport, Essex County* AMAZONSTONE: In the Cape Ann granite quarries.

   CITRINE QUARTZ: At Babson farm quarry.
- *Royalston, Worcester County* BLUE-GREEN BERYL: In Reynolds mine 2½ miles NE at Beryl Hill.
- *Stockbridge, Essex County* SMOKY QUARTZ: On Monument mountain 3 miles S via U.S. 7.
- *West Chesterfield, Hampshire County* SMOKY QUARTZ: W ¼ mile in road cut on Hwy 143.

   TOURMALINE: In Clark Ledge on Reed farm.
- *West Cummington, Hampshire County* * RHODONITE: The West Cummington manganese mine is ½ mile N of Hwy 9 on a mine road that leaves Hwy 9 roughly 3 miles from the fork of Hwys 9 and 112 just NW of Cummington. Rhodonite is found in the mine ore and on the dumps.

   TOURMALINE, LEPIDOLITE, CAT'S-EYE SPODUMENE: Farther E and just N of the hamlet of Lithia is the Barrus mine, the first farm N of Lithia on the right of Hwy 112. Take trail to the diggings alongside a small stream. (Obtain permission at the farmhouse to collect.)

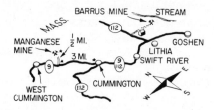

- *Westfield, Hampden County* AMETHYST: At Lane Traprock quarry with prehnite, datolite, and serpentine with bronzite inclusions.

   SERPENTINE: In Atwater quarry.

Michigan

Lower Michigan is quite level and not much elevated above the Great Lakes, and is underlain by sedimentary deposits of limestone, salt, and gypsum. Upper Michigan, however, is a rugged land of ancient igneous and metamorphic rocks, highly contorted and containing some of the world's richest iron and copper deposits, as well as a wealth of specimen minerals.

- •*Allouez, Keweenaw County* * CHRYSOCOLLA: From dump at Allouez Mine.

  AGATE: The Keweenaw beach agate is distinctive for its pastel shades. It is rarely large and is not easy to distinguish from the other pebbles on the beach. These agates are found along the NW shore from Tamarack waterworks to the tip of the peninsula.

  The best beach pickings are at Pete's Beach, reached by taking the Five Mile Point Road from Allouez to turnoff marked with sign and through woods to lake shore (fee).

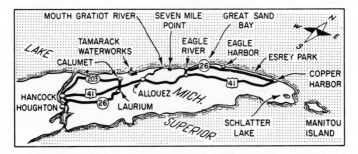

  At Gratiot River Beach, reached from Five Mile Point Road by turning S on very rough road.

  Also on Manitou Island.

  LEDGE AGATES: Larger and of a more conventional type. Found in the ledges that cross the road from Allouez to the lake shore.

  Also at High Rock Bay at Keweenaw Point.

  In the ledges back of Esrey Park on Agate Harbor.

  Inland from Seven Mile Point and on the N side of Schlatter Lake.

  PINK, GREEN THOMSONITES: Found on the Keweenaw, Pete's, and Gratiot River beaches. Also on Cedar Bay beach, from Ahmeek to thomsonite area near Eagle River.

- •*Alpena, Alpena County* FOSSIL CORAL (PETOSKEY STONE): In Rockport Quarry, 11 miles NE.

- •*Brighton, Livingston County* OOLITIC AGATE: E on Int. 96 to Kensington road, S ½ mile to the American Aggregate quarry.

• *Charlevoix, Charlevoix County* FOSSIL CORAL (PETOSKEY STONE): Take U.S. 31 to Bell's Bay road to Medusa quarry. Petoskey stones, a form of calcified coral, are widespread in eight counties—Benzie, Leelanau, Grand Traverse, Antrim, Charlevoix, Cheboygan, Presque Isle, and Alpena. They are most abundant along the S shore of Little Traverse bay from Petoskey to Charlevoix. They are also found in quarries along the bluffs on the shore from Petoskey to W of Charlevoix and in gravel pits S of this area, on beaches of Burt and Torch Lake, and in the area N of a line between Beulah and Manton on the S and W of Hwy 131 to Petoskey. A favorite spot is the Afton-Onaway district in Cheboygan and Presque Isle counties.

• *Copper Harbor, Keweenaw County* DATOLITE, GREEN EPIDOTE (SHOT THROUGH WITH COPPER), THOMSONITE: Datolite on Clark mine dump. Massive green epidote is found in many of these mines and makes an attractive cut stone. Thomsonite occurs in nodules and seams in the basalt.
AGATE: At northern point of peninsula, reached by taking logging road at northern end of U.S. 41 5 miles to clump of three birches at fork, and taking left fork 3 miles to point. Traffic is permitted only on Sundays.
Long hike to right around point leads to less picked area on Keystone Bay.

• *DeTour, Chippewa County* AGATE: Take ferry to Drummond Island. Collect on beach.

• *Grand Haven, Ottawa County* GEODES: E 12 miles in gravel pits.

• *Grandville, Kent County* ALABASTER: In gypsum quarry.

• *Ishpeming, Marquette County* JASPER, HEMATITE: The layered rock known as jaspalite is found widely but especially at Jasper Hill in Ishpeming. From U.S. 41 turn right on Hwy 28 and Division Street through the city to Jasper Street and turn right to foot of hill.
SERPENTINE: At Verd Antique quarry. Go W along U.S. 41 to Cooper Lake Road, turn right 2½ miles, then left on Rd. 572 for less than a mile to Ropes Gold mine and hike ⅓ mile to the serpentine quarry.
DOLOMITE: The rock known as Kona dolomite outcrops many places S of Marquette. The Lindberg quarries are reached by taking U.S. 41 to the Negaunee caution light then right on Rd 480 SE for 7 miles to a caution light then 1½ miles farther to the quarries.

- *Isle Royale* AMETHYSTINE AGATE: In Siskiwit Bay.
  On Thomsonite Beach.
  AGATE, CARNELIAN: At head of Siskiwit Bay.
  NE of McGinty Cove.
  N side of Amygdaloid Point.
  THOMSONITE: At point N of Stockly Bay.
  On main island S of Hawk Island.
  Near end of Scoville Point thomsonite has been found.
  CHLORASTROLITE: At Mott Island, Smithwick Island, Caribou Island, Rock Harbor, on S shore of Siskiwit Lake, at Scoville Point, Todd Harbor, Chippewa Harbor, and Tobin Harbor.
  (Isle Royale is a national park and collecting is forbidden there.)
- *Marquette, Marquette County* AGATE, JASPER: On point at N end of Presque Isle Avenue.
- *Michigamme, Marquette County* STAUROLITE: In road cut S of Lake Michigamme.
- *Mass, Ontonagon County* EPIDOTE ROCK: Green rock with copper inclusions on dumps of Mass and Minesota mines and other nearby mines.
- *Mohawk, Keweenaw County* DOMEYKITE: Several copper arsenides in white massive quartz are found in the dumps of the Mohawk, Seneca, and Ahmeek mines near towns of those names.
- *Newport, Monroe County* AMETHYSTINE QUARTZ: At Point aux Peaux.
- *Ontonagon, Ontonagon County* AGATE: On shores of Ontonagon and Gogebic counties, such as at Gull Point.
- *Oxford, Oakland County* OOLITIC AGATE: In gravel pits and also at Holly, Romeo, and Clarkston.
- *St. Johns, Clinton County* CHERT: N on U.S. 27 to Kinley av., E 1 mile to Scott road, then N ½ mile to Walling gravel pit.
- *Spalding, Menominee County* GARNET: In mica schist to W and N in Scott and Howe creeks.
- *Tahquamenon Falls State Park, Luce County* AGATE: On Lake Superior beaches from Whitefish Point to Crisp Point.

Minnesota

Southern Minnesota rises from the midwestern prairies into a rolling upland which, in the northwest, is dominated by the flat bed of the ancient extinct Lake Agassiz. In the northeast lies the Mesabi

iron range, and in central Minnesota the Cuyuna range. The whole
state is covered with lakes left by glaciers, which also left a rich deposit of Lake Superior agates on beaches and in gravel pits. This
deposit can be found generally wherever the soil has a reddish hue,
which is roughly from Duluth north to the Ontario line and west to
Hwy. 71, as well as a small area around the Twin Cities.

Areas marked on state map * are locations where there are
active gravel pits. Permission can usually be obtained to examine
the stock piles of gravel for agates of the Lake Superior type. These
are commonly brown or red, have fine stripes of several colors in
what is called fortification pattern, and usually are fist size or
smaller.

- *Beaver Bay, Lake County* AGATE: Whenever the lake builds a
  gravel beach agates are likely to be present. These
  beaches are formed and washed away by the waves.
- *Bloomington, Scott County* AGATE: S on Int. 35 to Exit 42, up
  ramp and turn left 1¹/₅ mile to Chicago avenue, turn
  right to Crystal Lake road, then left to farm and park.
  Hunt agates in gravel pit.
- *Bovey, Itasca County* AGATE: In mine dumps.
- *Buhl, St. Louis County* AGATE: Go E on U.S. 169 to Top's Tavern on N side of road, turn N on dirt road to Dormer
  dumps on left side of road.

•*Cloquet, Carlton County* AGATE: N 6 miles on Hwy 33, collect at Kinto Bros. pit and to S in Carter pit at Carlton.

•*Crosby, Crow Wing County* * BINGHAMITE: Silicified iron mineral known as binghamite at Evergreen (Portsmouth) mine dump. The mineral, which resembles red and yellow tigereye, is found in the dump, especially on the E side, and on the W side of the dump S of the road and near the pit.

Farther along a side road W from Hwy 6 and slightly S is the tipple and dump of the Louis Mine, where another form of the same material is obtained. William Perpitch, of the Yankee and Portsmouth Mine, knows the locations of this material in the area.

RHODOCHROSITE: Dump of Hopkins mine at Crosby-Ironton, and also at Pittsburgh-Pacific mine.

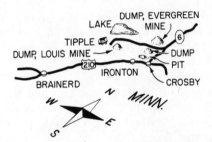

•*Duluth, St. Louis County* AGATE: In shoreline gravels (especially at low water) of Island Lake Reservoir 18 miles N.

Also at Coon Bros. gravel pit 8 miles NW at Munger, and Arrowhead pit 20 miles NW at Twig.

•*Grand Marais, Cook County* * THOMSONITE: 3 miles SW in ledges along road cut where power line crosses Hwy 61, above road in ledges. Also 6 miles S at Thomsonite Beach (fee).

In gravel of lake shore at point. (Permission to collect at shore difficult to obtain.)

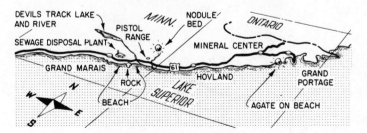

HOVLANDITE: Just beyond Grand Marais is the town's sewage-disposal plant on the lake shore and just beyond it is a small beach and a rock. An attractive dark-spotted rock known as hoylandite is obtained on the NE side of this rock.

AGATE NODULES: Beyond this spot lies the Devil Track River, and 1½ miles NE of its mouth is a side road to a pistol range. A dim road or trail N 150 to 300 feet from it leads to an area of agate nodules.

AGATE: At Paradise Beach, 13 miles E of Grand Marais, small banded agates can be dug from the basalt.

LINTONITE: Associated with thomsonite at Good Harbor Bay and elsewhere in this area.

- *Lanesburg, Fillmore County* QUARTZ: a mile E in road cut.
- *Little Marais, Lake County* * AGATE: In gravels at County Line Beach.

  Five miles SW at the Baptism River's mouth. Park just east of the state's blacktop depot and take trail down to the lake for blue agates. Stay S of the rock in the lake.
- *Mazeppa, Wabasha County* AGATE: Cold-water type agate in Zumbo River.
- *Mineral Center, Cook County* AGATE: Take side road to Grand Portage until it dips close to the lake. Here a faintly marked road leads through a shale ridge to the collecting spot on the beach.
- *Osseo, Hennepin County* AGATE: At Anderson Aggregate pit. S on Hwy 110, then W, and at two nearby pits.
- *Pipestone, Pipestone County* PIPESTONE (CATLINITE): In a national monument, no collecting.
- *Randall, Morrison County* AGATE: In gravel pits.
- *Red Wing, Goodhue County* QUARTZ CRYSTALS: In cavities in limestone bluffs along Mississippi River.
- *Royalton, Morrison County* STAUROLITE: In schist outcrops at Blanchard Dam; best under railroad bridge. Sieve gravel for staurolites, agate, and garnet.

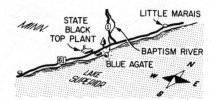

- *St. Paul, Hennepin County* AGATE: In gravel pit E on Hwy 12.
- *Tofte, Cook County* AGATE: In gravels at Two Islands Beach.
- *Two Harbors, Lake County* AGATE: NE 11 miles in gravels at Gooseberry Falls State Park beach.
- *Virginia, St. Louis County* * AGATE: Up a side road from U.S. 169 about 10 miles W of Virginia are the Atkins and the Wade mines. About 3 miles up this side road is a large spoil bank. On its W face Lake Superior agates can be dug.

  Beyond and to the left of this spoil bank is another which contains the same type of agates along its S face.

  JASPER: Take Hwy 135 from Virginia toward Biwabik, stop a mile short of Biwabik, take mine road marked "M.E." to Mary Ellen mine; look for jasper with swirl patterns on dump. Also on Hwy 135 1 mile W of Biwabik at Corsica mine.
- *Wabasha, Wabasha County* AGATE: In gravel pits.

Mississippi

Much of the state is built up of sand, gravel, and mud brought down by the Mississippi River and which has filled a great bay in the Gulf Coast. The surface rises from the Gulf Coast and the river toward the oldest sedimentary rocks in the state that form a ridge in the northeast counties. Thus, petrified wood and agates in river gravels are the major gem resources.

- *Anding, Yazoo County* AGATE, PETRIFIED WOOD: In Thompson and Perry creeks.
- *Carpenter, Claiborne County* PETRIFIED PALM WOOD, AGATE: S 3½ miles at Traxler Co. gravel washing plant at Bayou Pierre. Also banded chert.

- *Fair River, Lawrence County* AGATE, CHERT: N 3 miles of U.S. 84 and ½ mile W of Hwy 27, at Fair River gravel bars and Green Bros. gravel washing plant.
- *Fearn Springs, Winston County* OPALIZED WOOD: Along Hwy 25 near Webster in Mill Creek.
- *Georgetown, Copiah County* AGATE, PETRIFIED WOOD: W 2 miles to Green Bros. gravel washing plant just S of Hwy 28, collect in Copiah creek. Also collect in creek S of town and W of Hwy 27.
- *Greenville, Washington County* AGATE: In gravel dredged from Mississippi river. Feldspar moonstone is to be found in the Mississippi river gravels here and elsewhere.
- *Gulfport, Stone County* PETRIFIED WOOD, JASPER: In Bell Creek, 18 miles NW and generally in creeks to NW.
- *Meadville, Franklin County* AGATE, CHERT: to W at Middle Fork creek, also petrified wood.
- *Natchez, Adams County* AGATE, JASPER: Lake Superior agates and jaspers at St. Catherine Gravel Washing plant at Carthage Point.
- *North Foxworth, Marion County* AGATE, PETRIFIED WOOD: In gravels at Pearl River Washing plant.
- *Quentin, Franklin County* AGATE, PETRIFIED WOOD: S ½ mile of U.S. 84 in gravel bars in McCall Creek.
  AGATE: NW at gravel pit at Oldenburg and NE of Hamburg.
- *Tylertown, Walthall County* AGATE, PETRIFIED WOOD: At Walthall Gravel Washing plant on Bogue Chitto River just N of Louisiana line. Also chert.
- *Wesson, Copiah County* AGATE: E 6 miles, in Bahala Creek. W 4 miles, in gravel pit.
- *Yazoo City, Yazoo County* PETRIFIED WOOD, AGATE: Between Hwy 3 and 49 as far S as Hwy 433.
  Also in gravel terraces above Yazoo River at its tributaries.
  AGATE, CHERT: S on Hwy 49 to Little Yazoo, then W 4½ miles to Oil City, N for 2 miles and W 1⅓ miles to collect in gravel bars in river.

Missouri

Missouri north of the Missouri River is, like most of Illinois and Iowa, a fertile plain formed by glacial action and underlain by sedimentary rocks. Southern Missouri, however, contains not only an area of rolling plains to the west, as in Arkansas, but also the

Ozark Highland which becomes gradually rougher as it sweeps from southern Illinois southwestward into Arkansas and Oklahoma. These peaks and valleys expose not only sedimentary rocks but also granites.

- *Alexandria, Clark County* GEODES: S 8 miles on Hwy 61, in open pit on Scheffler's property (fee).
- *Cadet, Washington County* AGATE, QUARTZ: In barite mines, also at Potosi and Old Mines nearby.
- *Creighton, Cass County* PETRIFIED WOOD: In quarry on Cornett farm 3 miles E.
- *DeSoto, Jefferson County* AGATE: At Washington State Park. Take U.S. 21 to Hwy CC, then W on Hwy E to Tiff, then E across railroad to mine.
- *Farmington, St. Francois County* CHERT (MOZARKITE): W on Hwy W past Hwy 67, then in a block, turn N a block. Go 2⅕ miles W on blacktop road to fork, take right fork for ⅔ mile to road to right with chain across it. Collect to E and N where ground is bulldozed.
- *Gainesville, Ozark County* CHERT: At Timbered Knob.
- *Kahoka, Clark County* GEODES: N on Hwy 81 to nursing home, right 1 block, turn left, cross river, turn right, and then left at next corner to Easterday farm (fee).
- *Lincoln, Benton County* CHERT (MOZARKITE): To E in roadcuts or at Brice Patt farm (fee). (See James Melton at motel in Lincoln).
- *Malden, Madrid County* JASPER, CHERT: Go W on Hwy J for 5⅘ miles to gravel road to right, and N on ridge to pits on Crowley's Ridge.
- *Rolla, Phelps County* AMETHYST: S on Hwy 63 for 8 miles, then W on dirt road 2 miles to fork; take right fork to Moselle mine No. 10. Also quartz and jasper.
- *St. Francisville, Clark County* GEODES: At Sinotte property (fee).
- *St. Louis, St. Louis County* GEODES, JASPER. N on U.S. 67 to St. Ferdinand creek, search creek gravels.
- *Stanton, Franklin County* RUTILATED QUARTZ: At Cherry Valley iron mine.

Montana

The Rocky Mountains dominate the western part of Montana, crossing the state from northwest to southeast, and exposing a great variety of rocks. From them have come the gold, silver, copper, corundum, and other minerals which have caused Montana to be called the Treasure State. Eastward lie the High Plains, sloping eastward, formed of erosional deposits and broken by bluffs, gullies, and isolated mountains. In these areas are found moss agate and like materials.

- *Alder, Madison County* BANDED RHYOLITE (WONDERSTONE): Take road S along Ruby River from Alder 12 miles to righthand fork. Take road 8 miles; collect along road NW toward Dillon.
  ALMANDINE GARNET: In gravels of Ruby River above storage dam to S.
- *Anaconda, Deer Lodge County* AMAZON STONE: N 3 miles at falls of Lost Creek, in pegmatite.
  PETRIFIED WOOD: 2 miles E from French Gulch sign.
- *Butte, Silver Bow County* AMETHYST: To E in Little Pipestone Creek and in W fork of Rader Creek.
  At old Pohndorf mine reached by taking Hwy 10 E to 19 Mile Inn, then dirt road 1½ miles N.
  SMOKY QUARTZ: In pegmatites of Whisky Gulch N of Pohndorf mine. Also at Timber Butte, to S, and just E of railroad cut at Janney substation.
  SAPPHIRE: In Brown's Gulch to NW.
  RHODONITE: In Alice mine dumps and at Lexington mine.
- *Canyon Ferry Dam, Lewis and Clark County* GREEN SAPPHIRE: At Magpie Gulch, 1 mile above in Missouri River.
- *Columbus, Stillwater County* MOSS JASPER, PETRIFIED WOOD: To SE and E and W of bridge and on island in Yellowstone River.
- *Deer Lodge, Powell County* SAPPHIRE: To SE in Dry Cottonwood Creek.
- *Dillon, Beaverhead County* PETRIFIED WOOD: To NW in Frying Pan Basin.
  STAR CORUNDUM: 18 miles SW in Sweetwater Creek on the Rebish ranch.
  SILLIMANITE: E 13 miles at Christenson ranch.
  SOAPSTONE: SE ¾ mile on Sweetwater Road at Keystone quarry.
- *Dryhead, Carbon County* * AGATE: Take road N to ranch at foot of Pryor Gap. Agate is found on the rim rocks of the canyon where Dryhead Creek flows into the Big Horn River, and at the mouth of Big Horn Canyon. It is also scattered over much of the surrounding grazing area.

- *Elkhorn Hot Springs, Beaverhead County* AMETHYST: N 4 miles at Crystal Park.
- *Gardiner, Park County* AGATIZED WOOD: The Tom Miner basin collecting area lies 16 miles N on U.S. 89, then left 10 miles into Gallatin National Forest. From the campground hike up trail N and then NW above bluffs toward Ramshorn peak.
- *Helena, Lewis and Clark County* SAPPHIRE, GARNET: These can be found on a number of bars in the Missouri River, such as the American, Eldorado, Emerald, French, Metropolitan, Ruby, and Spokane bars. The Eldorado bar is reached from Helena by taking Last Chance Gulch Road N to N. Montana Street and on it to gravel road E; then N on road along the Missouri River to York bridge, cross it to York, and then N to Eldorado Sapphire Diggings (fee). SMOKY QUARTZ: SE 3 miles at Three-Mile Gulch.
- *Lewistown, Fergus County* SAPPHIRE: Near confluence of South and Middle forks of Judith River.
- *Livingston, Park County* PETRIFIED WOOD: In gravel halfway to Big Timber.
- *Manhattan, Gallatin County* ALABASTER (ONYX): 5 miles NW in quarry.
- *Miles City, Custer County* * MOSS AGATES: Montana moss agates are found all the way from the Big Horn River upstream on the Yellowstone River to beyond Sidney near the North Dakota line. They are in old gravel beds, on bluffs, and in ravines below bluffs. West of Miles City, the best collecting seems to be S of the Yellowstone, but farther E it ranges for 50 miles N of the river on ranches. Heavy ice in the winter and spring floods uncover new supplies of agate. The best months to collect are in April and in August when the water is low and the island

189

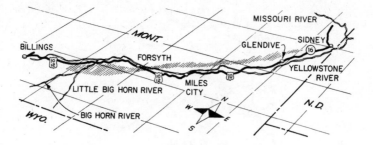

gravel beds are accessible. Heavy rains also lay bare agates in tributaries of the Yellowstone river and on hillsides far from the major highways. Most of the land is privately owned and permission to collect is needed. (Agate-bearing areas are shaded on the accompanying map.)

One recommended place to collect is S of Pompey's Pillar on Int. 94, where there are gravel banks, and another is farther E on Int. 94 at Hysham, where the collecting spot is S on Sarpy road in the hills.

- *Neihart, Cascade County* GREEN SPHALERITE: In Hartley mine.
- *Philipsburg, Granite County* SAPPHIRE: Take U.S. Alt. 10 S to Porters Corners, W 17 miles on Hwy 38 to bridge over fork of Rock Creek, follow sign to collecting area in Basin, Sapphire, Malay, Anaconda, and Coe gulches, where the gems are found in decomposing rock.

  Also S 6 miles on Hwy 26A to Hwy 28, then right for 17 miles to Chaussee Sapphire mine (fee).
- *Red Lodge, Carbon County* SERPENTINE: In chrome prospect dumps on Hellroaring Plateau.
- *Sula, Ravalli County* BERYL: In pegmatite 2 miles N via dirt road.
- *Twin Bridges, Madison County* QUARTZ CRYSTALS: W at Crystal Butte.
- *Utica, Judith Basin County* SAPPHIRE: 11 miles SW by gravel road to Yogo Gulch at foot of Little Belt Mountains, sapphire-bearing dike runs 5 miles E from Yogo Gulch. (fee).
- *Vaughn, Cascade County* BLACK AGATE, PETRIFIED WOOD: Along U.S. 89 and 91 E and S.
- *Warren, Carbon County* AGATE: N 5 miles, in the Pryor Mountains.
- *Whitehall, Jefferson County* SPHENE, SMOKY QUARTZ: 18 miles NW in Hay Canyon at the Gem Queen claim.

Nebraska

Nebraska is a plain sloping from northwest to southeast, including rich loess farmlands in the east backed by a region of sand hills to the west which lead into the more rugged bluffs, tablelands, and occasional mountains of the High Plains. In the extreme northwestern corner, Nebraska shares an area of badlands with South Dakota. Agates in stream gravels and petrified wood are the principal gem materials under such geological conditions.

- *Ashland, Saunders County* AGATE, PETRIFIED WOOD: In sand pits along Platte River and downstream to Louisville and LaPlatte.
- *Bayard, Morrill County* AGATE, PETRIFIED WOOD: In gravel beds along the N side of the Platte River all the way to Lake Guernsey, Wyo. Some of the wood is dendritic.
- *Beaver City, Furnas County* CHERT: Red and green material in the Niobrara chalk deposits.
- *Bridgeport, Morrill County* MOSS OPAL: Take Hwy 385 N to Angora Hill. Halfway up, turn E on dim road for 2 miles, then N up hill on another faintly marked road. Park here and walk to deposit on top of hill.
- *Chadron, Dawes County* CHALCEDONY: In northern part of county and as far W as Crawford and Harrison. Some of the chalcedony is blue.
- *Chappell, Deuel County* JASPER: Red and yellow float in South Platte river basin as far E as Hershey in Lincoln County.
- *Crawford, Dawes County* RED JASPER: Take Hwy 2 for 20 miles NW toward Orella railroad station, turn W ½ mile S of station, cross tracks and drive into badlands 2 miles W. Collect in hills.
  AGATE: Go ½ mile beyond Orella and turn E for 2 miles to Bald Butte. Also to NE near state line.
- *Fairbury, Jefferson County* JASPER, AGATE: In gravel pits as well as at Steele City, with petrified wood, and as far NW in Blue river basin as Ayr in Adams County.
- *Fullerton, Nance County* AGATE, PETRIFIED WOOD: In local gravel pits.
- *Gothenburg, Dawson County* PETRIFIED PALM WOOD: In sand pits.
- *Humboldt, Richardson County* AGATE: Along Nemaha River.
- *Kearney, Buffalo County* PETRIFIED WOOD: In sand and gravel pits as far west as Cozad and south to Holdrege.
- *Lincoln, Lancaster County* LAKE SUPERIOR AGATES: In gravel pits in nearby counties, especially near the cities of Win-

nebago, Norfolk, Fremont, Saunders, Wahoo, and Garland.

- *McCook, Red Willow County* PASTEL JASPER: In Republican river basin as far east as Franklin.
- *Mitchell, Scotts Bluff County* AGATE: In gravel terraces along the North Platte River.
- *Orella, Sioux County* AGATE: N 5 miles in Waldron Hills.
- *Palmyra, Otoe County* MOSS AGATE: In gravel pits here and at Dunbar.
- *Platte Center, Platte County* JASPER, PETRIFIED WOOD: In gravel pits and as float near junction of Loup and Platte rivers.
- *Plattsmouth, Cass County* SILICIFIED CORAL: Cream-colored material in limestone.
  ONYX: At Onyx Ace Hill quarry.
  CHERT (RICE AGATE): At Weeping Water and Lincoln.
- *Valentine, Cherry County* BLACK PETRIFIED WOOD: In hills along Minnechaduza Creek and the Niobrara River.
- *Waterloo, Douglas County* AGATE: In Lyman-Ritchie gravel pit to SW.

Nevada

Nevada is part of the Great Basin area of ancient sedimentary rocks that have been deformed and folded by granite intrusions, especially those associated with the Sierra Nevada uplift on the western edge of the state. Mineral occurrences are associated with the granite intrusions and the lavas. Much of the state is made up of arid plains and valleys broken by short mountain chains.

- *Battle Mountain, Lander County* CHALCEDONY, PETRIFIED WOOD: Go N across Southern Pacific railroad tracks, continue 18 miles to windmill, take E fork to bridge over Rock Creek and collect in and along creek.
  CINNABAR: Continue 7 miles farther, take left fork N for cinnabar in chert (myrickite) in washes and at dumps of Silver Cloud mercury mine.
  TURQUOISE: At No. 8 mine, 30 miles NE.
  At Blue Gem mine on Pedro claim, 4 miles SW on Hwy 8A.
  At Blue Matrix mine, 31 miles SE, near Tenabo.
  CINNABAR IN OPAL: At mercury mine to S.
  OBSIDIAN: NW 25 miles.

- *Beatty, Nye County* MARBLE: S 8⅓ miles on U.S. 95 to road E 3 miles to Carrara marble quarry.

  PETRIFIED WOOD: N 44½ miles on Hwy 95 past Stonewall Pass sign, then turn W 5 miles and S 4 miles.

- *Boulder City, Clark County* CHALCEDONY, ROSES, NODULES: S on Hwy 95 to road to Nelson, SE on it 8½ miles, then E and N on it 2 miles.

  AGATE: Cross Hoover Dam S and take Hwy 93 SE 3 miles, then W ¼ mile, park and hike over saddle into ravine to collect in lava on west hillsides.

- *Carlin, Elko County* GREEN TURQUOISE (FAUSTITE): NW 10 miles at Copper King mine in Tuscarora Mountains.

- *Coaldale, Esmeralda County* TURQUOISE, VARISCITE: NE 4 miles at Bonnie Blue mine on W side of canyon.

  JASPER: W 5 miles on Hwy 6, then N to collect on flats.

  OBSIDIAN: Hwy 6 W for 6 miles, turn S on Hwy 3A for ⅓ mile, leave paved road, angle left on bladed road 4½ miles to fork, keep right of Fish Lake, collect along road for 5 miles.

  OBSIDIAN, LIMB CASTS: Hwy 6 W for 6 miles, then S on Hwy 3A for 11½ miles and turn E to Sump Hole. Collect on north rim and in hills to W.

  AGATE: E on Hwy 6 for 7½ miles, S to Blair Junction and SW on road to Emigrant Pass for 6¾ miles, then S 2 miles to collect icicle agate on side of Silver Peak Mountains.

  PETRIFIED WOOD, AGATE: Take Hwy 6 7½ miles E, then N to Esmeralda Lake bed. From highway, take same side road but keep right 7 miles, watch for bluff; sagenitic agate is in debris from bluff face.

- *Cortez, Lander County* TURQUOISE: At Fox and Smith mines. At White Horse mine, 2½ miles NW.

- *Currie, Elko County* AGATE, QUARTZ: S on Hwy 93 to U.S. 50A and S to "Victoria Mine" sign, turn left to mine.

- *Denio, Humboldt County* FIRE OPAL: At Rainbow Ridge mine, 30 miles on Hwy 8A, then S 7 miles to trail from Virgin Valley to mine on side of Big mountain (fee).

  At Bonanza mine farther up Virgin Valley (fee).

  At Green Fire mine on E side of Virgin Valley.

  COMMON YELLOW OPAL: At Virgin Valley ranch.

  CARNELIAN: On hills above Denio road and Bonanza diggings.

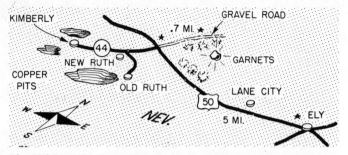

• *Ely, White Pine County* * GARNET: Take Hwy 50 NW from Ely
for 5 miles, then right on a gravel road ⁷/₁₀ of a mile
along the power line into canyon. Go to summit on foot.
The largest garnets are in rhyolite in area marked on
map.

Canyons N from Lane City for a mile in either direction
also contain garnet-bearing rhyolite.

BANDED RHYOLITE (WONDERSTONE): 40 miles W on U.S. 50
at Little Antelope summit.

• *Fallon, Churchill County* * BANDED RHYOLITE (WONDER-
STONE): Take U.S. 50 E and then SE for 11½ miles, turn
E through dump and 2½ miles into saddle to gravel pit.

GREEN AGATE: Mile south of the above gravel pit.

RED AND YELLOW JASPER: Continue on to turnoff 32 miles
S from Fallon on Hwy 50, 7 miles to road angling to E,

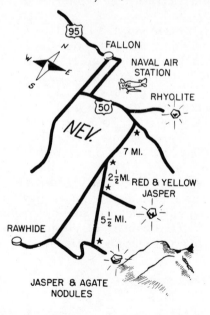

take a branch road E 2½ miles on and go to end for red and yellow jasper in weathered volcanic rock in canyon.

JASPER, AGATE NODULES: Come back to angling road and go 5½ miles to another branch road E. Take it into hills for jasper and agate nodules on hillsides.

- *Fernley, Lyon County* AGATE: On W side of Lake Lahontan and between lake and Fernley, 7½ miles S in hills E of U.S. 95A.

  PETRIFIED WOOD, AGATE NODULES. NE on Hwy 95A for 15½ miles; collect on flats and low hills.

  PETRIFIED WOOD, RHYOLITE: Hwy 95A SE 7½ miles to Fernley Park road, then W on farm road to Swartz ranch (fee). Return to Hwy 95A, go N nearly 1 mile to collect rhyolite (wonderstone).

- *Gabbs, Nye County* PETRIFIED WOOD: Take Hwy 23 N to road E to Broken Hills and Quartz Mountain, collect white wood around old LeFevre mine. Go back to Hwy 23, cross it and collect wood to W. Return to Hwy 23, take it a short distance toward Gabbs, then turn W again for green limb fragments.

- *Gerlach, Washoe County* PETRIFIED WOOD: Hwy 34 N for 41 miles past Black Rock desert. turn left to site of Leadville (fee).

  13 miles N on Hwy 34, collect in ravine.

  FIRE OPAL: Little Jo mine 40 miles N on Summit Lake road (fee). Get directions from Ray Duffield, 85 Tiger Dr., Carson City, Nev. 89701.

- *Goldfield, Esmeralda County* COLORFUL OPAL, AGATE: N on U.S. 95 2⅓ miles, then dirt road W 3½ miles (fee).

  PETRIFIED WOOD: S 18 miles on U.S. 95, at 3½ miles S of junction with Hwy 3 take dirt road W 6 miles, then W into red hills. Collect in ash beds.

- *Henderson, Clark County* GREEN JASPER: E past manganese plant a scant quarter of a mile, then NE 6 miles, park and walk to hill to N.

  BANDED CHALCEDONY: S 1⅔ miles on Hwy 93 turn W across tracks and go 4 miles, collect in hills.

  CHALCEDONY, NODULES: S on U.S. 95 to Hwy 2, take Hwy 2 8½ miles, turn E on dirt road through waste dump, park and collect chalcedony. Return to Hwy 2, continue SE 1 mile, collect nodules in hills W and S.

  OBSIDIAN, AGATE: S 7 miles on U.S. 95, W 13 miles, ignoring side roads.

- *Jackpot, Elko County* PINK LIMB CASTS: S 5 miles on road across

Trout Creek, then W for twig casts. Go 5 miles farther to dig limb casts from Granite range.

Also 2 miles S on Hwy 93, 3 miles E, S across bridge for 10 miles, turn E a mile, then S 6 miles to Texas Springs for pink limb casts.

• *Jarbidge, Elko County* AGATE: Take road N along Jarbidge River to Jack Creek, then trail into canyon SE to seam agate deposit near fork in creek. (Get permission, Rene Sprague in Jarbidge.)

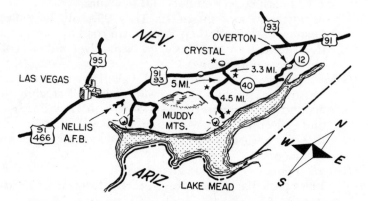

• *Las Vegas, Clark County* * BLACK AGATE: Take U.S. 91 to turnoff road to Nellis Air Force Base, then 2½ miles to entry road to Lake Mead Base. Go SE to Base hobby shop, turn left on unpaved road 4½ miles, then right to a gypsum wash. Walk S through gypsum piles to black agate field.

RED JASPER, PINK OPAL NODULES: Go back to U.S. 91 and continue N to Crystal, turn E for 3⅔ miles, then take right fork toward Muddy Mountains and go 5 miles to entrance to a canyon. Continue 4½ miles more to area where red jasper and pink opal nodules are found.

AGATE, JASPER: Collect by boat in gravels of N shore of Lake Mead between Las Vegas and Callville Bays.

• *Lida Junction, Esmeralda County* AGATE: Take road E from U.S. 95 for 1½ miles, collect along road for a mile.

• *Lovelock, Pershing County* AGATE, PETRIFIED WOOD: Take Western Avenue, then NW 10 miles, go W on same road 6½ miles to collect N of campsite in saddle.

AGATE AND OPAL: 2 miles W to fork, take left fork 16 miles, then N. Go back to fork, take right fork 20 miles for opal and plume agate.

JASPER, AGATE: Take road into Trinity Mountains for 15

miles NW and W to Eagle-Picher mine sign. About a mile farther collect on surface in saddles and canyon.

- *Luning, Mineral County* PINK THULITE, OPALIZED WOOD (HOWARDITE): Hwy 23 N almost to bridge, take left fork 34 miles to Rawhide, then 6 miles farther to ravine; collect in ash.
- *McDermitt, Humboldt County* PURPLE SAGENITIC AGATE: 4 miles W on Cordero mine road, collect in gravel pit. Also limb casts in nearby areas. Ask at McDermitt Rock Shop.
- *Midas, Elko County* CINNABAR IN OPAL: At Rand mine.
- *Mill City, Pershing County* AGATE GEODES: To S on Hwy 50 and then W to collect on E slope of Star Peak.
- *Millers, Esmeralda County* TURQUOISE: At Myers & Bona mine, 13 miles NW on W slope of Monte Cristo Mountains.
  At Petry mine, 11 miles NW in foothills of Monte Cristo Mountains.
  At Royal Blue mine, 12 miles NW on E edge of plateau.
  OBSIDIAN, CHERT: Take dirt road NW from U.S. 95, keeping NW at forks 9⅓ miles into pass, then follow faint tracks onto mesa.
- *Mina, Mineral County* SATIN SPAR: 3 miles S on Hwy 95, follow power line to mine.
  TURQUOISE: At Nevada Turquoise Co. mine.
  VARISCITE: Mile S of Candelaria and on E side of hill in Candelaria Mountains.
  COPPER MINERALS: In dumps of Wilson mine near Candelaria.
  JASPER, PETRIFIED WOOD: S on U.S. 95 to ruins of Sodaville, turn on road SW for 1 mile, then ½ mile up wash into Excelsior mountains.
- *Oreana, Pershing County* BLUE DUMORTIERITE: In quartz in Bullion Canyon.
- *Paradise Valley, Humboldt County* CHALCEDONY: At Coyote Springs.
  FIRE OPAL: 22 miles N at Firestone opal mine.
- *Reno, Washoe County* CINNABAR IN OPAL: S on U.S. 395 to Steamboat, backtrack to macadam road, go W ½ mile and take dirt road left across bridge into canyon to road junction. Collect in hills above road.
- *Rochester, Pershing County* PINK DUMORTIERITE: At Lincoln Hill.
- *Schurz, Mineral County* PETRIFIED WOOD: W on dirt road 19 miles to cattle guard, S on faint road.
- *Silver Peak, Esmeralda County* OBSIDIAN: SE 10 miles.

- *Tonopah, Nye County* TURQUOISE: At Smith Black Matrix mine, 3 miles NE.

  GREEN MOSS AGATE: W 26 miles on Hwy 6, N on Gilbert Road into canyon. Park at right-hand wash off canyon. Collect there and in hills to right.

  PETRIFIED WOOD: Take road NE past city reservoir, then follow power line over ridge into canyon. Fossil algae cover limbs.

  JASPER, AGATE: E 3 miles on U.S. 6, then N less than a mile to collect in hills and washes. Return to U.S. 6, go E 2⅓ mile, then N on Hwy 8A ⅓ mile and ½ mile W to collect petrified wood in wash.
- *Verdi, Storey County* QUARTZ: Go 5 miles NW on Dog Valley road to collect at Crystal Peak. Get permission from Mrs. E. G. Margrave, Reno Silica Company (fee).
- *Warm Springs, Nye County* THULITE, ZOISITE: SE on Hwy 25 for 58½ miles to road to Tempiute. Follow it to building by dry lake for a mile, then S on dirt road into mining camp in mountains.
- *Wendover, Elko County* CHALCEDONY: Take Hwy 50A S 38 miles, turn right at sign to Victoria, go N 12 miles to mine dumps.
- *Winnemucca, Humboldt County* AGATE, GEODES: Take U.S. 95 N to Hwy 8B and go through Paradise Valley to Hinkley Summit along road to N.

  JASPER, AGATE: Grass Valley road S 30 miles to hot springs, collect to E.
- *Yerington, Lyon County* OPALIZED LIMB CASTS: E on U.S. 95A to Hwy 3, S to second crossing of Walker River, then hike E into hills.

New Hampshire

The White Mountains of the Appalachians are the dominating geographical feature of New Hampshire. They occupy the north-central part of the state, an area of noteworthy mineral occurrences but of rocky, thin soil. Above the mountains is a region of ridges and valleys and south of them is the plateau characteristic of the New England upland. Glaciers have stripped the rocky granite highlands and created many lakes.

- *Acworth, Sullivan County* BERYL, ROSE QUARTZ: Less than 2 miles S at mine dump on W side of Beryl Mountain.
- *Alexandria, Grafton County* BERYL: In mine dump at 2,000 ft. level on N side of Hutchins Hill.

- *Alstead, Sullivan County* BERYL: In Beauregard mine (fee) and at Blister and Island mines.
- *Berlin, Coos County* JASPER: At cave W of trail and at 1,200 ft. level on S side of Jasper Mountain.
- *Center Strafford, Strafford County* BLUE BERYL, APATITE: At Foss mica mine mile NW. Go 2⅓ miles on Hwy 9, then mine road to right to Parker Mountain mine on Blue Hill.
- *Chatham, Carroll County* BROWN AND BLUE TOPAZ, PHENACITE, AMAZONSTONE: At 2,900 ft. level on E side of South Bald-face Mountain, in pockets where pegmatities meet talus slope.
- *Concord, Merrimack County* SMOKY QUARTZ: In Crowley granite quarry.
  RUTILATED QUARTZ: In New England Granite Works.
- *Conway, Carroll County* AMETHYST: At Redstone granite quarry, E of Hwy 302 between Conway and North Conway.
  At White Mountain granite quarry, at 700 ft. level on W side of Birch Hill.
  TOPAZ, SMOKY QUARTZ, AMAZONSTONE: Hwy 16 N ¼ mile, then left on Passaconaway road. Cross bridge, go ⅓ mile, then left to gravel road and N ¼ mile to collect in Lovejoy Pit.
  AMETHYST, SMOKY QUARTZ: 2 miles N of North Conway, then E on Hurricane Mountain road 3½ miles. Take trail from top ¼ mile W, follow old road and collect in ledges on Hurricane Mountain.
- *Danbury, Merrimack County* BERYL: At Wild Meadows mine.
- *Eaton Center, Carroll County* SMOKY QUARTZ: NE 2 miles at Randall lead mine.
- *Enfield, Grafton County* QUARTZ CRYSTALS WITH EPIDOTE INCLUSIONS: At Shaker Hill granite quarry.
- *Fitzwilliam, Cheshire County* RUTILATED QUARTZ: At Victoria White and Webb-Fitzwilliam granite quarries.
- *Franconia, Grafton County* JASPER: In Ammonoosuc River.
- *Gilsum, Cheshire County* GOLDEN AND BLUE BERYL: North of Gilsum along W side of road to Mill Hollow is a group of mines where golden and blue beryl has been found on dumps:
  At the Blister mine.
  At the Davis mine, ¾ mile N of Mica Mine School.
  At the Island Mica mine, 2½ miles N of Gilsum, 400 yards E of Hwy 10, and W of school on knoll between swamp and pond.
  At the Big mine, N of school.

At the Golding-Keene mine, NW of the Big mine.

S of Gilsum on E side of Hwy 10 at the J. White mine.

APATITE: At Fitzgibbon mine.

- *Grafton, Grafton County* BLUE BERYL: In dumps of mine 3 miles SW on E side of Melvin Hill.

  BLUE AND GOLDEN BERYL: At Kilton mine, reached via Ruggles Mine Road, crossing Manfeltree Brook, keeping right and then ¾ mile NE.

  At Ruggles mine on Isinglass Hill, reached by taking direct road W from Grafton Center 1½ miles to crossroads, then right across brook and up hill ¾ mile (fee).

  At Sargent mine, on N end of Horse Hill, reached by driving to top and taking ridge trail on foot.

  BLUE BERYL, ROSE AND SMOKY QUARTZ: At Alger mine, reached by taking road S where Ruggles Mine Road leaves Grafton Road and going mile.

- *Hanover, Grafton County* RUTILATED QUARTZ: At Moose Mountain.

- *Haverhill, Grafton County* QUARTZ CRYSTALS: In limonite at Black Mountain.

- *Hebron, Grafton County* BERYL, LEPIDOLITE: SW 2 miles at mine dump on E side of Hobart Hill.

- *Hinsdale, Cheshire County* PINK RHODONITE: Mile SE near Ashuelot River.

- *Keene, Cheshire County* BERYL: NE 5 miles in pegmatite of Bassett Hill.

  4½ miles E at Horse Hill.

  BERYL, SMOKY AND ROSE QUARTZ: At Keene granite quarry 3 miles SE.

  FLUORITE: At Will Wise mine. Hwy 9 W for 11 miles, pass Sherman Store, turn right at sign saying "1st Methodist Church in New Hampshire," go ½ mile, then right on dirt road 1½ mile, then left 3 miles, and a sharp left onto mine road. Park and walk up Bald Hill.

- *Lincoln, Grafton County* AMETHYST: On upper slopes of Mount Nancy.

- *Littleton, Grafton County* STAUROLITE: On hill ¾ mile W of Garnet Hill.

- *Marlboro, Cheshire County* ALMANDINE GARNET: Mile S at Webb granite quarry.

- *Marlow, Cheshire County* GREEN TOURMALINE: At Turner mine.

  ROSE AND SMOKY QUARTZ: In E cut of Windham mine.

- *Milan, Coos County* AMETHYST, TOPAZ: To W and 3 miles S at 1,700 foot level of Green's Ledge.

- *Milford, Hillsboro County* RUTILATED QUARTZ: In Bishop and Carlton granite quarries 2 miles NW.
  In Connoli granite quarry 3½ miles SW.
  In Kittridge granite quarry 1½ miles SW.
- *Newport, Sullivan County* BERYL, APATITE: At G. F. Smith mine and 3 miles E at Young's Hill (fee).
- *North Conway, Carroll County* TOPAZ, SMOKY QUARTZ, AMAZONSTONE: Take road W to Echo Lake, then jeep road W to Camp Albite, park and walk ¾ mile W to dig in Moat Mt. There is also collecting at South Moat and the hogback E of Middle Moat. (Now under Federal Bureau of Land Management supervision. Fee.)

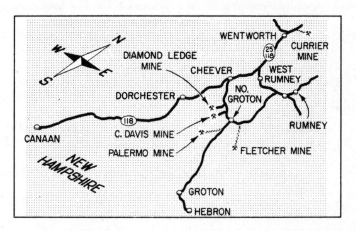

- *North Groton, Grafton County* * GREEN QUARTZ, APATITE, BERYL: SW 1 mile, then turn N less than a mile to Palermo No. 1 mine. Also at the Rice mine, a mile farther from North Groton.
  At the Charles Davis mine. About ¾ mile W of North Groton, the dirt road S from the Cheever Road leads to the mine. Lazulite here, too.
  At the Diamond Ledge mine, reached by a road a mile W of North Groton leading from the Cheever Road.
  At the Mica Products mine located on a hillside a quarter mile W of the Davis mine.
  At the Fletcher mine. Take the Rumney Road but turn off on a side road up Fletcher Mountain and go 1¼ miles.
  BERYL, APATITE: At the Valencia mine, located on the next hill NW of the Fletcher mine.

- *Orange, Grafton County* BERYL: At Keyes Mines, N 2½ miles on dirt road.

  Orford, Grafton County STAUROLITE: On Strawberry and Blackberry Hills.

  Ossipee, Carroll County SMOKY QUARTZ: In ledge S of road at Passaconway quarry near Albany.

- *Percy, Coos County* AMETHYST: On W slope of Hutchins Mountain.

  TOPAZ: NW 1¾ miles at Victors Head.

- *Raymond, Rockingham County* BERYL, GARNET, ROSE QUARTZ: Take Old Manchester road W, then Lane road a total of 2 miles to Chandler, Smith, Welch, and Blake mines.

  QUARTZ CRYSTALS: In boulders on ridge just N of Raymond-Nottingham town line and W of road.

- *Richmond, Cheshire County* CORDIERITE: In Richmond soapstone quarry.

- *Rumney, Grafton County* BERYL: At Belden mine.

- *Springfield, Sullivan County* GOLDEN BERYL, AMETHYST, SMOKY QUARTZ: At Columbia gem mine on N end of Springfield Mountain.

  AMETHYST, QUARTZ CRYSTALS: In soil at George Hill.

  BERYL, SPESSARTITE GARNET: At S end of Melvin Hill in ledge on Joe Hill farm.

  GREEN BERYL: At Playter mine on S end of Pillsbury Ridge.

  BLUE BERYL, GARNET, QUARTZ CRYSTALS: At Reynolds mine near top of NE slope of Robinson Hill.

  At Davenport mine just below.

  AMETHYST, SMOKY QUARTZ CRYSTALS: At Diamond Ledges on Long Mountain.

  SE on Hwy 4A for 1½ miles, then ½ mile N to Globe mine, collect on dump.

- *Stratford, Coos County* AMETHYST: Along road near Sugarloaf.

- *Sugar Hill, Grafton County* GREEN QUARTZ: S 1½ miles at Franconia iron mine.

  STAUROLITE: In slate near Franconia iron mine, S of summit of Ore Hill.

- *Sunapee, Sullivan County* RUTILATED QUARTZ: At Perry Sunapee quarry.

  At Spectacle Pond quarry.

- *Wakefield, Carroll County* BLUE BERYL: At Weeks mine ½ mile W of Province Lake.

- *Walpole, Cheshire County* ROSE QUARTZ: At Howe Lodge on W side of Derry Hill.

- *Warner, Merrimack County* ROSE QUARTZ: Near top of Mount Kearsarge.
- *Warren, Grafton County* GOLDEN BERYL, QUARTZ CRYSTALS: SW 1½ miles on SW side of Beech Hill.
- *Wentworth, Grafton County* BERYL: At the Currier mine. Take Hwy 25 N past railroad tracks, then first dirt road right ¾ mile. Park. (Ask permission to collect at houses nearby and take road through fields to mine.)
- *West Lebanon, Grafton County* RUTILATED QUARTZ PEBBLES: In Connecticut River.
- *Westmoreland, Cheshire County* AMETHYST, QUARTZ CRYSTALS: At Stoddard mine.
  STAUROLITE: At Park Hill.
- *Wilmot Flat, Merrimack County* BERYL: In mine dumps at Stuart Hill.
- *Winchester, Cheshire County* RHODONITE: Near top of Stony Mountain.

New Jersey

The northwest corner of New Jersey contains the famous Delaware Water Gap, where the river has cut through the Kittatinny mountain range of the Appalachians. Southeast of these mountains is a belt of ridgeland know as the Highlands, and paralleling it is a lowland marked by traprock ridges, such as the Watchung Mountains and the Palisades on the Hudson. Southeast New Jersey is coastal plain, much of it marsh. Glacial terminal moraines cross the central part of the state.

- *Andover, Sussex County* ACTINOLITE, SERPENTINE: Take road ½ mile N, turn right at Exxon station to Limecrest sign, go 6 miles crossing Newton-Sparta road, then 1½ miles to Limecrest quarry. It also contains corundum and tourmaline.
- *Bernardsville, Somerset County* AMETHYST: Take Hwy 202 for ¼ mile S to Somerset Crushed Stone Quarry.
- *Bound Brook, Somerset County* AGATE, AMETHYST, JASPER: At the New England quarry.
- *Cape May, Cape May County* QUARTZ (CAPE MAY DIAMONDS): In beach sand, expecially just S of sunken concrete ship at Cape May Point, and at Point Lookout, in water at waterline.
- *Clifton, Passaic County* AMETHYST, AGATE: 3 miles W and S of U.S. 64 at Houdaille Industries quarry.

- *Dover, Morris County* SUNSTONE: In Alan Wood iron mine dumps on Mine Hill.
- *Franklin, Sussex County* RHODONITE (FOWLERITE), VESUVIANITE (CYPRINE): In dumps of New Jersey Zinc Company mines. Best are Buckwheat dump outside Franklin and the Trotter dump.
   BLUE APATITE: In Atlas quarry.
- *Hawthorne, Passaic County* AGATE: In Braen's quarry.
- *Lambertville, Hunterdon County* PREHNITE, DATOLITE: In quarry to S on River Road.
- *Montville, Morris County* * SERPENTINE: Take U.S. 202 W to sign for Valhalla Lake. Turn up hill to a left turn between stone gate posts marked Valhalla Lake. Continue

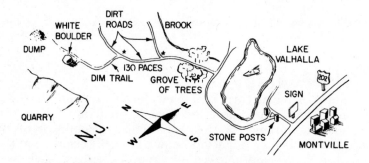

on hardtop road N and around lake for a mile to a brook. Park here and walk up a wagon road parallel to brook to a fork. Take left-hand trail for 130 paces. Here, a faint trail leads to the left ¼ mile to the top of the mountain and to a large white boulder. The dump is a few feet beyond. Yellow to green translucent serpentine in dumps.

- *Neptune City, Monmouth County* AMBER: In marl along Shark River.
- *Paramus, Bergen County* GARNET: At Green farm.
- *Phillipsburg, Warren County* GREEN SERPENTINE: At Royal Green marble quarry. Go NE to Harmony, take road to right marked Harmony Station, go 2 miles to quarry dumps.
- *Rudetown, Sussex County* DIOPSIDE, SERPENTINE: Take Quarry road to narrow bridge, cross and turn right to Edison quarry. Permission needed.
- *Sewell, Gloucester County* AMBER: In tributary of Mantua creek.
- *Sparta, Sussex County* UNAKITE: In dump S along Hwy 15.

- *Summit, Essex County* AGATE, PREHNITE, AMETHYST: In Houdaille Construction Materials Quarry.
- *Trenton, Mercer County* BLACK JASPER: N 9 miles on Hwy 29 in Delaware River at Washington Crossing State Park.
  AMBER: 4 miles S in lignite at Crosswicks Creek.

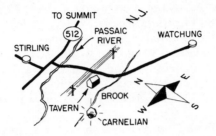

- *Watchung, Somerset County* * CARNELIAN, QUARTZ: Route 512 from Summit intersects the road S to Watchung just E of the road N to Stirling. Turn S on the Watchung Road. Cross the Passaic River, and go almost 2 miles toward Watchung to a power line over the road and past a tavern beside a brook. Park here and follow the brook S ¼ mile. Dig in the green sand about 18 inches down for carnelian and quartz crystal. It is convenient to dam off a bit of the bank, dig, and wash the sand in a screen.

New Mexico

New Mexico lies at the southern end of the Rocky Mountains, the Sangre de Cristo range extending down into the state from Colorado. Through the central part of the state, short chains of mountains run to the Mexican border, while another group parallels the Rio Grande River to the west. Plateaus cut by canyons form the borders with Texas and Arizona, and long plateaus lie between the central mountains. New Mexico owes its great variety of mineral and gem wealth to these exposures of many kinds of rock.

- *Abiquiu, Rio Arriba County* AGATE, PETRIFIED WOOD: Along Chama River and in hills ¼ mile N.
- *Albuquerque, Bernalillo County* PETRIFIED WOOD: Take road N across mesa toward old craters to the rim of the Rio Puerco valley. Collect on rim.
  JASPER NODULES: W on Int. 40 15 miles to Rio Puerco

bridge, turn N 16 miles in Rio Puerco valley, then left into low hills.

RED MOSS AGATE: W on Int. 40 to Rio Puerco bridge, go on further to white sign, turn N ½ mile to windmill, take side road to a white bluff.

RED AGATE, JASPER: NE on Int. 25 for 25 miles, then S up Tonque Arroya to old clay pit. Collect to S of pit.

UNAKITE: Through area traversed by Int. 40 on S slopes of Sandia mountains as far as Tijeras.

• *Aleman, Sierra County* PETRIFIED WOOD, AGATE: S to within mile of Dona Ana county line, then E toward Point of Rocks.

• *Ancho, Lincoln County* JASPER: N 2 miles.

• *Artesia, Eddy County* * QUARTZ (PECOS DIAMONDS): See Roswell entry.

• *Bernardo, Socorro County* OPALIZED WOOD: E on U.S. 60 3 miles, search banks of Rio Grande for gray wood.

• *Buell Park, McKinley County* * PYROPE GARNET, PERIDOT: The garnet area extends into three states.

Garnet Ridge lies close to the Utah border, and a few miles W of Mexican Water, Apache County, Arizona.

Ten miles N of Mexican Water, in San Juan County, Utah, is the Moses Rock field.

Best known of the areas, however, is Buell Park, a basin almost on the Arizona–New Mexico line and 10 miles N of Ft. Defiance. The garnets and peridot are found in the soil, and, to a lesser degree, W and N of Red Lake, and E and S of the lake to the edge of the Nacimiento desert.

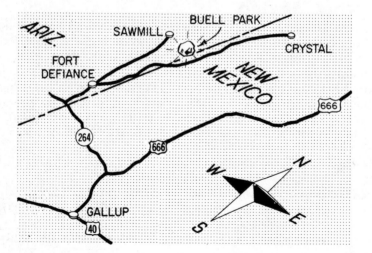

(Permission to collect in Indian reservation should be obtained at Chinle or Window Rock.)

•*Caballo, Sierra County* RHODONITE: Take Hwy 90 W to Hillsboro and collect at Comstock mine 10 miles W.

•*Cebolla, Rio Arriba County* AGATE NODULES: In canyon to E, take dirt road 2 miles S of Cebolla.

•*Cerrillos, Santa Fe County* PETRIFIED WOOD: At Sweet's ranch 3 miles E, and Keith ranch, which is E from Hwy 10 at ranch sign (fee).

　　TURQUOISE: Take Hwy 10 S for 12 miles, turn on to dirt road to dumps W at Mt. Chalchihuitl and to N at Castilian and Tiffany mines. (May be off limits.)

•*Chaco Canyon, McKinley County* JASPER: Just to N.

•*Columbus, Luna County* HONEY ONYX: At mine 4 miles W on N side of Hwy 9 (fee).

　　PURPLE AGATE: W on Hwy 9 20 miles and collect just E of railroad station in Hermanas.

　　DUMORTIERITE: In quartz, 13 miles NW in Tres Hermanas Mountains.

•*Cuba, Sandoval County* PETRIFIED WOOD: Along Hwy 44 to W and from Hwy 44 S in Rio Puerco.

•*Deming, Luna County* AGATE NODULES: Generally to S between Florida and Little Florida mountains. Specific locations, most of which charge fees for collecting, follow:
On Spanish Stirrup ranch 5 miles E on Int. 10.
On Spaulding property to SE.
At Baker ranch on Hwy 11.
At the Lindberg claims on Hilborn and Gore ranches. Take Hwy 11 for 8 miles S to Hermanas road, then E and S 30 miles to nodule beds.
Free collecting at the Rockhound State Park. Go S on Hwy 11, take road E to park for agate, carnelian, and amethyst in geodes.
　　CARNELIAN: Hwy 26 NE for 5 miles and then N on Cooks Peak road for 5 miles. Hunt in hills E of road and S of Cooks Peak.

•*Domingo, Sandoval County* JASPER, OPALIZED WOOD: Hwy 22 N 1½ miles, take right fork, pass Cochita Pueblo and take gravel road N and then W past Tent Rocks to Peralta Lookout. From there go 4 miles to Peralta Canyon and up canyon ¼ mile. Walk ½ mile N to tributary. Collect in it and along E side of canyon. Return to road, continue ½ mile, collect seam agate in ravine, and just beyond road is opalized wood in another ravine.

- *Eagle Nest, Colfax County* AGATE, APATITE: Take U.S. 64 to Mexican Gulch, which is first side canyon from Palisades and on right side of Cimarron Canyon.
- *Engle, Sierra County* TUBE AGATE: W 8 miles N on side of railroad tracks.

    PETRIFIED WOOD: In hills ½ mile W near road and to S as far as Cutter.
- *Ft. Sumner, DeBaca County* RED AGATE: N on U.S. 84 to Hwy 203, cross dam, turn N to fork, take W fork a mile to shallow valley.
- *Galisteo, Santa Fe County* JASPER: Along Galisteo River near Kennedy.
- *Glorieta, Santa Fe County* PETRIFIED WOOD: Along Glorieta River.
- *Grants, Valencia County* OBSIDIAN: Hwy 547 NE for 7½ miles past U.S. Gypsum mine sign, then less than a mile to dirt road W. Take it a mile and then S to fence. Collect to W outside fence on public land.
- *Hachita, Grant County* TURQUOISE: At Turquoise Montain 6 miles W on Hwy 9.
- *Hatch, Dona Ana County* MOSS OPAL: Drive S, then hike to diversion dam and dig opal from seams in side of arroyo.

    OPALIZED WOOD: To W of Hatch over wide area N and W.

    GREEN ALABASTER (ONYX): S 1½ miles on Mammoth Creek.

    RHYOLITE (WONDERSTONE): At S end of Caballo Mountains.
- *Laguna, Valencia County* AGATE: Along Rio San Jose.
- *La Madera, Rio Arriba County* NODULES: Turn right at general store across bridge and take Petaca road (Hwy 519) N for 1¾ miles to collect in mica mine.
- *La Union, Dona Ana County* PERIDOT: Take road W across Hwy 273 and continue about 7 miles W across railroad tracks, then follow road along tracks NW for 4 miles to a siding called Lanark. Turn W here for 8 miles to Kilbourne Hole.
- *Las Cruces, Dona Ana County* PETRIFIED WOOD: Along Hwy 478 S.

    FELDSPAR, PSILOMELANE, JASPER: Hwy 25 up Rio Grande valley for 31 miles to rail crossing; ½ mile farther is dirt dam. Collect to N of it in hills.
- *Lordsburg, Hidalgo County* AGATE NODULES: NW on U.S. 70 10 miles, turn W at ranch sign, go 20 miles to ranch house for permission to collect N about 3 miles.

FIRE AGATE, CARNELIAN: U.S. 70 NW for 25 miles, then take road SW for 18 miles, keeping to left at all forks, then turn right to Harry Day ranch. Collect at Round mountain (in Arizona).

• *Los Lunas, Valencia County* RED AGATE, JASPER: W on Hwy 6 16 miles. Collect in gravel along E side of river and to N of road.

AGATE, OBSIDIAN: Hwy 6 W for 9 miles to sign ¼ mile E of railroad overpass, turn S to Dalies and continue S, keeping right at all forks for 6 miles to Rio Puerco rim.

• *Luna, Catron County* AGATE: In San Francisco river N of Alpine and N, NE, and NW of Luna. One location is N of Luna 2 miles to road fork, take left fork 9 miles to road to left. Look here and along the road.

• *Magdalena, Socorro County* BLUE SMITHSONITE: On dumps of Kelly Mine 3 miles SE and also in the Graphic mine nearby (both fee).

PETRIFIED PALM WOOD: Take road N for 16 miles, then left on ranch road through ranch yard and 6 miles farther to collect in Bear Mountains area.

MOSS AGATE: Go 20 miles W on U.S. 60, then S 9 miles and turn right and go 27 miles to Farr ranch.

• *Mule Creek, Grant County* OBSIDIAN: W on Hwy 78 at Arizona line for silver sheen obsidian.

• *Orogrande, Otero County* TURQUOISE: To N in mines near Turquois.

• *Petaca, Rio Arriba County* BLUE BERYL: At Sunnyside Mine 3 miles S.

AMAZONITE, GARNET, QUARTZ: Take road to La Madera S for 3½ miles and W for 1½ miles; collect in dump of Cribbenville mine and nearby old pegmatite mines.

Also take Sawmill road W to old mines and prospects and N into La Jerita Canyon to other diggings.

• *Pilar, Taos County* * STAUROLITES, GARNETS: Just N of the hamlet of Pilar on the left side of Hwy 64 is a sign pointing out the Rio Grande Gorge. Continue 2 miles past this sign, then turn right into a dirt road and go 3 miles to a big sawdust heap. Park and take right-hand trail into Hondo Canyon. In this canyon and those to the S (Piedras Lumbres, Tierra Amarila and Agua Caliente Canyons) staurolites are plentiful in the schist, along with small garnets.

THULITE: In pegmatite, just S of Pilar on E bank of Rio Grande.

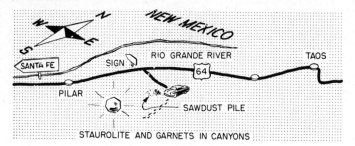

BERYL, LEPIDOLITE: S on U.S. 64, E on Hwy 75 7½ miles, then½ mile S to Harding mine. (Permission is needed.)

• *Playas, Hidalgo County* CHALCEDONY, AGATE: W at dry lake and S of road.

• *Portales, Roosevelt County* PETRIFIED WOOD: SW 68 miles on Hwy 70 to Bob Crosby Draw, go back 2½ miles and take dirt road S into Bitterlake wildlife refuge. Collect in hills.

• *Quemado, Catron County* CHALCEDONY ROSES, PETRIFIED WOOD: N 40 miles at Zuni Salt Lake.

• *Radium Springs, Dona Ana County* OPAL NODULES, SEAM OPAL: To N in Broad Canyon W of Hwy 85.

• *Ramon, Lincoln County* AGATE, JASPER: E 8 miles.

• *Redrock, Grant County* SERPENTINE (RICOLITE): Take road N across Gila River to first road E, follow it for 3 miles to Ash Creek canyon. A half mile W of main vein of green serpentine is one of yellow serpentine.

• *Raton, Colfax County* AMBER: In coal at Sugarite mine.

• *Red Hill, Catron County* AGATE, JASPER: Go N about 12 miles to windmill and red hill and collect on hillsides to NE.

• *Reserve, Catron County* * BANDED AGATE: Take Hwy 12 for 11 miles NE to Apache Creek; then take Hwy 32 NW for 5 miles to national forest fence. Park above fence, take trail to left to Lee Russell Canyon until it widens out into a flat, which is the best collecting area.
Also in hills N of highway and W of Apache Creek.
FELDSPAR (BYTOWNITE): W on Hwy 12 to U.S. 180, then S 6 miles to road toward Blue, Ariz. Search on mesa S of Pueblo Forest Campground for yellow faceting feldspar.

• *Rincon, Dona Ana County* GEM FELDSPAR, JASPER: Drive N on W side of railroad tracks and 2 miles into hills toward television tower. Collect between dam and new highway.

• *Roswell, Chaves County* * QUARTZ (PECOS DIAMONDS): In soil along Pecos River and in its gravels generally from Carls-

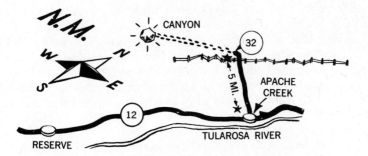

bad to Ft. Sumner. Specifically in hills W of river from Carlsbad to Artesia and on both sides of river to Roswell and Hwy 70, then over a cone-shaped area from Hwy 285 NE to Ft. Sumner. One good place is at Lake State Park SE of Roswell.

• *Santa Fe, Santa Fe County* RED JASPER, NODULES: Hwy 85 S for 30 miles, then E 7 miles up Tonque wash.

AGATE, OPALITE: 12 Miles SW at La Cienega as float in hills 2 miles to S.

- *Sheep Springs, San Juan County* NODULES: In Washington Pass to W.
- *Silver City, Grant County* MOONSTONE (SANADINE): Hwy 80 E to Noonday Canyon sign in Gila National Forest. Take canyon road, make hard left downgrade and park to continue in jeep beyond stream crossing and park. Take trail into Rabb Canyon to N to where stream splits and follow W side of N branch to a corral to dig. Another site ½ mile NW up small stream from left.

  AGATE, NODULES, CHALCEDONY: 8 miles N of Sapillo creek W of Hwy 15 and S of Gila Cliff Dwellings National Monument.
- *Socorro, Socorro County* DENDRITIC AGATE: Take Int. 25 N for 13 miles to San Acacia. Take frontage road 1½ mile W, then road W into arroya for 3 miles into canyon.

  AMETHYST: Take Int. 25 N across Rio Salado, follow ranch roads W, and collect on SW slopes of Ladrones Peak.

  OPALIZED WOOD: Continue N past the Rio Salado, and turn W before crossing Rio Puerco. Bear left around Ladron Peak after crossing cattle guard, passing broken windmill and cow skull nailed to tree, and go 1½ miles farther. Collect on both sides of road.
- *Tres Piedras, Taos County* OBSIDIAN: Hwy 285 for 7 miles N, then E to collect obsidian nodules (Apache tears) in perlite beds.
- *Truth and Consequences, Sierra County* OPALIZED WOOD: Along Rio Grande to N at Nogal Canyon.

  AGATE: Take U.S. 85 S to Hwy 90, turn W through Hillsboro and just past Perchas Creek to collect N of road on side and top of mountain.

  RHYOLITE (WONDERSTONE): To NW at Ellis claims and on E side of Cabollo Lake, reached by taking road N 1¼ mile after crossing dam.

  Also at Eagle Peak 20 miles SW on Chavez road.

  YELLOW AND BROWN PETRIFIED WOOD: In swamp at S end of Elephant Butte reservoir.
- *Tyrone, Grant County* TURQUOISE: In creeks and dumps all the way S to Leopold.
- *Valle Grande, Sandoval County* OBSIDIAN: In headwaters of Jemez River.
- *Wagon Mound, Mora County* AGATE, JASPER: Few miles E.
- *Winston, Sierra County* AMETHYSTINE QUARTZ: In Montezuma mine dumps at Chloride.

• *Youngsville, Rio Arriba County* VARICOLORED AGATE: From Hwy 96 turn SE on road to Canones, look for spotted agate along road and to W of Abiquiu Dam.

New York

More than half of New York State is a plateau sweeping down from the Adirondacks in the northeast and underlain by very old sedimentary rocks. The Adirondacks, however, are formed of crystalline rocks like the Laurentians in Canada. The central plateau rises from Lake Erie and Lake Ontario, becoming mountainous in the south and east, where the Appalachians enter the state, and where the plateau has been carved into the Catskill Mountains. The topography of lower New York is like that of New Jersey, except that Long Island is a part of the coastal plain.

• *Balmat, St. Lawrence County* APATITE: At Gouverneur Talc mine.
• *Bedford, Westchester County* ASTERIATED ROSE QUARTZ: Take Hwy 22 S, turn off on road to Greenwich, Conn., take first dirt road N and follow around old quarry to dump at mill ruins.
• *Blooming Grove, Orange County* BLOODSTONE: To S on Hwy 94 at Craigsville.
• *Canadice, Ontario County* LABRADORITE: On E side of Canadice Lake and 2 miles W of Honeoye Lake.
• *Clintonville, Clinton County* JASPER: Take Harkness road across first railroad tracks, just before reaching second tracks turn left up steep hill to Arnold mine. Collect jasper with martite in dumps.
• *DeKalb, St. Lawrence County* MOONSTONE, DIOPSIDE, BROWN TOURMALINE: In old marble quarries and to S at Richville. Also 5 miles SE at former Mitchell farm in talc.
• *Edwards, St. Lawrence County* HAUYNITE: In pockets in St. Joe Minerals Corp. mine.
• *Fonda, Montgomery County* * QUARTZ (HERKIMER DIAMONDS): Fonda and Middleville are the two areas where rocks are found containing the glittering quartz crystals known as Herkimer diamonds. There are several collecting sites near Fonda. Take Exit 28 from the New York State Freeway at Fultonville, cross bridge to Fonda, continue to creek and beyond it, take the first road right, Hickory Hill road, go right to Martin road to Stone Arabia road

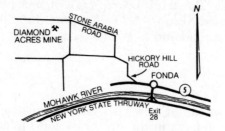

at left, cross England road and the Diamond Acres mine is at left (fee).

S of Fonda at Exit 28, take Hwy 55 SW to Sprakers. This is a fee area, as are most of the others, but there is a free area 1 mile E of Sprakers on the S side of Hwy 55 on the crest of a hill known as Little Nose.

- *Geneseo, Livingston County* CORAL: Silicified material is to be found 3 miles N in banks and bed gravels of a creek.
- *Gouverneur, St. Lawrence County* TOURMALINE, APATITE: Brown tourmaline and red and brown apatite in old quarries.
- *Johnsburg, Warren County* SERPENTINE: In asbestos mine to SW at Garnet Lake.
- *Keeseville, Clinton County* SERPENTINE: At Buttermilk Falls.
- *Malone, Franklin County* SUNSTONE: Take road SE to Owl's Head Village and make inquiry there for trail up mountain to iron mine. Collect in dumps.
- *Middleville, Herkimer County* * QUARTZ (HERKIMER DIAMONDS): Middleville is one of the two major areas for collecting the brilliant quartz crystals known as Herkimer diamonds. There are several collecting areas, mostly open for a fee.

  The Ace of Diamonds collecting area is within the village limits on Hwy. 28, and a mile S on Hwy 28 is the Atty area known as the Herkimer Diamond Grounds. Several other collecting areas have at one time or another been open N and NW of Middleville.
- *Mineville, Essex County* SUNSTONE: At Fisher Hill Mine.
- *Newcomb, Essex County* MOONSTONE, BROWN TOURMALINE: On S shore of Lake Harris.
- *North Creek, Warren County* ALMANDINE GARNET: Take Hwy 28 N for 4 miles, turn at Barton Mines sign, go 5 miles up Gore Mountain to shop.
- *Olmstedville, Essex County* MOONSTONE: 1 mile W on road to Minerva; pit is in outcrop on S side of road.
- *Pierrepont, St. Lawrence County* APATITE, BLACK TOURMALINE: At

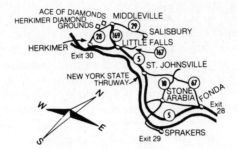

Powers Tourmaline Diggings ½ mile W on Hwy 68 (fee). Also at West Pierrepont.

- *Plattsburgh, Clinton County* MARBLE: Take Grand Island ferry S to Hwy 2 and SE to quarry for scenic "zebra" marble.
- *Port Henry, Essex County* ROSE QUARTZ: NW 6 miles.
- *Port Kent, Essex County* LABRADORITE: Along shore to S.
- *Rochester, Monroe County* AGATE: In limestone along E bank of Genesee river near Norton Street and past Avenue E.
- *St. Johnsville, Montgomery County* * QUARTZ (HERKIMER DIA-MONDS): At Crystal Grove campsite. Take Division Street, go 4½ miles to Crystal Grove, take right fork to Lassallsville and to picnic grove (fee).
- *Saranac Lake, Franklin County* MOONSTONE: Take Hwy 3 N for 4 miles to Leib's rock shop. Drive up hill and park and take trail to moonstone mine (fee).
  LABRADORITE: Along Indian Pass road off Kiwassa road.
- *Saratoga Springs, Saratoga County* CHRYSOBERYL: In pegmatite dike, 12 miles W of road intersection on Hwy 9 N of Saratoga Springs.
  QUARTZ CRYSTALS: In Maple Avenue (Gailor) quarry on W side of Hwy 9 on N edge of city.
- *Star Lake, St. Lawrence County* SILLIMANITE: In Benson mines to E.
- *Wading River, Long Island, Suffolk County* AGATE, JASPER: In beach pebbles at Wildwood State Park.
- *Wells, Hamilton County* LABRADORITE: In anorthosite boulders to N along Hwy 8 in E branch of Sacandaga River.
- *West Chazy, Clinton County* FOSSIL LIMESTONE: In old quarry.
- *Wolcott, Wayne County* LARVIKITE (FOSSIL LIMESTONE): Take new Hwy 104 to Hwy 414, then left on old Hwy 104, go N toward Lake Ontario, then right on Lummisville road to East Bay road and left on it to Chimney Bluff road to lake. Park and collect along shore. Epidote is also present there.

215

North Carolina

The eastern half of North Carolina is the low-lying coastal plain extending to the fall line, which divides it from the Piedmont plateau, a somewhat elevated level region containing the principal cities of the state. In the western part of the state the Blue Ridge escarpment rises abruptly to define the Appalachian Mountains, which in North Carolina form the greatest mountain mass in the eastern United States. In the varied rocks of these mountains are found most of the gem minerals in the state.

- *Alexis, Gaston County* RUTILE: At Lowe farm on Chubb Mountain on Hwy 27 between Lincolnton and Charlotte.
  KYANITE, LAZULITE, RUTILE: As float in fields 1½ miles E.

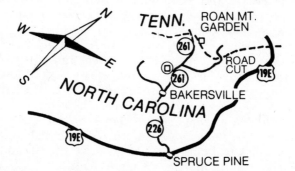

- *Bakersville, Mitchell County* GREEN FELDSPAR, THULITE, MOONSTONE: At Hawk Mine 1 mile N by road in Cave Creek valley. Also 12 miles NW on Hwy 261 at Roan Mountain Flower Garden and 12 miles NE on road to right at fork N of Bakersville.
  UNAKITE: N 10 miles at Roan Mountain.
  SUNSTONE: A mile N at Medlock Mountain.
  KYANITE: SE 4 miles on Hwy 226 in quartz near top of Yellow Mountain.
- *Balsam Gap, Buncombe County* KYANITE: S on Hwy 276 to Balsam Gap, then 1½ mile SE. Also on Lookout Mountain.
- *Bayleaf, Wake County* SOAPSTONE (STEATITE): W to Hwy 50, then 2 miles to Barton Creek crossing.
- *Beaver Creek, Ashe County* GOLDEN BERYL: At South Hardin Mica mine, 1½ miles SW on hill. Beryl is in the footwall of a pegmatite.
- *Bluff, Madison County* UNAKITE: On Roaring Fork Creek, ½ mile W of its junction with Meadow Fork, 2 miles SW of Bluff; also ⅓ mile N of Bluff.

- *Brasstown, Clay County* * STAUROLITE (FAIRY CROSSES): In bank along gravel road and nearby pastures and in matrix on mountainside. Get permission from Robert Trout to collect except along the road.

- *Bryson City, Swain County* KYANITE, STAUROLITE: 1½ mile N of Deep Creek campground, in schist.
- *Burch Station, Surry County* BLUE JASPER: On C. Greenwood farm 1½ miles off Hwy 268 to E, also along Yadkin river.

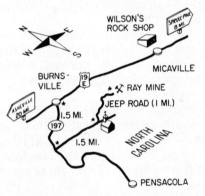

- *Burnsville, Yancey County* * AQUAMARINE, GOLDEN AND GREEN BERYL, AMAZONSTONE: Some of the best aquamarine in North Carolina comes from the Ray Mine. From Burnsville go E on Hwy 19E to traffic light opposite a funeral home. Turn S toward Pensacola for 1½ miles to a fork. Take left fork and go 1½ miles to a church on right-hand side of road. Opposite this church, a jeep road leads one mile to the mine.
- *Canton, Buncombe County* CORUNDUM: At Pressley Corundum mine. Take Main street to Newfound street, turn left

across Int 40, left again at first road past church, and left again on first gravel road. Pay fee at second house on left, mine is at end of next road left.

- *Casar, Cleveland County* RUTILATED QUARTZ: As float on ground 2 miles W and S.

  BERYL: At Elliott mine 3½ miles SW.

- *Cashiers, Jackson County* SAPPHIRE: 7 miles SE in Whitewater mine on Whitewater River.

  RUBY: E 7 miles on south shore of Sapphire Lake at Bad Creek mine.

  AQUAMARINE: At Rice mine.

- *Centerville, Franklin County* AMETHYST: SW on Hwy. 561 to Taylor farm.

- *Cranberry, Avery County* EPIDOTE, GARNET, KYANITE: At Cranberry Iron mine 1 mile S.

- *Danbury, Stokes County* CARNELIAN: In gravels of the Dan River.

- *Dysartsville, McDowell County* CORUNDUM: 1¹/₅ mile SE in stream on Mills farm on N side of Hwy 26.

- *Ellenboro, Rutherford County* ROSE QUARTZ, BERYL: Turn right on paved road off U.S. 74 W of Ellenboro, go a mile and then right to Dycus mine.

- *Franklin, Macon County* *

  The Franklin area is the most popular collecting area in North Carolina. Besides the diggings that charge a fee to allow collectors to wash gravel for ruby and sapphires, there are many other mines which offer a wide variety of gem materials.

  RUBY, SAPPHIRE: Take Hwy 28 N for 7 miles to the Cowee Creek road E at West's Mill. Follow road 2½ miles and then follow signs along gravel road to mines.

  Take Hwy 28 N 4 miles to Burningtown road, turn W 8 miles to Burningtown. From there take trail to Roy Mason's mine. (Fee)

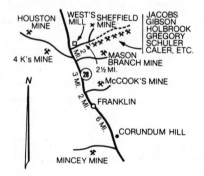

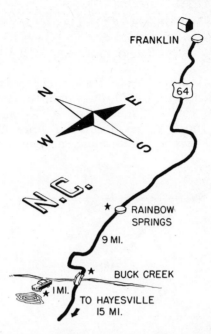

FRANKLIN

64

N.C.

★ RAINBOW SPRINGS

9 MI.

★ BUCK CREEK

★ 1 MI.

TO HAYESVILLE
15 MI.

CORUNDUM, ENSTATITE, PERIDOT: 6 miles SE on Hwy 28 to the Cullasaja mine at Corundum Hill. (Fee).

PYROPE, GARNET, RUBY IN SMARAGDITE: SW on Hwy 64 to Rainbow Springs, then 9 miles to bridge where Buck creek crosses highway. Turn right at bridge and go mile to another bridge. Park and hike up mountain to outcrops.

MOONSTONE: N 5 miles on Hwy 28, right to head of valley to Mason Mountain.

AMETHYST, AQUAMARINE: S 9 miles on Hwy 441 to Otto, E $3/5$ mile to Long and Connally Mines at Tessentee Creek.

AQUAMARINE: 10 miles E at Sheep Knob Mountain.

GARNET, SAPPHIRE: One of the most reliable locations for rhodolite garnet, one of the distinctive North Carolina minerals, is at the Mason Branch Mine formerly known as the Ried mine.

Take Hwy 28 NW from Franklin 5 miles to Mason Branch sign pointing to mine. Take road ¼ mile to mine. Rhodolite garnet is also found at McCook's mine to E of Hwy 28 2 miles N of Franklin, and star garnet at the 4K's mine to W of Hwy 28 on the Rose Creek road. Sapphire is also found at Houston's mine beyond the 4K's mine.

STAR CORUNDUM: 3 miles SE to Ellijay road; take it 3½

miles along Ellijay creek to Ellijay, turn right in town and right again to the Mincey mine. Gems have bronzy luster.

•*Gibsonville, Guilford County* GREEN QUARTZ: With inclusions of asbestos.

•*Hiddenite, Alexander County* * EMERALD, QUARTZ: Take Hwy 1001 N from Hwy 90, then right on Hwy 1498 and left on Hwy 1508 and follow signs to Rist mine on American Gems, Inc., diggings. Pay fee at office. On the way Hwy 1508 passes the Ellis mine, also owned by American Gems.

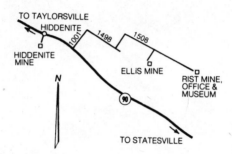

RUTILATED QUARTZ: Just S of the old Hiddenite mine and with beryl in dump of old Payne mine 1 mile S.

•*Highlands, Macon County* CORUNDUM: Hwy 106 SW 5½ miles to Scaly Mountain, search in mine dumps.

ALMANDINE GARNET: Hwy 64 E 3 miles, then take trail to Whiteside Mountain.

•*Hillsboro, Orange County* ANDALUSITE, LAZULITE, TOPAZ: At Piedmont Minerals mine.

•*Iron Station, Lincoln County* AMETHYST: N on Hwy 1314 to Hwy 73, turn right, then right on Hwy 1509, and right again on Hwy 1417. Pay fee at trailer and walk to digging area on Reel farm. Also nearby at Goodsen and Lynch farms.

•*Lexington, Davidson County* ORBICULAR GRANITE: W 10 miles and 1 mile W of Oaks Ferry on Yadkin River on Hairston farm.

•*Little Switzerland, Mitchell County* * EMERALD: Leave Blue Ridge Parkway at Little Switzerland exit, N on Hwy 1100 to Crabtree church, then 1 mile NE on Hwy 1104 to end of road, walk to Crabtree mine, dig in dumps. (Fee).

BERYL, THULITE, AMAZONSTONE: Return to Hwy 1104 and back to Hwy 1100–1104 to intersection, go W on Hwy 1100 to McKinney mine.

THULITE: Go W to Crabtree Road and N to sharp right

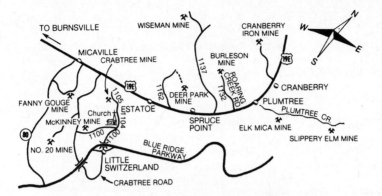

curve on steep downward slope, take road left here ¾ mile to No. 20 mine.

- *Marble, Cherokee County* MARBLE: 1⅓ mile N in Hyatt creek, and 1 mile S in Valley River and on Bettis farm.
- *Marshall, Madison County* ALMANDINE GARNET: N 6 miles on Redmon Dam Road. Cross dam, turn right, go to forks, take left fork to Lone Pine Mine.
- *Micaville, Yancey County* * AQUAMARINE, GARNET: U.S. 19 E for 2 miles across South Toe River, take Blue Rock Road, the first graded road, S a mile to Fanny Gouge and Spec mines.

  CORUNDUM: Hwy 80 S to Celo, collect in gravels of Toe river.
- *Morgantown, Burke County* GARNET: Go 5 miles S on Hwy 18 to Tweedy house on E side of road, pay fee and collect.

  AQUAMARINE, GOLDEN BERYL: 8 miles S and ½ mile E of Walker to the Walker Prospect.
- *Murphy, Cherokee County* SMOKY QUARTZ: At Voiles Cabins off Route 290 on Hiawasee Dam road.
- *Plumtree, Avery County* * GARNET: 2 miles E at dumps of Elk Mica mine and Slippery Elm mine on Plumtree Creek.

  MOONSTONE: 2 miles N on Roaring Creek road, at Burleson mine (fee).
- *Price, Rockingham County* QUARTZ, GARNET: U.S. 220 to road left that goes to Va. 692 at Virginia line, take it to Va. 691 to first dirt road, go left mile to Long Tom Smith mine.

  Also at Rosa Evans mine reached from Va. 691 by continuing a mile farther before turnoff.

  Also at Clifton mine mile W at state line.
- *Raleigh, Wake County* AMETHYST: U.S. 64 E to Wilder's Grove,

continue ½ mile, turn N a mile, and collect near the Neuse River.

•*Redmon, Madison County* ALMANDINE GARNET: 2 miles SW at mine on Little Pine creek.

•*Shelby, Cleveland County* EMERALD, RUTILATED QUARTZ: SW 5 miles on Hwy 18 to Stice Dam on the Broad River, then E 1½ miles to Turner mine on Allen property. Also at Old Plantation mine 1 mi NE of dam at bend in river.

QUARTZ: Hwy 18 S to Hwy 150, then W nearly 2 miles and S ½ mile. Also 1 mile S of Sharon Church.

SMOKY QUARTZ, RUTILE: Hwy 74 W to second stoplight, take Hwy 1313 past fiber plant to next road, turn left, cross creek, drive to mill with waterwheel and collect behind it on hillside below mine.

GARNET, MOONSTONE: Hwy 74 past town to second stoplight, turn S to stop sign, continue straight ahead to old school, go W around construction to site.

•*Sparta, Alleghany County* RHODONITE: Hwy 18 NE for 3 miles, then W for ½ mile to fork, take W fork ⅓ mile, collect in dumps.

•*Spruce Pine, Mitchell County* * AQUAMARINE: The Grassy Creek Mine near Spruce Pine has been a producer of fine aquamarine. Go S from Spruce Pine on Hwy 226 for 3 miles, turn left at church on dirt road and go ½ mile to mine.

MOONSTONE: Go 13 miles E on Hwy 19E, then left on Rt. 1132 ½ mile.

KYANITE: On surface loose in soil of Young farm.

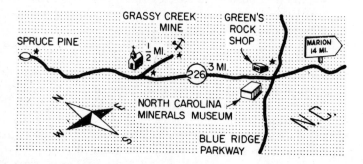

•*Statesville, Iredell County* AMETHYST: S 11 miles on Hwy 21. Collect in fields in vicinity of Sheperd's School and north to Oswalt and east to Smith Hill.

•*Valdese, Burke County* GARNET: At Tweedy's mine along Laurel creek.

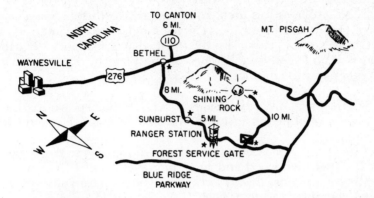

- *Waynesville, Haywood County* * ROSE QUARTZ: An outstanding locality for rose quartz is Shining Rock ledge. E on Hwy 276 for 7 miles to Bethel. S through Sunburst to U.S. Forest Ranger station. Get permit and key to gate and drive 10 miles to Shining Rock.

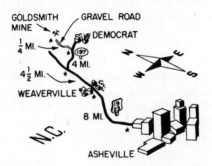

- *Weaverville, Buncombe County* * MOONSTONE: From traffic light go N on Hwy 19-23 for 4½ miles to junction with Hwy 197, then E on Hwy 197 4 miles and turn N on gravel road ¼ mile to Goldsmith mine.
  SERPENTINE: N 1⅔ miles to Pleasant Gap church, take next road E for ½ mile to mine on creek.

North Dakota

Eastern North Dakota lies in the level bed of the ancient Lake Agassiz, an area of rich farm land. To the west is a hilly plain, ridged with glacial moraines and dotted with lakes. An abruptly ris-

223

ing ridge separates this area from western North Dakota, which is part of the Missouri plateau, an almost unglaciated region of buttes and coulees culminating in the picturesque badlands. Petrified wood is found in the sandstones of the plateau, often associated with other quartz minerals.

- *Cartwright, McKenzie County* AGATE, PETRIFIED WOOD: Lime-coated agates in Little Missouri river gravels along with agatized wood.
- *Mandan, Morton County* PETRIFIED WOOD, AGATE: Worm-bored petrified wood and agate in gravel pits.
- *Medora, Billings County* PETRIFIED WOOD: In canyons S.
- *Minot, Ward County* JASPER: In gravel pits to S.
- *Mott, Hettinger County* PETRIFIED WOOD: In hills 11 miles NW along river.
- *Richardton, Stark County* CHALCEDONY: S 25 miles along Hwy. 8.
- *Tappan, Kidder County* AGATE: In gravel pits to E.
- *Watford City, McKenzie County* MOSS AGATE: In gravel pit ¾ mile E.
- *Williston, Williams County* MOSS AGATE, CHALCEDONY: On river bank near Hwy 85.

Ohio

Limestones and other sedimentary rocks underlie the state. They arch upward toward the west so that progressively younger rocks are exposed from west to east across the state. Most of the upper part of the state shows the typical appearance of midwestern glaciation. Fossils are abundant but, with one exception, gem materials are few.

- *Flint Ridge* * FLINT: Flint Ridge is an area about 8 miles long and ¾ mile wide in Licking and Muskingum Counties of central Ohio. It was the site of ancient Indian diggings for flint for artifacts and of the workshops where the artifacts were chipped out. Near the center of the area and on Ohio 668 is the Flint Ridge Memorial Park. The best collecting is on the corn fields S and E of this park, but it is also worthwhile to explore all along the E-W road E of Hwy 668.
  Three favorite places to collect are on the John Nethers farm, the Neibarger farm, and the Norris farm, all E of Hwy 278 and near the intersection of Hwys 292 and 277. Explicit directions can be obtained at the small museum

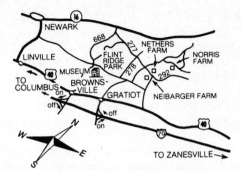

in the Flint Ridge park, which will introduce the collector to the nature of the flint deposit as well as the variety of the material itself. Collectors say that much well-colored flint has been picked up from the cornfields in the fall, when they are bare. There is a fee for admission to the park and for collecting at the several farms.

Oklahoma

Much of Oklahoma is rough and even mountainous. The Ozarks cross into the east central part of the state and die out in hills in the south central region occupied by a plateau known as the Arbuckle Mountains. Northwest of this area rise the steep Wichita Mountains and the Chautauqua Mountains. Northwest Oklahoma is part of the High Plains, and northeastern Oklahoma is a region of buttes and valleys carved from shales and sandstones. Despite this diversity of geological features, Oklahoma affords only a limited variety of gem minerals, mostly agate and petrified wood.

- *Ada, Pontotoc County* BLACK PETRIFIED WOOD: To S in Jack Fork and Canyon Creek.
- *Alva, Woods County* PETRIFIED WOOD, MOSS AGATE: To S and W.
- *Boise City, Cimarron County* AGATE: Take highway W toward Kenton to the Roberts ranch.
- *Buffalo, Harper County* AGATE: Go 3 miles S on Hwy 183 and then collect along highway for several miles.
  AGATE, PETRIFIED WOOD: W on Hwy 64 for 3½ miles to Ed Price place; collect on hill ½ mile W of ranch house. Aragonite crystals are found in Buffalo creek here. Go on 4 miles, then N 3 miles for agate in road cut.
- *Camargo, Dewey County* AGATE, JASPER: At Ames gravel pit.
- *Dougherty, Murray County* PETRIFIED WOOD, AGATE: At Makins gravel pit.

225

- *Hobart, Kiowa County* QUARTZ CRYSTALS: In quarries near Altus Reservoir.
- *Hollis, Harmon County* AGATE, JASPER: N 10 miles at Wilkerson pit.
- *Idabel, McCurtain County* PETRIFIED WOOD, JASPER: NE 9 miles at Mountain Fork River.
- *Jet, Alfalfa County* AGATE: S ½ mile at Cherokee Creek pit.
- *Kenton, Cimarron County* JASPER: Red dotted material with milky agate 5 miles S.
- *Lugert, Kiowa County* PETRIFIED WOOD: Generally in area.
- *Newcastle, Cleveland County* AGATE, PETRIFIED WOOD: In Dolese gravel pit.
- *Oakwood, Dewey County* PETRIFIED WOOD: S 6 miles at Gooch gravel pit.
- *Okemah, Okfuskee County* AGATE, PETRIFIED WOOD: NE 13 miles at Coffman gravel pit.
- *Orion, Major County* AGATE: In canyons cutting old shore line in hills N of Hwy 60.
- *Rosston, Harper County* ARAGONITE: So-called dollars. On twin buttes 1 mile E of Hwy 283 and 7 miles N of junction of Hwy 283 with Hwy 64.
- *Seiling, Dewey County* PETRIFIED WOOD: SE 7 miles at Carney gravel pit.
- *Talihina, Le Flore County* CHERT: To S along highway.
- *Taloga, Dewey County* AGATE: S 4 miles at Lovett gravel pit.
- *Welch, Craig County* JASPER: In Bill Patch strip coal mine 8 miles W.

Oregon

The Cascade Mountains, many of them extinct volcanoes, divide Oregon north and south into two diverse regions. West of the mountains, the land is well watered and contains the fertile Willamette Valley lying east of the Coast range, which merges in the south with California's Klamath Mountains. The eastern part of the state is a high plateau, generally arid, rugged, and made up of lava and rock debris, a region of salt lakes and even desert. Most of southeastern Oregon falls into the Great Basin. Oregon is celebrated for the agate formed in its lavas and the petrified wood and obsidian also associated with volcanic rocks.

- *Adrian, Malheur County* (Also see Homedale and Marsing, Ida.) AGATE: Nodules are found in area to S along the irrigation canal with red petrified wood to W at Alkalin

Lake. Canyon Road along Succor Creek passes diggings in the walls of the canyon S of Rockville.

•*Antelope, Wasco County,* AMETHYST, GREEN MOSS AGATE: Hwy 218 E toward Clarno, cross bridge, turn S at Antelope Agate Bed sign (fee).
RED JASPER: Mile E on Hwy 218, and ¼ mile S to old quarry.

•*Ashland, Jackson County* GREEN AGATE NODULES: E 7½ miles from Klamath Falls Junction on hills near road cut in Hwy 66.
AGATE: Along Jenny Creek near U.S. 66 in Goodsprings Mountain area.

•*Ashwood, Jefferson County* AGATE: A number of fee ranch diggings are nearby, including Norton ranch, 9 miles S, McDonald and Bedortha ranches just S, Swanson and Friend ranches, to the north, Palmer's Eagle Ranch and Forman's Indian Creek ranch with Brown's ranch nearby, and the Keegan ranch to the E.

•*Austin, Grant County* AGATIZED FERN: NW 17 miles in creek beds from Susanville to Bates.

•*Baker, Baker County* OPALIZED WOOD, ALMANDINE GARNET: Near Pleasant Valley.

•*Bandon, Coos County* AGATE, PETRIFIED WOOD: To N at Bullards Beach State Park beach. Take Hwy 101 N to Seven Devils Road to sign to Whiskey Run beach. Here and to S is brown petrified wood. Seven Devils Wayside Park is 2 miles farther N, for agates in creek and on beach.

•*Bend, Deschutes County* OBSIDIAN: At Glass Buttes, from milepost 72 to milepost 82 on U.S. 20. At milepost 79 take old road S into area, also at milepost 82. Another place to collect is reached by taking U.S. 97 S for 30 miles, then E and collect along road between Paulina Lake and East Lake.

•*Biggs, Sherman County* AGATE: At Fields farm 5 miles S on Hwy 97 (fee).
JASPER: Along E side of U.S. 97 2 miles S (private claim).

•*Brothers, Deschutes County* QUARTZ CRYSTAL: At Sugarloaf Mountain.

•*Brownsboro, Jackson County* * PETRIFIED WOOD, AGATE: Found W of the road NE from Brownsboro to Butte Falls and in the area E of the road and S of Butte Falls.
DENDRITIC AND CLEAR AGATE: In the desert 5 miles N of Medford and E of Hwy 62 in Antelope Creek and Little Butte Creek area.

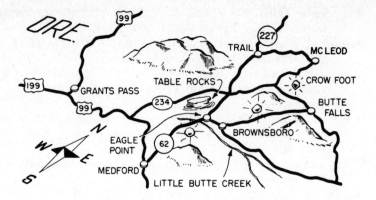

MOSS AGATE, JASPER, QUARTZ CRYSTAL GEODES: In the area S and W of Crow Foot, both in the creeks and washes and on the hills.

PETRIFIED WOOD: At Table Rocks on the side of Table Rock Mountain.

• *Burns, Harney County* AGATE NODULES: E for 23 miles on Hwy 20, then 4 miles S of Buchanan, at Robbins thundereggs diggings (fee).

PETRIFIED WOOD: Take Hwy 20 E for 28 miles to Stinking Water Summit, then S for 4 miles on BLM road, and jeep trail left to diggings.

PLUME AGATE: Hwy 20 to milepost 167, at foot of hill on N side of road (fee).

PETRIFIED WOOD: Hwy 20 to milepost 168, cross creek on bridge, take road S 7 miles, turn W on jeep trail to top of hill above Clear Creek. Hike to next ridge beyond Clear Creek, back up and take first trail right to diggings.

PLUME AGATE: Take Hwy 20 E for 40 miles, then S 26 miles on county road toward Warms Springs reservoir, turn W and go through two washes to collect on top of hill.

AGATE: Take Hwy 78 E for 1½ miles, S on Hwy 205 past milepost 16, then W 2 miles and N 2 miles to Wright ranch for snakeskin agate. Continue to milepost 24 on Hwy 205, take road E to Malheur Wildlife Refuge and collect in pumice on both sides of road. Just N of the Refuge, turn W, go 1½ miles around Eagle's Nest cliff and uphill on back of it to collect oolite and petrified wood, especially to S.

PETRIFIED WOOD: Take Hwy 205 to milepost 32, collect around Saddle Butte E of road.

OPALIZED WOOD: 18 miles N on Hwy 395 and W 7 miles at Silvies Canyon.

• *Canyon City, Grant County* SERPENTINE (VERD ANTIQUE): to S along Canyon Creek.

• *Chenoweth, Wasco County* PETRIFIED WOOD: NW at Johnson ranch.

• *Corvallis, Benton County* CARNELIAN, JASPER: Take Hwy 99W, watch for Keiger Island sign, cross bridge and keep right for access to river and bars, collect in gravel bars in middle channel of Willamette river between Keiger and Smith Islands. Also generally on bars in river from N of Salem to S of Corvallis.

• *Crabtree, Linn County* PETRIFIED WOOD, JASPER: E 4 miles to Brewster Station, N 5 miles to schoolhouse, then left a mile and N a mile to farmhouse (fee).

• *Durkee, Baker County* CHALCEDONY: In Shirttail Creek.

FIRE OPAL: To E where stream cuts through volcanic rocks.

• *Enterprise, Wallowa County* MARBLE: Black marble on Alder slope of Wallowa Mountains.

• *Estacada, Clackamas County* PETRIFIED WOOD, GREEN JASPER: In Clackamas River.

• *Gold Beach, Curry County* PETRIFIED WOOD: Follow road on S side of Rouge River 7 miles to Huntley Park to collect on river bar.

AGATE: S on Hwy 101 to Lone Ranch State Park, collect at Rainbow Cove around point at S end of beach.

• *Hampton, Deschutes County* GREEN MOSS AGATE, JASPER, PETRIFIED WOOD: Take U.S. 20 NW, then N 10 miles to Hampton Butte. Collect at next butte W.

• *Harper, Malheur County* AGATE GEODES, OPALIZED WOOD: S 32 miles at Skull Springs.

AGATE NODULES: S for 25 miles to Dryck, then W ½ mile to diggings.

• *Heppner, Morrow County* OPAL: At Opal Butte.

• *Holland, Josephine County* JASPER, MASSIVE GROSSULARITE GARNET: S 1½ miles in Althouse Creek.

• *Jamieson, Malheur County* PETRIFIED WOOD: Take road NE to Huntington sign, then 6 miles N to dig bogwood agate.

• *Lakeview, Lake County* BLUE AGATE: Take Hwy 395 S 4 miles and hike mile into hills.

AGATE NODULES: S 5 miles in Crane Creek Canyon to E of Hwy 395.

AGATE, PETRIFIED WOOD: W 36 miles on Hwy 140 at Quartz Mountain Pass.

JASPER AND QUARTZ CRYSTALS: Take Hwy 395 S to New Pine Creek, then Fort Bidwell Road to summit. Collect in old mine tunnels.

AGATE, ORBICULAR JASPER: In Bullard and Deadman canyons on outskirts.

AGATE: In Dry Creek area to W.

• *Lebanon, Linn County* CARNELIAN: Take Hwy 20 S to Central Ave., then W on Sodaville Road to Tyler ranch (fee). Also at Moore diggings nearby.

AGATE: Hwy 20 3 miles S, to Enco station, go on to stop sign, turn left on to Tin road, left again and next right to first gate on Tye road at Drummond Agate Beds (fee).

• *Madras, Jefferson County* AGATE NODULES: NE 17 miles on Hwy 97 almost to Willowdale, take road E to Priday ranch. [Diggings closed temporarily but agate for sale.]

Just S of Priday ranch is the Kennedy ranch for petrified wood and nodules (fee). Just N is the Richardson ranch, where new thunderegg diggings are open.

JASPER, NODULES: In Hay Creek area 11 miles E.

• *Maupin, Wasco County* AGATE: Take Hwy 216 16 miles W and then S to Sunflower Flats.

BLACK AGATE: In Deschutes River to N.

• *Medford, Jackson County* * GREEN JASPER: N on Hwy 62 to Hwy 234, then 1 mile farther and E on Butte Falls road 16 miles and S on Gunderson road to railroad tracks. Hike W to ravine to collect.

• *Newport, Lincoln County* BEACH AGATE AND JASPER: Dig at Beverly Beach just to N. Also generally N and S on other beaches.

• *Oceanside, Tillamook County* SAGENITIC AGATE: N of Maxwell Point and elsewhere on nearby beaches with petrified wood and jasper.

• *Oregon City, Clackamas County* GREEN AND RED JASPER: In gravel bars of Clackamas River.

• *Plush, Lake County* * AVENTURINE LABRADORITE: Take road N 10 miles, go right ½ mile, take left fork NE 9 miles to fork, take left fork, go 5 miles, passing Rabbit Creek dam, hike ½ mile up dry wash to collect sunstone fragments in soil and decomposed basalt. The collecting area is in the Rabbit basin in Warner Valley.

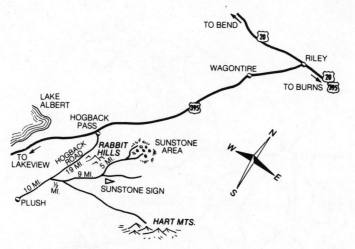

CHALCEDONY NODULES: Go 9 miles N, take the right fork 18 miles to refuge headquarters and S to Hart Mountain area. Hike to top and collect nodules in slopes of five canyons facing W.

FIRE OPAL: Collect in basalt on W rim of canyons.

• *Prineville, Crook County* * Prineville has organized its numerous collecting spots into a tourist attraction with camping facilities and town-owned collecting areas. Some of them are:

DENDRITIC AND ANGEL WING AGATE: At Eagle Rock. Take Post (Combs Flat) Road 18 miles to Eagle Rock, turn right past rocks, and follow a sharp incline left 1¼ miles.

PETRIFIED WOOD: At Bonnieview ranch, 6 miles short of Post. (Fee, get directions at Recreation Unlimited in Prineville.)

Likewise for Dick ranch claim 14 miles past Post.

AGATE, PETRIFIED WOOD: E on Post Road mile past Post, right across bridge and left on Shotgun Road to Booton ranch (fee).

RED, GREEN AND MOSS AGATE: At Maury Mountain. E on Post Road 8 miles past Post to Milepost 33, turn right over wooden bridge, continue over 5 cattle guards to first road right past national forest sign, go a mile and then right a mile to diggings.

LIMB CASTS: At Milepost 43 on Crooked River Hwy, take Camp Creek Road S and then W to plateau. Dendritic and colored limb casts found in area between creeks both sides of S Fork of Crooked River.

MOSS AGATE: At Reservoir Heights. Take Juniper Canyon road SE to road just N of reservoir; follow it to end to collect.

PETRIFIED WOOD: Take road S along Crooked River to dam, then N and go S and E to Bear Creek road past Little Bear Creek and on to point shortly after road leaves creek. Go left on rough road to collect at its end.

LIMB CASTS: Continue E on main road to McCormack ranch, take road along Soldier Creek E to turnoff S along Middle Fork of Camp Creek to collect at Smoky Mountain. Return N to turnoff, go 1½ mile, then S 2 miles to collect at South Pole Creek.

AGATE NODULES: At White Fir Spring. Take U.S. 26 E 9 miles, turn left at store onto Mill Creek Road 10 miles, then right across bridge 4½ miles to road junction and collect a few hundred yards ahead.

MOSS AGATE: U.S. 26 E 31 miles to Marks Creek Guard Station, turn left and follow Viewpoint signs on Road 127 to Whistler Spring dig. Road 125 leads to Road 123 (at sign) to the Valley View and Lucky Strike fee claims for thundereggs.

MOSS AGATE: U.S. 26 NE 31 miles to Marks Creek Guard Station, then Road 127 1 mile, NW on Road 123 to Road 1203 and N to Road 1256 and E to campground. Dig in Ochoco Mountains 2 miles W.

BLUE AGATE AND NODULES: At White Rock Spring. Turn left at White Fir Spring junction 2 miles to campsite, then rough road mile to diggings.

WHITE AGATE: At Sheep Creek. U.S. 26 16½ miles E, angle right on gravel road 3 miles, turn right on Wolf Creek Road to Sheep Creek sign and take Cadle Road to Arvid Nelson Road and left to 21 mile sign.

JASPER: At Coyle Spring. Take Hwy 26 E to fork at Marks Creek road; do not take it but take right fork on Ochoco Creek road. Continue to Road 13026 and go left on it to collect.

MOSS AGATE: At Shotgun Creek. Take Post road past Booton ranch to Road 1728, go S to road W, continue on it to fork and then go right ¾ mile.

NODULES: At Dry Creek: Take Hwy 26 to Road 133 N just past Ochoco Reservoir, go 5 miles, and left to Road 13015 and continue to creek. Return to Road 133 and take it N and then NW along Harvey Creek to Harvey Gap, then NE on Road 1307 to collect. Backtrack on Road 133 about a mile and collect in Harvey Creek. Also from the turn NW off Road 133 is a rough road E. Take it to end and then hike a mile E to Forked Horn Butte for nodules.

MOSS AND WHITE PLUME AGATE: At Bear Creek. S down Main Street 20 miles over Prineville Dam and continue on new road until it joins old road. Turn left on old road several miles to Bear Creek and collect in diggings on W side of bank.

PETRIFIED WOOD: At Swartz Canyon petrified forest. W to Redmond Hwy to road sign indicating turnoff to left.

• *Rockaway, Tillamook County* AGATE, JASPER: Pebbles on beach.

• *Rogue River, Jackson County* RHODONITE: Take road along

Evans Creek N for 15 miles to mine, collect in road cut and creek.

- *Rome, Malheur County* AGATE (SNAKESKIN): Hwy 95 SW to a mile E of rest area and just E of Crooked creek. Go S 1 mile and then take right fork a mile, turn left to end of road. Rake agate from soil.
- *Roseburg, Douglas County* PETRIFIED WOOD, AGATE: In North Umpqua River to Glide.
- *Rufus, Sherman County* AGATE: In gullies mile S of Hwy 30.
- *Salem, Polk County* PETRIFIED WOOD, JASPER: At River Bend Sand and Gravel company works.
- *Scio, Linn County* PETRIFIED WOOD: E on Hwy 226 for 3 miles to Richardson Gap road, turn right, then left on next paved road, go 1½ miles to first gravel road. Take it left to end and dig at Rogers Mountain.

  PETRIFIED WOOD, AGATE: Go 9 miles SE to hunt at Prospect Mountain Mine, which is 2 miles NW of Roaring River hatchery (fee).
- *Seaside, Clatsop County* AGATE, JASPER: Pebbles on beach.
- *Sweet Home, Linn County* BLUE AGATE: Take Hwy 228 for 4 miles SW to Holley school, then right a bit more than 2 miles, and again right 2 miles to farmhouse. Hike logging road for 1 mile to site. Another location is at end of a gravel road from Holley to river. Walk across river and dig.

  PETRIFIED WOOD: At Belveal farm 5 miles SW on Hwy 228 and 1⅓ miles E of Holley church (fee). Another location is just N of Hwy 228 bridge over Calapooya River and then E 1⅓ miles.
- *Tillamook, Tillamook County* ORANGE AGATE, JASPER: Take Third Street to Bay-Ocean Road to its end and collect at Tillamook bar.
- *Trent, Lane County* AGATE WITH REALGAR: S on Hwy 58, then ½ mile to road E to Snyder ranch to dig agate (fee).
- *Unity, Baker County* AGATE: Take Hwy 26 NW to Hwy 7, then NE 6 miles to road N through Whitney toward Sumpter, collect in dredge dumps and river gravels.

  BLUE AGATE: In rhyolite in area SE to Ironside.
- *Vale, Malheur County* PETRIFIED WOOD: Take road S 25 miles to sign reading "Owyhee Dam 8 Miles," go W 2 miles and S in creek bed to collecting area.

  OPALIZED WOOD: NW 12 miles at Willow Creek.
- *Vernonia, Columbia County* AGATE: S on Hwy 47 to bridge, turn right on logging road nearly a mile to farm gate. Ask

permission to cross farm, collect in Clear Creek gravels and banks.

CARNELIAN: In Nehalem River to N.

• *Wasco, Sherman County* JASPER (SCENIC): 1 mile outside town in new road cut; jasper is like Owyhee jasper.

• *Wedderburn, Curry County* MASSIVE GROSSULARITE GARNET, JASPER, PETRIFIED WOOD: In gravels at mouth of Rogue River, at Gold Beach, and on beaches and in coves for 6 miles N.

• *Willowdale, Jefferson County* MOSS AGATE: S 1 mile on U.S. 97, then S 5 miles and E 2 miles to Palmer ranch (fee).

PETRIFIED WOOD: At Folmsbee place. N on Hwy 97 for a mile, then E on Antelope road 7 miles.

• *Yachats, Lincoln County* SAGENITIC AGATE, JASPER: On Cummings Creek Beach.

MOSS AGATE, MASSIVE GROSULARITE GARNET, PETRIFIED WOOD: At Big Creek, 10-Mile Creek, China Creek, and Squaw Creek beaches to S.

Pennsylvania

Eastern Pennsylvania falls within the coastal plain made up of marine deposits, and lying west of it is the Piedmont plateau, resting on crystalline metamorphic rocks and sedimentary rocks. The highlands are formed of crystalline and volcanic rocks and culminate in the Allegheny plateau, largely sedimentary rocks, which forms nearly half the state and is its most rugged region. The belts or regions cross the state from northeast to southwest.

• *Avondale, Delaware County* * AQUAMARINE, GOLDEN BERYL, GARNET: In dumps of old Leiper (now Faccenda) quarry on E side of Crum Creek.

QUARTZ CRYSTALS: In quarry to SE on W side of Crum Creek.

AMETHYST: 1 mile W in quarry on George Sharpless farm.

• *Bart, Lancaster County* SMOKY QUARTZ: E of ruins of smelter ¾ mile N of Gap Nickel Mines.

• *Black Horse, Delaware County* AMAZONITE, GARNET: In exposures on Mineral Hill along road from Media.

SUNSTONE: S ¼ mile at old corundum pits, and ½ mile E on J. Smith farm.

GREEN QUARTZ: At quarry ½ mile NE of Black Horse.

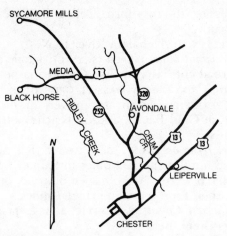

- *Boothwyn, Delaware County* AMETHYST: At J. B. Okie's farm 2 miles N.

  At Armstrong farm ½ mile N.

  RUTILATED QUARTZ: Loose in soil at McCay's farm.

  QUARTZ CRYSTALS, GARNET: In pits on W side of E branch of Naaman's Creek.
- *Bridgeport, Montgomery County* JASPER, QUARTZ: SE ½ mile on Hwy 202 in Dolomite quarry of the Bethlehem Steel company.
- *Carlisle, Cumberland County* BANDED AGATE: On S side of Hwy 11, a mile E of the Carlisle interchange on Pennsylvania Turnpike.
- *Chester, Delaware County* AMETHYST, BERYL, SMOKY QUARTZ: At Shaw & Esrey's Quarry ¼ mile S.

  ALMANDINE GARNET: In soil above Peter's Mill Dam in Green Creek and in creek mile S of Chester Heights Station.
- *Coatesville, Chester County* BERYL, AMETHYST, SMOKY QUARTZ: In quarry 1½ mile NW and just S of U.S. 30 bypass.
- *Cornog, Chester County* BLUE QUARTZ, SMOKY QUARTZ: With epidote as stringers in gneiss at Keystone Trap Rock quarry just SE.
- *Darlington Corners, Chester County* SERPENTINE, BERYL: In Brinton quarry to SW.
- *Darby, Delaware County* BERYL: Near White Horse 3 miles S.
- *Easton, Northampton County* TOPAZ, SERPENTINE: To N at Chestnut Hill in Verdolite and other quarries.
- *Eureka, Bucks County* SMOKY QUARTZ: At Eureka quarry to NE.
- *Gladhill, Adams County* COPPER IN RHYOLITE: At Bingham mine

½ mile NE of Piney Mountain on W side of road to Maria Furnace.

- *Glendale, Delaware County* BERYL: In quarry on Glendale road just N of place where road parallels Darby creek and mile S of where Hwy 3 meets the creek.
- *Harrisburg, Dauphin County* AGATE, GARNET: Take Int. 83 S across Pennsylvania Turnpike to overpass, then 1 mile farther to Fairview church, collect from weathered material.
- *Jenkins Corner, Lancaster County* SERPENTINE (WILLIAMSITE): At Cedar Hill quarry, reached from Hwy 222 by going E on road along Pennsylvania-Maryland line and following signs to mine. Get permission D. M. Stoltzfus & Son, Talmadge, Pa.
- *Kennett Square, Chester County* SUNSTONE: At Pierce's paper mill ½ mile SE.
  At Cloud's farm 2 miles SE.
  TOURMALINE: At Bailey's farm SW of Willowdale.
- *King of Prussia, Montgomery County* QUARTZ: With malachite in McCoy quarry.
- *Knavertown, Chester County* ACTINOLITE, QUARTZ: N past St. Peter's to dumps of French Creek mine.
- *Kunkletown, Monroe County* QUARTZ: Just to S in clay pit E of sand pits, and along stream banks. Permission at Sheesley's Minerals.
- *Leiperville, Delaware County* BLUE AND GOLDEN BERYL, THULITE, QUARTZ CRYSTALS: At Deshong's quarry ½ mile W on E side of Ridley Creek.
- *Lemont, Centre County* QUARTZ: In Neidgh quarry and loose in soil.
  OOLITIC CHERT: To W in fields of university farms.
- *Lenni, Delaware County* SUNSTONE, AMAZONSTONE, MOONSTONE: In cut on railroad ⅜ mile E of station.
  AMETHYST: W ½ mile of Crozierville on S side of Chester Creek.
- *Ligonier, Westmoreland County* QUARTZ CRYSTALS: W 3 miles at quarry on Hwy 30.
- *Media, Delaware County* AMETHYST: NE 1½ miles on Crum Creek road on James Worral, Morgan Hunter and Randolph farms.
  AMAZONSTONE, MOONSTONE: A mile W at Mineral Hill W of Ridley Creek, in quarry N of Crump's Quarry on grounds of School for the Feeble Minded.
  BERYL: At Blue Hill 2½ miles NW and in boulders along

Crum Creek. Take Paper Mill road to end, park near bridge over creek and take trail to S bank.

- *Morgan Station, Delaware County* AMETHYST: In quarries to W and near Crozierville and Chad's Ford.
- *Morgantown, Berks County* GARNET, EPIDOTE, QUARTZ: E 1¼ miles at Grace mine of Bethlehem Steel Company.
- *Mt. Holly Springs, Cumberland County* AGATE, NODULES: Take Hwy 34 W at bank, go ½ mile, take right fork about a mile to farmhouse, get permission and collect in fields S of house.
- *Neshaminy Falls, Bucks County* MOONSTONE: N 2 miles at Van-artsdalen's Quarry.
- *New Ringgold, Schuylkill County* QUARTZ: In hill nearby.
- *Oxford, Lancaster County* SERPENTINE (WILLIAMSITE): In dumps at Wood's Chrome mine 9 miles SW, and in nearby mines. The mine is ½ mile N of the state line in a meander of Octorara Creek. (See Maryland for other serpentine localities.)
- *Pocopson, Chester County* AMETHYST: E of station ¼ mile in field NW of Minshall Painter's house.
  At Darlington's farm ¼ mile W.
- *Quarryville, Lancaster County* SERPENTINE (WILLIAMSITE): Take Hwy 472 SE through Kirkwood to Union, then W to fork, take left fork ½ mile. Stillwell quarry is just over bridge on Gables Run.
- *Redington, Northampton County* CAT'S-EYE QUARTZ: On South Mountain.
- *Rock Springs Run, Lancaster County* MOSS AGATE, CARNELIAN: In small branch of run 1¼ miles N of Rock Springs, Md.
- *Stromville, Monroe County* QUARTZ: At Crystal Hill.
- *Stroudsburg, Northampton County* * QUARTZ CRYSTALS: Steep, wooded area located on the Christian Armitage farm S of Stroudsburg. Crystal Hill is reached by taking Rt 611 E from Stroudsburg to a blinker light and turning S on Hwy 191 for 3.1 miles, then keeping right 1.4 miles to Armitage house. Walk up steep hill to site where quartz crystals are loose in fine-grained quartz conglomerate (fee).
- *Sycamore Mills, Delaware County* SMOKY QUARTZ: W ½ mile on Walker Yarnell's farm for smoky quartz.
  AMETHYST: S ½ mile on Marshall farm near Dismal Run.
  GREEN QUARTZ: S ¾ mile at J. Tyler's farm.
- *Trainer Station, Delaware County* SMOKY QUARTZ, QUARTZ CRYSTALS, GREEN BERYL: At William Trainer's farm ½ mile N.

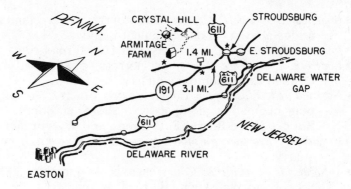

- *Unionville, Chester County* CORUNDUM, SERPENTINE: NE 2 miles on Northbrook Road at Corundum Hill.
- *Upper Darby, Delaware County* SMOKY QUARTZ: Along West Chester Pike ½ mile W.
- *Valley Forge, Chester County* AMETHYST: W 1½ miles at abandoned Jug Hollow Mine.
- *Vera Cruz, Lehigh County* JASPER: At quarry to N, along creek and in fields E of road and N of creek. Generally in area from Durham to Kutztown.

Rhode Island

Once a plain not much above sea level, Rhode Island has been uplifted and its surface carved by stream action into low hills and valleys; some of the latter have become ocean bays. Glaciation has completed the work of forming the surface.

- *Cumberland Hill, Providence County* QUARTZ, AGATE: Take Hwy 120 to Hwy 114, then N through Diamond Hill and left into state park to collect in dumps of quarries across road.
  SAGENITIC QUARTZ: At Diamond Hill Granite quarry in dumps.
  SERPENTINE: At Iron Mine Hill quarry. With diopside at Sneech Pond. Take Copper Hill road W to West Wrentham road, N ½ mile and W ¼ mile to Ballou Meeting House.
  AMETHYST: At Iron Hill mine dumps.
  SMOKY QUARTZ: At McLaughlin's Ledge.

239

- *Jamestown, Newport County* STAUROLITE: Near Jamestown bridge abutments on Conanicut island.
- *Johnston, Providence County* BERYL: In Hwy 6 road cuts.
- *Limerock, Providence County* SERPENTINE, QUARTZ, AGATE: In Conklin Lime Company quarry.
- *Narragansett, Washington County* BERYL, QUARTZ: In outcropping pegmatites along eastern shore, at Bonnet Point, Bonnet Shore Beach, Ft. Varnum and Watson Pier.
- *Providence, Providence County* QUARTZ: At Wanskirch Granite quarry.
- *Spragueville, Providence County* BERYL: At junction of Mann School and Wanskuck Hill roads in road cut.
- *Tiverton, Newport County* RUTILATED QUARTZ: In quarry of Fish road.
- *Westerly, Washington County* BERYL: At Westerly Granite quarry.
- *West Greenwich, Kent County* AMAZON STONE: At Nooseneck, Weaver Hill road and Int. 95.

South Carolina

Near the ocean, South Carolina is a region of islands and marshes in the coastal plain. Behind this is the upcountry, the rolling Piedmont plateau, while the northwest corner of the state rises abruptly into the Blue Ridge Mountains of the Appalachian system, adjoining noted gem areas in Georgia and North Carolina. Most of the gem locations lie in the more mountainous northwestern part of the state.

- *Allendale, Allendale County* CHERT: Take Hwy 301 SW across the Savannah River, turn NW for 8 miles to where road makes sharp turn S, continue ahead on dirt road 12 miles and collect along road. Other favored collecting spots include King's Creek Landing on the Savannah river.
- *Anderson, Anderson County* EMERALD: At J. M. McConnell place 3½ miles NE in schist.
  BERYL: At Ferguson mine 5⅔ miles N on Hwy 187, and ½ mile SW of McConnell place in pegmatite.
  GARNET, QUARTZ: N 9 miles near dam on 26-Mile Creek.
  AMETHYST, GARNET: S 15 miles on Hwy 28 where road cuts dike near lake.

- *Antreville, Abbeville County* AMETHYST, SMOKY QUARTZ: Go 3 miles W on Hwy 284, then a mile N on S-1-72, and ¾ mile farther and right to house, pay fee, return to next road S and go E and N a mile to mine.
- *Blacksburg, Cherokee County* SAPPHIRE: In pegmatite 2½ miles NW on Hwy 83 at Andrew Moon place.
- *Blenheim, Marlboro County* PETRIFIED CYCAD: In sand pits 4 miles S.
- *Buffalo Church, Cherokee County* AMETHYST: At W. T. Gibbons place just to W and in stream gravels.
- *Columbia, Richland County* AMETHYST: At Lake Murray.
- *Cross Hill, Laurens County* AMETHYST: N on Hwy 39 to crossroads with large white house, turn right 3 miles until road takes sharp turn. Stop at farmhouse just before turn, get permission to collect, make turn, go ½ mile to road right into pines. Dig in field to right of road.
- *Due West, Abbeville County* AMETHYST: At Ellis-Jones Amethyst mine, by permission of the Williams family.
- *Easley, Pickens County* SOAPSTONE: In schist.
- *Edgefield, Edgefield County* SERPENTINE: In Turkey Creek within sight of Hwy 25.
- *Gaffney, Cherokee County* SAPPHIRE: At Porter's Hill, on Bowen river.
  GARNET: At Troy Blanton mine 8 miles SW.
- *Greenville, Greenville County* QUARTZ, GARNET: N 5 miles at E end of Paris Mountain State Park in pegmatite at junction of two creeks.
- *Greenwood, Greenwood County* AMETHYST: At Wrenn's place.
  CHALCEDONY: At Harper's place at powerhouse.
  GARNET: At Stockman's Quarry.
  QUARTZ CRYSTALS, SMOKY QUARTZ: At Milford place.
- *Iva, Anderson County* BERYL: Go 3 miles to country store on bank of Lake Secession, get permission and directions to collect nearby.
  BERYL: NW 1¾ miles on Wilson's Creek, and on Hwy 413 at Frank Pruitt place, and at J. B. Anderson farm 3 miles SW.
  AMETHYST: SW 8 miles at Sherard place.
- *Jefferson, Chesterfield County* YELLOW AND BLUE TOPAZ: 3 miles W at Brewer Mine for topaz.
- *Laurens, Laurens County* CORUNDUM: At New Cemetery and inside city at Dead Man's Cut in railroad.
  PYROPE GARNET: At Dead Man's Cut.

• *Liberty Hill, Lancaster County* SMOKY QUARTZ: Near Wateree reservoir in pegmatite near creek. Also take Hwy 21 S to Hwy 97, go 8¼ miles, then right on dirt road for 2¼ miles and right on dirt road 1½ miles, walk to mine.

• *Lowndesville, Abbeville County* AMETHYST: To E at McCalla place and 1⁴/₅ miles N at Barnes place.

• *Pelzer, Anderson County* AQUAMARINE, GREEN TOURMALINE: S 1 mile.

• *Piedmont, Greenville County* BERYL: At the D. D. McNeely place.

• *Princeton, Laurens County* AMETHYST: At spring 1½ miles SW.

• *Saluca, Greenwood County* UNAKITE: On W shore of Lake Greenwood.

• *Seneca, Oconee County* SILLIMANITE: N 2 miles on LeRoy property. Collect in soil and dike. Material will cut cat's-eyes. Get permission King's Rock shop, Franklin, N.C.

• *Shoals Junction, Greenwood County* AMETHYST: SE 1½ miles on road to Donalds at the Hadden place, and 1 mile SW at the Dunn place.

South Dakota

East of the Missouri River, South Dakota is a fairly level, glaciated plain; to the west of the Missouri lies rolling prairie broken along the White River and north of it by the Badlands, and in the far south and central west by granite mountains known as the Black Hills. One of them, Harney Peak, is the highest point in the United States east of the Rockies. The agates of the prairies and the pegmatite minerals of the Black Hills are the principal gem resources of the state.

• *Ardmore, Fall River County* * AGATE, JASPER: Generally in area to S along state line and down into Nebraska. Take dirt road E for 7 miles toward the best known collecting spot, known as Sugarloaf Butte.

• *Custer, Custer County* * AGATE: Take U.S. 16 E to State Park, turn off toward State Farm, go beyond cattle gate, search in hills to right.

PYRITE, BARBOSALITE: Showy black and golden materials in Bull Moose mine dumps 5 miles SE.

ROSE QUARTZ: At White Elephant Mine. S on Hwy 385 7½ miles to fork, take right fork to mine on ridge. Collect on dumps.

AGATE: For Tepee Canyon agate, go 14 miles W on U.S. 16 to campground on left. Continue 1 mile to road on

right up canyon. Collect at top of hill left, or go up canyon to small gully and collect on hill left. Also go back to U.S. 16, drive W to logging road on right. Agates are in limestone.

GARNET, TOURMALINE: Go 7 miles W on U.S. 16, turn N at Deer Camp sign, go ¼ mile, and search in stream, or take trail up steep hill and look in mica schists.

• *Fairburn, Custer County* * AGATE: The brightly colored Fairburn agates were never plentiful and they are now difficult to find. Experts advise that the best place to look is where the agates have been found before, and that the fall of the year, after the grass has died back, is the best time. Fairburn-type agates have been found over a three-state area (shown by dotted line on map) extending down into Nebraska and Wyoming. Well-patterned jaspers and agatized fossils are also found in the agate beds.

To reach the original collecting location, leave Fairburn on Hwy 79, go E 3½ miles to left fork and follow French Creek 5½ miles to McDermand ranch. Continue to picnic grounds, enter and drive across creek nearly a mile, and collect in the gravelly knolls.

• *Hot Springs, Fall River County* * PETRIFIED WOOD: At Fall River Canyon.

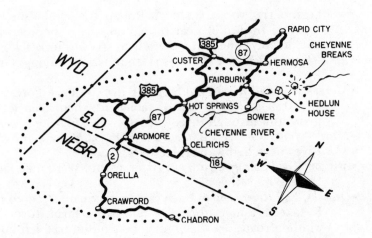

- *Interior, Jackson County* AGATE: Take Hwy 40 W, go ¾ mile farther after it becomes gravel. Along road pick up agates which look like wads of gum.
- *Keystone, Pennington County* * ROSE QUARTZ: In pegmatite dikes along gravel road connecting Alt. 16 and Hwy 87 near Mount Rushmore National Monument.

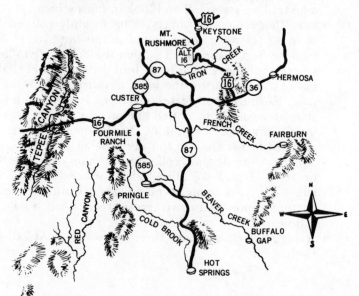

LEPIDOLITE, TOURMALINE: At Robert Ingersoll Mine.
GARNET: In dumps near tunnel on Alt. 16 between Hwy 16 and Keystone and generally in streams in Black Hills.
- *Little Eagle, Corson County* PETRIFIED WOOD: Along Grand River.
- *Minnekahta, Fall River County* FOSSIL CYCAD: Take Forest Service trail to left to top of tableland, then keep left on main trail through three gates to collecting site.
- *Murdo, Jones County* CHALCEDONY: On sand bars in White River near highway bridge to S.
- *Mission, Todd County* BLACK PETRIFIED WOOD: W 12 miles along Little White River.
- *Oelrichs, Fall River County* * AGATE: Go S in main street to road E, take it 1 mile, then S 2 miles to a farm, turn E on winding road to a sharp turn, take a dim trail left and N a mile then W to buttes to collect. A similar place is Lone Butte, reached by going 4 miles E to a ranch gate, then ½ mile S to collect on N and E sides of butte.

•*Pringle, Custer County* * AGATE: Along Hwy 89 between Pringle and Minnekahta, and to NW and W of Pringle and near Custer State Park to NE.

•*Rapid City, Pennington County* RUTILATED QUARTZ: To E in Box Elder Creek.

PETRIFIED WOOD: To W and N along Hwy 14.

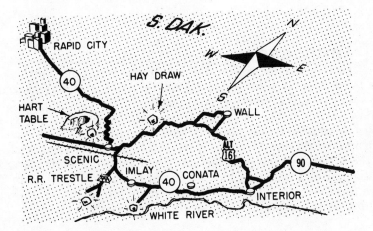

•*Scenic, Pennington County* * BLACK AGATE: West of Scenic 2 miles and N of the railroad is a formation known as Hart Table, where black agate is found in the gullies and eroded bluffs.

AGATE, PETRIFIED WOOD, ROSE QUARTZ: Loose on ground 3 miles S, mile off road in either direction.

GEODES: On Hwy 40 E from Scenic, the road reaches a pass. Turn S from here and past a railroad trestle for geodes.

BLACK, WHITE AGATE: Farther E past Imlay, a road turns S toward White River for black and white agate along banks.

NODULES: Northeast of Scenic on the road to Wall, the road passes a formation known as Hay Draw. Here nodules are found in a clay ironstone matrix, both in the stream and in its banks.

JASPER, AGATE: Hwy 40 W 1 mile to place where red hills are seen to right. Park, walk to them and collect along the way.

245

AGATE: To W in the breaks of the Cheyenne River is the Hedlun log cabin. Ask permission to collect to N for Fairburn agates.

- *Sioux Falls, Minnehaha County* JASPER, AGATE: In gravels of Big Sioux River.
- *Spearfish, Lawrence County* ONYX: To W on Crow Peak.
- *Whitewood, Lawrence County* AMETHYST: Nodules in Whitewood creek.

Tennessee

East Tennessee rises in the mountains along the North Carolina border, an area of folded crystalline rocks, and extends across the valley of the Tennessee, cut in sedimentary rocks, to the Cumberland plateau. This plateau, bordered by steep escarpments, encloses a central basin running from northeast to southwest, in which Nashville lies. The basin rises to highlands on the west, cut by the lower Tennessee River, and then falls to a bluff along the Mississippi in a plateau which is part of the Gulf coastal plain. Except for the narrow belt of Appalachian Mountains in the east, Tennessee is formed mostly of sedimentary rocks.

- *Beechgrove, Coffee County* CHALCEDONY NODULES AND FRAGMENTS: S and W of U.S. 41.
- *Bluffton, Cocke County* UNAKITE: In nearby streams and granite outcrops.
- *Bristol, Sullivan County* ONYX: At bypass road cut in Hwy 421.
- *Cookeville, Putnam County* JASPER, AGATE: In nodules in streams from Cumberland Plateau.
- *Copper Hill, Polk County* STAUROLITE: Take road to Ducktown for 1 mile, look on right side for a rough place in bank.
- *Erwin, Washington County* JASPER: Go 5 miles N on Hwy 81, cross river and turn left at Embreeville to Bumpas Cove for dark variegated material with blue areas.
- *Friendsville, Blount County* MARBLE: In waste piles of many quarries close to village.
- *Frog Pond, Unicoi County* UNAKITE: N on U.S. 23 1 mile, collect in road cut and creek fill to left. Also at Chandler mine 2¾ miles NW.
- *Jamestown, Fentress County* ONYX: Take U.S. 127 to road W at S edge of town to Herbert Tipton farm in Buffalo Cave area (fee).

- *Jellico, Campbell County* AGATE: In road cut between bridge and tavern outside town on LaFollit road.
- *Kingsport, Sullivan County* JASPER: Take Hwy 11W past U.S. 23 intersection, then 1⅔ miles to road N to Lambert quarry.
- *Memphis, Shelby County* AGATE: Material of Lake Superior type in Mississippi river gravels at Richardson's Landing.
- *Murfreesboro, Rutherford County* AGATE NODULES: In chert in road cuts and ditches.
- *Oakley, Cumberland County* GEODES: Go 13 miles N to Dale Hollow lake, dig on south central shore.
- *Roan Mountain, Carter County* UNAKITE: Take Hwy 143 going N to second roadside table on Tennessee side of Roan Mountain. Also collect in Rock Creek and along U.S. 19S.
- *Shelbyville, Bedford County* IRIS AGATE, CARNELIAN: To E and N between Fairfield Turnpike and Hwy 64. Best in valleys off Pannell Ridge, such as those crossed by Horse Mountain road from the mountain to Wartrace. Also on road from Horse Mountain road around Philippi church on way to Wartrace and SW of Wartrace in Stokes Branch section, agate is found in streams and fields, such as along Duck river and its tributaries.
  One specific place to collect is at the Velmer Curvow farm, on Rt. 2 (fee).
  FOSSIL CORAL: To W at bridge over Sugar Creek on Hwy 64.
- *Sparta, White County* JASPER: Take U.S. 70 S 1 mile to White Company limestone quarry.
- *Townsend, Blount County* EPIDOTE: In road cuts and stream gravels.
- *Woodbury, Cannon County* GEODES: On farms 5 miles E on U.S. 70S, and in Stone river tributaries.

Texas

Sandy sediments typical of the coastal plain make up southeastern Texas. Behind this lies the Llano uplift, a region of crystalline rocks. The Grand Prairie and Edwards plateaus, primarily sedimentary rocks, link the Llano uplift to the north central plains and, toward the Panhandle, the High Plains themselves. In far western Texas is the Trans Pecos, formed of rugged mountains, both igneous and sedimentary in their structure. The great variety of sedimentary areas affords a wealth of agate and petrified wood, while in the Llano area occur topaz and garnet and other minerals characteristic of crystalline rocks.

- *Alpine, Brewster County* AGATE: At Woodward ranch 14 miles S on Hwy 118 and turn at sign.
  Also at Anderson ranch 21 miles S and to left at sign.
  At Henderson ranch 32 miles S and to left at sign.
  At Cocoanut ranch 33 miles S on Hwy 118.
  PETRIFIED WOOD: At Aqua Fria ranch 58 miles S on Hwy 118, then right 10 miles.
  At Tooter Hill ranch 66 miles S on Hwy 118, then turn at sign 8 miles to ranch.
  AGATE: E on Hwy 90 for 8 miles, then N on Hwy 67 26 miles and W to Hovey ranch.
  All these collecting spots charge a fee.
  POMPOM AGATE: At Needle Peak, 115 miles S of Woodward ranch between end of Hwy 118 and Rio Grande River. This is just W of Big Bend National Park. (By arrangement with Woodwards.)
  YELLOW LABRADORITE: S 20 miles and loose in soil.
  OPAL: In seams in rhyolite 16 miles S.
- *Amarillo, Potter County* AGATIZED WOOD: SE 50 miles near Palo Duro Canyon.
- *Austin, Travis County* SERPENTINE: Just S of Beecaves, reached by taking Hwy 290 to Oak Hill, then NW on Hwy 71.
  LIMESTONE: Fossiliferous material is found on hill 1½ miles upstream from Barton Springs in Barton creek.
- *Balmorhea, Reeves County* BLUE AGATE: Take access road SW to Toyahvale, then E to collect between Lake Balmorhea and Hwy 290. Agate is also found SE of the lake loose in the soil.
- *Bedias, Grimes County* TEKTITES: Found in a large irregular area as far SW as Gonzales County.
  BEDIASITE: The variety found here, takes its name from this town.
- *Borger, Carson County* FLINT: Varicolored Alibates flint is found in Plum Creek canyon reached by taking Hwy 1913 to sign to Plum Creek Recreation park, then S to bottom of Plum Creek Canyon and right 4 miles to campground. Hunt in creek and in soil.
- *Brackettsville, Kinney County* JASPER: Near town and in Rio Grande gravels.

• *Caldwell, Burleson County* PETRIFIED WOOD: To S between Hwys 21 and 36.

• *Calliham, McMullen County* PETRIFIED WOOD: W along Hwy 72 as far as Tilden and NE and SW of Falls City.

• *Carmine, Fayette County* PETRIFIED WOOD: Take road N ½ mile, then left ¼ mile and right ¼ mile to dirt road, follow it ½ mile to gate on left; go to creek and hunt in creek and along banks.

• *Columbus, Colorado County* PETRIFIED WOOD: In gravels 10 miles W.

• *Cross, Grimes County* PETRIFIED WOOD: To N along Hwy 39 all the way to Normangee and to NE along Hwy 90 to Madisonville.

• *Eagle Flat, Hudspeth County* AUGITE: Gem grade with black spinel.

• *Eagle Pass, Maverick County* AGATE, JASPER: In gravel pit on Rio Grande and at Hill ranch (fee) 9 miles NW on Hwy 277 to collect south of buildings.
    BROWN AMBER: In cretaceous coal deposits.

• *El Sauz, Starr County* PETRIFIED PALM WOOD, AGATE: To S along Hwy 649.

• *Fredericksburg, Gillespie County* AMETHYST, CITRINE: To NE at Amethyst Hill.
    ALMANDINE GARNET: In stream gravels.

• *Freer, Duval County* PETRIFIED WOOD: At Stevenson Ranch.
    FIRE OPAL: Seams in rhyolite.

• *Giddings, Burleson County* PETRIFIED WOOD: Take U.S. 290 E to Ledbetter and Rd 2145 S to Matejonsky farm to hunt palm wood (fee).

• *Hemphill, Sabine County* PETRIFIED WOOD: To S along E edge of Rayburn reservoir and W edge of Toledo Bend reservoir.

• *Johnson City, Blanco County* FOSSIL MARBLE: Black material near Cypress Mill and 5 miles S at Honeycut Bend.

• *Karnes City, Karnes County* PETRIFIED WOOD: In fields and in streams to N and E toward Falls City and Helena. Tessman ranch (fee) is 10 miles E of Falls City on Hwy 792, the Pavelick farm is S of Falls City (fee), and the Erdman's Rock Haven in Falls City offers guide collecting service.

• *LaGrange, Fayette County* * PETRIFIED PALM WOOD: LaGrange is near the center of a belt of gravels 100 or more miles inland from the Gulf of Mexico and extending from

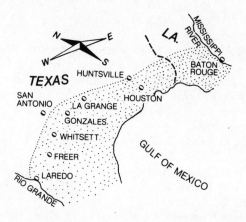

Huntsville, 50 miles N of Houston, through LaGrange, Gonzales, Whitsett and Freer. In this area, called the Catahoula formation, fossil wood, including palm, is found on the surface and in creeks. Near LaGrange it is found to N along Rabs Creek and to SW toward Muldoon.

•*Laredo, Jeff Davis County* AGATE, PETRIFIED WOOD, JASPER: One of the prime collecting areas in the United States lies along the Rio Grande from Mission and Sullivan City in the south to Laredo in the north. Gem materials are found in fields, along side roads, and railroad cuts, and in the gravel pits along the river. Often they are coated with a white limy layer. Some specific localities:

W 3 miles of Sullivan City take first road left to Garcia ranch (fee). Also at Fordyce gravel pits.

W 4 miles of Rio Grande City and N along road to El Sauz. Collect along road.

E 12 miles on Hwy 83 to road S to Grulla. Just before reaching railroad track take road E and N to collect in gravel.

NW on Hwy 83 to river gravels at Roma.

At Falcon, where gravel from the dam was dumped.

At Lajitas behind store and in wash to W.

At Laredo, 10½ miles from turnoff from Hwy 83 to Rd. 1492, then left over cattle guard to Diaz ranch (fee).

N 9 miles from Laredo on Delores road, then left to river to collect. Farther along Delores road is Singing Hills ranch (fee).

(Also see Zapata entries.)

- *Llano, Llano County* GRANITE (LLANITE): In dikes, fields, and streams N near Hwy 16, such as 10 miles N in quarry just W. Also 15 miles S at Enchanted Rock (fee).
- *Marathon, Brewster County* AGATE: S on U.S. 385 to Hwy 2627 then SE 6½ miles to Stilwell ranch (fee). Nearby is a similar collecting place, the Brushy Creek ranch.
- *Marfa, Presidio County* AGATE: Take U.S. 67 to Hwy 169, then left 18 miles to Bishop ranch (fee).

    AGATE: Along Hwy 67 S of intersection with Hwy 169.

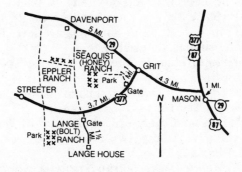

- *Mason, Mason County* * TOPAZ: White to blue topaz is found on several ranches in Mason County, near Mason, Grit, Katemcy, and Streeter. Specific directions are: Take Hwy 87 NW to Grit, then SE on Hwy 377. The first ranch on N side of road is the Seaquist (Honey) place, 1 mile from Grit to gate. Get key and pay fee at 400 Broad St., Mason, and collect in streams or dig in granite hills W of parking lot, or in Hickory branch of Honey Creek and the Gulch. Go W from Seaquist gate 3½ miles to dirt road on left into Ernest Lange (Bolt) place. Take it 1½ miles to Lange house, pay fee. Hunt in ravine behind house and ¾ mile back on dirt road.

    Across from the Lange ranch is the Eppler place.

    For directions to Schwanke place, see Robert Raspberry in Mason. The place lies N of Grit.

    The Davenport ranch lies N of the Eppler place. It is on Hwy 29. Take Hwy 29 out of Grit 5 miles, turn left and collect in dry gravel and in creek in S end of the ranch. Get key from Mrs. Loeffler in Grit.

    Another collecting place is in the Giersch ranch S of Hwy 377 at Streeter.

Nearby at Katemcy is topaz at the McWilliams ranch on Hwy 1222.

- *Oxford, Llano County* AMETHYST: In quartz veins near old town site.

  SERPENTINE: To N in quarry near Hwy 16.

- *Pecos, Reeves County* PLUME AGATE: Along roads N and S of Toyah, 19 miles W of Pecos.

- *Pumpville, Val Verde County* AGATE, JASPER, PETRIFIED WOOD: On Sidney Smith ranch N of Hwy 90.

- *San Saba, San Saba County* LIMESTONE: Limestone containing crinoid fossils is found on the C. B. Lambert ranch. Take Hwy 190 W 2 miles, then 7 miles S on Rt. 1030, and then E to ranch (fee). SE of San Saba are several quarries containing similar material.

- *Sierra Blanca, Hudspeth County* TURQUOISE: NW 8 miles in Sierra Blanca Mountains.

- *Smithville, Bastrop County* PETRIFIED WOOD: in creeks and gravels near town.

- *Terlingua, Brewster County* YELLOW AMBER: In Terlingua Creek. RUIN AGATE: Along Hwy 170 E on way to Big Bend National Park.

- *Tilden, McMullen County* PETRIFIED PALM WOOD: To E along course of Frio and Nueces Rivers.

- *Voca, Mason County* QUARTZ: Near the town and in Katemcy creek. Often asteriated.

- *Whitsett, Live Oak County* PETRIFIED PALM WOOD: To N and along Hwy 99.

  To E in creeks and gullies for petrified palm wood.

- *Trinity, Trinity County* PETRIFIED PALM WOOD: Along Hwy 405 toward Huntsville, and to N in road cuts toward Groveton and Lovelady.

- *Zapata, Zapata County* AGATE, JASPER, PETRIFIED WOOD: Collect in two hills between Hwy 83 and the Rio Grande 15 miles to S.

  Take Hwy 83 E for 13 miles to signs for Bob's Knob, follow signs for 9 miles (fee).

  Cross Rio Grande and go 8 miles to Guerrero, Mexico, and collect along road.

  At Hines Ranch 23 miles NW on Hwy 83, then S at gate (fee). (Also see Laredo entries).

Utah

Utah falls into two grand divisions, the plateau, east of a line from the middle of the northern border running to the southwestern corner and for a long way following the Wasatch Mountains, and the Great Basin region to the west of this line. The Great Basin, formerly the bed of a lake of which Great Salt Lake is a remnant, is level except for isolated mountains. To the north the plateau is bounded by the wild Uinta Mountains, which descend into the sandstone buttes and cliffs that in southern Utah form the fantastic regions of erosion seen in Zion and Bryce Canyon National Parks and in the Grand Canyon of the Colorado. These sandstone areas are rich in fossils and petrified wood.

- *Beaver, Beaver County* AGATE: Take left-hand road past city dump and then next right-hand road for 2 miles.
- *Blanding, San Juan County* BLACK PETRIFIED WOOD: Hwy 95 W through Natural Bridges National Monument, then 18 miles farther past monument entry road into White Canyon.
- *Boulder, Garfield County* AGATE, PETRIFIED WOOD: In canyons to E and S.
- *Cainesville, Wayne County* AGATE, CONGLOMERATE: Hwy 24 6 miles E to small canyon, collect just W of canyon and to S of road. Best material is S of small creek.
- *Cedar City, Iron County* AGATE: Take rim road in Cedar Breaks National Monument to gate and cattle crossing. Turn outside monument into field and take first turn right toward Brian Head. Collect in washes below peak. Also found on W side of road leading from S gate of monument.
  BLUE AGATE: N on access road to Int. 15, through gates and E into Fiddler's Canyon. Farther N and just E of access road are several gates on way to summit that mark roads E to red agate collecting areas in hills.
- *Central, Washington County* AGATE NODULES: Take Hwy 18 to Dixie National Forest sign, turn left through gate before reaching sign, and take left fork N into canyon. Go ½ mile and search on hill to left. Go on, take left hand road to camp at end of road to collect S and W of camp. Go back to fork, take right fork into canyon, and then into a second canyon and follow ditch to diggings.
- *Cisco, Grand County* * JASPER: Take Hwy 128 S for 7 miles, then take left fork to river and drive into canyon. Jasper is in ledges on sides of canyon.

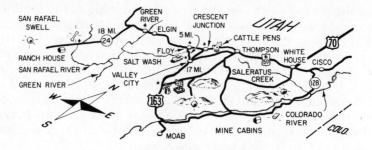

RED AGATE PSEUDOMORPHS: Farther west in the hills are red agate pseudomorphs after barite concretions.

AGATE, PETRIFIED WOOD, AND DINOSAUR BONE: Some 17 miles S of Thompson is a windmill and former CCC camp. In the hills E and SE of the windmill, agate, petrified wood, and petrified dinosaur bone weather out of the Morrison formation.

LACE AND GRAPE AGATE: Farther W and about five miles S of a deep wash across the road S from Floy, park and go into the wash and hills to S for agate.

RED AGATE, SEPTARIAN NODULES: Take Hwy 163 S 13 miles from Crescent Junction to Seep Spring sign, then E 4 miles and right to collect in creek.

AGATE: Farther S, a dim road cuts S from the road that swings from Thompson to Hwy 163 N of Moab. After crossing a wet wash on this dim road, look in the hills to S for agate.

Below Green River, take Hwy 24 S until it crosses the San Rafael River (about 18 miles). In the hills just N of the reef is agate; to the W, dinosaur bone.

JASPER-AGATE: Farther S on Hwy 24 the road passes several ranches and then plunges into the San Rafael Swell. In this area jasper-agate is loose on the desert floor.

• *Delta, Millard County* * TOPAZ: To reach the Thomas Mountain collecting area, go NE on Hwy 6 for 10 miles, turn left and go NW for 40 miles to a gravel road, turn right 2 miles to a track N, follow it a mile to fork, take left fork a mile, then N in dry wash. In the valley or amphitheater of the mountain is a white knoll W of the campsite. Sherry-colored topaz can be dug out of the rhyolite there, and on slopes ½ mile W and ½ mile E are complex crystals. A mile NE of the knoll is a saddle where yellow etched crystals are found. Garnet is found with the topaz

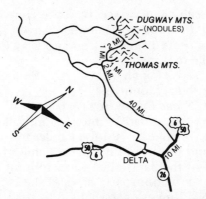

midway between the knoll and the V of Topaz Mountain, and on the W side of the mountain above the fluorite mine. The crystals are found in the rhyolite and loose in the sand, but those exposed to sunlight are bleached white.

NODULES: The Dugway nodule location is reached by going from Topaz Mountain E 2 miles on the Jericho road, then N 15 miles to a road W. Follow it 8 miles to a sign to the nodule bed.

•*Deseret, Millard County* * YELLOW LABRADORITE: S on Hwy 257 to cinder mounds 1 mile N of Clearlake Station, cross tracks to E and search flats for transparent gems.

•*Escalante, Garfield County* AGATE, JASPER: N 2 miles, collect along fence. Go on toward campground for jasper in hills, then SE to collect near ranch road. The road circles back to Escalante.

•*Eureka, Juab County* RHYOLITE (WONDERSTONE): Take Hwy 36 N 17 miles, cross railroad tracks, go right 2 miles to dig in ridges.

AGATE: Go 4 miles NE to a gravel road NW, cross railroad tracks and drive into Pinyon Canyon. Collect on surface.

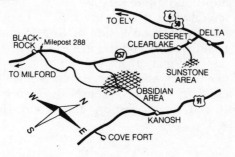

- *Fairfield, Utah County* VARISCITE: Take Hwy 73 N 4 miles, then left on dirt road up Manning Canyon past old gold mine and continue 1 mile to trail into Clay Canyon. Take trail $1/10$ mile to mine.
- *Grantsville, Tooele County* VARISCITE: S 9 miles at Amatrice Hill in Stansbury Mountains.
- *Green River, Grand County* AGATE, JASPER: W on Int. 70, then S on Hwy 24 to road W into Goblin Valley.

  AGATE: W on U.S. 70 for 11 miles to overpass, turn S on road and hunt W of it. Go on 4 miles farther to road SE and N of the San Rafael River to hunt in hills.

  PETRIFIED WOOD, FOSSIL BONE: Take U.S. 70 $3\frac{1}{2}$ miles W, then N 17 miles on Hwy 6-50 to road W under railroad tracks, follow it $6\frac{1}{2}$ miles and collect in hills to S.

  AGATE: Hwy 70 E for 12 miles, then S under power line for 6 miles, and E $\frac{1}{2}$ mile to dig pink agate. Go back to road and continue 7 miles S, then mile E to collect red-spotted agate.
- *Hanksville, Wayne County* AGATE: W on Hwy 24 for 3 miles, then N 4 miles to collect red agate in Muddy Creek area. Return to Hanksville, go $26\frac{1}{2}$ miles S to sign for Star Springs Park, then W to fork, take S fork a mile to collect near dam and in cliffs W of dam.

  JET: S 10 miles in Coaly Basin.
- *Heber City, Wasatch County* RED HORN CORAL: N on Hwy 40 to Hwy 35, then E 7 miles to Francis and 3 miles more to Woodland. Go 2 miles to gate, park and walk 2 miles to site in Riley's Canyon, which is W of Camp Kildare in the Kamas district of the Wasatch National Forest. The coral is in limestone scarps or loose on the ground.
- *Hurricane, Washington County* FLOWER AGATE: Go 5 miles W, then S $1\frac{1}{2}$ miles through 2 gates and S 2 miles through another gate and collect to right of road in red dunes. Fawcett Hobby Shop in Hurricane advertises it will give directions and guide service.
- *Jericho, Juab County* CHALCEDONY ROSES: Take road W for 35 miles and collect on S side of Keg Mountain. On the N side obsidian and nodules are found.

  AGATE: To E just off Hwy 6.
- *Kanab, Kane County* AGATE, PETRIFIED WOOD: Take U.S. 89 E for less than 16 miles, then N through gate $6\frac{1}{2}$ miles to collect red agate, jasper, and wood along Vermilion Cliffs.

Continue on U.S. 89 13 miles to rest area, go through gate and NE 7 miles to hills for petrified wood.

• *Leeds, Washington County* PETRIFIED WOOD: Take U.S. 91 NE a mile to a road S, cross two pole lines in first ½ mile, turn right through gate into canyon.

• *Levan, Juab County* BLACK AGATE: Take Hwy 28 S 13 miles, then mile E on dirt road into valley. Collect to the right beyond buildings in ravines and on ridges.

• *Lucin, Box Elder County* VARISCITE: NW 5 miles at Utahlite Hill (private claim).

• *Milford, Beaver County* * OPAL: Take Hwy 257 N to McDonald ranch (fee).

QUARTZ CRYSTALS: E 12 miles at Mineral Mountain in Miner's Basin.

OBSIDIAN: Take Hwy 257 N for 23 miles, E across railroad tracks, then nearly 2 miles farther to poor road S to collect snowflake obsidian in hills. Go back to Hwy 257, continue N 11 miles, then E 2½ miles to a big sink for more obsidian.

• *Mt. Carmel Junction, Kane County* SEPTARIAN NODULES: Go NE 1⅔ miles on U.S. 89, then N 3 miles to gate and 2½ miles farther, park, and collect nodules in steep canyon to right and canyons opening into it.

• *Moab, Grand County* AGATE, FOSSIL BONE: Take U.S. 163 to road E a mile below airport, and continue into Burro Seeps, and S in valley to collect.

• *Nephi, Juab County* FOSSIL PALM WOOD: Take Hwy 132 W for 12 miles toward Delta, turn S at gravel pit, go 8 miles to a gate, then a mile farther to a fork. Take left fork a mile and dig for wood. Return to fork, take right one and walk E into hills for agate.

RED ONYX: Go E on Hwy 132 for 6 miles, then N on Mt. Nebo road 3½ miles to a cattle guard. Park, climb to shelf, and then go left to diggings.

• *Panguitch, Garfield County* JASPER, AGATE: Take road to Panguitch Lake to end of pavement; then go ½ mile to camp grounds and collect S of camp.

• *Parowan, Iron County* AGATE: Take road E up Parowan canyon to second fork, then left to top of ridge. Also farther along road on way to Cedar Breaks National Monument.

• *Pelican Point, Utah County* BLACK CALCITE ONYX: Along Utah Lake.

• *St. George, Washington County* AGATE: Go E on Hwy 17 for 17½

miles to dirt road S, continue 4 miles to red dunes.
BANDED RHYOLITE (WONDERSTONE): At quarries.
MALACHITE: In Dixie Apex Mine.
- *Salina, Sevier County* RHYOLITE (WONDERSTONE): Go 3 miles SE,
  then take right turn S for 3 miles and take right fork to
  ranch. Collect to E.
- *Thompson, Grand County* PETRIFIED WOOD, BARITE PSEUDO-
  MORPHS: Take Int. 70 E 6 miles, then dirt road SE 8½
  miles to collect. Another area, the Yellow Cat area, is
  reached from Int. 70 by going S 10 miles and then E a
  mile.
- *Washington, Washington County* SANDSTONE: Scenic sandstone is
  mined on the W side of Virgin oil dome and SE of Hurricane on Little Creek mountain.
- *Wendover, Tooele County* PLUME AGATE: Take U.S. 40 N for 8
  miles and search hillsides in Nevada. Also take Int. 80 E
  ½ mile and turn 2 miles N to collect.
- *Woodside, Emery County* JASPER, PETRIFIED BONE AND WOOD: S 5
  miles on Hwy 50, then NW 5 miles on dirt road to Castle
  Dale; hunt on slopes.

Vermont

Much of the area of Vermont is broken up by the Green
Mountains and, parallel with them in the west, the Taconic Mountains. As a result of its rugged topography and glaciation, Vermont
has a number of lakes, of which Lake Champlain is the largest. Its
soil is thin, so that underlying rock is often exposed.

- *Barre, Washington County* GRANITE, RUTILATED QUARTZ: At
  Wheaton Granite quarry in Cobble Hill quarry group.
- *Burlington, Chittenden County* JASPER: N 9 miles at Eugene Par-
  rot farm.
- *Chester, Windsor County* KYANITE, STAUROLITE: In quarries.
- *Eden, Lamoille County* VESUVIANITE, SERPENTINE: At Belvidere
  Mine of Vermont Asbestos Company, on Belvidere
  Mountain.
- *Grafton, Windham County* SERPENTINE, KYANITE: In quarries.
- *Lowell, Orleans County* GARNET, DIOPSIDE: In dump at gate of
  Ruberoid Asbestos mine.
- *Milton, Chittenden County* JASPER: At Parrott quarry 6 miles SW
  on U.S. 2.
- *Proctor, Rutland County* MARBLE: In local quarries.

- *Rutland Station, Rutland County* AVENTURINE QUARTZ: In saddle on N side of Round Hill 3¾ miles SE.
- *South Alburg, Franklin County* QUARTZ: On shore of Lake Champlain.
- *Williamsville, Windham County* AGATE: In road cut E of bridge over Adams Brook on way to East Dover. Also mile N of bridge just above where Bemis Brook empties into Adams Brook.

Virginia

Drowned valleys along the coastal plain of Virginia form long bays and, in the southeast, swamps such as the Great Dismal Swamp. Behind the coastal, sandy plain lies the Piedmont plateau, its rolling surface broken by ridges of crystalline rocks. This passes into the Blue Ridge Mountains, running from northeast to southwest, and the Allegheny Mountains, with a great valley between them. Gem minerals in the crystalline rocks and caves in the sedimentary regions are notable occurrences.

- *Altavista, Pittsylvania County* BERYL: SW 6 miles in a pegmatite along Hwy 29.
   STAUROLITE: In cliffs 8 miles upstream in Roanoke river near its junction with Old Woman Creek.
- *Amelia, Amelia County* * AMAZONSTONE, MOONSTONE, SPESSARTITE, BERYL: The Rutherford mine NE of Amelia is famous for its brilliant green amazonstone, moonstone, apatite, and gem-quality spessartite garnet. To the SE is the Morefield mine where excellent amazonstone can be found.
   The Rutherford mine is 1½ miles NE on Hwy 360 and then N on Hwy 609 (fee). The Morefield mine is 3½ miles NE on Hwy 360 and then S on Hwy 628 (fee).

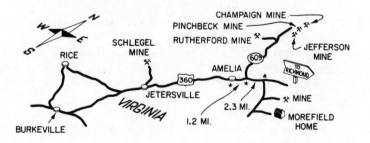

Nearby are many other mines, such as the Ligon mine 9 miles NE, notable for star quartz, the Champion mine, the Anderson Mica Prospect, and the Winfree Prospect, which is reached by Hwy 360 to Hwy 627 to Smack's Creek, then right, and the Vaughan Beryl Prospect, which is 2¾ miles due E on the W side of Hwy 627. Nearby are the Flippen Mica-Beryl Prospect ⅓ mile W of Hwy 628 and 3½ miles NE, and the Dobbin prospect near it. N of the Rutherford mine is a group shown on map.

AMETHYST: Via Hwy 638 to SE on Duncan farm.

• *Amherst, Amherst County* AMETHYST: E for 3 miles to Hwy 604, take it S to Hwy 659, then Hwy 659 to a cross road and sign to Schaar farm (fee).

• *Arrington, Nelson County* AMETHYST: At Saunders farm 8½ miles NW.

• *Bedford, Bedford County* APATITE: At Mitchell mine 6½ miles SE.

QUARTZ: In Peaksville mine 5 miles NW.

MOONSTONE: SE 6½ miles via Hwy 714, together with thulite.

GARNET: At quarry on W bank of Falling Creek 4 miles SE and ½ mile N of Hwy 714.

• *Bent Creek, Appomattox County* CRYPTOMELANE: At Enterprise mine to S.

• *Bland, Bland County* AGATE: Near Point Pleasant N side of Walker Mountain.

• *Brokenburg, Spotsylvania County* BERYL: In dumps of Edenton Mica mine ½ mile E of Brokenburg and Hwy 208.

• *Brookneal, Campbell County* AMETHYST: On Lacey Rush farm ⅓ mile NE and Clay farm 10 miles NE.

• *Browntown, Warren County* UNAKITE: As float in fields and pebbles in streams.

• *Central Plains, Fluvanna County* RHODONITE: Take Hwy 6 W 1 mile to Kids Store, then right-hand fork to Hwy 620 for ½ mile and trail to right (fee).

• *Centreville, Fairfax County* PREHNITE: At Fairfield quarry 4 miles W via Hwy 29 and 211.

• *Charlotte Court House, Charlotte County* AMETHYST: W on Hwy 40 for 2½ miles to Vassar house, take trail S to collect. Also 2½ miles NW at Donald plantation.

KYANITE: NW 12 miles.

• *Charlottesville, Albemarle County* QUARTZ: Behind 7–11 Store on Hydraulic road W of U.S. 29. Also in construction zone

NW of the intersection of Ivy road and Hwy 29, and in greenstone in road cut W of Hwy 20 and U.S. 64 intersection.

- *Coatsville, Hanover County* KYANITE, GARNET: At Saunders No. 2 mine on S shore of Little River 2½ miles NE.
- *Collinsville, Henry County* STAUROLITE: Take Hwy 57 W to Fairy Stone park, collect in area outside park.
- *Cullen, Charlotte County* BERYL, GARNET, QUARTZ: In mica mines to S, as well as the Crews No. 1 a mile N.
- *Deerfield, Bath County* QUARTZ: Take Hwy 629 S to Hwy 640, then left to the third farm, collect on Chestnut Ridge.
- *Farmville, Prince Edward County* KYANITE: At Willis Mountain.
- *Flat Rock, Powhatan County* BERYL, QUARTZ: Take Hwy 613 NE 3½ miles to Herbb No. 3 mine and Herbb No. 1 nearby.
  STAR QUARTZ: To NE at White Peaks mine.
  TOPAZ, AMAZONSTONE: In Herbb No. 2 mine.
- *Front Royal, Warren County* UNAKITE: As veins in exposed granite and as gravel in streams.
- *Galax, Grayson County* KYANITE, GARNET, CORUNDUM: At J. C. Pierce Prospect ⅓ mile N of West Galax and at Nuchols place 1 mile SW.
  GARNET: In veins on Higgins and Phipps farms to SW.
- *Glade Hill, Franklin County* APATITE: Yellow crystals in schist 1⅓ miles S of Glade Hill school.
- *Goose Creek, Loudoun County* SERPENTINE: In Virginia Lime and Marble quarry to S.
- *Grant, Grayson County* UNAKITE: NW 1½ miles along Hwy 16.
- *Hillsboro, Albemarle County* STAR QUARTZ: Blue material in quarry S of Yancey's Mill.
- *Horse Pasture, Henry County* GARNET: At Wilson quarries to N.
- *Ida, Page County* JASPER: NW 1 mile along road and near Hoak Hill.
- *Ladysmith, Caroline County* BERYL: In Last Chance mine on Lawrence Beazeley farm 6 miles SW by Hwy 229 for 4½ miles to Hwy 603 a mile and then a mile on dirt road.
  UNAKITE: At quarry to S.
- *Laurel Fork, Carroll County* QUARTZ: On A. G. Vaughn farm 6⅔ miles N and a mile E, and at Guy Barnard place 3¾ miles E and a mile S, as well as the Marvin Marshall farm 1 mile NW and the Henry Hall farm ³/₅ mile NE of the Marshall farm.
- *Leesburg, Loudoun County* PREHNITE: At Arlington Stone quarry reached by Hwy 659 S a mile from Hwy 7, and at Belmont Traprock quarry 4 miles SE on Goose Creek.

- *Luray, Page County* * UNAKITE: Go E on U.S. 211, then S on Hwy 689, cross stream just N of Ida; turn W several miles on dirt road; collect in stream bed and on hillside. BLOODSTONE, JASPER: In Naked Creek on Rockingham County line.
- *Lowesville, Amherst County* AMETHYST: NE 2½ miles.
- *Lynch Station, Campbell County* CRYPTOMELANE: In prospects E of the old Bishop mine.
- *Lynchburg, Campbell County* CRYPTOMELANE: At Bell mine 6 miles S and 1 mile W of Hwy 29. Also at the Piedmont mine 10 miles E.
  AMAZONSTONE: On T. Graves place 6 miles SE.
  KYANITE: S 7½ miles.
- *Martinsville, Henry County* BERYL: Golden beryl on Williams prospect 3 miles SW and ⅓ mile S of U.S. 58.
  STAUROLITE: SE 9 miles in road cut near S bank of Smith River.
  EPIDOTE: S 2 miles along Hwy 229.
- *Moneta, Bedford County* AMAZONSTONE, GARNET: One mile SE at Young mine.
- *Mountsville, Loudoun County* SERPENTINE: E to Hwy 733, then to Highcamp road 1½ mile, at marble quarry.
- *Newport, Giles County* SMOKY QUARTZ CRYSTALS: SW 3½ miles on Spruce Run.
- *Oliver, Hanover County* MOONSTONE, GARNET: Take Hwy 738 from U.S. 1 for 7⅔ miles, hunt in stream N of house and left of barn at Harris Mica mine (fee).
- *Petersburg, Prince George County* PETRIFIED WOOD: In gravel pits to E.
- *Rice, Prince Edward County* AMETHYST: Take Hwy 619 N for 3 miles at Smith place. Amethyst is also found on H. D. Hodges farm; take Hwy 307 for less than a quarter mile, take first road left.
  KYANITE: In old mica mines 1 mile N.
- *Rich Valley, Smyth County* QUARTZ: Loose in soil near Portersfield quarry.
- *Rileyville, Page County* SERPENTINE, EPIDOTE: In copper prospect on W side of Hwy 662, 2½ miles from Rileyville and 1 mile E of junction with Hwy 605.
- *Roseland, Nelson County* BLUE STAR QUARTZ: E ½ mile at American Rutile company quarry, with apatite.
- *Saltville, Smyth County* QUARTZ: At Worthy mine. Some is scepter quartz.

- *Schuyler, Nelson County* SOAPSTONE: In quarries here and in a belt trending NE 30 miles long.
- *Springfield, Page County* ORBICULAR JASPER: Go 2 miles E to collect in Jeremiah creek.
- *Stanley, Page County* UNAKITE: At Fisher's Gap S of Marksville on road from Hwy 680 to Bailey Mountain.
- *Stuart, Patrick County* STAUROLITE: In belt of schistose rocks extending from SW of Stuart for 20 miles NE.
  Another similar belt runs from about 9 miles NE of Stuart across Henry County. Many of the stones are loose in the soil.

- *Syria, Madison County* * UNAKITE: Material from Fisher's Gap is found in the Rose River. Take the river road and collect in the stream. One place is at the Graves farm.
- *Troutsdale, Grayson County* UNAKITE: SE 2½ miles as outcrops along Rd. 16.
- *Vesuvius, Rockbridge County* * UNAKITE: Some of the best is found near here below the Blue Ridge Parkway. It is found along Hwy 56 in road cuts and in a quarry 2 miles W of the Tye River Gap.
  CHERT: At South River mine.
- *Willis, Floyd County* QUARTZ: At A. T. Moles farm 6 miles SW and a mile E of Buffalo Mountain Church.
- *Willkie, Nelson County* UNAKITE: E of Skyline drive at its intersection with Hwy 56.

Washington

The Cascade Mountains, containing a number of extinct volcanoes and ranging north from the Columbia River to Canada, divide the state into two regions. To the east of the mountains is a plain rising from the Columbia River, formed of lava beds and extending to the Okanogan highland to the north. West of the mountains is the great basin in which lies Puget Sound, cut off from the ocean by the rugged Coast range and Olympic Mountains. Washington's lavas are the matrix of rich petrified wood and agate materials.

- *Aberdeen, Grays Harbor County* FLOWER JASPER: On beaches and in stream banks all the way to Raymond.
- *Adna, Lewis County* CARNELIAN, PETRIFIED WOOD: Take Bunker Creek road N 4 miles, then W on Ceres Hill road 4 miles to McCoy farm (fee).
  AGATE: In road cuts and ditches on Hwy 6 on way to Pe Ell, and along the Chehalis River.
- *Anacortes, Skagit County* JASPER PEBBLES: On beach.
- *Beverly, Grant County* OPALIZED LOGS: In volcanic ash on slopes of Saddle Mountains S of hwy from Beverly to Corfu. Go S to Mattawa, then E 3 miles and N to collecting area. (Fee).
  PETRIFIED WOOD: Take Hwy 243 S 14 miles to Vernita ferry. Drive up bluffs on W side of river to cafe, ask way to Bennett claim (fee). Or go 6 miles upstream to wooden bridge over Crab Creek and collect on N bank of creek or in hills.
- *Bucoda, Thurston County* AGATE, CARNELIAN: Take road S to Tono, then 5 miles over hill to coal mine spoil piles. Dig by creek bed, or go to right to dig under clay stratum.
- *Castle Rock, Cowlitz County* CARNELIAN: Take Hwy 504 E to Kid Valley State Park, then E to Beaver Creek.
- *Centralia, Chehalis County* AGATE: On ground 4½ miles E.
- *Chehalis, Lewis County* CARNELIAN: Take Alpha road to Lucas Creek sign, go on to gate, then N to dig S of trail and N and S of creek. Then go on farther N and W to dig.
  Also go 5 miles S on Hwy 99 and E 4 miles to bridge, and collect in gravels of N fork of Newaukum River.
- *Clay City, Pierce County* AMETHYST: E 1 mile on Siegmund ranch.
- *Clearwater, Jefferson County* AGATE, PETRIFIED WOOD: As pebbles on Kalaloch Beach.
- *Cle Elum, Kittitas County* * BLUE AGATE: Widely distributed from Leavenworth along Hwy 97 S to Yakima. Some specific locations: Take Hwy 97 3 miles NE to steel bridge, cross, take road left 15 miles to Jack Creek sign. Turn right on this road and continue for 5 miles up mountain to a fork. Take left road almost 1 mile. Dig nodules in cliff up the bank or through woods on right.

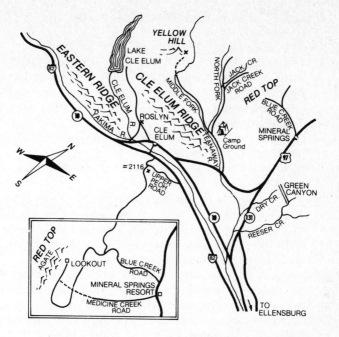

Also take Hwy 97 NE turning off left on Blue Creek Road at Mineral Springs resort station for 9 miles. Park, take upper trail to Red Top Lookout, and dig beyond it. Also take Hwy 97 N, turn right on Horse Canyon road beyond second bridge that crosses creek. Walk ¼ mile up road and to left up hill. Dig in red brown basalt cliffs along Dry Creek, Green Canyon, Reeser Creek, and Horse Canyon roads.

AGATE: Leave U.S. 10 at Roslyn interchange, take first logging road to left off overpass ramp and drive to crest of ridge. Dig S and E of beacon.

RED AGATE: Take Teanaway road from U.S. 97, turn left on first road beyond bridge. Turn onto Middle Fork of Teanaway road at Casland, go 4 miles, cross river on Hwy 2110, and take jeep road to Yellow Hill. Dig in bulldozed area and in canyons.

NODULES: At Roslyn interchange to W take first logging road to left off overpass ramp and go NW to crest of ridge. Dig S and E of beacon on side hill.

BLUE AGATE: Go S through South Cle Elum to Upper Peoh Point road, follow it to the second High Line Canal bridge, and walk S to base of steep ridge to S. Collect along ridge.

- *Colton, Whitman County* SMOKY QUARTZ: In sandpit.
- *Concrete, Skagit County* JADE, SERPENTINE: Take Dallas Bridge Road S 10 miles toward Darrington, keeping left at fork. Take Finney Creek Road right and follow creek on left 13 miles, using Gee Point Road to parking area. Collect in first creek.
  Washington Gem and Mining company of Darrington has claim in this area.
- *Cumby, Kittitas County* JASPER-AGATE: On middle fork of Teanaway River.
- *Duvall, King County* BLACK PETRIFIED WOOD: Take Hwy 203 N, stay N at fork for 3 miles, cross Cherry Creek, and go 2½ miles more to road E up hill. Take it 1 mile to fork, then right to second fork, and stay right to locked gate. Hike 1 mile through woods to creek to collect.
- *Ellensburg, Kittitas County* PETRIFIED WOOD: Take Hwy 97 S for 13 miles to parking area on right where footbridge crosses river. Dig on hillsides across river.
- *Forks, Clallam County* ORBICULAR JASPER: Go N on Hwy 101 to Calawah and Soleduck rivers, collect in gravel and along banks.
- *Gilmore Corners, Cowlitz County* BLOODSTONE, CARNELIAN: Take Sightly Road S until it turns E, continue E to first road S, take it to Walter Swift farmhouse. Collect in area to E. (Fee.)
- *Goodnoe Hills, Klickitat County* CHERT: Go SW to small bridge, follow E bank upstream ½ mile to collecting spot.
- *Grays Harbor, Grays Harbor County* AGATE: N and S on beaches around Westport and Grayland.
- *Grays River, Wahkiakum County* AGATE: On Gorley ranch (fee).
- *Issaquah, Kings County* AMBER: Go S on Hobart road 3 miles, turn E on Tiger Mountain Road for 1½ miles and then N on dirt road. Go ½ mile to E side of Fifteen-Mile Creek, collect in place and on E side of road. Farther up road ½ mile is blue agate.
- *Kalaloch, Jefferson County* BEACH AGATE, PETRIFIED WOOD: N and S to Queets along beach.
- *Kalama, Cowlitz County* AGATE: In area E of Cowlitz River.
  NODULES: Take cemetery road NE for 1½ miles and dig in cliff. Then go S on Green Mountain road 4 miles to Johnson road and turn N ¼ mile to dig geodes and agate.

- *La Push, Clallam County* SPHERULITIC JASPER: In gravels at mouth of Quillanute river, 6½ miles W of Lake Crescent in the rock, and 1 mile NW of the W end of Lake Crescent in gully as boulders.
- *Liberty, Kittikas County* JASPER-AGATE: Take Boulder Creek road to meadow, then jeep road to right up Robinson Gulch for 2 miles and take trail to top of ridge. Dig to left at top of Crystal Mountain.

  FLUORESCENT QUARTZ: Take U.S. 97 to the summit, turn right on Lion Rock road No. 2107 and the Road 2101 to Lookout. Dig on either side of road about 2 miles beyond slide area on way to Lookout.

  BLUE AGATE: For several miles to S along Hwy 97 in road cuts and hills.

  NODULES: At heads of Williams and Boulder creeks and on Table Mountain.
- *Lyle, Klickitat County* AGATE, JASPER, PETRIFIED WOOD: To N 10 to 15 miles in gullies and on hillsides.
- *Mondovi, Lincoln County* OPAL: NW 1 mile and also 1 mile N in vesicular basalt.

  AGATE: Take road toward Capps Talc Mine near Spokane River and dig 2 miles below mine for vein material in cliffs along river.
- *Mount Vernon, Skagit County* JADELIKE MATERIAL: In talc on SW side of Cultus Mountain. Take road from Clear Lake E 3½ miles to mine.

  AGATE, GEODES: Take Hwy 538 S to Walker Valley road past Big Lake, then S 2 miles to diggings.
- *Newport, Pend Oreille County* AMETHYSTINE QUARTZ: On W bank of Pend Oreille River 2 miles NW.

  AGATE: With jasper in beaches along Yaquina Bay park.
- *Okanogan, Okanogan County* AVENTURINE QUARTZ: Take road N along Salmon Creek, then turn right to Happy Hill (fee).
- *Olympia, Thurston County* AGATE, PETRIFIED WOOD: In sand to S at Tono.
- *Oso, Snohomish County* JADE: Along Deer creek upstream from bridge.
- *Palisades, Douglas County* OPALIZED WOOD: To W of road at Moses Coulee and S to Appledale.
- *Pasco, Franklin County* AGATE: In bluffs on E bank of Columbia River to NW.
- *Prosser, Benton County* OPALIZED WOOD: In volcanic ash in canyons of Horse Heaven Hills.

- *Pullman, Whitman County* AMETHYST: To NE on hill W of Ringo Station.

  SMOKY QUARTZ: In sand pit with corundum at Bald Butte to S of Pullman and E of Hwy 195.
- *Riverside, Okanogan County* PINK THULITE: To NE at Tunk Creek.
- *Roosevelt, Klickitat County* PETRIFIED WOOD: Take Hwy 12 7 miles E to Pine Creek, turn N up road on left bank to canyon and 2 miles to Ford Creek. Dig in E bank of creek.
- *Sedro Woolley, Skagit County* SERPENTINE: NE 6 miles.
- *Silver Lake, Cowlitz County* AGATE, PETRIFIED WOOD: In nearby fields and stream beds.
- *Snoqualmie Pass, King County* QUARTZ: Go to Curtiss campground at Denny Mountain, then take Denny Creek trail 1½ miles to gorge, and collect in talus. There is also some amethyst.
- *Sunnyside, Yakima County* PETRIFIED WOOD: Take Hwy 12 SE to Vernita Ferry road, turn N on it for 9 miles to Anderson ranch cabin (formerly The Old Hard Rock Bennett) (fee) on right-hand side of road, dig on ranch. There are free diggings farther along road 13 miles to dig on left of road, and farther beyond it on road is another road on right. Take it 4 miles to collect.

  The Silver Dollar diggings are near Sunnyside (fee).
- *Tenino, Thurston County* CARNELIAN, JASPER: Go to Johnson Creek Road, then 5½ miles E to Rocking B ranch. Collect above creek. Also take Hwy 507 S to Skookumchuck Road, go E for 7 miles to Johnson Creek Road, then N ⅓ mile to Anderson house (fee).
- *Toledo, Lewis County* CARNELIAN: Take any road E or N to Salmon Creek, collect in river bars.
- *Valley, Stevens County* RED MARBLE: Take Waits Lake Road W to Carr's Corner, go left 6 miles to quarry.
- *Vantage, Kittitas County* PETRIFIED WOOD: Take Wanapum Road 2 miles to Petrified Logs Trail sign, enter gate to right into Game Department land through stone pillars, go 2 miles to another gate and look for digging area.
- *Warwick, Klickitat County* CARNELIAN, GREEN JASPER: W 2 miles at bridge over wash in Hwy 8. Collect in fields and wash.
- *Whidbey Island, Island County* JADE, AGATE: On beaches.
- *Wiley, Yakima County* PETRIFIED WOOD: To S in Ahtanum canyon in L.T. Murray Wildlife Recreation Area. Collect on surface only. No digging.

• *Woodland, Cowlitz County* CARNELIAN: Go N on U.S. 99 5 miles to Cloverdale, then E on Todd Road to Cloverdale Road and N and E to Green Mountain Road. Collect in Cloverdale Creek.
• *Yakima, Yakima County* OPALIZED WOOD: In wash 33 miles E and mile N of Hwy 24 at Yakima Ridge.

West Virginia

The western two-thirds of West Virginia is a rough area of hills and valleys cut in sedimentary rocks and forming a part of the Allegheny plateau that extends from New York to Alabama. The eastern part lies in the Great Valley, in which mountain ridges and valleys have been the result of intense folding and erosion of the sedimentary rocks.

• *Baker, Hardy County* QUARTZ: 5 miles NW on E slope of Branch Mountain.
• *Berkeley Springs, Morgan County* QUARTZ: NE along U.S. 522 for 4 miles; access to Pennsylvania Glass Sand Corp. mines is by road 1 mile NE of company offices. Also in quarry on U.S. 522 2 miles N of Cacapon Mountain State Park entrance.
• *Charlestown, Kanawha County* PETRIFIED WOOD: Take Hwy 14 W for 4 miles to bridge and hunt in creek banks along road to country club.
• *Huntersville, Pocahontas County* CHERT: SE 1½ miles and 1 mile from Hwy 89.
• *Marlington, Pocahontas County* AGATIZED CORAL: SW 8 miles on U.S. 219 to Mill Point quarry N of intersection of Hwy 219 and Hwy 39. Also 2 miles SW of Hillsboro to Locust Creek road, then left 1½ miles to stone bridge to collect in Locust creek.
• *Romney, Hampshire County* QUARTZ: S 3 miles on U.S. 220 at Tonoloway quarry.
• *Union, Monroe County* QUARTZ: Along Turkey Creek and on Fullen Brothers farm.
• *Willowtown, Mercer County* ONYX: In quarry.

Wisconsin

Wisconsin is a rolling plain laid down on sedimentary rocks and broken in places by upthrust igneous and metamorphic rocks, such as the Baraboo Hills in the south central region, the granite exposures in Waushara and Marathon counties, and the gneisses of the northeastern part of the state. Wisconsin's extensive glaciation is shown by its many lakes and the famous moraine district west of Milwaukee.

• * LAKE SUPERIOR TYPE AGATES (DERIVED FROM GLACIAL GRAVELS): Are found in a number of places in Wisconsin. Among them are:
Along Hwy 64 E of New Richmond and generally from Hudson to New Richmond.
Just W of Hudson at gravel plant in Minnesota.
On gravel bars of the Hay River.
H. Turner and Son Plant at Cassville S on Hwy 133.
At Rush River Plant where Rush River crosses Hwy 10.
At Durand and Chippewa Falls in gravel pits.
At the River Falls Sand and Gravel Plant.
At Owen in gravels of Black River.
At Dillman Plant on Villa Louis Road in Prairie du Chien 3 blocks S of Hwy 18 and at Prairie City Gravel Co. pit ¼ mile N.
Bock Bros. Plant at Eagle Corners.
At Pepin on Deer Island and Lake Pepin beaches.
At LaCrosse in gravel dredging operations.

- *Afton, Rock County* AGATIZED CORAL: At gravel pit in village and at nearby quarries along road. Also at Shopiere to E in gravel pits.
- *Cascade, Sheboygan County* AGATE: S 2 miles at Bluhm Gravel pit.
- *Dickeyville, Grant County* ONYX: Take Hwy 151 for 4 miles, then dirt road right to pine tree on hill at quarry.
- *Hayward, Sawyer County* EPIDOTE, JASPER: N on Hwy 27 to Denver road, then W about 5 miles to mine road S and E across Ounce river to County mines and Skrupty mine for copper in epidote and jasper.
- *Janesville, Rock County* AGATIZED CORAL: Take Hwy 51 to junction with Hwy 14, then take first road left 1 mile to gravel pit.
- *Mosinee, Marathon County* UNAKITE: N 1 mile from where Hwy 153 and Hwy H meet.
- *Pittsville, Wood County* RED AND GREEN AVENTURINE QUARTZ: To S.
- *Powers Bluff, Wood County* QUARTZITE: Red, yellow, and black dendritic material SW of Arpin.
- *Spooner, Washburn County* AGATE: In lake area to NW and in roads and gravel pits, especially County Hwy C and P and at the Scott Township dump.
- *Redgranite, Waushara County* PINK GRANITE: In quarries to NW.
- *Waupaca, Waupaca County* RED AND GREEN GRANITE: N 5 miles in quarry.
- *Wausau, Marathon County* MOONSTONE: W on Hwy 29 to Hwy O, then N to Hwy U and W to collect in road fill banks. PERISTERITE: At Anderson Bros. & Johnson quarry.
- *Wisconsin Rapids, Wood County* SERPENTINE: N on Hwy 34 to Hwy C at Rudolph, then E to collect in outcrops along road.
- *Wittenburg, Shawano County* LABRADORITE: In boulders.

Wyoming

Much of Wyoming consists of rolling prairie more than a mile above sea level, broken by occasional buttes and erosion ridges. The northeastern part is a continuation of the Black Hills, while through the central part from east to west runs a long pass or valley below the Big Horn Mountains in north central Wyoming. Northwestern Wyoming is a complex region of igneous intrusions and upturned sedimentary rocks which holds the marvels of Yellowstone Park, the majesty of the Tetons, and the beautiful Wind River range to the south. Agate and petrified wood of many types exist in the gravels of all the regions, and jade in the eroded mountain ridges of the south central part.

- *Boslar, Albany County* JASPER: E 10 miles on Hwy 34. See Slim's Rock Shop in Boslar.
- *Buffalo, Johnson County* PETRIFIED WOOD: SE 12 miles along Crazy Woman Creek.
- *Casper, Natrona County* PETRIFIED WOOD: Along N bank of North Platte River E to Glenrock.
  CARNELIAN: To W in area between Poison Spider Creek and S fork of Casper Creek.
- *Cheyenne, Laramie County* CHALCEDONY: In gravels to W.
  QUARTZ CRYSTALS: In Cheyenne Pass.

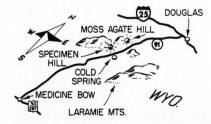

- *Douglas, Converse County* * BLUE MOSS AGATE: Two collecting localities near graded road S to U.S. 30: first, Moss Agate Hill, about 30 miles SW of Douglas, a prominent hill W of road.
  Second, S of this locale about halfway to a place known as Coldspring lying in the Laramie Mountains—Specimen Hill, for dark blue moss agate in masses. E of road black agate is found on the ground.
- *Dubois, Fremont County* PETRIFIED WOOD: Drive 27 miles N to Wiggins Fork Creek, take road to forest service campground. Collecting is done by wading in Wiggins Fork and Frontier Creeks, searching flats along creek, and hiking up the mountain beyond the Wilderness Boundary. On the mountain is a petrified forest where collecting is not allowed.
- *Farson, Sweetwater County* * PETRIFIED WOOD: Farson is the center of a notable collecting area for limb casts and other petrified wood. N 9 miles on Hwy 187, turn E on dirt road 3 miles past end of Big Sandy reservoir, continue to fork, and take right hand one to collect near

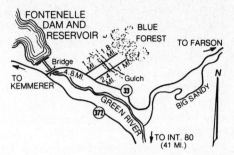

road for several miles. Also near Arandel reservoir No. 2.

Take Hwy 28 NE 15 miles to Hay Ranch sign, take ranch road, then new road around ranch buildings and go E to collect in hills. Ranch is occasionally closed to visitors.

Take road SW 25 miles toward Fontenelle Dam, turn N to dig limb casts in Blue Forest area.

• *Glendo, Platte County* CHALCEDONY: NE in hills along North Platte River.

• *Guernsey, Platte County* QUARTZITE: Go 2 miles W on Hwy 26, then N, keeping right at fork for 8½ miles to W shore of Lake Guernsey, for youngite, a quartzite, as well as jasper and agate. The material is also reported from the NW shore of the lake near caves.

AGATE: Along W side of the road N to Hartville and farther N on left-hand fork. Also in quarry along road.

• *Jeffrey City, Fremont County* *MOSS AGATE: Go 3 miles E on Hwy 287 to ranch road leading N. Go through ranch gate and

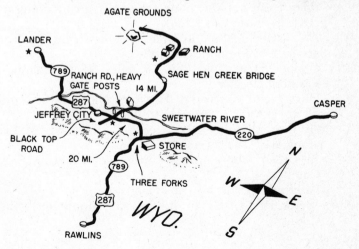

yard and beyond to collect the Sweetwater type fluorescent moss agates in flat. Or take Bureau of Land Management road 8 miles E. Recently a deposit of limb casts has been discovered N and E of this collecting area. The agates are covered with a white coating and lie along Sage Hen creek watershed.

AGATE, JADE: Ten miles farther W on U.S. 287, a road turns S to Crooks Gap, where agate and some jade have been found.

• *Kemmerer, Lincoln County* PETRIFIED ALGAE: E 10 miles on Hwy 30 near town of Opal.

• *Lander, Fremont County* NEPHRITE JADE: Over wide area in Wyoming in place or as boulders. Dark colored float jade is found along the course of the Sweetwater River between Crook's Creek on the E and the Wind River Mountains on the W.

BLACK JADE: Is found generally in the Granite Mountains and N of Split Rock.

LIGHT GREEN JADE: Has come from the Crook's Mountain area 65 miles SE of Lander and from the E side of Cottonwood Creek wherever black diorite boulders appear. To reach this area, take Hwy 287 12 miles past the Sweetwater River crossing and turn S for 8 miles.

NEPHRITE JADE: Abernathy claims, Fremont County, 40 miles SE of Lander, in diorite dike in granite, the material contains quartz crystals.

Curtis and Marion claims, Sec. 13, 18, T. 30, R. 92, 93 W; black, olive green outcrop ½ mile SW of this one.

Lucky Strike Claim, Secs. 19, 20, T. 30 N., R. 92 W., 61 miles from Lander, olive green pieces containing quartz crystals, at apex of a fold.

As float near Marston Lake, 40 miles from Lander, and at Moneta, Fremont County.

Copper Chief Gold Mine: 3 miles NE of Atlantic City, Fremont County.

Olive green, outcrop of East fork NE of Dubois and NE of Circle Ranch, Fremont County.

As float along Beaver Creek, 25 miles SE of Lander along Hwy 287, Fremont County.

In Green Mountains, 20 miles W of Bairoil, Fremont County.

Pathfinder Dam, Natrona County.

Along Dry Creek in Rattlesnake Mountains, Natrona County.

JADE, NEPHRITE, BLACK: As float over large area S of upper drainage of Sulfur Creek, 30 miles W of Bairoil, Fremont County.

PETRIFIED WOOD: Hwy 28 S for 35 miles to Bridger Wilderness sign, take dirt road left and stay on main road 9 miles toward two flat-topped buttes W of the road. At sharp turn in road, park and walk E and S for petrified wood, algae, and agate.

• *Medicine Bow, Carbon County* PETRIFIED WOOD, AGATE: N 18 miles and take right fork 13 miles to petrified forest to W of road.

PETRIFIED WOOD, BONE: To E at Como Bluff.

• *Moran, Teton County* JADE: Go S to Gros Ventre River, hike up bed 6 to 7 miles.

• *Riverton, Fremont County* MOSS AGATE NODULES: Take dirt road that runs W to Hwy 287; park where wires cross above road and collect in washes to NE.

PETRIFIED WOOD, AGATE: In gravels and streams in area between Hwy 287 N from Lander and Hwy 26 W from Riverton.

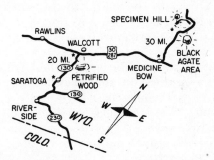

• *Saratoga, Carbon County* * PETRIFIED WOOD: On flats along Hwy 130 N to Walcott. The flats from Saratoga N to Walcott are strewn with petrified wood and chalcedony, especially on the E side just N of a road cut.

• *Shell, Big Horn County* PETRIFIED WOOD AND BONE: N 4 miles at Elkhorn ranch.

• *Sheridan, Sheridan County* GRANITE (LEOPARDITE): W 25 miles in dikes N of Burgess ranger station.

• *Shoshoni, Fremont County* AQUAMARINE: In dikes 15 miles NE in Bridger Mountains.

• *South Pass City, Fremont County* PETRIFIED WOOD: To N on divide between Hall and Twin creeks.

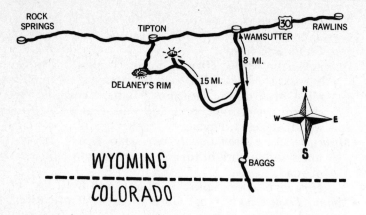

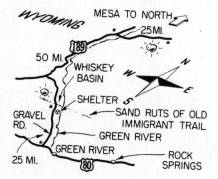

• *Split Rock, Fremont County* RUBY: In schist on Sweetwater divide.

JADE: In place at American Jade Company claim N of junction of Longs Creek and Sweetwater River.

• *Tipton, Sweetwater County* * ALGAE AGATE, TURRITELLA AGATE: Drive S for less than 2 miles, take right-hand fork for 4 miles to within sight of Cathedral Bluffs on Delaneys Rim. Drive up the bluffs to top, turn left, and collect oolite, brown algae agate in outcrops on rim, as well as the silicified Oxytrema fossil shells known as turritella agate.

The area can also be approached from Wamsutter by going S 8 miles on the road to Baggs, then W on a ranch road 15 miles past barn and over ridge a mile to the Rim. There is black petrified wood in gullies and along the road.

• *Wheatland, Platte County* MOONSTONE: With labradorite to S and W along Hwy 34.

- *Whiskey Basin Area, Sweetwater and Sublette Counties* * AGATE: A gravel road that takes off N from Int. 80 a few miles W of Green River leads in 25 miles to the ruts of the old immigrant trail and to an area known as Whiskey Basin. To the W are hills where agate is found.
- *Worland, Washakie County* CHALCEDONY: To W of town.

Canada

Alberta

Most of the province is a part of the vast continental plain of Canada, but on the west its boundary is set by the Rocky Mountains, which rise in places to 10,000 feet. The southern part of the plain is prairie, while the northern part is rolling and wooded.

- *Calgary* PETRIFIED WOOD: E 90 miles in Red Deer River Valley. The wood is limb sections like Eden Valley wood.
- *Drumheller,* PETRIFIED WOOD, BONE: To NW in Valley of the Dinosaurs.
  AGATE: To E in seams in the Hand Hills.
  Note: Make a border declaration of any polished stone or jewelry taken into Canada or it may be dutiable on return to the United States.

British Columbia

Mountains cover almost all of British Columbia, from the Rockies to the Coast ranges. These were formed by giant granite masses forcing up the Coast and Selkirk ranges, and the overthrust toward the east that created the Rockies. Later, lavas poured into the lower part of the province, as they did in the United States farther south, and the exposed rocks were carved into valleys by glaciers of the ice ages. Most of the mineralization has been in the western ranges, while vast quantities of quartz, jade, and petrified wood are contained in the enormous deposits of gravel along the rivers.

- *Agassiz* The bars in the Fraser River from Chilliwack on the south to above Lillooet in the north contain pebbles and boulders of nephrite jade, rhodonite, agate, and vesuvianite. Many are inaccessible except in times of low

277

water in the late winter and early spring. Specific localities are described below under entries by cities.

There are several collecting spots at Agassiz. To get to
one, take the road to Seabird Island, turn at the sign,
then right at the first fork and left at the crossroads. Go
over the dike to a long narrow bar. Can be reached only
by boat at other than low-water times.

Take the road to Seabird Island and then the gravel
road N to Waleach Station and turn on road to the river.
Or continue past the station 3 miles to a construction
camp, then right to the river.

•*Chilliwack* AGATE, JADE: In gravel bar by Fraser River bridge
and downstream at sand bar at mouth of Ruby creek.

•*Clinton* AGATE NODULES: Take Hwy 97 N 11 miles to Gang
Ranch turnoff, go NW for 55 miles to Fraser river, cross
to Empire valley road, take it S for 20 miles to Bryson
ranch and collect thundereggs and jasper 14 miles S at
Freeze property (fee).

AMETHYST: Continue 13½ miles S, then E through farm
yard 4½ miles to Scottie Creek, follow along bank and
dig in bluff on right bank.

•*Hope* JADE, AGATE, RHODONITE: Take road SW to Flood, then
road to airport and on to Fraser River to search in several bars offshore. The same gem materials are found in
the Coquihalla river E of Hope.

RHYOLITE (WONDERSTONE): E 10 miles in slide debris.

•*Kamloops* AGATE: Take Hwy 97-1 E to Barnhart Vale road,
then it to Robbin Range road; follow the latter a mile,
then E on ranch road to collect seam agate in hills to N.
Go back to Barnhart Vale road, take it 3 miles farther
beyond Buse Lake, follow road S and path W around
lake to collect blue agate in hills S of lake.

AGATE: Take Hwy 97 SE 30 miles to Monte Lake, collect
nodules and seam agate close to highway along lake.

JASPER, AGATE: Take Hwy 1 W to Tunkwa Lake road S,
follow it to Indian Garden ranch road and take it W for 5
miles; park, follow pipeline to third slope to collect.

•*Keremeos* RHODONITE, JASPER: In slide material along highway
on W edge of village.

•*Lillooet* JADE, AGATE, ETC.: In rock piles on Lillooet side of
bridge over Fraser River and in bar downstream. Also
take road toward Seton river and hunt in Fraser River
bar, as well as upstream in Bridge River and at its mouth.
Upstream where the Yalakom River flows into the Bridge
River is an excellent collecting spot for serpentine.

- *Lytton* * JADE, AGATE, ETC: Cross Fraser River on ferry, go toward Stein River 1½ miles, turn right past corrals to road, take it ¼ mile and hike to Spences ranch bars. Then continue on Stein River road and down to Fraser River for more bars.

  AGATE: E on Hwy 1 to the Nicoamen river bridge, go 1 more mile, take dirt road right for 5 miles where there is a row of bluffs. Park and search below bluffs and in outcrops. Prase is reported here, too.

- *Paldi* RHODONITE: In old mine near Duncan on top of mountain.

- *Penticton* AMETHYST, GEODES: W 8 miles on Green Mountain Road.

- *Prince George* JASPER, AGATE: In gravels of delta of Nechako River within city limits, and 8 miles W at Miworth gravel pit on S side of river, and 7 miles W on N side of river.

- *Princeton* LIMB CASTS, AGATE: N across on Hwy 5, then Coalmont road left 2 miles, park and follow trail on N side of river 1¼ miles just past turn, collect in Vermilion Bluffs for limb casts and ½ to a mile farther N for agate on sides of bluffs.

  AGATE: Take Copper Mountain road S, turn left on dirt road on top of Wolfe Creek hill, cross Willis Creek and take logging road along the creek to sign "Jeep Road to Agate Mountain." Go 4 miles to top and collect agate and petrified wood in rock slides and bluffs on N side of mountain.

279

- *Quesnel* AGATE: In Fraser river to S opposite Macalister, as well as on E side.
- *Rosedale* AGATE, JADE, ETC.: Take Hope road 6 miles to Peters road and follow it to the Fraser river to collect on bars. A mile beyond this spot is another large bar. Yellow serpentine and rhodonite are also found here.
- *Shaw Springs* AGATE: N on Hwy 1, for a mile, take dirt road E for 5 miles to collect in small cliffs of mountain. On return go 2½ miles, take dirt road N to Soap Lake for agate on hill to left. Return to Shaw Springs, go a mile S to a culvert, walk E ⅓ mile along creek to collect agate in basalt cliffs.
- *Sidney* RHODONITE: Take ferry to Salt Spring Island and collect at Hallings farm near Fulford harbor.
- *Squilax* AMETHYST, AGATE: S to fork in road, take left fork to logging road and park after 1¾ miles. Look for agate and amethyst here. Walk 2 miles NE to collect in road cuts. Return to fork, go S to Turtle Valley road, at second junction take trail E and follow creek to top.
- *Takla Landing* JADE: E 16 miles in Vital Creek in Omenica mining district.
- *Trail* PREHNITE: In Le Roi mine 7 miles W at Rossland.
- *Vancouver* AGATE: On beach to W with jasper at Tsawwassen, where ferry docks.
- *Vancouver Island* BRECCIA: A rock known locally as dallasite is found at Qualicum Beach and at Horne Lake. Take road 8 miles N from Qualicum Beach to a store, then gravel road 4 miles to collect on surface and in creek.
- *Vanderhoof* JASPER, PETRIFIED WOOD: In dry bed of Nechako river 60 miles S and just N of Kenney dam.
- *Victoria* PORPHYRY: Pebbles known as chrysanthemum rock on beaches of southern Vancouver Island, specifically on beach at foot of Dallas road.
  JASPER: N 8 miles at Mill Bay.
- *Watson Lake* JADE: Take Alcan Highway to Milepost 644, then S to Cassiar for jade in asbestos mine dumps, then W to Dease Lake to hunt within 50-mile radius.
- *Westwold* AGATE: S on Douglas Lake road 7 miles to collect W of road. Go 8 miles farther and collect in long row of cliffs W of road.

Manitoba

Northeastern Manitoba is covered by rocks of the great shield that forms much of central Canada, but below Lake Winnipeg these dip below the limestones, which form a more fertile region. The southwest corner of the province is a plateau of younger sedimentary rocks.

- *Cedar Lake* AMBER: On beach on SW edge near mouth of Saskatchewan River.
- *Lac du Bonnet* BERYL, APATITE: At Bernic Lake mine. Take Hwy 11 to junction with Bird Lake road. Take it 25½ miles, then S to mine on N shore of lake and another on E end of lake. S of Bernic Lake 1¾ miles is Shatford Lake, with beryl and topaz in pegmatite on N side.
- *Lamprey Falls* BERYL: Go 4¾ miles by boat along the Winnipeg river, then S 1¼ miles to Lake and Grace claims and at Silver Leaf property. About ⅓ mile E of Silver Lead property is the Huron claim with zoisite and black quartz as well as beryl, and ¼ mile NE are the Annie Claims. E of Lamprey Falls 6¼ miles a trail leads ¼ mile S of the Winnipeg River to Green Lake and beryl at its SE end at the Grace claims.
- *Souris* AGATE, PETRIFIED WOOD: In Janz brothers gravel pits along the Souris River. Look for Montana type agate and jasper in the oversize dumps (fee).

New Brunswick

Most of the province is a lowland of sedimentary rocks, but granite rocks are exposed in the western areas and the more rugged southern coast.

- *Cross Creek, York County* TOPAZ, BERYL: At Burnt Hill Tungsten mine. Take Hwy 25 for 3 miles, then W 5 miles on gravel road to Maple Grove Station. Register at the Miramichi Lumber company office, go 15½ miles on gravel road to a Department of Fisheries camp, then right on mine road ½ mile and right again to mine.
- *Dalhousie, Restigouche County* AGATE, JASPER: On beach between Peuplien Point and Pin Sec Point. Take Hwy 11 NW to CIL plant, turn E to beach on rough road. There are agates on the beach NW as far as Campbelltown and in seams in the cliffs, and on the beaches of Chaleur Bay. SERPENTINE, AGATE: On Belledune Point and as far SE as Nash Creek.
- *Grand Manan Island, Charlotte County* BLOODSTONE, AGATE: At Whale Cove and up the shore toward a cliff known as

Seven Days Work. The island is reached by ferry from St. John.

- *Hillsborough, Albert County* ALABASTER: In gypsum quarry.
- *St. John, St. John County* AGATE: In basalt as far west along shore as Blacks Harbor.
  QUARTZ: On E side of Musquash.
- *St. Martins, St. John County* JASPER: In conglomerate on beach.
- *Woodstock, Carleton County* MANGANESE ROCK, RHODOCHROSITE: At Plymouth Iron mine. Take Hwy 5 W for 4¾ miles, turn N on Plymouth road 1½ miles to trail opposite farmhouse to collect at mine. The two materials are also found at Moody Hill and other pits. Take Hwy 275 N 3 miles to road left, go 1 mile to pits in clearing.
- *Upsalquitch, Restigouche County* AMETHYST: Above forks of Upsalquitch River 7 miles.

Newfoundland

Newfoundland is the northernmost extension of the Appalachian Mountain system which skirts the Atlantic Ocean in the United States. The province is a low plateau of ancient rocks rounded and scraped by extensive glacial action which has filled the valleys with drift. Labrador, which is administered as a part of Newfoundland, is the eastern tip of the great shield of ancient Laurentian crystalline rocks which are the source of most of Canada's mineral wealth.

- *Lawn, Placentia West County* AMETHYST: In dumps of LaManche mine.
- *Nain, Labrador* LABRADORITE: On Tabor's Island in Grenfell quarry, 20 miles SE. Also on Black and Paul islands and at Ford's Harbor.

Northwest Territories

The northeastern part of this large region is an arctic prairie of thin soil and almost entirely devoid of trees. Most of the rest of the territories is covered with forests, except the desolate Arctic Islands of which Baffin Island is the principal example.

- *Ellsmere Island* AMBER: In coal seams along Gilman River near Lake Hazen.
- *Fox Islands, Great Slave Lake* SAPPHIRE: At Philmore Mine.

Nova Scotia

Like southeastern Quebec and New Brunswick, Nova Scotia shows the Appalachian topography which dominates the eastern landscape of the United States. It is an ancient mountain land, much folded and intruded by granite, especially south of Halifax. Erosion has created the valleys that are the routes of communication, and sinking of the land has further left its mark in the harbors and offshore islands.

- *Digby, Digby County* * JASPER: Generally at beaches in area known as Digby Neck. Some specific localities are breccia jasper on shore of Long Island near Tiverton; lace agate less than a mile from the Tiverton ferry slip along dirt road; S on Hwy 217 toward Central Grove from Tiverton and right ½ mile toward Bear Cove beach; on beach at Centreville, and red chalcedony at St. Mary Bay.

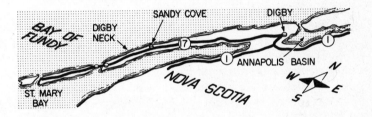

- *Halls Harbor, Kings County* AGATE, JASPER: Take road to Kentville, then road left to Glenmont and dirt road left for 3 miles to Ross Creek to collect on beach.
  AMETHYST: Take road to Glenmont and N to Scott's Bay. Ask directions at farm to beach and Amethyst Cove. Another location is near Hall's Harbor. Turn right just before bottom of hill and take dirt road along shore, bearing right to road to beach. Collect at second rock fall. Ask directions of Everett Dunham to another location.
  BLUE AGATE, AMETHYST: Take road to Lower Blomidon, collect on rocky beach. Start after peak of tide, get back before next tide.
- *Parrsboro, Cumberland County* * AGATE: Take Golf Course road 4½ miles to turnoff to right just beyond bridge. Go to cottage for permission, then take steep trail to beach, turn left and walk ¼ mile to Wasson's Bluff and farther on to collect. Return to road, go on to first right hand

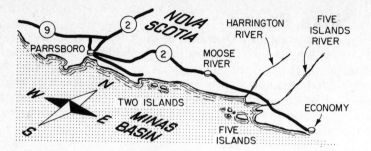

turn, park and walk to beach and go left past sandstone cliffs to McKay Head and beyond for agate and quartz. From here it is possible at low tide to wade to Two Islands to collect.

AMETHYST: Drive to Partridge Island, go right above marshy area to coves at beach to collect. Watch tides carefully. Return to the causeway, take path behind camp, turn right into woods and collect in stream.

BLUE AGATE, AMETHYST: Take Main Street W, go 7 miles to fork, take west fork to parking area and walk to West Bay beach to hunt on beach to right.

AGATE, AMETHYST: Moose Island is across the inlet from the Island View Motel at Lower Five Islands. Bruce Patterson of the motel will take collectors to the island by boat.

Ontario

Southeastern Ontario is a fertile area of glacial soils bordering the Great Lakes. To the northeast lies more rolling country set off by a great ridge known as the Niagara escarpment. North and west of Lake Superior, however, Ontario is part of the vast Laurentian shield of granite and other crystalline rocks containing gold and industrial minerals.

- *Atikokan, Rainy River County* QUARTZ: In limestone to N at Steep Rock iron mines at Steep Rock lake.
- *Bancroft, Hastings County* SODALITE: At Cancrinite Hill. E on Hwy 500 for 2⅓ miles, then right for ⅓ mile to vacant house, walk across stream to clearing and follow trail ⅓ mile to outcrop. Nearby is another outcrop at Davis Hill. At Princess quarry (fee). Take Hwy 100 2½ miles E and

turn N from highway to mine store. At the Golding-Keene quarry, which is on the W bank of the York River just N of Hwy 500, and at the Morrison quarry on the E bank and 1½ miles N of the highway.

AMETHYST: In dumps along the York river to the N.

PERISTERITE: At the Faraday mine. Take Hwy 28 SW for 4½ miles, then ½ mile N.

MARBLE: At the Stewart quarry. Take Hwy 62 S for 2¾ miles, then E a mile.

• *Batchawana, Thunder Bay County* EPIDOTE: Pebbles at mouth of the Montreal River and the Agawa River on the Lake Superior shore.

• *Bird Creek, Hastings County* DIOPSIDE: Drive W ¼ mile to first road N, cross creek, go to end and hike along E side of McFalls Lake to N end to collect on side of cliff.

• *Bruce Mines, Algoma County* CONGLOMERATE: E 2½ miles of the intersection of Hwys 17 and 561, and also W and N of Bruce Mines. The conglomerate contains jasper pebbles.

• *Craigmont, Renfrew County* CORUNDUM: In quarries on Craigmont Mountain, 7 miles S of Combermere and just E of Hwy 517.

• *Dryden, Kenora County* SOAPSTONE: On hill on W side of Barritt Bay on Wabigoon Lake, just W of Wabigoon. Also on SE and NW shore of Miles Lake and on islands in Trap Lake, reached by boat.

BERYL: In pegmatite on E shore of Medicine Lake on the property of E. Zabeski of Kenora. Reached by taking Hwy 17 to Gordon Lake road for 1½ miles to cabin on property.

• *Eganville, Renfrew County* AMAZONSTONE: On A. Berger farm on road to Germanicus 2 miles N of intersection of Hwys 41 and 60. Also at the Smart mine. Take Lake Clear road toward Foymount; at first dirt road past bridge turn left to end, and right 2½ miles to mine.

• *Foymount, Renfrew County* APATITE: At Turner's Island. Take Lake Clear road left for 3¼ miles to road to Goulet's cabins. Rent boat. After landing, go to left of boat landing at NW end of island. Dig in pits.

• *Gananoque, Leeds County* QUARTZ: At Marble Rock quarry. Go N on Hwy 32 to side road marked Marble Rock. Cross iron bridge, keep right to first farm gate on left, enter and go to gravel bed, park and take path to quarry.

• *Gooderham, Haliburton County* SODALITE, APATITE: Take Hwy

500 from Tory Hill for ¾ mile, then S 2½ miles to barn; dig in pits ½ mile SW of barn.

• *Griffith, Renfrew County* SCAPOLITE: At Spain mine. Take Hwy 41 for 6 miles NE. Mine is on S side of highway.

• *Hybla, Hastings County* AMAZONITE: In pit in pegmatite on R. McCormack farm E of the railroad and a mile S of Hybla. Also at the Woodcox farm 2¼ miles E and S of the road to Monteagle Valley.

• *Kaladar, Lennox and Addington Counties* DIOPSIDE, KYANITE, STAUROLITE: On S side of road W from Hwy 41 just S of railroad crossing S of Kaladar. Also take Hwy 41 N for 11 miles, then right on Hwy 506 for 12 miles and left on access road E of Fernleigh. Go ¼ mile to rocky slope on left to collect.

• *Ludgate, Parry Sound County* SUNSTONE: In gneiss on N shore of Lake Huron 20 miles E of the French River.

• *Lyndhurst, Leeds County* QUARTZ: At Black Rapids (Steele) mine. Take road to Lansdowne 5½ miles to bridge, cross and take road to La Rosa bay on E side of the bridge at Black Rapids for 1½ miles to Steele house, where J. A. Steele will sell specimens but no longer allows collecting. There are other pits S and E of Black Rapids.

• *Madoc, Hastings County* MARBLE: Go S on Durham Street ½ mile, right on Seymour Street for 1⅓ miles and keep right to Jones quarry for black marble. There are six other Jones quarries in the area.

• *Marathon, Thunder Bay County* LAURVIKITE (SYENITE): A rock that has a schiller like labradorite. Found in road cuts along Hwy 17 from a mile W to the bridge over the Little Pic River, and in road cuts from 2 to 4 miles W of the Marathon turnoff and to E of the turnoff.

• *Matachewan, Timiskaming County* PORPHYRY: Found 19 miles W and just N of Rahn Lake.

• *Michipicoten Island, Thunder Bay County* AGATE, AMETHYST: Reached by plane or boat from Wawa. Land at Quebec harbor. Agates are found on extreme SW end but the best collecting is on the islets offshore, for which a boat is needed. Agate Islet in Quebec Harbor, the W end of Schafer Bay and along Channel Lake are favored spots.

• *Nipigon, Thunder Bay County* AGATE: On beaches of West Bay on Lake Nipigon, just W of Kelvin Island.
AMETHYST: E 9 miles where Hwy 17 crosses the Jackfish River and on E bank of river 1½ miles above Canadian Pacific bridge. Best reached by boat.

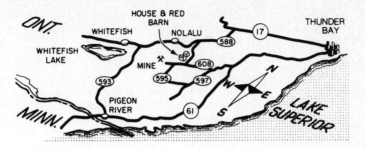

- *Nolalu, Thunder Bay County* * JASPER: Material that often is bloodstone is found on Arrow Lake 28 miles W, in Whitefish River 1¾ miles W and 2 miles E, and in Peerless Creek at the Hwy 588 bridge.
  AMETHYST: Take road E to Aleck Teukula house, get permission to collect at mine.
- *Ouimet, Thunder Bay County* AMETHYST: Go 6 miles S on Hwy 17 and left on Hwy 69-13 to railroad tracks and walk ⅕ mile along tracks to mine dump.
- *Perth, Lanark County* PERTHITE: To S in pegmatites between Otty and Adam Lake. Also take Hwy 7 W for ½ mile to Lanark road, turn right to Balderson and then left to crossroad and drive 1½ miles to Bell Corners, turn right 1 mile and then left ⅔ mile to school, where right turn for ¼ mile will reach mine. Other mines are nearby.
- *Quadeville, Renfrew County* BERYL, ROSE QUARTZ: At Canadian Beryllium and Alloys mine, 2 miles W on Hwy 515 and then N 1¼ miles (fee).
- *Rossport, Thunder Bay County* AGATE, PREHNITE, PUMPELLYITE: Along S shore of Copper Island, at E end of S shore of Wilson island and at Greenstone Beach, at Salter Island just W of Old Man's Pocket Harbor, at Harry Island in cove on W end, along S shore of Simpson Island and W of McKay Cove, and on Bowman and Agate islands and at Agate Point on E shore of Black Bay Peninsula.
  Agates are also found in basic lavas on the islands E of Sibley Peninsula and S of Rossport.
  AMETHYST: In road cuts on Hwy 17 1½ miles W of turnoff and also just W of Billy Lake 9 miles E on N side of the highway. Also 8 miles W in road cuts at Rossport Provincial park.
- *Sault Ste. Marie, Algoma County* CONGLOMERATE: In boulders

on Lake Superior shore N of Goulais Bay, in the St. Mary's river 4 miles W of Campment d'Ours, and at quarry near E end of Echo Lake.

• *Spragge, Algoma County* STAUROLITE: E 4½ miles on Hwy 17 and S of highway.

• *Stanley, Thunder Bay County* AMETHYST, ROSE QUARTZ: Take Silver Mountain road SW to Victoria mine N of road. Nearby are the Beaver Jr., West Beaver, Climax, and Badger mines, all S of the road.

• *Superior Junction, Kenora County* JASPER (JASPALITE): With magnetite on S side of Minnitaki Lake, 12 miles S.

• *Sydenham, Fontenac County* APATITE, DATOLITE: At Lacey mine 7 miles NE on E side of Eel Bay in Sydenham Lake.

• *Terrace Bay, Thunder Bay County* JASPER: Pebbles on W shore of the largest, Slate Island, which is 8 miles S.

• *Thunder Bay, Thunder Bay County* * AMETHYST: There are many locations for digging amethyst in the area once known as Port Arthur and Fort William and now as Thunder Bay. The most publicized location is a fee mine reached by taking Hwy 17 N, then right at the first intersection for 8 miles, and right 2 miles following signs to the Thunder Bay mine near Loon Lake.

Other locations include amethyst at the mouth of the McKenzie river 10 miles NE of Thunder Bay, in the Current River, and on the outskirts of Thunder Bay between Boulevard Lake and Trowbridge Falls Park.

Another is 13 miles N on Hwy 17 to Silver Harbor road, cross railroad tracks, then drive left and walk along tracks ½ mile to pits E of tracks.

At Jarvis River, take Hwy 61 S 3¼ miles to Jarvis Bay road, go 5½ miles to Jarvis Bay resort, and follow shore to headland of Prince Bay and mine on hill.

There are prospect hole and mine dumps 4 miles NE of Little Gull Lake, on the N side of Sunset Lake, ½ mile S of the E end of Whitefish Lake, 1½ miles SE of Silver Mountain railroad station, and E of Ancliff. Some of these locations also yield agates, and oolitic jasper is found in taconite in the bed of the McIntyre River.

• *Vermilion Bay, Kenora County* GARNET: On shore of Garnet Bay at N end of Eagle Lake, reached by boat. Soapstone deposit on W shore of the lake.

• *Verona, Frontenac County* PERISTERITE, QUARTZ: N on Hwy 38 1 mile and then right on Desert Lake road for 4⅔ miles, go left at church to Richardson Feldspar quarry. Also nearby on Abrams farm.

- *Wawa, Algoma County* EPIDOTE, QUARTZ: As pebbles on beaches of Coldwater River at park 40 miles S. Also in the Agawa river.
- *Wilberforce, Haliburton County* APATITE: At Cardiff Uranium mines 1¾ miles S on Hwy 500 to gravel road E for 1 mile. Also in calcite in dumps on ridge ¾ mile SW, and at Fission and Liscombe mines.
  PERISTERITE: E 4 miles at Richardson mine.

Quebec

Most of Quebec lies within the Canadian or Laurentian shield, a vast area of ancient granites and gneisses, covered with thin glacial deposits and dotted with typical glacial lakes. A part of this region near Lake Abitibi, near the Ontario border, is rich in minerals. Most of the population of the province lives in the sedimentary St. Lawrence River basin which was the bed of the former Champlain Sea. Eastern Quebec is Appalachian, like much of eastern Canada, formed of sedimentary rocks broken by granite hills.

- *Asbestos, Richmond County* GARNET: At Jeffrey mine of Johns Manville company. Also at same company's Union mine near Thetford. Also collect serpentine and vesuvianite in dumps.
- *Black Lake, Megantic County* SERPENTINE: In Megantic mine.
- *Coleraine, Megantic County* SERPENTINE: Gem quality serpentine at Continental mine. Take road W toward Vimy Ridge 1½ miles to sign to Demerco mines, turn right to mine. Also at nearby Windsor mine. Take Rue Martel E to Av. St. Joseph, then left ⅓ mile and left on gravel road 1 mile to road junction, then left ⅓ mile to junction and right a mile to the mine.
  Also at Montreal Chrome pit. Take Hwy 1 for 2¼ miles N, then E on Petit Lac St. François road for 3¾ miles. Take right fork ½ mile, then left at gravel pit 1½ miles to mine.
- *East Broughton, Beauce County* SERPENTINE: At Quebec Asbestos Corp. pits. Take road NW from Hwy 1 for 1½ miles. Also at Fraser mine near Broughton Station.
- *Chandler, Gaspé East County* CRINOIDAL LIMESTONE: In road cuts SW to Port Daniel and in bay shore rocks, in quarry and beach pebbles.
- *Gaspé East County* JASPER, AGATE: In beach pebbles here and to N and W, and especially to S at Pointe St. Pierre, Belle Anse, and Cap-d'Espoir.

- *Hull, Hull County* SCAPOLITE, APATITE: At Headley mine. Take mine road 4⁴/₅ miles, then trail ¾ mile to flooded pit.
- *Kilmar, Argenteuil County* SERPENTINE, MARBLE: At Canadian Refractories mine.
- *Kipawa, Temiscamingue County* AMAZONSTONE: E of Kipawa on S side of island in N end of Lac Sairs. It is accessible by plane or canoe. Get permission from Tasso Komossa in Toronto.
- *Labelle Station, Labelle County* GARNET: In quarry 2 miles S on Canadian Pacific Railroad right-of-way.
- *Laurel, Argenteuil County* DIOPSIDE, VESUVIANITE: W 2 miles on S side of road to Lost River.
- *Maniwaki, Gatineau County* QUARTZ: On Britt farm. Take Hwy 11E to E side of Gatineau River, turn N for 4½ miles, take right fork and go ½ mile to farmhouse.
- *Matane, Matane County* EPIDOTE: Pebbles with flint on St. Lawrence beaches.
- *Mont St. Hilaire, Rouville County* SODALITE: In Desourdy quarry with albite on NE slope of mountain.
- *Notre Dame de la Salette, Papineau County* STAR QUARTZ: N on Hwy 35 to sharp bend in road just beyond Mine de Mica, hike NW to hill to collect in Villeneuve mine.
- *Ottawa, Federal District* APATITE: At Forsyth mine 10 miles N, also at Laurentide mine, and the Scott mine N of the latter, and the McConnel mine a mile N of the Scott mine.
- *Otter Lake Village, Pontiac County* CORDIERITE, APATITE: W on the A. Richards farm. See Richards in the village. Also apatite and diopside at Yates Uranium mine 9 miles N, then W for 2½ miles.
- *Phillipsburg, Missisquoi County* MARBLE: At Phillipsburg marble quarries. Take St. Armand road E, turn left at church and drive ⅔ mile to quarries. Also at Missisquoi-Lautz quarries ¾ mile N. There are other quarries at South Stukey.
- *Pointe au Chene, Argenteuil County* SCAPOLITE, DIOPSIDE: At McGill farm N 3 miles.
- *Ste. Anne des Monts, Gaspé West County* PORPHYRY: Red material 40 miles S on Hwy 299 in Berry Mountain Brook.
- *St. Denis de-Brompton, Shefford County* SERPENTINE: At Webster Lake mines. Go S to trail around N end of Lac Montjoie (Webster). The pits and dumps are on the NW side.
- *St. Ludger de Milot, Lake St. John West County* MOONSTONE: In outcrops of gneiss near No. 4 bridge 70 miles N on W side of road to Passe Dangereuse.

- *St. Pierre de Wakefield, Gatineau County* AMAZONSTONE, TOURMALINE: In Le Duc quarry.
- *Scotstown, Compton County* NORDMARKITE (AUGITE SYENITE): A Dark rock with a schiller like labradorite in Scotstown Granite company quarry.
- *Sheldrake, Saguenay County* LABRADORITE: On N shore of St. Lawrence river. Also to NE around La Garnier and N to Lac Rougemont.
- *Sherbrooke, Sherbrooke County* JASPER-MAGNETITE: In pits behind lighted cross on De La Breiere street.
- *Wakefield, Gatineau County* TOURMALINE: At Le Duc mine on ridge 2½ miles W.
  SERPENTINE: SE 2 miles at Canadian Aluminium Company quarry.

Mexico

Most of Mexico is a high plateau, underlain by folded sedimentary rocks and extensively altered by thick layers of volcanic rocks. Mountains linked with American ranges border both coasts. Baja California, for instance, is a continuation of the California Coast range. Between the mountains and the sea on both coasts are narrow lowlands. Southeastern Mexico belongs to the mountainous Central American plateau. Yucatán is a low limestone plain. In many respects Mexico resembles the Great Basin area of the United States.

Baja California

- *El Marmol* ONYX: In quarry 5 miles away at Volcan Springs.
- *El Rosario* TURQUOISE: E 2 miles at El Aguajito.
- *Ensenada* PREHNITE: S 50 miles at Punta China.
- *Puertocitos* ONYX: Go to Oakie's Landing 29 miles away, then 4 miles to mine W of Route 5.
- *Rancho Viejo* TOURMALINE: In pegmatite 2 miles S at Socorro mine.
  SPHENE, TOURMALINATED QUARTZ, EPIDOTE: At Pino Solo near Rancho Viejo in pegmatite pits 100 yards N of landmark tree and 300 yards W.
  ALABASTER: Take Hwy 1 SE to San Agustin, then 10 miles E to quarry for alabaster (onyx).
  TURQUOISE: S 23 miles in dumps of La Turquesa mine.
- *Tecate* PETRIFIED WOOD: On S side of red hill just S of Pinto Wash near U.S. border.

RHYOLITE: In Cerro Pinto ridge in Pinto Basin, E of Tecate.

TOPAZ, QUARTZ: In pegmatites 25 miles E on Route 2.

AXINITE: Take Route 2 to El Condor, then S 40 miles, staying right at forks to El Topo road, then stay left to La Olivia mine.

Chiapas

• *San Cristobal las Casas* AMBER: Around Simojovel.

Chihuahua

AGATE: On privately owned ranches crossed by the highway from Juárez to Chihuahua City. These begin S of Villa Ahumada, especially at Gallego, Oja Laguna, and Moctezuma. Other areas are SW of Parral, NE of Alameda, W of Camargo, SW of Zaragoza, W of Rosario, and SE of Reforma. Collecting is rarely permitted.

• *Naica* MOSS AGATE: In nearby diggings.

• *Santa Eulalia* QUARTZ: At San Antonio mine, 4 miles away.

Durango

• *Durango* AGATE, JASPER: In creek beds to N along Hwy 45, especially near Rodeo.

AGATE NODULES: Take Mazatlán Highway 17 miles to first bridge, then 1¾ miles more, collect in road cut to right.

Guanajuato

Miners at the Valenciana mine will sell quartz crystals and amethyst. Cherry opal and fire opal are found nearby in rhyolite.

• *Apaseo* OBSIDIAN: A green variety to N.

Guerrero

• *Real del Monte* CAT'S-EYE OBSIDIAN: At Aztec obsidian mine.

Hidalgo

• *Hidalgo* FIRE OPAL: In rhyolite, at Barranca de Tepezala in Atotonilco district.

• *Huichapan District* PETRIFIED WOOD: At Salitera mine.

GARNET: Near Laguna Haso Cherhuahan and Zimapan-Canhardo.

- *Pachuca* OBSIDIAN: S 30 miles at Huasca. Also at Cerro de la Navajas, 10 miles S.

  Also 3 miles N of San Miguel Regla in cornfields at N end of lake.

  RHODONITE: On dumps of Real del Monte mine, 6 miles S.
- *Rosarito* AGATE: On beach one mile N of hotel.

Jalisco

- *Guadalajara* OBSIDIAN: Take Tepic-Mazatlán Highway 16 miles, collect before reaching Tequila.
- *Tequila* OPAL: Go on Route 15 to La Magdalena area, then 4 miles W and 3 miles N to San Simeon mine near village of the same name.

  Also at the Cinco mine near Hosta.

Morelos

GARNET: Pink grossularite at Rancho San Juan, near Xalostoc, Sierra Tlayacac.

Nueva Leon

- *Guerrero* AGATE, JASPER: The road from the U.S. border customs office winds through the hills. Collect along the road and also on the road to the Uribe ranch.

Puebla

- *Tecali* ONYX: Turn off Route 150 at Tepeaca to La Pedrara quarry in mountains to S.

Queretaro

- *San Juan del Rio* OPAL: Several mines are near Trinidad, reached from San Juan del Rio by taking Morelos Oriente avenue NE, then at 7½ miles crossing bridge, and going ½ mile farther left to Trinidad. Two miles W is La Carbonera mine, and nearby are La Guadalupana and Bernal mines. The Simpatica mine is at Esperanza. 30 miles NW and nearby is the Rosario mine. For entry to the La Guadalupana mine, see Senor Cabrera at La Guadalupana lapidary shop, 16th of Sept. st, in San Juan del Rio.

CHALCEDONY: At Granadas.

OBSIDIAN: Along highway from Queretero to San Juan del Rio.

San Luis Potosí

• *San Luis Potosí* FIRE AGATE: S 45 miles on Route 57 at Tula Hill. Take Route 57 to kilopost 359, and turn off road to the hill on E side of highway as far as kilopost 361.

AGATE NODULES: Take Hwy 80 SW 12 miles to dam, then backtrack ½ mile and collect on N side of road.

TOPAZ: S 30 miles at Tepetate.

Sinaloa

• *Culiacan* AMETHYST: In nearby diggings.

Sonora

• *Magdalena* OPAL: At La Unica, San Simeon, and La Estancia mines. Opal is also mined at Tequila, Etzatlán, San Marco, and Hostotipaquillo.

• *Cananea* SPHALERITE: Transparent crystals at the Manzanal and Chivera mines.

Vera Cruz

GARNET: At Las Vagas and Escobar.

Zacatecas

• *Concepcion del Oro* CHRYSOCOLLA, TURQUOISE: On dumps of San Elijio mine N of Salaverna, and Socovan mine between Salaverna and Bonanza.

• *Zacatecas* AMETHYST: N 6 miles in dumps of El Bote mine gem material is found.

Note: Visitors to Mexico should get a permit at any Mexican consulate and should have a birth certificate, car title if driving, and evidence of smallpox vaccination. Tetanus shots are also advisable, as well as halazone tablets to purify water. Car insurance should be obtained in Mexico for the duration of the visit. It is wise to keep the gas tank full, to carry small-denomination traveler's checks, and make payments in Mexican money. A permit to collect should be obtained at the site and should be shown when leaving Mexico. Collecting of ancient carvings and artifacts is forbidden and even possession of them is illegal. In Mexico the people should be treated with every courtesy, and ability to speak some Spanish and to show a friendly attitude is very helpful. Use of guides whenever possible is invaluable in making contacts and avoiding trouble. Cigarettes and candy (for children) are much appreciated small gifts.

glossary

Abalone: a shellfish of the genus *Haliotis,* noted for the variegated color of its pearly shell.

Acicular (a-sick'-u-ler): needle shaped, referring to mineral.

Activator: foreign substance that causes mineral to fluoresce.

Adamantine (ad-a-man'-teen): having luster like diamond.

Aggregate: mass including several rocks or minerals.

Alluvial (a-lew'-vi-al): sand or silt deposited by running water.

Amorphous (a-mor'-fus): without crystal structure.

Amphibole (am'-fi-bole): a group of silicates that are common rock-forming minerals, usually dark.

Amygdaloid (a-mig'-dah-loyd): volcanic rock containing small round gas cavities, which are often filled with other minerals.

Andalusite: an aluminum silicate, of which chiastolite is a variety.

Angstrom unit: unit used to measure wave lengths of light; equals $1/250,000,000$ inch.

Aragonite (a-rag'-o-nite): a mineral composed, like calcite, of calcium carbonate, but differing in crystallization and physical properties.

Arroyo (a-roi'-oh): creek, or its dry channel.

Asparagus stone: yellowish green apatite.

Asteriated (as-ter'-i-a-ted): showing starlike pattern.

Axis: imaginary line fixing structural direction in crystal.

Bar: sand or gravel bank in stream.

Basal: cleavage parallel to the base of the crystal.

Basalt (bah-sawlt'): dark, fine-grained igneous rock formed principally of feldspar and iron and magnesium minerals.

Batholith (bath'-o-lith): igneous rock formation of vast extent that was formed deep underground.

Birthstones: January—garnet, February—amethyst, March—bloodstone, April—diamond, May—emerald, June—pearl, July—

ruby, August—sardonyx, September—sapphire, October—opal, November—topaz, December—turquoise.

Bladed: elongated, flat, thin.

Blank: a slice or slab of gem material cut to the basic shape of the stone.

Botryoidal (bot-ri-oi'-dahl): shaped in rounded, grapelike masses.

Buff: a wheel of felt, wood, or leather for polishing gem stones.

Breccia (brech'-i-ah): rock containing angular fragments, usually of another type of rock.

Brittle: Easily broken.

Butte (beaut): isolated hill or small mountain with very steep sides.

Cabochon (ka'-beau-shon): gem cut with convex, rounded, unfaceted surface.

Capillary: hairlike, referring to a crystal.

Carat: unit of weight, usually 200 milligrams (about $1/150$ ounce).

Carbonate: a salt of carbonic acid; that is, a compound of a metal with carbon and oxygen.

Cast: mineral taking shape of cavity left in rock by decay of plant or animal.

Cat's-eye: a gem showing a sharp streak of light across it caused by reflections from fibers within the stone.

Cattle guard: loose pipes laid parallel on the ground at gate or opening to stop cattle, which are frightened by uncertain footing.

Chalk: a soft limestone of earthy character.

Chatoyant (sha-toi'-aunt): reflecting light in form of moving or undulating streak—like a cat's eye in the dark.

Chlorite: group of hydrous silicates, usually green.

Cleavage: parting of a mineral along a smooth plane surface.

Color zone: striping or segregation of color within a crystal.

Columnar: like a column, referring to crystal.

Compound: distinct substance formed by union of two or more elements in definite proportions.

Conchoidal (kong-koi'-dahl): concave, like inside of bivalve shell; referring to shape of fracture of a substance.

Concretion: lump of unlike material in sedimentary rock.

Contact metamorphism: change in rock in contact with intruding igneous rock.

Coulee (cou'-lee): steep-walled valley.

Craze: tendency of a gem material to develop fine cracks on the surface.

Crust: outer rocky layer of the earth.

Cryptocrystalline (kript'-oh-kris'-tal-in): composed of crystals so minute that they are not visible without magnification.

Crystal: solid bounded by planes that meet at characteristic and definite angles, expressing an orderly arrangement of atoms.

Crystalline: having definite visible crystal structure.

Cubic: having the form of a cube, as many of the isometric system crystals.

Delta: Deposit of sand and gravel at mouth of a river, often a large tract of land.

Dendritic (den-drit'-ik): branching, treelike; referring to patterns produced in a mineral by a foreign mineral, or a branching form of a mineral.

Diaphaneity (die-ah-fa-nee'-i-tee): ability of a substance to pass light, expressed as transparent, translucent, or opaque.

Dichroscope (die'-crow-skope): optical device for splitting light refracted by gem into its constituent colors.

Diggings: place where excavation has been made, as by a prospector.

Dike: vertical, tabular body of rock cutting through major rock mass.

Dip: angle at which inclination of rock bed departs from the horizontal.

Dop: a metal or wooden rod to which the gem blank is cemented for holding in the cutting and polishing process.

Drift: mass of rock materials deposited by glacier.

Drusy (droo'-zi): rock surface covered with minute crystals.

Ductile: capable of being drawn, as into wire.

Dump: pile of waste rock at mine or other excavation.

Effervescence: bubbling gas in a liquid, such as that generated by reaction of acid with a carbonate.

Electron: very small, lightweight particle of negative electricity that is a part of all matter.

Element: simplest natural unit of ordinary matter, such as iron or hydrogen.

Emery: natural aluminum oxide used as abrasive.

Erosion (e-ro'-zhun): wearing away of rocks at earth's surface by action of natural agents.

Escarpment: a long cliff, especially one formed by faulting.

Euclase: a beryllium and aluminum silicate.

Extrusive: form of igneous rock forced to surface while molten.

Facet: a flat face cut on a gem; a style of cutting with facets.

Fault: displacement of rocks in earth's crust along a fracture zone.

Felsite: igneous rock composed of quartz and feldspar.

Fibrous: mineral formed of thread or needlelike crystals.

Fire: brilliance of a gem, caused by its ability to split up light.

Flat: a level area, especially in a desert.

Flaw: an imperfection in a gem material, such as a crack or inclusion.

Flexible: having the ability to bend without breaking.

Float: rock fragments found on surface some distance from outcrop or vein from which they came.

Flower: a form of agate showing a pattern variegated in color and design resembling a bouquet.

Fluorescence: emission of light by a substance when it is exposed to ultraviolet rays.

Foliated: capable of being separated into thin sheets, like mica.

Fortification: a form of agate with a pattern of angular stripes resembling battlements on a castle.

Fossil: evidence of past life preserved usually in rocks.

Fracture: texture of a freshly broken surface of rock or mineral.

Friable: separating easily into grains.

Geode (gee'-owed): mineral shell lined with crystals or filled with mineral.

Geology: science of the origin, history, and structure of the earth and life as they are recorded in the rocks.

Glacial drift: earth, sand, and stones transported and deposited by a glacier.

Glaciated: subjected to glacial action.

Glacier: ice field moving down a slope or covering a continental area.

Glassy: vitreous, resembling the luster of glass.

Gneiss (nice): crystalline metamorphic rock having banded appearance because of segregation of its minerals.

Grain: unit of weight used for pearls, equal to ¼ of a carat.

Gram: metric measure of weight; there are 28.35 grams in an avoirdupois ounce.

Granite: light-colored crystalline rock composed mainly of quartz and feldspar, with mica and hornblende.

Ground mass: the fine-grained mass of a rock in which crystals, such as those of a porphyry, have formed.

Gulch: sharply cut bed of a torrent, a ravine.

Habit: characteristic manner of occurrence of a crystal.

Hackly: a jagged fracture like that of cast iron.

Hardness: degree of resistance of surface to being scratched.

Herkimer diamond: quartz crystal from the Herkimer County (N.Y.) region.

Hexagonal: belonging to a crystal system in which a vertical axis is intersected at right angles by three axes intersecting one another at 60 degrees.

High grade: to pick out the high value, choice ore, or gem material.

Hornblende: commonest of the amphiboles, a black or dark green constituent of many granites.

Hydrous: containing chemically combined water.

Igneous (ig'-nee-us): type of rock formed by solidification of molten material from deep within the earth.

Inclusion: a foreign particle in a mineral.

Inorganic: derived from or pertaining to the inanimate world.

Intarsia: pattern or picture made by fitting precisely cut pieces of stone together, like mosaic.

Intrusive: form of igneous rock that has hardened before reaching surface.

Iridescence: rainbow play of colors, like that of a soap film.

Iris: a form of agate that shows rainbow colors when light passes through it.

Isometric (eye-so-met'-rik): crystal system in which all three axes are equal in length and meet at right angles.

Lamellar: composed of thin layers stacked like the leaves of a book.

Lap: a plate of metal or plastic revolving horizontally for cutting and polishing gem stones, usually used in faceting.

Lapidary: the craft of fashioning a gem stone, and the person who does it.

Lava: molten rock extruded to the surface, as by a volcano.

Lenticular: shaped like a flat bean.

Limestone: sedimentary rock formed mainly of calcium carbonate.

Lode: an ore deposit occurring within definite boundaries, a vein or ledge or reef.

Loess (low'-ess): soil composed of silt deposited by wind.

Luminescence (lew'-mi-nes-ens): light emitted by a substance because of any stimulation except heating; a more general term than fluorescence.

Luster: appearance by reflected light of a fresh surface of a mineral.

Magma: molten rock deep inside the earth from which igneous rock comes.

Malleable: capable of being shaped by hammering.

Massive: lacking definite crystal structure or form.

Matrix (may'-trix): rock in which a mineral is imbedded or to which it is attached.

Melt: molten rock material, known as magma, deep within the earth, from which igneous rocks are derived.

Mesa: flat-topped hill with steep sides.

Metamorphic: rock altered from its original state by the action of heat, pressure, solutions, or gases.

Microscopic: visible only under a microscope.

Mineral: a natural, inorganic substance, with a definite chemical composition, which expresses itself by orderly internal structure and definite external shape.

Mineralogy: the study of minerals.

Monoclinic: crystal system in which the axes are unequal in length, and two meet at right angles while the third meets them at an oblique angle.

Moraine: accumulation of stones and earth deposited by a glacier.

Nacreous: pearly.

Nodule: small roundish lump of mineral, often formed in a rock cavity.

Octahedron: a solid enclosed by eight triangular faces.

Oolitic: composed of small concretions like fish roe, usually in limestone.

Opalescent: having a bluish milky appearance, like common opal.

Opaque: incapable of passing light.

Orbicular: marked with circular, eyelike patterns.

Ore: mineral or rock deposit that can be mined at a profit.

Organic: derived from or pertaining to living organisms.

Orient: Luster of a pearl; also to position a gem by its crystal structure.

Orthorhombic: a crystal system in which the axes are all of unequal length but they all meet at right angles, as in an oblong.

Outcrop: exposure of rock.

Overburden: rock or soil which must be removed to mine by open-pit method.

Oxide: compound of oxygen with another element.

Pan: to wash earth and gravel in a pan in search of gold and other heavy materials.

Pearly: having luster like that of a pearl.

Pegmatite (peg'-ma-tight): igneous rock of coarse granite composition and texture, usually found as a dike.

Perfect: term for cleavage that is readily started and leaves a smooth surface.

Petrifaction (pet'-ri-fak-shun): process of fossilization in which original cell tissue remains but cells are filled with mineral; also called permineralization.

Phosphate: compound of phosphorus and oxygen with one or more other elements, which are usually metallic.

Phosphorescence: luminescence that persists after exciting cause is removed.

Pisolitic: composed of rounded pealike masses.

Pitch: dip or inclination of a mineral vein or bed at right angles to its strike.

Placer: stream segregation of heavy minerals.

Plateau: high tract of level land of considerable extent, a tableland.

Playa: undrained desert basin that may occasionally contain water, a dry lake.

Pocket: cavity in rock.

Point: Diamond weight, $1/100$ of a carat.

Porphyry (por'-fi-ree): igneous rock containing well-developed crystals embedded in a fine-grained ground mass.

Precious: of great value; the precious stones are diamond, ruby, sapphire, emerald, and opal.

Prism: solid in which faces are parallel to one axis, usually longer than broad, and usually four- or six-sided and terminated by flat surfaces.

Prospect: unproved mineral property, or partly developed mine.

Pseudomorph (sue'-do-morf): mineral that has replaced another mineral but has kept the replaced mineral's crystal form.

Pyrite (pie'-right): iron sulphide, commonly called fool's gold.

Pyroxene (pie-rocks'-een): a group of silicates that are common rock-forming minerals.

Quadrangle: the four-sided tract of land represented by an atlas sheet map of the U.S. Geological Survey.

Quarry: open excavation to remove rock, usually for industrial uses.

Radiating: fanning out from a center, like rays from a light.

Ravine: steep-sided valley, larger than a gully and smaller than a canyon.

Refraction: the bending of light as it passes from one medium, such as air, into another, such as a gem material.

Refractometer: instrument for measuring bending of light passing through gem mineral.

Reniform (wren'-i-form): rounded, kidney-shaped mineral surface.

Replacement: fossilization in which tissue of organism has been removed and replaced simultaneously by mineral substance.

Resinous: having luster like that of resin.

Reticulated: having the form of a lattice or network; used to describe crystals.

Rhyolite (rye'-oh-light): fine-grained volcanic rock composed of quartz and feldspar, the equivalent of a granite.

Rock: a natural inorganic solid from the earth's crust.

Rough: uncut gem material.

Rutilated (rue'-ti-late-ed): crystal shot through with needles of rutile (titanium oxide).

Sagenitic (saj-eh-nit'-ik): crystal containing needlelike crystals of a foreign mineral.

Sandstone: a sedimentary rock formed of grains of sand compacted together.

Scarp: see escarpment.

Schist (shist): metamorphic rock containing mica flakes arranged in layers so that rock readily splits along micaceous surface.

Seam: thin layer, stratum, or vein of mineral.

Sectile: capable of being cut into shavings.

Sedimentary: rock formed of sediments or the debris of other rocks.

Segregation: a grouping of like minerals by natural processes.

Semiprecious: materials cut and worn as gems, other than those ranked as precious.

Shaft: vertical or inclined entrance to a mine.

Shale: laminated sedimentary rock formed from silt or clay.

Silica: silicon oxide.

Silicate (sil'-i-kate): mineral composed usually of one or more metals combined with silicon and oxygen.

Silicify: to replace substance by chalcedony or opal.

Silky: having luster like that of silk.

Sixling: twinning of six crystals into a pseudohexagonal form, as in chrysoberyl.

Skeletal: a crystal with faces not fully formed.

Slate: cleavable metamorphic rock formed by compression of clays and shale.

Slurry: a thin, watery mixture.

Soil: decomposed rock, sand, and decayed vegetable matter.

Spar: a lustrous, cleavable, nonmetallic mineral, such as fluorspar (fluorite) or satin spar (gypsum).

Specific gravity: comparison of the weight of a substance with the weight of an equal volume of water.

Spectroscope: instrument for analyzing chemical composition by measuring wave length of radiant energy (usually light) that is emitted or absorbed by the specimen.

Stalactite: Column hanging from roof of a cave; its opposite is a stalagmite.

Stalactitic: mineral formed into columns resembling stalactites.

Star: an asteriated gem, or one that reflects a four- or six-rayed star from fibers embedded in the stone.

Stellated: Starlike, radiating from a center.

Stratification: bedding of sedimentary rock.

Stratum (straight'-um): a distinct layer or bed of sedimentary rock (plural is strata).

Streak: color of powder left on unglazed porcelain when mineral specimen is rubbed across it.

GLOSSARY

Striation (stri-a'-shun): one of parallel lines or ridges formed in development of a crystal face.

Strike: compass direction at which inclined rock bed crosses the horizontal; perpendicular to the direction of dip.

Sulphide: compound of sulphur and a metal.

Symmetry (sim'-eh-tri): correspondence in size, shape, and relative position of parts that are on opposite sides of a dividing line or median plane.

Synthetic: man-made, referring to a gem material that has the same physical and chemical qualities as a natural gem.

System: one of six groups into which crystals are classified.

Tableland: broad, level, elevated region, for example, a plateau.

Tabular: tablet shaped.

Talus (tay'-lus): rock debris at base of cliff or slope.

Tarnish: surface change, usually of color, of a mineral.

Template: a plate pierced with holes of various shapes for marking dimensions of a gem before cutting it.

Tenacity: ability of a substance to hold together under stress, such as pulling or pounding.

Termination: face or faces at end of a crystal.

Tetragonal (te-trag'-oh-nawl): belonging to a system in which only two axes are equal in length, and all three axes intersect at right angles.

Texture: size, shape, and pattern of a rock's components.

Thunderegg: nodule with agate core and surface of rhyolite or jasper.

Topographic map: map that shows surface features of an area, especially elevations and depressions, by means of contour lines connecting points of equal elevation from sea level.

Translucent: able to pass light but not the image of an object.

Transparent: able to pass light so that objects can be seen through it.

Traprock: any of several dark, fine-grained igneous rocks, such as basalt.

Triclinic: belonging to a crystal system in which all three axes are unequal in length and in which they meet one another at oblique angles.

Trisoctahedron: crystal formed of 24 faces arranged so that three take the place of each face of a regular octahedron.

Truck collector: one who removes more gem material than he needs or can use.

Tumble: process of polishing gem material in a revolving barrel.

Twin: compound crystal composed of two or more crystals or parts of crystals in reversed positions with respect to each other.

Ultraviolet: having wavelengths shorter than those of visible light.

Vein: mineral deposit in the form of a thin sheet or stringer.

Vitreous (vit'-re-us): luster like that of glass.

Wash: gravel or sand spread out like a fan, often at the mouth of a canyon.

Wasty: gem material that yields only a small proportion of its bulk as finished stones.

Water: the clarity of a diamond; a diamond that is perfectly transparent is described as of the first water.

Weathering: action of water, wind, and temperature in altering form, color, or texture of exposed material, such as rock.

Zeolite: a group of fairly soft hydrous silicates usually found in cavities in lavas.

OFFICIAL STATE STONES

Following are the gemstones, minerals and rocks adopted as their official choices by the various legislatures:

State	Gem	Rock (or Stone)	Mineral
Alabama			Hematite
Alaska		Jade	Gold
Arizona	Bola Tie		
Arkansas	Diamond	Bauxite	Quartz Crystal
California	Benitoite	Serpentine	Gold
Colorado	Aquamarine		
Florida	Moonstone		
Idaho	Star Garnet		
Illinois			Fluorite
Indiana		Limestone	
Iowa		Geode	
Maine	Tourmaline	Red Granite	Galena
Maryland	Williamsite (Serpentine)		
Michigan	Chlorastrolite	Petosky Stone (Hexagonaria Coral)	
Minnesota	Lake Superior Agate		
Missouri		Mozarkite	Galena
Montana	Sapphire	Montana Agate	
Nebraska	Blue Agate	Prairie Agate	
New Mexico	Turquoise		
New York	Garnet		
North Dakota		Teredo Fossil Wood	
Ohio	Flint		
Oklahoma		Barite Rose	
Oregon	Thunderegg		
Rhode Island		Cumberlandite	Bowenite
South Carolina	Amethyst	Granite	
South Dakota	Fairburn Agate		Rose Quartz
Texas	Blue Topaz	Palmwood (Petrified)	
Utah	Topaz		
Vermont		Greenstone (Serpentine)	Talc
Wisconsin		Red Granite	Galena
Wyoming	Nephrite Jade		

sources of information and supply

State geological publications, maps, and public displays of minerals are among the best means the gem hunter has to prepare himself for a field trip. Many displays are in colleges, where an appointment may be necessary to see the collection (which is primarily for teaching purposes). Following is a list giving (1) the state geological agency to which application should be made for printed and map material on state mineral resources, and (2) museums having mineral displays, and the cities in which they are located.

United States

Alabama: (1) Geological Survey of Alabama, University. (2) Alabama Museum of Natural History, University; Alabama Polytechnic University, Auburn.

Alaska: (1) Division of Mines and Minerals of Alaska, Box 1391, Juneau. (2) State Museum in the State Capitol, Juneau.

Arizona: (1) Bureau of Mines, Tucson. (2) Museum of Northern Arizona, Flagstaff; Petrified Forest National Monument, Holbrook; Fairgrounds Museum, Mineral Building, Fairgrounds, Phoenix; Public Museum, Tombstone; Meteorite Museum, Sedona; University of Arizona, Tucson.

Arkansas: (1) Resources and Development Commission, State Capitol, Little Rock. (2) University of Arkansas Museum, Fayetteville; Hendrix College, Conway.

California: (1) Division of Mines and Geology, Resources Building, Sacramento. (2) University of California, Berkeley; Western Trails Museum, Knott's Berry Farm, Buena Park; County Museum, and Museum of Science and Industry, both in State

Exposition Building in Exposition Park, and University of California and University of Southern California, all in Los Angeles; Public Museum, Oakland; California Institute of Technology, Pasadena; Municipal Museum, Riverside; Natural History Museum, Balboa Park, San Diego; Division of Mines Museum in Ferry Building, Academy of Science Museum in Golden Gate Park, Junior Museum at 16th and Roosevelt Way, Recreational Museum, Wells-Fargo Bank, all in San Francisco; Natural History Museum, Santa Barbara; University of Santa Clara Museum, Santa Clara.

Colorado: (1) Bureau of Mines, State Services Building, Denver. (2) University of Colorado Museum, Boulder; Colorado College, Colorado Springs; Museum of Natural History, State Museum, and Bureau of Mines in State Capitol, all in Denver; Colorado School of Mines, Golden.

Connecticut: (1) Geological and Natural History Survey, Box 128, Wesleyan Station, Middletown. (2) Bruce Museum, Greenwich; Trinity College, Wadsworth Athenaeum, both of Hartford; Wesleyan University, Middletown; Peabody Museum and Geology Laboratory, Yale University, New Haven; and the Choate School, Wallingford.

Delaware: (1) Geological Survey, University of Delaware, Newark. (2) Robinson Hall of University of Delaware, Irenée DuPont collection, Penny Hall, University of Delaware, Newark.

District of Columbia: (1) Geological Survey and Bureau of Mines, both in the Department of the Interior, Washington 25. (2) National Museum of the Smithsonian Institution; Interior Department museum.

Florida: (1) State Board of Conservation, Division of Geology, Tallahassee. (2) John B. Stetson University, De Land; University of Florida, Gainesville; Geological Survey Museum and Geology Department of Florida State University, Tallahassee.

Georgia: (1) Department of Mines, Mining and Geology, Agricultural Building, Atlanta. (2) State Museum, Atlanta; University of Georgia, Athens.

Hawaii: (2) Bernice P. Bishop Museum, Honolulu, Oahu Island.

Idaho: (1) Idaho Bureau of Mines and Geology, Moscow. (2) State Capitol, Boise; University of Idaho, Moscow.

Illinois: (1) State Geological Survey, Urbana. (2) Southern Illinois University, Carbondale; Academy of Sciences, Field Museum of Natural History, both in Chicago; Lizzadro Museum of Lapidary Arts, Elmhurst; Augustana College, Rock Island; Funk Museum, Shirley; State Museum, Springfield; Natural History Museum in Natural Resources Building at University of Illinois, Urbana (on the campus).

Indiana: (1) Geological Survey, Indiana University, Bloomington.

(2) Indiana University, Bloomington; Hanover College, Hanover; State Museum in the State Capitol, Children's Museum, both in Indianapolis; School of Engineering at Purdue University, Lafayette; Earlham College, Richmond.

Iowa: (1) Geological Survey, Geological Survey Building, Iowa City. (2) Iowa State Teachers College, Cedar Falls; Coe College, Cedar Rapids; Public Museum, Davenport; Museum of State Historical Building, Straight Memorial Museum at Drake University, both at Des Moines; Grinnell College, Grinnell.

Kansas: (1) State Geological Survey, Lawrence. (2) St. Benedict's College, Atchison; Baker University, Baldwin; Kansas State Teachers College, Emporia; Fort Hays Kansas State College, Hays; Natural History Museum and Geology Departmental Museum at University of Kansas, Lawrence; Ottawa University, Ottawa; Kansas State Teachers College, Pittsburg; Smoky Hills Historical Museum, Oakdale Park, Salina; State Historical Society, Memorial Building, Topeka; Historical Museum Association, Wichita.

Kentucky: (1) Geological Survey, 120 Graham Avenue, Lexington. (2) Baker Hunt Foundation, Covington; Geology Department, University of Kentucky, Lexington; Public Library Museum, Louisville.

Louisiana: (1) Geological Survey, Baton Rouge. (2) Louisiana State University Geology Museum, Baton Rouge; Louisiana State Museum in Jackson Square, Tulane University, both in New Orleans.

Maine: (1) Department of Economic Development, State House, Augusta. (2) State Museum, Augusta; Bates College, Lewiston; University of Maine, Orono; Hamlin Memorial Hall, Paris; Portland Natural History Society Museum, Beach Museum, both of Portland; Colby College, Waterville.

Maryland: (1) Department of Geology, Mines and Water Resources, Johns Hopkins University, Baltimore. (2) Johns Hopkins University Geology Department, Natural History Society, and Academy of Sciences, all in Baltimore.

Massachusetts: (1) Geology Department, University of Massachusetts, Amherst. (2) Pratt Museum of Amherst College, Amherst; Society of Natural History, Children's Museum in Jamaica Plain, both in Boston; Mineralogical Museum of Harvard University, Cambridge; Smith College, Northampton; Peabody Museum, Salem; Mount Holyoke College, South Hadley; Museum of Natural History, Springfield; Williams College, Williamstown; Natural History Museum, and Clark University, Worcester.

Michigan: (1) Department of Conservation, Lansing. (2) Mineralogical Museum of the University of Michigan, Ann Arbor; Kingman Museum, Battle Creek; Cranbrook Institute of Science, Bloomfield Hills; Fort Wilkins State Park Museum, Copper Harbor; City Museum, Wayne State University, both in Detroit; City Museum, Grand Rapids; Michigan Technological University, Houghton; Michigan State University Museum, State Historical Museum, both in East Lansing; Public Museum, Kalamazoo; Northern Michigan College, Marquette.

Minnesota: (1) Department of Conservation, Division of Lands and Minerals, Centennial Office Building, St. Paul. (2) Museum of Natural History at University of Minnesota, Science Museum at Public Library, and Walker Art Center, all in Minneapolis; Carleton College, Northfield; Science Museum, St. Paul.

Mississippi: (1) Geological Survey, University. (2) Mississippi State College, State College; University of Mississippi, University.

Missouri: (1) Division of Geological Survey and Water Resources, Rolla. (2) University of Missouri, Columbia; Missouri Resources Museum, Jefferson City; City Museum, and Geological Museum, University of Missouri, Kansas City; School of Mines, Rolla; Educational Museum of the Public Schools, Washington University, Museum of Science and Natural History, all in St. Louis; Palmer Little Museum, Webb City.

Montana: (1) Bureau of Mines and Geology, Butte. (2) School of Mines, Anaconda Employes' Club, both of Butte; Historical Society, Helena; State University, Missoula.

Nebraska: (1) Division of Conservation and Survey, University of Nebraska. (2) State Museum, Lincoln.

Nevada: (1) Bureau of Mines, University of Nevada, Reno. (2) Lake Mead Natural History Association, Boulder City; State Museum, Carson City; Mackay School of Mines Museum, Reno.

New Hampshire: (1) Planning and Development Commission, Concord. (2) Woodman Institute, Dover; University of New Hampshire Geology Department, Durham; Wilson Museum of Dartmouth College, Hanover; County Historical Society; Institute of Arts and Sciences, Manchester.

New Jersey: (1) Department of Conservation and Economic Development, Trenton. (2) Museum of the Newark Mineralogical Society, Newark; Rutgers University, Geology Department Museum, New Brunswick; New Jersey Mineralogical Society, Paterson; Princeton University Geology Department Museum, Princeton; State Museum in State House Annex, Trenton.

New Mexico: (1) Bureau of Mines and Mineral Resources, Campus Station, Socorro. (2) University of New Mexico, Albuquerque;

Museum of New Mexico in Palace of the Governors, Santa Fe; New Mexico Institute of Mining and Technology, Socorro.

New York: (1) State Museum and Science Service, Albany. (2) State Museum, Albany; Museum of Science, University of Buffalo, both of Buffalo; Knox Museum of Hamilton College, Clinton; Museum of Natural History of Colgate University, Hamilton; Cornell University, Ithaca; American Museum of Natural History, Columbia University Geology and Mineralogy Museum, Metropolitan Museum of Art, all in New York; Vassar College, Poughkeepsie; University of Rochester Museum of Geology, Museum of Arts and Sciences, both of Rochester; Union College, Schenectady; Rensselaer Polytechnic Institute, Troy.

North Carolina: (1) Department of Conservation and Development, Raleigh. (2) Colburn Mineral Museum, Asheville; University of North Carolina, Chapel Hill; Duke University, Durham; Museum of North Carolina Minerals of National Park Service at Gillespie Gap, Spruce Pine; North Carolina State College, State Museum, both of Raleigh.

North Dakota: (1) Geological Survey, Grand Forks. (2) University of North Dakota, Grand Forks.

Ohio: (1) Department of Natural Resources, Division of Geological Survey, Ohio State University, Columbus. (2) Ohio University Museum of Natural History, Athens; Bowling Green State University, Bowling Green; Museum of Natural History, Cincinnati; Department of Geology of Case Institute of Technology, Museum of Natural History, Western Reserve University, all of Cleveland; State Museum, Orton and Lord Halls of Ohio State University, both of Columbus; Johnson-Humrickhouse Memorial Museum, Coshocton; Oberlin College, Oberlin; Miami University, Oxford; Clark County Historical Society, Springfield; Heidelberg College Science Hall, Tiffin.

Oklahoma: (1) Geological Survey, Norman. (2) Woolaroc Museum, Bartlesville; Gould Hall and Stovall Museum of the University of Oklahoma, both in Norman; University of Tulsa, Tulsa.

Oregon: (1) Department of Geology and Mineral Resources, State Office Building, Portland. (2) Oregon State College, Corvallis; University of Oregon, Eugene; Museum of Science and Industry, State Department of Geology and Mineral Resources, Lewis and Clark College, all in Portland.

Pennsylvania: (1) Department of Internal Affairs, Bureau of Topographic and Geologic Survey, Harrisburg. (2) Lehigh University, Bethlehem; Bryn Mawr College, Bryn Mawr; Dickinson College, Carlisle; Lafayette College, Easton; Geologic Survey, Harrisburg; North Museum, Franklin and Marshall College, Lancaster; Allegheny College, Meadville; Delaware County Institute of Science, Media; Academy of Natural Sciences, University of Pennsylvania, Wagner Free Institute of Science, all in Philadelphia; Carnegie Museum, Pittsburgh; Mineral Industries Building, Pennsylvania State University, University Park.

Rhode Island: (1) Development Council, Roger Williams Building, Providence. (2) University of Rhode Island, Kingston; Roger Williams Park Museum, Rhode Island Hall of Brown University, both of Providence; Public Library, Westerly.

South Carolina: (1) Division of Geology, State Development Board, Wade Hampton State Office Building, Columbia. (2) Howard Collection at University of South Carolina, Columbia.

South Dakota: (1) Geological Survey, Science Center, University, Vermillion. (2) School of Mines and Technology, Rapid City; Geology Department of State University of South Dakota, Vermillion.

Tennessee: (1) Department of Conservation, Division of Geology, State Office Building, Nashville. (2) University of Tennessee Geology Department, Knoxville; Vanderbilt University Geology Department, State Division of Geology, State Museum in War Memorial Building, all in Nashville.

Texas: (1) Bureau of Economic Geology of University of Texas, Austin. (2) Texas Memorial Museum, Austin; Centennial Museum, El Paso; Natural History Museum, Houston; Witte Museum, San Antonio; Baylor University, Waco.

Utah: (1) Geological and Mineralogical Survey, Mines Building, University of Utah, Salt Lake City. John Hutchings Museum, Lehi. (2) Geology Museum of the University of Utah, Westminster College, both in Salt Lake City; Fieldhouse of Natural History in Vernal State Park, Vernal.

Vermont: (1) Geological Survey, East Hall, University of Vermont, Burlington. (2) Fleming Museum of University of Vermont, Burlington; State Cabinet Building, Montpelier; Fairbanks Museum, St. Johnsbury.

Virginia: (1) Division of Mineral Resources, Box 3667, Charlottesville. (2) Holden Hall of Virginia Polytechnic Institute, Blacksburg; Brooks Museum of the University of Virginia, Charlottesville; Washington and Lee University, Lexington.

Washington: (1) Division of Mines and Geology, General Administration Building, Olympia. (2) State Capitol Museum, Olympia; University of Washington, Seattle; Grace Campbell Memorial Public Museum, Spokane; Washington State Historical Society, Tacoma; Ginkgo Petrified Forest Museum, Vantage; Whitman College, Walla Walla; North Central Washington Museum, Wenatchee.

West Virginia: (1) Geological and Economic Survey, Morgantown. (2) Geology Museum of Marshall College, Huntington; West Virginia University, Morgantown.

Wisconsin: (1) Geological and Natural History Survey, Science Hall, University of Wisconsin, Madison. (2) Lawrence College, Appleton; Beloit College, Beloit; University of Wisconsin, Madison; Public Museum, University of Wisconsin—Milwaukee, both of Milwaukee.

Wyoming: (1) Geological Survey, University of Wyoming, Laramie. (2) State Museum, Cheyenne; Geology Building of University of Wyoming, Laramie; Norris Museum, Yellowstone Park.

In addition to these museums listed above, most national parks and monuments in the United States have nature exhibits and museums which often include excellent displays of native rocks and minerals.

Canada

(1) Geological Survey of Canada, Ottawa, Ontario. (2) Alberta—University of Alberta, Edmonton; British Columbia—University of British Columbia, City Museum, and British Columbia and Yukon Chamber of Mines, all Vancouver; Mineral Museum, Victoria. Manitoba—Museum in Civic Auditorium, Winnipeg. New Brunswick—New Brunswick Museum, St. John; University of New Brunswick, Fredericton; Mount Allison University, Sackville. Newfoundland—Memorial University, St. John's. Nova Scotia—Museum of Science, Dalhousie University Museum, Halifax. Ontario—National Museum of Canada and Victoria Museum, Ottawa; Miller Hall of Queen's University, Kingston; Royal Ontario Museum, Toronto. Quebec—Redpath Museum of McGill University, and College de Montréal, both Montréal; Musée de Minéralogie of Laval University, Quebec.

Sources of Supply

Below are listed a number of dealers serving the various aspects of the collecting hobby. These have been chosen because they have been in business for a number of years and have a reliable reputation. There are many other dealers who undoubtedly have the same reliability, variety of materials, and other attributes as the ones listed. In the lists, "General" means that the dealer stocks equipment, jewelry findings and tools, some minerals and gems, and so on. "Gems" and "Mineral" categories overlap; those in either classification may have what the collector wants. "Lapidary Equipment" and "Books" are self-explanatory; most of the former are manufacturers; the latter are dealers who have a special interest in books.

General

Aleta's Rock Shop, 1515 Plainfield Ave. N.E., Grand Rapids, Mich. 49505

Compton Rock Shop, 1405 S. Long Beach Blvd., Compton, Calif. 90221

Francis Hoover, 12445 Chandler Blvd., North Hollywood, Calif. 91607

Geode Industries, P.O. Box 158, New London, Ia. 52645

Gordon's, 1741 Cherry Ave., Long Beach, Calif. 90804

Grieger, 900 S. Arroyo Parkway, Pasadena, Calif. 91109

Mid-America Rock Shop, 4503 Milwaukee Ave., Chicago, Ill. 60630

Minnesota Lapidary Supply Co., 524 N. 5th St., Minneapolis, Minn. 55401

Mueller's, 1000 E. Camelback Rd., Phoenix, Ariz. 85014

Shipley's Mineral House, Gem Village, Bayfield, Colo. 81122

Stewart's Gem Shop, 2620 Idaho St., Boise, Ida. 83706

Tom Roberts Rock Shop, 1006 S. Michigan Ave., Chicago, Ill. 60050

Treasure of the Pirates, 7125 Wisconsin Ave., Bethesda, Md. 20034

Trowbridge Crafts, 4 E. McDonald Rd., Prospect Heights, Ill. 60070

Ward's Natural Science Establishment, P.O. Box 1712, Rochester, N.Y. 14600

Gem Minerals

Amber Guild, 80-19 31st Ave., Jackson Heights, N.Y. 11372

American Gems and Minerals, P.O. Box 16057, Ft. Worth, Tex. 76132

Bergsten Jade Co., Box 2381, Castro Valley, Calif. 94546

Harry Bookstone, 22 W. 48th St., New York, N.Y. 10036

Commercial Minerals Corp., 22 W. 48th St., New York, N.Y. 10036

Goodnow Gems U.S.A., 3608 Sunlite, Amarillo, Tex. 79109

Hodson's of Scottsdale, 7116 1st Ave., Scottsdale, Ariz. 85251

Art House, P.O. Box 22066, Cleveland, O. 44122
Walter Johansen, P.O. Box 907, Morgan Hill, Calif. 95037
Murray American Corp., 15 Commerce St., Chatham, N.J. 07928
Pala Properties, 912 S. Live Oak Ave., Fallbrook, Calif. 92028
Parser's, P.O. Box 2076, Danbury, Conn. 06810
Plummer's Minerals, 4720 Point Loma Ave., San Diego, Calif. 92107
Perham's, West Paris, Me. 04289

Minerals
Dawson's Minerals, 215 Buena Creek Rd., San Marcos, Calif. 92069
Minerals Unlimited, P.O. Box 877, Ridgecrest, Calif. 93555
Norm's Treasures, 409 Shepard Terr., Madison, Wis. 53705
H. Obodda, P.O. Box 51, Short Hills, N.J. 07078
Harry Sering Co., Hwy 135, Morgantown, Ind. 46160

Books
Don Faust, 703 N. Main St., Adrian, Mich. 49221
Gemological Institute of America, 11940 San Vicente Blvd., Los Angeles, Calif. 90049
Kytes' Collections, P.O. Box 3227, Alexandria, Va. 22302
Peri Lithon, P.O. Box 9996, San Diego, Calif. 92109

Machinery & Tools
Covington, 112 First St., Redlands, Calif. 92373
Craftool Co., 1421 W. 240th St., Harbor City, Calif. 90710
Estwing Manufacturing Co., 2647 Eighth St., Rockford, Ill. 61101
Henry B. Graves Co., 1190 S, Old Dixie Hwy., Delray Beach, Fla. 33444
Highland Park Manufacturing Co., 12600 Chadron Ave., Hawthorne, Calif. 90250
Lapibrade Inc., 8 E. Eagle Rd., Havertown, Pa. 19083
Lortone, 2854 N.W. Market St., Seattle, Wash. 98107
Pacific Test Specialties, 13449 Beach Ave., Marina del Mar, Calif. 90291
Raytech Industries, River Rd., P.O. Box 84, Stafford Springs, Conn. 06076

Miscellaneous
Althor Products, 2260 Benson Ave., Brooklyn, N.Y. 12214 (plastic boxes)

SOURCES OF INFORMATION AND SUPPLY

Craftstones, P.O. Box 547, Ramona, Calif. 92065 (wholesale tumbled stones)

J. J. Jewelcraft, 4959 York Blvd., Los Angeles, Calif. 90042 (mountings)

Ultra-Violet Products, San Gabriel, Calif. 91778 (ultraviolet lamps)

for further reading

Every gem hunter and collector needs reference material on geology, minerals, gems, and related subjects. The following material forms a well-rounded working library:

The Agates of North America, edited by Hugh Leiper. Lapidary Journal, San Diego, Cal., 1962.
The Book of Agates, Lelande Quick. Chilton Book Company, Philadelphia, 1963. 232 pages.

> Both books are by former editors of the Lapidary Journal and contain the most up-to-date information available when they were published. Their illustrations are helpful.

Collecting Rocks, Minerals Gem and Fossils, Russell P. MacFall. Hawthorn Books, New York, 1963. 156 pages.

> A general book useful for the beginner because of its how-to-do-it illustrations and identification data.

Dictionary of Gems and Gemology (6th edition), Robert M. Shipley. Gemological Institute of America, Los Angeles, 1972, 261 pages.

> Reliable and up-to-date source of information by an authority.

Encyclopedia of Minerals, Willard L. Roberts, George R. Rapp Jr. and Julius Weber. Van Nostrand-Reinhold Company, New York, 1974, 693 pages.

> Comprehensive treatment in tabular form of all known minerals by an authority with excellent photographs. Brings all other authorities up to date.

A Field Guide to Rocks and Minerals (3d edition), Frederick H. Pough. Houghton Mifflin Co., Boston, 1960, 349 pages.

> Useful field guide for identification of minerals, especially American ones. Color illustrations vary in quality.

Fossils for Amateurs, Russell P. MacFall and Jay C. Wollin. Van Nostrand-Reinhold Company, New York, 1971, 1972. 341 pages.

> Useful for its discussion of the federal and state laws affecting all kinds of collecting, as well as for its general prospecting hints.

317

Gems (2d edition), by Robert Webster. Archon Books, Hamden, Conn., 1971. 836 pages.

    Sumptuous and expensive compendium by an English authority. The illustrations are mostly examples of costly jewelry.

The Gem Kingdom, Paul Desautels. Random House, New York, 1971, 252 pages.

    Informal account of gems by an official of the Smithsonian Institution. The color plates are sumptuous.

The Gemmologist's Compendium (4th edition), Robert Webster. N.A.G. Press, London, 1971. 228 pages.

    A less costly reference book by an English authority, published in England.

Gems and Gem Materials (5th edition), Edward H. Kraus and Chester B. Slawson. McGraw-Hill Book Co., Inc., New York, 1947. 332 pages.

    Widely used textbook and reference by two University of Michigan faculty members.

Gems and Precious Stones of North America, George F. Kunz. Dover Publications, New York, 1968.

    Reprint in paperback of a classic first published in 1892, with the original color plates.

Gemstones (14th edition), George F. H. Smith. Pitman Publishing Corp., New York, 1958. 560 pages.

    New edition of an important general work by a former British Museum curator of gems. Revised by F. C. Phillips.

Gemstones of North America, John Sinkankas. Van Nostrand Reinhold Company, New York, 1959. 675 pages.

    Comprehensive work with some special features by a widely known mineralogist.

Geology (2d edition), William C. Putnam. Oxford, 1971. 585 pages.

    Exceptionally well organized textbook. Revised by Ann B. Bassett.

Handbook for Prospectors (5th edition), Max W. von Bernewitz. McGraw-Hill Book Company, New York, 1973. 472 pages.

    All about prospecting and locating a claim. Revised for this edition by Professor Richard M. Pearl.

Prospecting for Gemstones and Minerals, John Sinkankas. Van Nostrand Reinhold Company, New York, 1969. 285 pages.

    A how-to book, well written and well illustrated.

Precious Stones, Max Bauer. Dover Publications, New York, 1968. 2 volumes.

    Paperback edition of a German classic on gems, translated by L. J. Spencer. With color illustrations.

The Rockhound's Manual, Gordon S. Fay. Barnes and Noble, New York, 1972. 290 pages.
> Paperback or hardback ·editions of a general book for amateurs with names and addresses of governmental organizations.

Rocks and Minerals, Joel Arem. Bantam Books, New York, 1973. 155 pages.
> Excellent paperback strong on basic theory and very well illustrated.

Rocks and Minerals, Richard M. Pearl. Barnes and Noble, New York, 1956.
> Revised edition of a general discussion of the field, by a widely known geologist.

Rocks and Minerals, Herbert S. Zim and Paul R. Shaffer. Golden Press, New York, 1957. 160 pages.
> An excellent inexpensive guide with color photographs.

A Textbook of Mineralogy (4th edition), Edward S. Dana. John Wiley & Sons, New York, 1932. 851 pages.
> The revision of Dana's textbook by William E. Ford, badly out of date but still useful.

Ultraviolet Guide to Minerals, Sterling Gleason. Van Nostrand Reinhold, New York, 1960. 244 pages.
> Best elementary work on the subject, somewhat dated but useful for its tables.

Regional and State Guides

Since the *Gem Hunter's Guide* first appeared in 1946, its example has been followed by the issuance of a number of regional and local guides to gem locations. Because no national guide can hope to be as detailed as a specialized local guidebook, the reader is advised to consult such of these publications as will be useful wherever he plans to hunt for gem materials. Most of them are pamphlets or paperbacks.

REGIONAL GUIDES
Appalachian Mineral and Gem Trails, June Culp Zeitner. Lapidary Journal, San Diego, 1968. 134 pages.
Desert Gem Trails, Mary Frances Strong, a guide to the gems and minerals of the Mojave and Colorado deserts. Gembooks, Mentone, Cal., 1966.
A Field Guide to the Gems and Minerals of Mexico, Paul Willard Johnson. Gembooks, Mentone, Cal., 1965.

FOR FURTHER READING

Gem and Mineral Localities of Southeastern United States, Leon
D. Willman. Anniston, Ala., Vol. 1, 1963, 97 pages; Vol. 2, 1970,
271 pp.
Gem Hunters Atlas, H. Cyril Johnson. Scenic Guides, Susanville,
Cal. Three guides issued: Northwest (4th edition), 1960; Southwest
(revised edition), 1960; and California-Nevada (revised edition),
1961.
Hunting Diamonds in California, Mary Hill. Naturegraph Pub-
lishers. Healdsburg, Cal., 1972. 80 pages. (Paper)
Northwest Gem Trails, Henry C. Dake. J. D. Simpson & Co., West
19–27th Ave., Spokane, Wash., 1956.
Roadside Geology of the Northern Rockies, David D. Ault and
Donald W. Hyndman. Mountain Press, Missoula, Montana, 1972.
The Rock Collector's Nevada and Idaho, Darold J. Henry. J. D.
Simpson & Co., West 19–27th Ave., Spokane, Wash., 1953.
Southwest Mineral and Gem Trails, June Culp Zeitner. Lapidary
Journal, San Diego, 1972. 146 pages.

CANADIAN
B.C. Gem Trails, Howard Pearsons. Capilano Gem Shop, North
Vancouver, n.d.
Geology and Scenery along the North Shore of Lake Superior,
E. G. Pye. Geological Circular 10, Ontario Department of Mines,
Toronto, Ontario, 1962.
Nova Scotia Mineral Locations No. 1, Minas Basin area, Bryce
Rumery, 1967.
Rock and Mineral Collecting in Canada, Vol. 2, Ontario and
Quebec, Anna P. Sabrina. Geological Survey of Canada, Misc. Re-
port 8, rev. 1971.
Rocks and Minerals for the Collector, Anna P. Sabrina. Depart-
ment of Energy, Mines and Resources, Ontario, Paper no. 87-51,
1968.
**Rocks and Minerals for the Collector: Eastern Townships and
Gaspe, Quebec and Parts of New Brunswick,** Anna P. Sabrina.
Geological Survey of Canada, Paper no. 66-51, 1967.
Rocks and Minerals for the Collector: Sudbury to Winnipeg,
Anna P. Sabrina. Geological Survey of Canada, Paper no. 63-18,
1963.
200 Mineral Locations in Southern Ontario, Harley Leach. Kingston, Ontario, n.d.

STATE GUIDES
Rocks and Minerals of Alabama. Circular 38, Alabama Geological
Survey, University, 1966.

Arizona Gem Fields (2d edition), Alton Duke. P.O. Box 1402, Yuma, Ariz., 1959.

Minerals of Arizona, F. W. Galbraith and D. J. Brennan. Physical Science Bulletin No. 4, University of Arizona, Tucson, 1959.

Mineral Resources of Arkansas. Bulletin 6, Arkansas Geological and Conservation Committee, Little Rock, 1942.

Rockhounding Out of Bishop (Calif.), Cora B. Houghtaling. Chalfont Press, Bishop, 1967.

California Gem Trails (3rd edition), Darold J. Henry. J. D. Simpson & Co., Spokane, Wash., 1957.

Gem and Lithium Bearing Pegmatites of the Pala District, R. H. Jahns and L. A. Wright. Special Report 7-A, California Division of Mines and Geology, Resources Building, Sacramento, 1951.

Minerals of California, Joseph Murdoch and R. W. Webb. Bulletin 173, Division of Mines and Geology, Resources Building, Sacramento, 1956. Plus several supplements.

Colorado Gem Trails and Mineral Guide, 3d ed., Richard M. Pearl. Sage Books, Denver, 1972.

Minerals of Colorado, Edwin B. Echel. Bulletin 1114, U.S. Geological Survey, Washington, D.C., 1961.

Connecticut Minerals, Julian A. Sohon. Bulletin 77, State Geological and Natural History Survey, Middletown, 1951.

Connecticut Mines and Minerals, John Hiller, Jr. Shelton, Conn., n.d.

Gem Minerals of Idaho, John A. Beckwith. Caxton Printers, Caldwell, 1972.

Field Tripping in Illowa Territory (Illinois and Iowa). Illowa Gem and Mineral Society, Davenport, Ia., n.d.

Minerals of Indiana, R. C. Erd and S. S. Greenberg. Bulletin 18, Indiana Geological Survey, Bloomington, 1960.

Kansas Rocks and Minerals. Geological Survey, Univ. of Kansas, Lawrence.

Gems and Minerals of Oxford County, Maine, Jane Perham Stevens. Privately printed, 1972. 216 pages.

Maine Mineral Collecting. Geological Survey, Augusta, Maine.

Maine Minerals and Mineral Locations, Phillip Morrill. Dillingham Natural History Museum, Naples, Maine.

Minerals of Maryland. Natural History Society of Maryland, Baltimore, 1940.

Rocks and Minerals of Michigan. Publication 42, Department of Conservation, Lansing, Mich., 1953.

Collecting Michigan Minerals. Tourist Council, Mason Building, Lansing.

FOR FURTHER READING

Guide to Mineral Collecting in Minnesota, G. R. Rapp, Jr., and D. T. Wallace. Minnesota Geological Survey, Minneapolis, 1966.
Meanderings of a Montana Rockhound, Paul Fry. Miles City, 1972.
Minerals and Gemstones of Nebraska, Roger K. Pabian, Ed. Circ. 2, University of Nebraska Conservation and Survey Division, Lincoln, 1971.
Geology of New Hampshire, Part 3, "Minerals and Mines," T. R. Myers and G. W. Stewart. State Planning and Development Commission, Concord, 1956.
New Hampshire Mines and Mineral Locations, Phillip Morrill. Dillingham Natural History Museum, Naples, Maine.
The Minerals of New Mexico, S. A. Northrup. Bulletin, Geological Series, Vol. 6, No. 1, University of New Mexico, Albuquerque, 1942.
New Mexico Gem Trails, Bessie W. Simpson. Gem Trails Publishing Co., Box 157, Glen Rose, 1961.
Let's Hunt for Herkimer Diamonds, C. H. Smith. Geneva, N.Y.
The Rubies of Cowee Valley, North Carolina, Lou Harshaw. Hexagon Company, Asheville, N.C., 1973. 75 pages.
Mineral Collecting Kit. North Carolina Travel and Promotion Division, Raleigh.
100 Minerals, Rocks and Fossils from Oklahoma, W. E. Ham. Geological Survey, Norman, Okla., 1942.
Mineral Collecting in Pennsylvania (2d edition), David M. Lapham and Alan R. Geyer. Bureau of Topographic and Geologic Survey, Harrisburg, Pa., 1965.
Common Rocks and Minerals of Pennsylvania. Topographical and Geological Survey, Main Capitol Annex, Harrisburg.
Minerals of Rhode Island, Clarence E. Miller, ed. by Don Hermes. University of Rhode Island, Kingston, 1972.
Mineral Resources of the Colorado River Industrial Development Association Area (Texas), J. W. Dietrich and John T. Lonsdale. Bureau of Economic Geology, University of Texas, Report 37, 1958.
Texas Rocks and Minerals, an Amateur's Guide, Roselle M. Girard. Guidebook 6, Bureau of Economic Geology, University of Texas, 1964. 109 pages.
Gem Trails of Texas (3d edition), Bessie W. Simpson. Gem Trails Publishing Co., Glen Rose, 1968.
Utah Gem Trails, Bessie W. Simpson. Gem Trails Publishing Co., Glen Rose, 1972.
Utah Fact Book. Utah Travel Council, Council Hall, Capitol Hill, Salt Lake City.

Minerals of Virginia, R. V. Dietrich. Research Division, Bull. 47, Virginia Polytechnic Institute, Blacksburg, 1970.
Mineral and Rock Collecting in Wisconsin. Geological and Natural History Survey, University of Wisconsin, 1815 University Ave., Madison.
Wyoming Mineral Resources, F. W. and Doris Osterwold. Bulletin No. 45, Geological Survey. Laramie, Wyoming, 1952.

Magazines
Earth Science. P.O. 1815, Colorado Springs, Colo. 80901.
Gems and Gemology. Gemological Institute of America, 11940 San Vicente Boulevard, Los Angeles, Calif. 90049. Quarterly.
Gems and Minerals. Box 687, Mentone, Calif. 92359.
Lapidary Journal. Box 80927, San Diego, Calif. 92138. Also publishes **Rockhound Buyers Guide** annually in April.
Mineralogical Record. P.O. Box 783, Bowie, Md. 20715.
Mineral Digest. 155 E. 34th St., New York, N.Y. 10016.
Rocks and Minerals. Box 29, Peekskill, N.Y. 10566.
Rock and Gem. Behn-Miller Publishers, 16001 Ventura Blvd., Encino, Calif. 91316.